ON CAPITALISM

ON CAPITALISM

Edited by Victor Nee and
Richard Swedberg

Stanford University Press
Stanford, California
2007

Stanford University Press

Stanford, California

Printed in the United States of America on acid-free, archival-quality paper

Library of Congress Cataloging-in-Publication Data

On capitalism / edited by Victor Nee and Richard Swedberg.

    p. cm.

  Includes index.

  ISBN 978-0-8047-5664-8 (cloth : alk. paper)—ISBN 978-0-8047-5665-5 (pbk. : alk. paper)

  1. Capitalism. I. Nee, Victor, 1945– II. Swedberg, Richard.

HB501.O584 2007

330.12′2—dc22

2007003024

Typeset by Thompson Type in 10/14 Minion

Contents

List of Tables

List of Figures

Chapter 4

Chapter 7

Chapter 8

Chapter 11

Acknowledgments

WE GRATEFULLY ACKNOWLEDGE THE SUPPORT OF THE JOHN Templeton Foundation in generously funding the "Conference on Norms, Beliefs, and Institutions of Capitalism: Celebrating Weber's Protestant Ethic and the Spirit of Capitalism." The conference was convened at Cornell University, October 8–9, 2004, to mark the 100th anniversary of Max Weber's *The Protestant Ethic and the Spirit of Capitalism.* The question raised by Weber's work—the relationship between values, economic institutions, and performance—is the central theme of this book. Special thanks to Barnaby Marsh for his steadfast encouragement and interest in helping us conceive and assemble the conference. We also are appreciative of the keen and attentive interest of Drs. John and Josephine Templeton, who attended the conference at Cornell. We thank Diane Masters for providing administrative support for the planning of our conference in 2004 and for the preparation of this book.

Contributors

VICTOR NEE IS THE GOLDWIN SMITH PROFESSOR OF SOCIOLOGY and Director of the Center for the Study of Economy and Society at Cornell University.

Richard Swedberg is Professor of Sociology at Cornell University.

Robert J. Barro is the Paul M. Warburg Professor of Economics at Harvard University, a senior fellow of the Hoover Institution of Stanford University, and a research associate of the National Bureau of Economic Research.

Bruce G. Carruthers is Professor of Sociology at Northwestern University.

Robert H. Frank is the Henrietta Johnson Louis Professor of Management and Professor of Economics at the Johnson Graduate School of Management, Cornell University.

Mark Granovetter is the Joan Butler Ford Professor of Sociology at Stanford University.

Terence C. Halliday is Senior Research Fellow at the American Bar Foundation and Adjunct Professor of Sociology at Northwestern University.

Russell Hardin is Professor of Politics at New York University.

Ronald Jepperson is Associate Professor of Sociology at the University of Tulsa.

Barnaby Marsh is Research Fellow at New College, Oxford, and is adjunctly affiliated with the Center for the Study of Economy and Society at Cornell University.

Rachel M. McCleary is Director of the Project on Religion, Political Economy, and Society, Weatherhead Center for International Affairs, Harvard University, and Research Fellow of the Hoover Institution, Stanford University.

John W. Meyer is Professor of Sociology, emeritus, at Stanford University.

Michael Novak holds the George Frederick Jewett Chair in Religion, Philosophy, and Public Policy at the American Enterprise Institute in Washington, D.C., where he is Director of Social and Political Studies.

Sonja Opper is the Gad Rausing Professor of International Economics and Business at the School of Economics and Management at Lund University and member of the Lund Resarch Institute (Sweden).

Charles F. Sabel is Professor of Law and Social Science at Columbia Law School.

Duncan J. Watts is Professor of Sociology at Columbia University, where he directs the Collective Dynamics Group, and an external faculty member of the Santa Fe Institute.

ON CAPITALISM

Introduction

Victor Nee and Richard Swedberg, Cornell University

THE DEMAND FOR ECONOMIC GROWTH—AS MUCH ECONOMIC growth as is possible and sustainable—is nearly universal. Governments practically stand and fall with their success in handling such growth in their countries, and the growth rates of the countries that are moving ahead the fastest—yesterday, Japan and today, China and India—are the envy and worry of all the rest. The idea that modern economic growth is essential for a nation's wealth and power is uncontroversial. Even the critics of capitalism, whether they base their arguments on ecological, distributive, or some other ground, support growth that is sustainable. A century ago Max Weber predicted that the West's emphasis on creating rapid economic growth through capitalist economies would soon be universally adopted, and it now appears he was right.

Max Weber also predicted that only a very special type of capitalism had the actual capacity to uniformly and steadily increase economic growth: what he called rational capitalism, which he characterized as predictable, methodical, and deeply agnostic when it comes to divisions along ethnic, gender, or religious lines. What Weber called traditional capitalism and political capitalism differed on each of these three points (Swedberg 1998). Rational capitalism also has a universal quality that makes it not only suitable to each and every country but also deeply international in spirit. Although capitalist economies thrive in different cultural and institutional settings, the hallmark traits of calculable, predictable, and methodical pursuit of profit define the edges of dynamic growth in global capitalism.

The global economy has expanded dramatically since the end of the Cold War. The integration of Russia, China, and India into global capitalism has doubled the supply of labor available worldwide for capitalist production. In 2005, emerging economies led by China and India surpassed the developed economies in world output, according to the *Economist,* based on computing purchasing-power parity, which provides a more reliable measure of the size of the economy and living standard than does gross domestic product (GDP; January 21, 2006: 69–70). In sum, globalization has resulted in a rapid diffusion of the modern capitalism that emerged first in the West. What Weber termed *rational capitalism,* in other words, is what today in many cases goes under the name of *global capitalism.*

Although agreement that more economic growth is better seems practically universal today, knowledge of how to make a country initiate dynamic economic growth (to "take off") or to ensure a high and steady rate of economic growth still eludes us. There is a huge literature on patterns of growth rates among developed countries as well as on former developing countries that have suddenly taken a qualitative leap ahead, the way that Japan once did and that the Asian Tigers and China are presently doing (e.g., Dowrick and Nguyen 1989; Korpi 1996). Despite massive scholarly work on these issues by economists for a very long time, the key to what launches a country's economy on the course of modern economic growth still evades confirmation. Japan, for example, was moribund in the 1990s in terms of economic growth, and it is not clear why this was the case; inversely, China is currently in a very dynamic stage of development, and the reasons for this are similarly not well understood.

Neoclassical growth theory dominated the economic profession in the 1950s and 1960s, but is generally viewed today as insufficient and lacking on many points. It assumed that economic development was a linear process of capital accumulation to catch up in terms of capital/labor output with the advanced Western economies (Solow 1956). Later development economists criticized the neoclassical growth model for overlooking issues of income distribution and the historical and cultural conditions of underdevelopment (i.e., Meier 1976; Fields 1980; Wilber 1973). However, the development-as-growth approach has regained favor among economists in recent years (Swan 2002). Schumpeter's old idea that economic growth must be seen as endogenous is for example fully accepted today (e.g., Romer 1986; Aghion and Howitt 2005). The idea that economic change can be brought about by import, be it in the form of technology, capital, or whatnot, has in other words been supplanted with the notion that what you need is a center of inner dynamics.

A number of scholars, including Douglass North, Mancur Olson, and Avner Greif, have also argued that economic growth is intimately connected to institutions and that an analysis of economic growth that does not pay proper attention to institutions is bound to fail (i.e., North 1990; Olson 1982; Greif 2006).

An economic system, it has for example been argued by North, can be likened to a football game in which the rules are represented by the institutions, and the players by organizations. The rules specify the incentive structure for organizational actors; they are the constraints that provide the scaffolding of the economic order. Only if the rules are the right ones—and this is a most important point for our concerns here—will the game result in gains not only for the players but also for society at large. The new institutional approach highlighting the positive effect of political institutions on economic growth has had broad influence in the social sciences and also in international development agencies such as the World Bank (Knack and Keefer 1995; Dollar and Kraay 2003; Rodrik 2003).

The emphasis on institutions as the key to economic development has been challenged by some mainstream economists. Glaeser et al.'s (2004) empirical tests of the "institutions-matter" approach fail to confirm the claim that institutions cause economic growth. Rather, they infer from their empirical analyses, it is economic growth that causes improvement in the quality of institutions. Hence a pro-growth communist reformer like China's Deng Xiaoping first succeeds in launching self-sustaining economic growth; this later is followed by successors' efforts to improve the economic and political institutions. These economists revisit Lipset's (1960) hypothesis positing the importance of human capital in fostering the more benign politics that rely on stable political institutions. Better-educated people tend to promote political orders that are favorable to sustained economic growth. However, if human capital is the deeper cause of economic development, as Glaeser et al. (2004) argue, then the former Soviet Union, with its huge urban scientific and technical workforce, should have been the first post-Communist country to experience economic takeoff. Instead, China, which radically disabled its educational system during the Cultural Revolution, with a per-capita educational spending about the same level as Bangladesh's, has far outstripped Russia in economic growth in recent decades. In other words, the rise of China as the fastest-growing capitalist economy in the world was due not to high levels of human-capital accumulation prior to economic take off but to other factors that have eluded economists (see Victor Nee and Sonja Opper's chapter in this volume).

Mainstream economists have also during the last few decades started to investigate the role of law and religion in furthering economic growth. It has, for example, been argued that countries with legal systems that draw primarily on the common law tradition will be more supportive of shareholder rights, and thereby also foster economic growth, than will countries that draw on the continental tradition (e.g., La Porta et al. 1998). Similarly, there is empirical support for the idea that countries with stern religions that emphasize beliefs about heaven and hell tend to do better when it comes to economic growth than countries with soft religions (Barro and McCleary 2003). Despite these innovative attempts by mainstream economists to look for the key to economic growth in various new places, what accounts for economic growth is still very much an open question. As Krugman (2004) states, we simply do not know why certain developing countries have been able to take off, while others have not; and why certain countries can maintain high economic growth over long periods, while this has not been possible for others. What is needed in a situation of this type, we argue, is to look very widely for deep—including challenging-to-measure—factors that may help to explain dynamic transformative economic growth. For this reason, this volume contains a variety of articles that are all concerned with solving the mystery of economic growth in one way or another. As we see it, it is only by casting the analytical net very wide that the discussion of dynamic economic growth can be decisively moved forward.

What we are looking for are not so much local descriptions of what has made capitalism function in various places, as the general mechanisms that help to account for dynamic or rational capitalism. Many chapters in this volume were originally presented at a conference organized by the Center for the Study of Economy and Society at Cornell University in October 2004, in celebration of the centenary of Max Weber's *The Protestant Ethic and the Spirit of Capitalism*. Our intention with this conference was not so much to draw attention to the particulars of Weber's famous study but to encourage and try to engage in the kind of the creative and bold theorizing about capitalism that is the hallmark of this work. Weber's Protestant ethic-thesis sought to identify the difficult-to-measure religious spirit that motivated the founding of rational capitalism in Europe. The enduring legacy of Weber's scholarship is perhaps not so much the Protestant ethic-thesis, but the view that the mechanisms motivating and facilitating today's capitalism are rooted not in the materialist domain of incremental capital accumulation, but in the realm of ideas and institutional structures.

Although our need today is for a modern version of Weber's study to address the dynamics of this new era of capitalism, a few words about its qualities and contributions are nonetheless warranted, so that we may convey to the reader a better sense of what we are looking for. Weber's study, first of all, seems exemplary to us in that it attacks the problem of transformative economic growth in both a sociological and an economic manner. As sociologists we focus attention on the centrality of social relations for the analysis of economic phenomena; but we also support the attempt in contemporary economics to join together the sociological with the economic approach (i.e., Mansky 2000; Gibbons 2005; Basu forthcoming). We furthermore agree with Weber that the sociological approach has to be structural in the sense that institutions are central to an understanding of what goes on in the economy.

But there is more to Weber's analysis of what made Western capitalism take the decisive step to become dynamic as well as a model for modern capitalism than attention to social relations and institutions. Whether right or wrong, Weber argued that there was also another factor, a separate force that helped to ignite dynamic capitalism, namely a new type of religion. More precisely, this role was played by ascetic Protestantism, most famously in the form of Calvinism that first spread from continental Europe to England and then took the step over the Atlantic with the Pilgrims. We say *whether* Weber was right or wrong in his argument about the link between Protestantism and Western capitalism, because we want to sidestep the huge debate that has been raging about this issue since the publication of *The Protestant Ethic* in 1904–1905 and instead emphasize the effort from Weber's side to strike out in new theoretical directions to account for the dynamic nature of modern capitalism.

Another contribution of Weber's study that deserves emphasis here has to do with the role that unintended consequences play in his argument, which we find very suggestive for analyses of dynamic capitalism. According to Weber, members of various ascetic Protestant sects inadvertently helped to bring about a new attitude to economic affairs in their efforts to behave as good Christians. He thus viewed Western capitalism primarily as an unintended consequence (Hirschman 1986). Furthermore, Weber's argument that what was an intensely private affair for the religious individual translated into something very different at the macro-level of the economy is similar to more recent arguments about micro-motives and macro-behavior. According to this type of analysis, which seems very useful in dealing with the problem of dynamic economic growth, micro-motives often have little to do with the macro-behavior that they end up producing (Schelling 1978).

At the very core of Weber's argument is also the interesting idea that under certain circumstances it is simply not enough to only have the "right" kind of institutions; something more is needed for dynamic economic growth to take place. In Weber's particular case, special religious values originated *outside* the main institutions of western European societies, captured the hearts of people, and influenced their actions in a dynamic manner. At first, according to Weber, these novel religious ways of acting emigrated to the existing economic institutions and invested these with a new dynamic. Eventually, the already existing economic institutions in sixteenth- and seventeenth-century Europe (early forms of banking, early forms of the firm, and so on) changed their structure and became anchored in a new type of work ethic ("the Protestant ethic").

We have briefly mentioned above the efforts in mainstream economics to account for economic growth. Something also needs to be said about those of globalization studies, development economics, and economic sociology. In globalization studies no sharp conceptual line is drawn between the economy and the rest of society; the emphasis is instead on ongoing attempts to go beyond the individual nation state, be it in cultural matters, political practices, communication, or something else (e.g., Held and McGrew 2000). We agree with this and find it useful. But we also feel that today's discussion of global capitalism needs to be better connected to the core insights of sociology than it is in globalization studies, in order to move beyond the current impasse when it comes to the analysis of economic growth. The way that this can be done, as we see it, is primarily by forging links to economic sociology, especially the type of economic sociology that is concerned with the dynamics of capitalism.

The field of development economics is generally considered to have been in crisis since many years back, and it is clear that no new and convincing general theory has emerged, even though a number of important insights have been produced (e.g., Sen 1999; Sachs 2005). Several surveys and discussions of the current state of development economics exist (e.g., Evans 2005). The only point we would like to add is that from our perspective with this volume, which is centered on the idea of a dynamic capitalism, the very idea of having one theory for developed countries and another for underdeveloped countries seems wrong. Most countries, for example, have dynamic as well as non-dynamic sectors, and an increasing number of corporations, regardless of where they are located, have to be internationally competitive today.

As a field, economic sociology grew out of an attempt to deal precisely with the new type of capitalism that had developed in the West. We are primarily thinking of the works of Karl Marx, Max Weber, and Joseph Schumpeter (who like Marx and Weber did important work not only in economics but also in economic sociology). Today's economic sociologists, with a few exceptions such as Neil Fligstein and Fred Block, have however shown little interest in capitalism as an economic system in its own right and instead have focused on middle and micro issues. This is a tendency that we have criticized and tried to correct in an earlier volume, entitled *The Economic Sociology of Capitalism* (Nee and Swedberg 2005a), which also originated in a conference arranged by the Center for the Study of Economy and Society.

We suggested that capitalism and its dynamics may be captured with the help of Karl Polanyi's concepts. Economies are traditionally viewed as consisting of three interrelated processes—production, distribution, and exchange—but these three processes, we argue, can only become dynamic under certain circumstances. These circumstances involve production and consumption, but first and foremost it is the way that the *distribution* of what has been produced is organized that is decisive. It is at this point that Polanyi's famous concepts of reciprocity, redistribution, and exchange come into the picture because each constitutes a different way of institutionalizing the process of distribution. An economy where what is produced is being redistributed (say by the state) will have difficulties in being dynamic because the decision of what goods should go where is taken by a political actor. The same is true for an economic system where what has been produced is distributed via institutions of reciprocity, for example in a household-type economy such as the family. It is only when what has been produced is being distributed by the market, in the form of exchange, that the profit motive is released from political and familial constraints and can be used to produce more profit and nothing else. In economic systems where the distribution of what has been produced is organized through a market, there is a feedback loop that makes the system dynamic (see Figure I-1). This view is confirmed by the remarkable economic growth in China, and also in other poststate socialist economies, following transitions to market capitalist economies.

A. The Universal Economic Process

B. The Economic Process where "Redistribution" (Polanyi) is Predominant

C. The Economic Process where "Reciprocity" (Polanyi) is Predominant

D. The Economic Process where "Exchange" (Polanyi) is Predominant

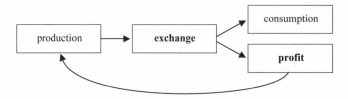

FIGURE I-1 Capitalism and other ways of organizing the economic process

Comment: The economic process in any society is often defined as consisting of *production, distribution,* and *consumption.* The distribution or passing on of what has been produced can be organized in fundamentally three ways, and which of these is chosen will have an enormous impact on the productivity of the economy. Following Polanyi, we may call these *redistribution* (by, e.g., the state), *reciprocity* (in, e.g., a family), and *exchange* (in a market). Exchange characterizes the capitalist organization of the economy, and this type of economy derives its dynamic from the fact that the end goal of the economic process is not exclusively consumption, but also profit. The more that this profit is reinvested into production, the more dynamic the economy will be. The two key mechanisms in capitalism, in other words, are *organized exchange (the market)* and *the feedback loop of profit into production.* It is the use of these two, it should be stressed, that makes the organization of economic interests in the form of capitalism into such effective machinery for transforming economic reality.

Following this model, modern capitalist economies consist of various sectors. There is, first of all, the leading corporate sector, where exchange dominates. There is also a nonprofit sector, which is based, among other things, on redistribution. The state accounts for a huge part of gross national product (30–50%), and what can be called the state economy is primarily based on redistribution. The household economy is based on a mixture of redistribution and reciprocity.

This simple model is international in nature, in the sense that accumulation is not in any important way dependent on national boundaries, and therefore fits today's global capitalism quite well. Nonetheless, one issue that it has difficulties with is *why* profit is continually reinvested. Weber solved this problem for his era by assuming that capitalists as well as consumers were originally puritanical and adverse to consumption and that these motivations were later translated into a new work ethic. Neither of these, however, is a persuasive explanation today.

What is clear is that without continuous reinvestments, profits will fall; there is also an institutional mandate today that corporations have to make a profit. Nonetheless—and we here have to return to the kind of motive that Weber had in mind when he spoke about "the spirit of capitalism"—it would also seem that the imperative of reinvesting has to be deeply anchored in people and not only in institutions. Institutions, to be effective, have to be grounded in a number of phenomena that we may provisionally refer to as values, attitudes, and norms. Without this anchorage, institutions become empty shells and do not have the capacity to shape the way that society moves.

What we are arguing for, in brief, is a revision of the common view of institutions in sociology and other social science disciplines that institutions are *the* key to what is happening in society in the long run (i.e., North 1990; Hall and Soskice 2001; Höpner 2005; Nee and Swedberg 2005b). We want to rectify this by arguing the Tocquevillian point that if institutions are not properly anchored in the mores of society, they are without much force and power. There is also the fact that under certain circumstances these noninstitutional phenomena may even acquire a certain priority when it comes to society's development and may eventually lead to the creation of new institutions. One way that this can happen is illustrated by Weber in *The Protestant Ethic* with its argument that religious sentiments coming from outside the dominant institutions reanimated these and turned them in a new direction.

This volume is organized into four parts to give emphasis to various thematic areas where new research can contribute to the understanding of capitalism. In Part 1 we group three chapters broadly focused on exploring the dynamics and contradictions of capitalism. In the first of these, "The Systemic Anticulture of Capitalism," Russell Hardin asserts that while Weber's Protestant ethic-thesis may offer a persuasive explanation of the rise of rational capitalism in northern Europe, this does not imply that capitalism requires a religious or cultural motive to sustain its dynamic expansion as a worldwide economic order. Once established, he argues, rational capitalism takes on a systemic quality. Like science and mathematics, rational capitalism as a global economic order is not bound to a particular local culture, but it assumes universality in its dynamics and systemic features as an abstract system. In essence, rational capitalism is transcultural despite its origins in northern Europe. As an economic system, capitalism thrives not on greed but on calculable and methodical pursuit of profit-making by firms. It is a globe-spanning economic engine dedicated to production and profitability, and there is no country-specific culture of global capitalism per se.

Hardin concurs with James Scott that local knowledge and culture are undermined through globalization. However, he asserts that what he terms the anticulture of global capitalism does not stem from old-fashioned European imperialism, but from its systemic features. Global capitalism may undermine local knowledge by offering a transcultural repertoire of choices, but the choice to participate in the international division of labor offers the best route out of poverty. Hardin argues that the large capitalist enterprise provides the only countervailing force against the state as an organized system of power and authority. The capitalist capacity for greatly improving productivity operates as a constraint on the political choices of states and also on the greed of managers of capitalist enterprises. Runaway greed on the part of corporate managers leads to the downfall of firms as effective competitors in global capitalism, as seen in the bankruptcy of Enron. Hardin concludes that capitalism's dominant message, "be profitable or die," makes the spirit of capitalism culturally undefined in today's global economy.

Richard Swedberg's close reading of Tocqueville's study of economic behavior in early nineteenth-century America offers a counterpoint to Hardin's emphasis on capitalism as an abstract system "unmoored" from the particular cultural boundaries of national societies. In his interpretation of Tocqueville's *Democracy in America*, arguably the most widely read account of the United States, Swedberg examines the spirit of capitalism in America from the ground up, through the lens of a young French aristocrat. What emerges from Tocqueville's ethnographic study of economic behavior is a remarkably astute and insightful account of the spirit of American capitalism in the formative stage of modern economic growth. Tocqueville describes the spirit of enterprise as economic action characterized by excited, impatient restiveness in pursuit of profit, passionate love of material well-being, an all-pervasive work ethic in which every type of work is considered honorable, and a proclivity for audacity and boldness going beyond the realm of rational action in the pursuit of economic gain. Like Weber, Swedberg shows, Tocqueville also sought to establish a positive link between religious belief and the methodical pursuit of economic goals; e.g., "the Americans are a Puritan and a commercial people." But Tocqueville traces the spirit of capitalism to the ordinary and continuous features of daily life. Thus Tocqueville's sense of the motivating drive in America's dynamic capitalism resonates with Schumpeter's conception of "animal spirit" as the essential motor driving nineteenth-century entrepreneurial capitalism.

Tocqueville's bottom-up ethnography of American capitalism sheds light on the spirit of capitalism that still eludes the efforts of social scientists to measure and analyze. The difficulty of identifying, detecting, and measuring fundamental features of the physical world is widely acknowledged in the natural sciences. In the social sciences, we are still at an early stage of recognizing that mechanisms difficult to identify and observe may have huge causal significance in explaining transformative changes. Causal mechanisms as intangible and difficult to measure as the "spirit of enterprise" or "animal spirit" may explain the sequencing and location of capitalist economic takeoff in the global economy. Yet they are omitted from the development economist's tool kit. If Tocqueville were alive today, and were to travel to China, he would find many similarities between the Chinese "spirit of enterprise" and the excited restiveness, love for material well-being, pervasive work ethic, and the qualities of boldness and audacity in the conduct of business that he observed in America in 1830. By contrast, neither the human-capital nor the institutions-matter approach is persuasive in explaining the rapid pace of economic growth in China over the past quarter century (Glaeser et al. 2004; North 2005; Greif 2006). The problem is reverse causality. China's human-capital stock and political and economic institutions were severely depleted and damaged by the decade-long tumultuous Cultural Revolution that preceded economic takeoff in China after the death of Mao.

In the hedonism of consumer culture in advanced capitalism, the Protestant ethic confronts a deepening cultural contradiction, wrote the sociologist Daniel Bell—a cultural contradiction that he predicted will eventually undermine the ethics and values that made American capitalism so dynamic. In a similar vein, Robert Frank's essay argues that the rapid increase in income inequality during the closing decade of the twentieth century is a social contradiction causing self-destructive tendencies that weaken the viability of American capitalism as a dynamic economic order. The distribution of household income in America previously supported a large and prosperous middle class. However, the post–New Deal trend in the expansion of the middle class ended in the early 1980s. Technological change and globalization fueled the emergence of a "winner-take-all" market, leading to a rapid increase in the earning power of the top income bracket. Growing income and wealth inequality have reached such an extreme that the sharp increase in relative inequality now poses a deepening threat to the well-being of the middle class. Middle-class Americans find the good life increasingly beyond their financial means, even though by world standards they remain privileged. They feel worse off because they are pressured to compete both in winner-take-all markets and in "expenditure cascades" that have lifted the bar of the good life beyond their reach. Frank concludes that a return to the economic institutions inspired by the Protestant ethic is needed to constrain the effects of these markets.

In Part 2, Victor Nee and Sonja Opper analyze in "On Politicized Capitalism" recent economic developments in China in an effort to assess whether its economic system is in a stable phase or in a stage of transition. They depict China's economy as a hybrid institutional order, with the state not only setting the rules for the firms but also intervening in firms' activities. Many factors account for China's current economic success, such as modernization of the bureaucracy and the introduction of an efficient tax system that operates along the lines of fiscal federalism. The state has also improved education, invested heavily in science and technology, allowed foreign investment, and created special economic zones. Drawing on interviews as well as quantitative data to investigate the state's involvement in firms, both in their market transactions and in their governance structure, Nee and Opper find that firms that are closely tied to the state have incentives to remain so, whereas this is not the case with firms that lack these ties. Although there are sectors that have an interest in the stability of the current economic system, the overall tendency in China's economic system is one of dynamic transition to market capitalism.

In their chapter, "Law, Economy, and Globalization: Max Weber and How International Financial Institutions Understand Law," Bruce Carruthers and Terence Halliday examine how international financial agencies and organizations have implicitly affirmed and extended core propositions of organizational sociology through policies that legitimate and promote the importance of rational-legal institutions in the global economy. Although Adam Smith has received recognition for the continuing significance of his contribution to neoliberal economic policies, there has been virtually no recognition of Weber's intellectual legacy. Yet Weber in his pioneering comparative study of bureaucracy and law provided the first systematic analysis of the importance of legal calculability, predictability, and transparency in modern capitalism. Carruthers and Halliday argue that taking Weber's intellectual legacy seriously draws attention to the close articulation between law and markets in global capitalism. Rational capital accounting, involving the valuation of assets and liabilities, means that there is the capability for precise assessment of profits (or losses) to guide the firm's strategic decisions and actions. Rational-legal rules allow for precision in calculating *ex ante* transaction costs arising from specific contractual agreements. Carruthers and Halliday focus on modern corporate bankruptcy law as a case study of what they interpret as a neo-Weberian turn in global capitalism. Bankruptcy law provides a useful example of the importance of calculability and predictability of law, because it enables economic actors to liquidate and reorganize bankrupt firms in an orderly and rule-governed manner. Calculable and predictable rules governing the distribution of assets among competing claimants following corporate bankruptcy reduces economic uncertainty.

A sociological analysis of corruption offers a useful counterpoint to the discussion of rational-legal institutions. Mark Granovetter shows in "The Social Construction of Corruption" that corruption is a special type of social network exchange involving the exchange of money or gifts and the discharge of public duties perceived as wrongdoing. As such, corruption typically takes place in political markets in which bribery or extortion lubricates the exchange between economic and political actors. In principle, the "rule of law" and effectiveness of rational-legal institutions are perverted or undermined through corruption. However, the adage "money talks and nobody walks" is not unfamiliar to politicians and entrepreneurs in modern capitalism. In practice, corruption to a greater or lesser extent is an incorrigible feature of all capitalist economies, not only because of the expectation that self-interested actors will seek to benefit from opportunities, but also because both entrepreneurs and capitalist enterprise have an interest in securing favorable government action and policies.

Granovetter shows that the boundaries between legitimate and illegitimate transactions in political markets depend on the social construction of the exchange. In political markets actors often reciprocate gifts in exchange for services rendered in a *quid pro quo*. This norm leaves a large grey area for the determination of what constitutes corruption, defined as the give-and-take between economic and political actors that is proscribed by the law or in violation of local moral standards. It is common for actors to engage in exchanges of quid pro quo that they believe to be fair and in conformity with norms of reciprocity and distributive justice. However, what may appear to be appropriate or legitimate at the time of the exchange may later be socially constructed by observers as corrupt behavior in the light of public scrutiny.

The main point of the chapters in Part 3 that discuss the relationship between religion and the economy is that moral and spiritual factors must definitely be taken into account in understanding motivating conditions for economic growth. If this is not done, the analysis will be incomplete. Different ways for approaching the link between religion and economy exist. In the first article are suggested, In "Beyond Weber," Michael Novak both praises and criticizes Weber's *Protestant Ethic* argument, which he finds bold and suggestive but also mistaken in the monopoly that it assigns to Protestantism in advancing the modern economy. Catholicism has also played a positive role in this process, according to Novak, not least during the Middle Ages, when asceticism spread from the Catholic monasteries to lay people. The most important factors that have helped Catholicism contribute to modern economic life, he argues, are closely related to its emphasis on joy, creativity, and what Novak calls "the Don Quixote factor." All of these factors, (which Tocqueville describes in *Democracy in America*), are very different from the methodical and ascetic qualities of Protestantism that Weber discusses.

"Political Economy and Religion in the Spirit of Max Weber" by Robert Barro and Rachel McCleary also takes its departure from *The Protestant Ethic*. Whereas Novak bases his argument primarily on theological insight and knowledge, Barro and McCleary analyze aggregate country-level data from cross-national surveys conducted between 1981 and 2003. They look at how economic growth may affect religion and, conversely, how religion may affect economic growth. They find, importantly, that as gross domestic product (GDP) per capita increases, various measures of religiosity decline—which means that the currently popular critique of the secularization thesis is incorrect. An exception from this trend is the United States (as well as Singapore and Poland). In looking at the impact of religion on economic growth, they find that although belief in hell has a significantly positive effect on the GDP, attendance at religious services has a significantly negative effect. This means that Weber was correct in singling out religious beliefs as being more important for economic growth than is attendance at religious services. Their empirical analysis shows some indication that the work ethic of a country is affected by religious beliefs, but not honesty and thrift.

In the next chapter Barnaby Marsh argues that, in order to advance the current discussion of economic growth, one does not so much need more information as to locate and analyze new factors of consequence. One such factor is spiritual capital; for while this factor cannot by itself advance economic growth—other types of capital are needed for this, not least physical capital—neither can economic growth be properly understood without taking spiritual capital into account. As Marsh defines it, spiritual capital includes religious beliefs but is not restricted to these; it consists of "the outlooks, ideals, and beliefs held either individually or collectively" (p. 175). Each of these, Marsh shows, drawing on interdisciplinary literature that includes evolutionary thought, economics, psychology, and sociology, may influence the way that the individual perceives the outer world and also become an important social force when many individuals act upon it.

Part 4 is devoted to methodological and conceptual issues. In "The Collective Dynamics of Belief," Duncan Watts severely criticizes two types of reasoning that are quite common in social science: the historicist (common in history, sociology, and political science) and the rationalist (common in economics). Causality in the former is often constructed by starting with the end result of some event and its context, and then working backwards to the preferences of individuals. In economics, the procedure is nearly the opposite; here you start with a rational individual and then aggregate up to a rational outcome. What is wrong with both of these types of reasoning, according to Watts (a sociologist with a background in physics), is that aggregation between the level of the individual and the level of the collective (assuming only two levels!) is nonlinear as well as stochastic. There are many reasons for this, all related to the elementary fact that the decisions of individuals are dependent not only on what the individual prefers or believes but also on what *other actors* prefer or believe. This last fact is absolutely crucial to the understanding of any social process, be it stock markets, winner-take-all situations, or products in the cultural markets such as bestsellers and popular movies. The complexity of social life, he concludes, is such that it is simply impossible to explain single outcomes; only a little of social reality can actually be explained (44).

In "Analytical Individualism and Explanation of Macrosocial Change: From Weber to Theories of Global Capitalism," Ronald Jepperson and John Meyer argue similarly that popular attempts to analyze economic change at the macro-level are often deeply mistaken and that the reason for this has to do with the conceptual tools that are used. This goes for the literature on globalization today, just as much as for the literatures on European economic development or religious history yesterday. Like Watts, Jepperson and Meyer criticize the use of the rational actor and argue that a multilevel type of analysis is necessary. However, whereas Watts advocates the use of recent social science methods that explicitly take social interaction into account, with the help of methods that are often inspired by physics and are mathematical in nature, Jepperson and Meyer advocate a cultural and organizational type of analysis. Western culture, they suggest, has over the last few centuries come to glorify the individual in various ways, and this includes Western social science, especially in the United States. Today's social science tends to reproduce this Western cultural logic by depending far too much on the individual in its analyses (*analytical individualism*). The remedy for this is to use a multilevel type of analysis that adds an organizational level, where roles are central, and an institutional level, where more vital and important roles can be found.

If emphasis in this chapter is primarily on the role of culture in better understanding the dynamics of economic growth, it is on institutions in the final chapter, "Bootstrapping Development: Public Intervention in Promoting Growth," by Charles Sabel. Many sociologists and economists argue today that institutions are absolutely central to economic growth and that development will come once you have the right institutions. This ("the endowment view," as he calls it) is not the view of Sabel. The current emphasis on the centrality of institutions to economic growth is quite wrong he asserts, because it is built on the assumption that once a country has the right type of institutions, its economy will takeoff more or less automatically. The experiences of Russia and East Germany contradict this view he argues; and the successes of countries such as India and China suggest a very different "emergent process or bootstrapping view of growth" (4). Institutions do not automatically create their own positive environment for growth, but have to be constantly changed and adjusted to their context in order to be effective. What is at issue is not so much to set a country on the right path through well-designed institutions, but to initiate a process of social learning that presupposes institutions that are adjusted to their specific context and that also are constantly changed. The political authorities also have a positive role to play in this new approach to economic development, and this is to support business by removing constraints to growth.

References

Aghion, Philippe and Peter Howitt. 2005. *Endogenous Economic Growth*. Cambridge, MA: MIT Press.

Barro, Robert and Rachel McCleary. 2003. "Religion and Economic Growth Across Countries." *American Sociological Review* 68:270–81.

Basu, Kaushik. Forthcoming. "Identity, Trust and Prosperity: Sociological Clues to Economic Development." Cornell University.

Bell, Daniel. 1976. *The Cultural Contradictions of Capitalism*. New York: Basic Books.

Dollar, David and A. Kraay. 2003. "Institutions, Trade and Growth." *Journal of Monetary Economics* 50(1): 133–162.

Dowrick, Steve and Duc-Tho Nguyen. 1989. "OECD Comparative Economic Growth 1950–1985: Catch-up and Convergence." *American Economic Review* 79:1010–30.

Evans, Peter. 2005. "The Challenges of the 'Institutional Turn': New Interdisciplinary Opportunities in Development Theory." Pp. 90–116 in Victor Nee and Richard Swedberg (eds.), *The Economic Sociology of Capitalism*. Princeton, NJ: Princeton University Press.

Fields, Gary S. 1980. *Poverty, Inequality, and Development*. New York: Cambridge University Press.

Gibbons, Robert. 2005. "What Is Economic Sociology and Should Anyone Care?" *Journal of Economic Perspectives* 19,1:3–7.

Glaeser, Edward L., Rafael La Porta, Florencio Lopez-de-Silanes, and Andre Shleifer. 2004. "Do Institutions Cause Growth." *Journal of Economic Growth* 9:271–303.

Greif, Avner. 2006. *Institutions and the Path to the Modern Economy*. Cambridge, UK: Cambridge University Press.

Hall, Peter and David Soskice. 2001 "An Introduction to Varieties of Capitalism." Pp. 1–68 in Peter Hall and David Soskice (eds.), *Varieties of Capitalism*. New York: Oxford University Press.

Held, David and Anthony McGrew (ed.). 2000. *The Global Transformations Reader*. Malden, MA: Polity.

Hirschman, Albert O. 1986. *Rival Views of Market Society and Other Essays*. New York: Viking.

Höpner, Martin. 2005. "What Connects Industrial Relations and Corporate Governance: Explaining Institutional Complementarity." *Socio-Economic Review* 3:331–58.

Knack, S. and Phil Keefer. 1995. "Institutions and Economic Performance: Cross-Country Tests Using Alternative Measures." *Economics and Politics* 7(3):207–227.

Korpi, Walter. 1996. "Eurosclerosis amd the Sclerosis of Objectivity." *Economic Journal* 106:1727–46.

Krugman, Paul. 2004. "The Future of Neoliberalism." Speech on August 17 at the Annual Meeting of the American Sociological Association, San Francisco.

La Porta, Rafael, Florencio Lopez-de-Silanes, Andrei Shleifer, and Robert Vishny. 1998. "Law and Finance." *Journal of Political Economy* 106:1113–55.

Lipset, S.M. 1960. *Political Man: The Social Basis of Politics*. New York: Doubleday.

Mansky, Charles 2000. "Economic Analysis of Social Interactions." *Journal of Economic Perspectives* 14,3:115–36.

Meier, Gerald. 1976. *Leading Issues in Economic Development*. New York: Oxford University Press.

Nee, Victor and Richard Swedberg (eds.). 2005a. *The Economic Sociology of Capitalism*. Princeton, NJ: Princeton University Press.

———. 2005b. "Economic Sociology and New Institutional Economics." Pp. 789–818 in Claude Ménard and Mary Shirley (eds.), *Handbook of Institutional Economics*. Berlin: Springer.

North, Douglass. 1990. *Institutions, Institutional Change and Economic Performance*. New York: Cambridge University Press.

———. 2005. *Understanding the Process of Economic Change*. Princeton, NJ: Princeton University Press.

Olson, Mancur. 1982. *The Rise and Decline of Nations: Economic Growth, Stagflation and Social Rigidities*. New Haven, CT: Yale University Press.

Rodrik, Dani (ed). 2003. *In Search of Prosperity: Analytic Narratives of Economic Growth*. Princeton, NJ: Princeton University Press.

Romer, Paul. 1986. "Increasing Returns of Long-Run Growth." *Journal of Political Economy* 94:1002–37.

Sachs, Jeffrey. 2005. *The End of Poverty: Economic Possibilities for Our Time*. New York: Penguin.

Schelling, Thomas. 1978. *Micromotives and Macrobehavior*. New York: Norton.

Sen, Amartya. 1999. *Development as Freedom*. New York: Oxford University Press.

Solow, Robert. 1956. "A Contribution to the Theory of Economic Growth." *Quarterly Journal of Economics* 70,1:65–94.

Swan, Trevor W. 2002. "Economic Growth." *Economic Record* (Economic Society of Australia) 78 (243):375–80.

Swedberg, Richard. 1998. *Max Weber and the Idea of Economic Sociology*. Princeton, NJ: Princeton University Press.

Weber, Max. 1958. *The Protestant Ethic and the Spirit of Capitalism*. New York: Scribner's.

Wilber, Charles K. (ed). 1973. *The Political Economy of Development and Underdevelopment*. New York: Random House.

I THE DYNAMICS AND CONTRADICTIONS OF CAPITALISM

1 The Systemic Anticulture of Capitalism[1]

Russell Hardin, New York University

MUCH OF MAX WEBER'S *THE PROTESTANT ETHIC AND THE Spirit of Capitalism* can be read as an account of the culture of capitalism—indeed, of the Protestant culture of capitalism. Although Weber seems to license it, I think that such a reading is a distortion of what he actually claims in his strongest arguments. What Weber gives us, rather, is an account of the rise of capitalism in northern Europe and not of the content or culture of capitalism once it is underway. Once it is underway, firms are driven by their need for profitability if they are to survive in the competitive world of capitalism. Profitability depends in part on a firm's own incentive structures as defined by their effects on the interests of the firm's personnel. Profits and interests can generally be defined as money, which can readily be measured and compared. Protestants might have been driven to create capitalist enterprises in a past era, but the drive for corporate profits is not itself a Protestant drive. Indeed, it is a systemic drive and not strictly an individual drive at all. The systemic drive is survival, which requires profitability. It is a mistake therefore to focus on capitalists and their motivations rather than on capitalism and what it forces firms and their personnel to do if the firms are to survive.

Weber's conception of capitalism is spelled out against the supposition, which he rightly thinks erroneous, that capitalism is based in and driven by greed. Greed is an individual, not a systemic, matter ([1904–05] 1958, 17):

> The impulse to acquisition, pursuit of gain, of money, of the greatest possible amount of money, has in itself nothing to do with capitalism. This impulse

exists and has existed among waiters, physicians, coachmen, artists, prostitutes, dishonest officials, soldiers, nobles, crusaders, gamblers, and beggars. One may say that it has been common to all sorts and conditions of men at all times and in all countries of the earth, wherever the objective possibility of it is or has been given . . . Unlimited greed for gain is not in the least identical with capitalism, and is still less its spirit . . . But capitalism is identical with the pursuit of profit, and forever *renewed* profit, by means of continuous, rational, capitalistic enterprise. For it must be so: in a wholly capitalistic order of society, an individual capitalistic enterprise which did not take advantage of its opportunities for profit-making would be doomed to extinction.

Weber's view is a forerunner of Joseph Schumpeter's ([1942] 1950, 81–86) argument that capitalism leads to creative destruction. Unprofitable firms die and leave the field to those that are profitable. A firm can fail because it fails to compete with others in its industry, or it can fail because its whole industry is in decline, for example, as a result of changing technology. Schumpeter says that "this process of Creative Destruction is the essential fact about capitalism. It is what capitalism consists in and what every capitalist concern has got to live in" (83). Capitalism "is by nature a form or method of economic change and not only never is but never can be stationary" (82). Capitalism is to be understood at the system level, not the individual level. This is true even though it is also true that economic results are the product of individual actions. System-level results and the system itself are generally unintended consequences of those individual actions. Indeed, Schumpeter says, Karl Marx's economic interpretation of history does not require that people act from economic motives, and Weber's arguments in *The Protestant Ethic* fit perfectly into Marx's account (10–11).

On this account, capitalism is abstract, and therefore it is a system that is unmoored in any particular culture, although it might radically affect any culture that is under its sway. Just as greed can be transcultural, so too capitalism can be and by definition is. Some cultures might entail, say, asceticism that would work against both greed and capitalism. However, the commitments to greed and capitalism are not themselves inherently aspects of any particular culture. They are potentially universal. The Protestant ethic is not the necessary spirit of capitalism, although it seems to have been consistent with the rise of capitalism in northern Europe and North America and may have supported capitalism's rise there. In Weber's account, Protestantism contributed to savings and accumulation that nonconsuming Protestants invested. Such accumulation is necessary for capitalism. Capitalism has risen later in many other places that are not and have never been significantly grounded in the Protestant ethic, however, such as many nations of east Asia, that are not and have never been significantly grounded in the Protestant ethic and it seems to be on its way to the conquest of the Chinese economy at an astonishingly fast pace. One could be a capitalist out of strong commitment to the welfare of oneself, one's family, or one's ethnic group, or even out of a commitment to perfectionism in production.

Note in passing that Weber's claim that capitalism is not about greed fits recent scandals in which greed has destroyed capitalist enterprises. A capitalist enterprise might enable one to act on one's greed in perhaps new and destructive ways, but it cannot withstand the full-blown attack of the massively greedy that destroyed Enron and numerous other capitalist corporations in the United States around the turn of the current century.

Against any too easy association of capitalism with a particular culture, note that one can be a capitalist in a society in which few others are capitalists. Indeed, probably *all capitalists are themselves unusual in their own societies.* The vast majority of any society's population or workforce are not capitalists. It would therefore be very odd to say that it is the culture of a particular society that leads people to be capitalists, although there could be a culture that militates against the commitments of capitalism, and there are probably cultures that are more nearly enabling for capitalists than are some other cultures. But clearly any cultural claim here must be finely nuanced, or it must be trivially false. The impact of a relatively small percentage of capitalists in a society causes us to label the society and its economy capitalist. That is an extraordinary testimony to the great impact of even those few capitalists. They set the tone for the whole society economically. Even agriculture, which in most times and places has been primarily for subsistence and little more, is driven to be capitalist despite the false and irrelevant ideology of the small family farm in North America and Europe.

Interests as Money

Before going further in the argument here, I should clarify the use of the term *interests.* A massive literature debates the meaning of interests. Much of this literature argues that interests are largely defined by culture, and much of it defines interests as Aristotle might, as ends rather than as means. I will use the term here exclusively to refer to means or resources for doing things we want to do. I will not be concerned with what anyone wants to do—the list of things is long and complex, and culture might tell us a lot about what people in different societies want. I will only be concerned with enabling them to do those things and not with the choices of things to do. To a large extent, such enabling comes from resources, which can often be summarized as money. Georg Simmel ([1900] 1978, 219) notes that the "German language very subtly terms those who own a considerable amount of money *bemittelt,* that is, equipped with means."

Interests is one of a triumvirate of terms that capture the sense of benefits to people. The other terms are *consumptions* and *welfare.* Interests enable me to consume things, and the consumption of those things adds to my welfare (see further, Hardin 2001). We do not need an elaborate discussion of these terms to make sense of the main issues here. It is merely clear that *interests,* seen as resources and means, is a very simple term. It does not have the qualities that could be lumped under the term to account for the fact that the things that you would think improve your life may be different from the things that would improve someone else's life. For example, you want wonderfully complex gourmet food, whereas another wants an ascetic and supposedly healthful diet. The differences in this case are differences in consumptions rather than in simple interests seen as resources.

Money has the enormous value for capitalism that it allows a measure of the success of any change in production. That measure is of two different things: the reduced costs of producing something and the increased profits from selling it. The "forever *renewed* profit" that Weber mentions in the quote cited earlier gets its meaning and its measure from money. Money is the ultimate abstraction of the notion of interests. It generally has no value in its own right. It has value only in what it can help us consume or do. Strangely, however, in the context of a reasonably stable world, it makes sense to say that the value of money is objective or abstract whereas the values of the things that it purchases are subjective. The values of these things are subjective because their value derives only from the fact that we want them. If we stop wanting them, they stop having value to us. We do not want money in the same way. We want it only as a means to supply our other, subjective wants. As long as we want *any* other things, we will not stop wanting money, and it will not cease to have its value.

Here culture can come in very strongly in our evaluations of the things we might consume, but it has little role otherwise in setting the value of money.

Money therefore crosses cultural boundaries with great ease, whereas many commodities lose much of their value at relevant borders. Those commodities that have the character of resources, such as energy, have more in common with money than with ordinary consumer goods. They are abstractly valuable, and they have no cultural valence. Some goods that are strictly consumer goods cross borders almost as readily as money and energy, and they may finally affect cultural commitments. For example, blue jeans have become nearly universal and gender neutral in their appeal even though they do not fit easily within the culture of Islam or of other traditional societies in which clothing is strongly associated with identity and with gender.

Incidentally, the role of money was unstable through most of history because its availability was fraught with difficulties. When the U.S. greenback was introduced as a federally backed currency in 1863, merchants were enabled to deal very differently with their customers. Before all paper money was the same greenbacks rather than the variously valued notes of many banks, face values were not reliable. Notes were discounted according to the financial stability of the issuing banks, which might go bankrupt at any time. Under such circumstances, you cannot safely accept retailers' claims that they will let you return goods they have sold you for a full refund, because they might repay you in less valuable notes than those you used to buy the goods originally. Having a uniform currency makes our dealings strategically clearer.

Capitalism

Weber sang the praises of capitalism even while romantic criticism of it was the norm in his time. It "has been the unequivocal criterion of economic modernization since the Middle Ages," Weber (1994, 145) insists. He says some people childishly want a romantic communal economy to counter capitalism. (In the United States, the main counters to capitalism in Weber's time were progressivism to put the state in charge of capitalism and antimonopoly sentiments that often generalized into demands for state management of the economy.)[2] He dismisses them as profoundly ignorant of the nature of capitalism because they wrongly focus on momentary and opportunistic corruption, which they wrongly see as the core motivation of capitalism. The particular corruption they see at the time of Weber's writing is the greed of various business leaders in gaining contracts from the state during wartime. Again, he insists that the true core of capitalism is the calculation of profitability (which, as Simmel might insist, is easier if there is money as a measure). The "robber capitalists" who are tied entirely to politics are no different from greedy scavengers in all eras, whereas bourgeois capitalism is the product of modern Europe and is a progressive force (Weber 1994, 89). Indeed, it is moral in ways that greed clearly is not. The profitability of capitalism is grounded in an understanding of the maxim "honesty is the best policy" (a phrase that Weber renders in English [90; see further, Mueller 1999]), a maxim that the executives at Enron scorned.

Among the romantic critics of capitalism were many of those who supported or welcomed the coming of World War I, in which vast numbers of them died. Arthur Conan Doyle has Sherlock Holmes express his praise of the coming war. In "His Last Bow," set in 1914, Holmes says to Watson, "There's an east wind coming . . . , such a wind as never blew on England yet. It will be cold and bitter, Watson, and a good many of us may wither before its blast. But it's God's own wind none the less, and a cleaner, better, stronger land will lie in the sunshine when the storm has cleared" (Doyle [1914] 1986, 803). Adam Gopnik quotes Rupert Brooke, who died horribly and wrote, "Now, God be thanked Who has matched us with His hour." As Gopnik (2004, 82) says, these intellectuals did not want the "moral equivalent of war; they wanted war as a way of driving out moral equivalence—ending [the] familiar evils of a shopping and pleasure-seeking society." They wanted war, politics, and states to take control of economies, not to communize society but to recommunalize it, as though escaping the tethers of traditional communities through economic progress had been a bad thing, a great loss. Their romanticism was finally murderous beyond imagination.

Before the era of totalitarian state control, Weber insisted that the end toward which these romantic ideas would lead is the elimination of private capitalism and rule by the state alone, without any countervailing force, giving the state's rationalizing tendencies free reign. Thus, the romantic populists would find themselves not freer but less free before an all-powerful, uncontestable, pervasively hierarchical state. "The situation would resemble that of ancient Egypt, but in an incomparably more rational and hence more inescapable form" (Weber 1994, 157–8). He seems to have gotten the twentieth-century possibilities entirely right. There were two contending forces: the state and the capitalist economy. Where the latter was subjugated to the state, individuals were commonly brutalized and their hopes for economic progress were stymied. In at least one instance, India, there was only economic harm without massive direct attacks on individual liberties. Nevertheless, history has so far been much too kind to Nehru and his crippling leadership (Das 2000).[3]

Economic growth in India after economic liberalization in 1991 surpasses all the growth for the previous four decades (while much of east Asia boomed), when economic growth rates did not differ substantially from population growth rates, an appalling fact that suggests the numbers in poverty grew steadily throughout the vaunted era of Nehru and his Congress Party successors. Growth rates in India now rival those of China.[4] Education, however, still lags, and India has extraordinarily high levels of illiteracy in comparison to east Asian norms. And agriculture, which supports two-thirds of the population in 2004, is still under government control.[5]

In one of the great ironies of social theory, capitalism is a liberalizing force just because large capitalist enterprises can stand against the state. Jennifer Nedelsky (1990) argues that private property has this role of countervailing power under the U.S. constitution, although later politics has undercut its power. But private property in the form, say, of gigantic estates has little force to offer against government. When James Madison extolled private property, he presumably had in mind almost only large landed estates such as those of southern plantations and the estates of the Anti-Federalists of upstate New York. They are essentially gone, and they play no real role in politics today. Capitalist property, however, which is inherently put to use in production, plays a massive role.

Weber's insight here seems more compelling than Madison's or Nedelsky's because private capitalism may be equal to government in many ways. Sweeping the economy under government control would likely kill the entrepreneurial spirit of capitalism. Without private capitalism, individualism, freedom, and democracy would all be at greater risk. Politics and government would also suffer. As Charles Lindblom (1977) argues, not only can capitalists be a countervailing force against the state but the state also must turn to them to provide what government needs: production and income for workers. In a market society, business is therefore not merely another among many interest groups. It has power and resources far beyond what such groups have; it is the necessary partner of government, and where government intrudes too heavily in controlling it, government loses. Moreover, capitalism has greater possibilities for spontaneity than government has. "In market systems, tiny minorities of one can innovate, but they cannot veto" (Lindblom 1977, 348). Hierarchical government can more readily suppress innovations. "It is extremely rare for a businessman to be so intent on selling what he thinks the public ought to have that he is willing to lose his business rather than sell the public what it wants. Only in politics is there place for the ideologue or the doctrinaire" (218).

To play this countervailing role it is the *regime* of capitalism that matters and not its particularities in one or another *firm*. Individual capitalists can be greedy enough to try to override the regime in their own particular favor. Weber's commitment to capitalism is in its collective or systemic role, not merely its individual firm's role. Yet it is the incentive structure of capitalist production in general that induces individual firms to act in ways that are collectively supportive of capitalism—*unless* individual firms or industries can mobilize government to intervene to block capitalist moves by others.

Finally, note that capitalism can prosper even when the individual capitalist entrepreneurs are soon replaced by managers of large firms. Adolf Berle and Gardner Means (1932) characterize the development toward managerial capitalism, a development that has continued since their writing, so that many of the best-known corporate leaders of our time are in fact managers whose ownership of parts of their firms comes to them as part of their managerial compensation. The developments that Berle and Means chronicle and analyze might lead one to change the discussion to focus on large corporations rather than on capitalism. But many, perhaps most, of the innovative explosions of the recent technological revolution are genuinely exercises in capitalism and not in corporate managerialism. In any case, it is private holdings in productive firms that pose a counter to the power of government. The chief obstacle to keeping the countervailing power of capitalism effective is the one Weber sees in wartime Germany. Corporations seek benefits from government and thereby distort their function and the entire economy. They also often are able to use government to oppose other firms or the potential capitalist development of other firms. The biggest internecine attacks on capitalism by capitalists have arguably been those of the era of gigantic monopolistic trusts and now the era of so-called intellectual property.

Culture

Culture may be seen de facto as a body of knowledge, beliefs, and values that is shared by a group of people who are in close interaction with each other. If we are in the same society, we may believe roughly the same things and have roughly the same values in many ways. Constraints and commitments follow from that knowledge and give culture its bite. There need be little system in the development of a group's group-specific knowledge—that knowledge is apt to differ in highly idiosyncratic ways from one group to another. It is the differences in central parts of one group's knowledge and in another group's knowledge that define them as essentially different groups.

If we are communally to organize ourselves in a way that maintains particular cultural values and practices, we will generally have to do so spontaneously through interpersonal relations that are not backed by powerful institutions of government. We will need endogenous, spontaneously motivated reasons or incentives for adhering to our culture. Spontaneous organization even for what is generally agreed to be a simple collective benefit is likely to be very difficult (Olson 1965; Hardin 1982). To sustain it over generations seems likely to be nearly impossible if we assume that the individual members of the cultural group must primarily be motivated by personal concern with the collective benefit of the culture. And yet, many cultures seemingly have survived many generations with only modest change over time.

The main obstacle to maintenance of such a strong set of governing beliefs is that they must often run against the immediate short-run interests of many of us in the culture. We could partially overcome this obstacle if we could develop close, trusting relationships with enough people. To do so is virtually impossible in even a moderately complex society. As Adam Smith remarks, in civilized society the individual "stands at all times in need of the cooperation and assistance of great multitudes, while his whole life is scarce sufficient to gain the friendship of a few persons" (Smith [1776] 1976, 26).

The most obviously effective way to counter the incentive to follow contrary individual interests would be to introduce other incentives, including sanctions, that would over-weigh the incentives to violate the norms and practices of the culture. What capitalism and globalization do to us is give us new knowledge that counters some of the shared knowledge that we previously had. Some of us may now reject our past knowledge and accept the new knowledge that is in some sense embodied in the new experiences and consumptions that we get from globalization. It is our own preferences that change. Globalization itself is substantially enhanced and aided by capitalism in its Weberian quest for profitability. Globalization does not impose anything on us, but it offers us many things, including new employments and new consumptions, some of which some of us now accept as part of our own daily lives. It has to do this, or we will not buy or take the jobs.

We may or may not in some stronger sense reject much of the cultural knowledge we previously had, but we now have additional knowledge that might sometimes be contrary to bits of that prior knowledge. The central motor in so-called cultural imperialism may be nothing more than the appeals of openness to new ideas and new consumptions. Such openness goes against the conservatism of maintaining some set of cultural beliefs and practices. It may especially appeal to the young, who have not yet made more or less final epistemological commitments to central tenets of their society's culture. A culture's future depends on the eventual commitments of the young, however, so their openness may be death to much of the culture of their forebears. To call this imperialism is odd; it is more nearly adoption. Efforts to block it can succeed only by constraining the next generation. Not even the ayatollahs of Iran have been able to do that very effectively.

Often, defenders of culture against the impact of economic change seem to mean little more than the preservation of local practices and knowledge that, in the larger scheme of things, have little or no value because there are radically better ways to accomplish what those practices and knowledge do for us. James Scott (1998, chap. 9) deplores the loss of local knowledge in the economic transitions that are affecting much of the world—especially, in Scott's concerns, the third world. If we think of knowledge as essentially useful to us, destruction of some of it may not be a loss if that knowledge can no longer be profitably put to use. Local knowledge does, of course, get destroyed in economic and technological transitions, but much of what is lost is local knowledge that has no value once economic progress comes. Most of us in advanced industrial societies know almost nothing of traditional agricultural practices, and we are better off for that lack of knowledge.

Scott extols the rich local knowledge that an Andean potato farmer applies to small bits of poor mountain land to produce a substantial crop of varied potatoes (Scott 1998, 301; see van der Ploeg 1993). In the face of poverty and necessity, as when most of the workforce is in agriculture, that knowledge is valuable. In a better economy in which agriculture is the work of a tiny fraction (currently under 2 percent in the United States), however, that knowledge—and possibly those bits of land—would be worthless because the potatoes the knowledge produces cost far too much in human labor and essentially guarantee the poverty of the human laborers who produce them. It would be a good thing if prosperity saved the next generation from needing and having this bit of local Andean knowledge. Scott seems to agree with this general point in some contexts when he notes that the knowledge of how to start a fire with tinder and flint stones is well lost once matches become available (335), as is much of the knowledge of peoples in many places and historical eras who have faced great beneficial change.

Many of the poor whose perspective Scott (1976, 1985) takes face massive economic transitions that supersede old ways of doing things and that relieve the next generations of the grim life of relative poverty. The transitional generation, however, may suffer massively from the transition that makes life better for future generations. One might meaningfully say that they lose their culture. If that is what the opponents of globalization mean, even in part, their objection is misguided because the only way to allay it is to keep many societies in grim subsistence agriculture and poverty.

Often an additional criterion for defining or at least defending culture is the claim that it is morally valued by those who share in it. They think that it is right or good and that it should be maintained therefore because something good would be lost if it faded from our practices (see further, Hardin 1995, chap. 7). Unfortunately, as seemingly attractive as this criterion of the morality of culture might be, it is not finally compelling. Virtually everything that people do as a matter of habit or even merely as a matter of frequency is commonly seen to be good or right through a conservative claim that what is is good or, even worse, what was is good just because it was. We begin to expect you to do what you have generally always done, and we judge you as morally blameworthy if you now do otherwise.

Even more forcefully, we might be hostile to changes that de facto force us to give up prior practices, even though the force is a matter of our own preferences as aggregated from our own individual actions. Such reactions to sudden economic changes must be common and must be strengthened by the fact that accommodating oneself to change, especially to a major transition, is not easy and must be fraught with a sense of insecurity. The result can be great nostalgia for former conditions, even though those conditions were not good and even though one would not willingly return to them. Many chronicles of such unease and nostalgia sometimes border on morally judgmental criticisms. Changes are so fast in India today that it offers a complex of enjoying the improvements in life with wariness of the changes that are enjoyed (see for example, Traub 2001).

Capitalism or Culture?

Ronald Gilson (1999; more briefly, see McMillan 2002, 111–15) argues that entrepreneurs in the high-tech industrial area called Silicon Valley in California took leadership in developing the computer era away from entrepreneurs along Route 128 in Massachusetts because of differences in intellectual property law. Massachusetts has an intellectual property law that prohibits employees from taking knowledge gained on the job to other firms. Employees often have to sign a covenant agreeing not to work in a competing firm within some time after leaving a job, and such covenants are legally enforceable. The terms typically are for a few years, which is long enough to make one's human capital in the high-tech world obsolete. In California, such covenants are not enforceable, and people in Silicon Valley have moved quickly from one firm to another (Gilson 1999, 607–09, 615–18).

Covenants that block employee mobility pose a collective action problem. Sharing ideas benefits the entire industry, making us all more productive. But each instance of sharing an idea might harm one firm relative to others. In Massachusetts, many well-known firms used the background threat of government enforcement on their behalf to kill local capitalist development, eventually even killing themselves as a consequence of efforts to kill competitors. It is the natural instinct of courts to turn intellectual property into a legal rather than an economic issue, and it is the long history of Massachusetts case law that establishes the enforceability of covenants not to compete and that generalizes this principle to job hopping. The courts have acted against the economic interests of Massachusetts and its high-tech corporations. Hence, although high-tech development started much bigger along Route 128, it stagnated relative to the burst of activity in Silicon Valley. Much of that activity was in start-ups created by employees who left major firms to create their own firms to do particular things that the larger firms were not doing. Such mobility to create start-ups was almost unheard of along Route 128 (Gilson 1999, 592; Saxenian 1994, 63), although there were academics who still started new firms. Academics are presumably not subject to covenants not to compete, even in Massachusetts (Gilson 1999, 606–07).

World economic development historically would likely have been grievously obstructed if analogs of Massachusetts law had always governed economic activity.[6] To exaggerate the issue somewhat, imagine a university system in which anyone who leaves one university is barred from working for a competing institution. It seems plausible that the proliferation of great universities in the United States has substantially been spurred by its unusually high level of professional mobility. If we were to vote on the rule that would generally benefit everyone, we would most likely vote for easy employee mobility. India currently benefits from the return of many Indians who bring their human capital, which they developed in the United States and other nations, to India to help its economic growth, especially in high-tech sectors. The return of expatriates is encouraged by the Indian government. The annual income of the twenty million Indians living abroad is 35 percent of India's gross domestic product (GDP; Amy Waldman, "India Harvests Fruits of a Diaspora," *New York Times,* 12 January 2003, 1.4). Bringing their productivity to India is possibly the fastest way for India to grow economically and to become a competitive force in the world economy.

Anna Lee Saxenian (1994, 111–17) attributes the differences in the growth patterns of Route 128 and Silicon Valley during the several decades after 1965 to differences in the business cultures of the two areas. Silicon Valley supposedly had a culture of mobility and open "architecture," whereas Route 128 had a culture of career-long employment and vertically integrated firms. In part she uses these features *to explain themselves,* as is commonly done in so-called cultural arguments. Such an explanation is not necessarily wrong; there could be feedback mechanisms that lead to replication of an established pattern of behavior. Gilson (1999, 578 and passim) explains these features as the result of different laws on the enforceability of covenants on employment. Those laws were themselves accidental in a meaningful sense for this comparative history in that they were on the books long before the high-tech explosion occurred and provoked efforts to constrain job-hopping workers.

The supposed cultures of the members of these groups were arguably basically the same in that they were essentially capitalist; they came from all over the United States and even, increasingly, the world; and most of them had high-tech educations at more or less the same universities, especially at Massachusetts Institute of Technology (MIT) and Stanford. They faced different legal constraints, however. The constraints in Silicon Valley enabled capitalist development through *restraints on employers* that prevented them from blocking job hopping; the constraints in Route 128 substantially blocked capitalist development through *restraints on employees* that prevented them from job hopping. One might suppose that the culture argument is so weak that it would not have kept innovative employees along Route 128 from hopping the continent to create start-ups in California. Indeed, in Gilson's (1999, 588–9) account, Silicon Valley was virtually created by Frederick Terman, whose roots were in both the wartime MIT and the prewar Stanford engineering communities. He fit very well in both places, neither of which constitutes a culture. Culture is a very weak constraint in the face of capitalist development. Furthermore, there may be no such cultures; there are only behaviors in response to legal provisions and other constraints and enablers. We might look to the apparently huge cultural differences between India and the United States and wonder why capitalism in the high-tech sector flourishes in both societies, unless we suppose that it is capitalism—along with states that do not interfere too much—that drives the developments and not culture.

Some of those who moved from one firm to another in Silicon Valley must have thought it their moral (and not merely political) right to do so, and many of those who opposed their movement in Massachusetts must have insisted just as forcefully that it was morally wrong, a form of theft, for them to do so. Both these positions are moralistic and likely solipsistic. People hold the view that fits their own interests or roles, not one that fits an overarching moral principle or theory. Anyone might stand back and ask, What is generally beneficial? and would be hard pressed to formulate an argument for why either job hopping or a ban on it is wrong in principle without attention to the larger effects of it. The job hopping that might soon help lift India into the prosperous world of capitalist development cannot be bad prima facie. Indeed, the job hopping that has made California's Silicon Valley the emblem of economic progress and benefits to vast numbers of people cannot trivially be dismissed as immoral on any account. Both sides evoke libertarian rights to defend their position. The libertarian rights of corporations and their owners to control the fruits of human capital conflict with the libertarian rights of employees to be mobile. Lawyers and courts may often side with owners; legislators who are concerned with the general welfare of their polities apparently should side with employees. If Gilson's (1999) account of the facts of the Silicon Valley and Route 128 histories is correct, then utilitarians must have an easy time concluding in favor of the California legal position against enforcing covenants on the transfer of human capital.

The Division of Labor

The standard complaint that capitalism bulldozes traditional cultures is probably true, as Scott (1976, 1985) and many others argue convincingly for specific historical cases. Therefore, it is anticulture. It does this, however, not through an attack on culture, as many opponents of globalization seem to suppose, but rather through the remaking of the values of individuals, most of whom presumably are simply seeking better prospects. Even then, the change in values or preferences comes from little more than being given new choices that were not previously available. Among the most important of these choices is opportunity to participate in the international division of labor. In societies in which subsistence agriculture employs the large majority of all citizens, this opportunity is potentially extremely valuable.

Perhaps the largest part of the anticulture of capitalism comes through the division of labor that greatly enhances productivity. With many others, including Adam Smith ([1776] 1976, book 5, chap. 1, article 2, pp. 782–8), Marx ([1849] 1977, 225), and Emile Durkheim ([1893] 1933), Simmel notes that "the product is completed at the expense of the development of the producer. The increase in psycho-physical energies and skills, which is the result of specialized activity, is of little value for the total personality, which often even becomes stunted because of the diversion of energies that are indispensable for the harmonious growth of the self" ([1900] 1978, 454). At the same time, however, the producer is rewarded with money, not with cultural artifacts or bartered goods. The actions of the producer are increasingly abstract and specialized, whereas the rewards to the producer are increasingly abstract and generalized. Craftsmanship and barter both play ever-decreasing roles in a developing capitalist world.

Indeed, at the core of capitalism, the technological and managerial drive for enhanced productivity is on a par with the inventive drive to create new goods. Capitalism is primarily a machine for enhanced production. These are the elements of the capitalist enterprise that Weber says must take advantage of its opportunities for profit making or be doomed to extinction. Along with technological advances in production techniques, refinements in the division of labor allow perhaps the greatest opportunities for making the same goods cheaper and often of better quality.

Location theory in economics and sociology commends putting similar firms near one another to facilitate the transfer of human capital from one firm to another to the benefit of all, as in the example of Silicon Valley discussed previously.[7] Alfred Marshall ([1890] 1964, 223) thinks this is part of the development of the division of labor. In the Silicon Valley, with its laws blocking restraints on employment, the density of high-tech firms gives opportunity not merely for the mobility of human capital but for its extremely quick development and for the quick development of industrial capital and capacity.

Concluding Remarks

Weber ([1904–05] 1958, 13–17) remarks on the development of science, geometry, and other intellectual disciplines as having begun their ascent to abstraction from any culture after their virtual invention by the Greeks. It is part of the great appeal and power of these disciplines that they lack any significant residues of the cultures that have in some sense produced them. Their content is largely independent of culture once they are underway.[8] Cultures can come crashing down on them, as the still-medieval Catholic Church of Galileo's time came crashing down on his abstract science, which ran against a science that was little more than the ignorant opinions of Aristotle, and as Nazi and Soviet states attempted to crush much of the science that was produced by Jews or that ran against the stupid views of Stalin, who thought his political theory must be reified in biological science. However, there is no Catholic, Nazi, or Soviet science or mathematics; there is only science and mathematics. Culture may affect what is discovered. It does not substantially affect the content of science beyond the moment of discovery, although it can hold up progress, as with the Greek and generally Western opposition to the idea of zero (Seife 2000, esp. chap. 2). Similarly, culture does not substantially affect the content of capitalism beyond the moment of its creation or rise.

Within the capitalist system, individuals will naturally compete with one another for advantage in ways unrelated to the central core of the system, but the Dennis Kozlowskis (Tyco), Andrew Fastows (Enron), and Scott Sullivans (WorldCom), who greedily plundered their firms, were enabled to do so by their managerial positions and enticed to do so by the wealth of those firms. Theirs was a particularly capitalist form of greed in the era of managerial capitalism, as analyzed by Berle and Means, who actually predicted such abuses in the transformation of capitalism into the corporate form. This form creates "a new set of relationships, giving to the groups in control powers which are absolute and not limited by any implied obligation with respect to their use." Through their absolute control of a corporation, the managers "can operate it in their own interests, and can divert a portion of the [corporation's income and assets] to their own uses," and we face the potential for "corporate plundering" (Berle and Means 1932, 354–5).

Moreover, the managers must often view their tenure as relatively brief, so that they may see themselves as being at endgame. No long-run future will haunt them for their actions now, so long as their actions are legal, as Jack Welch's greedy personal profiteering at General Electric may well have been. At endgame, you take what you can and say farewell. The grand entrepreneurial capitalists, such as John D. Rockefeller and Andrew Carnegie, reached endgame only when they died, and even then they could often bind their wealth to their own children or to foundations to honor their names, thus extending the lifetime of their enterprises beyond their own lifetimes and extending the concern with profitability.

Managerial capitalism is often constrained by entrepreneurial capitalism at new firms and even at new industries, so that some firms, perhaps especially new firms, are a countervailing force against one another just as they are against government. This check may not be sufficient to block the abuses of managerial capitalism altogether, especially when particular firms manage to infiltrate government.[9] The first few years of the twenty-first century in the United States presented an appalling failure of capitalism in its managerial form. Greed can thrive within capitalism, but capitalism does not thrive through greed. The worst problem capitalism presents to us now may well be the corporate abuses that are enabled in managerial capitalism and that were analyzed by Berle and Means (1932) at the height of the U.S. Great Depression. Keeping open the possibility of the unfettered struggle of entrepreneurs that characterized the early centuries of capitalism may be the best check against managerial abuses. That possibility largely depends on technological innovation that opens opportunity for new entrepreneurs, although a large part of the innovation that we see is governed hierarchically by extant large corporations, such as Toyota and DuPont.

Yet, even in the face of the spectacle of greed at Enron, Tyco, and various other firms, it is still true—"it must be so," Weber says—that capitalist organization that focuses on corporate profitability must dominate firms in which greed distorts profitability. Plundering is the right word for the ill that Berle and Means recognize. Plundering is for a city or a firm that has been vanquished, and a firm that is plundered cannot long be part of a thriving economy. The plundering suffered by Enron and various other corporations in recent years wrecked them not merely because it took vast sums of money from them but because it cost them so much that they could no longer compete with other corporations in their industries. Another energy supply company chose not even to buy the shell of Enron because its liabilities were so great that owning its assets would be too costly, or at least too risky. That is the correct message of capitalism: Be profitable or die. It is this systemic fact that makes capitalist market economics generally less corrupt and venal than the Enron and other recent cases make it seem. As Weber ([1904–05] 1958, 57) remarks, "The universal reign of unscrupulousness in the pursuit of selfish interests by the making of money has been a specific characteristic of precisely those countries whose bourgeois-capitalistic development . . . has remained backward."[10]

We could ask speculatively what the circumstances are in which the seeming conservatism of culture that might block or slow capitalism would be overcome. There are two partially separate issues: overcoming it at the individual level and overcoming it at the societal level. First, for an individual, it is important that others are open to and also quest for new knowledge and that there is feedback from revision of knowledge to show its payoff. The invention of science and the scientific method by Copernicus, Galileo, and others set Europe on the road to constant change from the innovations of individuals. Second, for a society, openness to capitalism is likely a coordination or tipping phenomenon. If enough societies are open, it is easy and natural to be open. Capitalism is organized for innovation and revisions of our ways of doing things. Capitalist successes in producing basic goods and reducing poverty virtually guarantee that individual innovators will be rewarded so that there is feedback to personal incentives. Capitalism is in some ways similar to science. Its successes are virtually self-evident and hard to forego once they are available. Culture cannot readily block either science or capitalism unless it gains control of government and its powers of blocking innovations.

Money is emblematic of the nature of capitalism in that it does not embody particular cultural values. It is culturally neutral and universally useful in acquiring other things, including things whose value is defined by their cultural role or roots. The ethic and spirit of capitalism are culturally undefined. They do not include Protestantism or any other values other than the need for profits and change if firms are to survive. And we may want a particular firm to survive merely because it gives us our lifestyle or our resources for doing other things. Science is an engine for discovery, and capitalism is an engine for production and for profitability. Jointly, they are historically the main engine for economic progress and for increasing welfare. From the time of the rise of capitalism, they have fed each other and they have stood together outside religion and any strong culture, both of which have often opposed both science and capitalism. As has been true also for science, capitalism has often stood against politics, sometimes being subjugated in a particular society, such as the Soviet Union and Nehru's India. Stalin has become reviled for the harms—economic and personal—that he brought onto the Soviet peoples, and Nehru may soon enough also begin to be reviled for his arrogant economic harms (Das 2000). Any political regime that wants to prosper and *to bring prosperity to its people* has little choice: It must rely on the powers of capitalism, which is the engine for increasing productivity.

References

Barro, Robert J., and Xavier Sala-i-Martin. 1995. *Economic Growth.* New York: McGraw-Hill.

Berle, Adolph A., and Gardner C. Means. 1932. *The Modern Corporation and Private Property.* New York: Macmillan.

Chace, James. 2002. *1912: Wilson, Roosevelt, Taft, and Debs—The Election That Changed the Country.* New York: Simon and Schuster.

Das, Gurcharan. [2000] 2001. *India Unbound.* New York: Knopf.

Doyle, Arthur Conan, Sir. [1914] 1986. "His Last Bow," in *The Annotated Sherlock Holmes,* edited by William S. Baring-Gould, vol. II. New York: Clarkson N. Potter: 792–803.

Durkheim, Émile. [1893] 1933. *The Division of Labor in Society.* New York: Macmillan.

Gilson, Ronald. 1999. "The Legal Infrastructure of High Technology Industrial Districts: Silicon Valley, Route 128, and Covenants Not to Compete." *New York University Law Review* 74 (June): 575–629.

Gopnik, Adam. 2004. "The Big One: Historians Rethink the War to End All Wars." *New Yorker* (23 August): 78–85.

Hardin, Russell. 1982. *Collective Action.* Baltimore, Md.: Johns Hopkins University Press for Resources for the Future.

———. 1995. *One for All: The Logic of Group Conflict.* Princeton, N.J.: Princeton University Press.

———. 2001. "The Normative Core of Rational Choice Theory." In *The Economic World View: Studies in the Ontology of Economics,* edited by Uskali Maki. Cambridge, UK: Cambridge University Press: 57–74.

Lindblom, Charles E. 1977. *Politics and Markets: The World's Political-Economic Systems.* New York: Basic.

Marshall, Alfred. [1890] 1964. *Principles of Economics.* 8th ed. London: Macmillan.

Marx, Karl. [1849] 1977. "Wage Labour and Capital," in Karl Marx and Frederick Engels, *Collected Works.* New York: International Publishers, 9:197–228.

McMillan, John. 2002. *Reinventing the Bazaar: A Natural History of Markets.* New York: Norton.

Mueller, John. 1999. *Capitalism, Democracy, and Ralph's Pretty Good Grocery.* Princeton, N.J.: Princeton University Press.

Nedelsky, Jennifer. 1990. *Private Property and the Limits of American Constitutionalism: The Madisonian Framework and Its Legacy.* Chicago: University of Chicago Press.

Olson, Mancur, Jr. 1965. *The Logic of Collective Action.* Cambridge, Mass.: Harvard University Press.

Saxenian, Anna Lee. 1994. *Regional Advantage: Culture and Competition in Silicon Valley and Route 128.* Cambridge, Mass.: Harvard University Press.

Schmitt, Frederick, ed. 1994. *Socializing Epistemology: The Social Dimensions of Knowledge.* Lanham, Md.: Rowman and Littlefield.

Schumpeter, Joseph A. [1942] 1950. *Capitalism, Socialism and Democracy.* 3rd ed. New York: Harper.

Scott, James C. 1976. *The Moral Economy of the Peasant: Rebellion and Subsistence in Southeast Asia.* New Haven, Conn.: Yale University Press.

———. 1985. *Weapons of the Weak: Everyday Forms of Peasant Resistance.* New Haven, Conn.: Yale University Press.

———. 1998. *Seeing Like a State: How Certain Schemes to Improve the Human Condition Have Failed.* New Haven, Conn.: Yale University Press.

Seife, Charles. 2000. *Zero: The Biography of a Dangerous Idea.* New York: Penguin.

Simmel, Georg. [1900] 1978. *The Philosophy of Money.* Translated by Tom Bottomore and David Frisby. Boston: Routledge and Kegan Paul.

Smith, Adam. [1776] 1976. *An Inquiry into the Nature and Causes of the Wealth of Nations.* Oxford: Oxford University Press; Indianapolis, Ind.: Liberty Classics, 1981, reprint.

Traub, James. 2001. "Keeping Up with the Shidhayes." *New York Times Magazine* (15 April): 32–7.

van der Ploeg, Jan Douwe. 1993. "Potatoes and Knowledge." In *An Anthropological Critique of Development,* edited by Mark Hobart. London: Routledge, 209–27.

Weber, Max. [1904–05] 1958. *The Protestant Ethic and the Spirit of Capitalism.* Translated by Talcott Parsons. New York: Scribner's Sons.

———. 1994. *Political Writings,* edited by Peter Lassman and Ronald Spiers. Cambridge, UK: Cambridge University Press (the essays cited here date from 1917).

Notes to Chapter One

1. Prepared for presentation at the conference "The Ethic and Spirit of Capitalism," Cornell University, 8–9 October 2004. I thank Huan Wang for energetic and creative research assistance in writing this paper.

2. James Chace (2002) argues that the U.S. presidential election of 1912 pitted these three visions in the contest among the trustbuster Theodore Roosevelt, the federal regulator Woodrow Wilson, and the small-government and economic-libertarian William Howard Taft. Taft insisted there are limits to government capacity to make the economy flourish by trying to run it. The total vote implicitly in favor of government intervention swamped the vote for Taft.

3. Das ([2000] 2001, 175) tells of a meeting at which an industrialist, Rahul Bajaj, is threatened with jail for producing more scooters than his quota allowed. He retorts, "Sir, my grandfather went to jail for my country's freedom. I stand ready to do the same for producing on behalf of my motherland."

4. The compounding effect of these rates is astonishing. At 7 percent growth per year, the Indian economy doubles in size in a decade. India is now in its second decade of such growth, and if it continues for two decades it will have grown by a factor of four. "If the United States had begun in 1870 at a real per capita GDP of $2,244 and had then grown at a rate of 0.75 percent per year over the next 120 years, then its real per capita GDP in 1990 would have been $5,519, only 2.5 times the value in 1870 and 30 percent of the actual value in 1990 of $18,258. Then, instead of ranking first in the world in 1990, the United States would have ranked 37th out of 127 countries with data. To put it another way, if the growth rate had been lower by just 1 percentage point per year, then the US real per capita GDP in 1990 would have been close to that in Mexico and Hungary and would have been about $1,000 less than that in Portugal and Greece" (Barro and Sala-i-Martin 1995, 1).

5. See Saritha Rai, "India Sets a Fast Pace, Expanding 8.2% in Year," *New York Times,* 1 July 2004, W.1; Amy Waldman, "In India, Economic Growth and Democracy Do Mix," *New York Times,* 23 May 2004, 4.3.

6. Much of the legal concern with employee mobility makes good sense. For example, an insurance agent working for a firm could set up a competing firm by enticing clients from the earlier to the new firm (see further, Gilson 1999, 616–18). The issue in the high-tech industries of the Silicon Valley is much more clearly about human capital than about mere economic information. Hence, the laws that came into place to deal with taking secrets from one firm to another are not strictly suited to the movements of people with very general skills and knowledge gained on the job. The law could directly penalize the movement of proprietary information, such as names of insurance clients, without going after all cases of job hopping.

7. Hence, the political proposal to spread financial firms around after September 11, rather than having them rebuild to stay concentrated in the southern tip of Manhattan, is probably a bad idea.

8. This claim is contested, of course. Also, one school of epistemologists argue that social conditions influence what we look for and what we find, but these social epistemologists do not argue that we thereby determine the truth of what we find. See, for example, contributions to Schmitt 1994.

9. Enron donated campaign funds to so many officeholders who might have been charged with investigating and prosecuting it that U.S. Attorney General John Ashcroft and most of the U.S. attorney's office in Houston, Texas (Enron's headquarters), were forced to recuse themselves from pursuing the case. *New York Times,* "Cleaning Up after the Debacle," editorial page, 20 January 2002, p. 4.12.

10. On the rise of virtue in retailing, see Mueller 1990, 77–93.

2 Tocqueville and the Spirit of American Capitalism

Richard Swedberg, Cornell University

D EMOCRACY IN AMERICA HAS FOR A LONG TIME BEEN RE-
garded as a classic in the United States, and there exists a huge
secondary literature on what Tocqueville has to say about various aspects of
American life, especially its politics, religion, and organizational life. What
Tocqueville says about the U.S. economy has, in contrast, rarely been singled
out for special attention. At the most, individual aspects of his analysis have
been scrutinized, such as Tocqueville's observation that wealth was as quickly
made as it was lost in the United States and his prophecy that, if a new aristocracy is ever to come into being in a democracy, it will be in the form of an
industrial elite (e.g., Pessen 1971, 1982; Drescher 1968:73ff.).

The purpose of this chapter is to show that Tocqueville's analysis of
economic life is a subject worthy of its own interest and that Tocqueville,
contrary to what has been suggested, did have a coherent view of economic
matters.[1] Tocqueville, as I will attempt to show, had a very original and
suggestive way of looking at the economy that was part of his more general analysis of society, and this analysis is well worth paying attention to
(cf. Hereth 1977). Tocqueville "painted to a considerable extent in economic
colours," as Joseph Schumpeter elegantly put it in *History of Economic Analysis* (Schumpeter 1954:820). This comes out in his analysis of the United States
and the French Revolution as well as in some of his minor writings, such as
his famous memoir on pauperism and his less known writings on the French
railroads (e.g., Tocqueville [1835] 1997, 1995). In this paper, however, I will

limit myself to *Democracy in America,* and I shall try to make the following two points: (1) that Tocqueville's analysis may help to improve the status of the concept of the spirit of capitalism, which is currently very low in the social sciences; and (2) that Tocqueville can also be of help in further developing this concept so that we better understand what a vigorous spirit of capitalism means.

Finally, as part of making these two points, I will show that Tocqueville established a direct link between the strength of U.S. capitalism and Puritanism. In this context I also want to remind the reader very strongly that in Weber's day it was common to point to the positive relationship between Protestantism and capitalism. Because this is not the case any longer, and Weber's thesis in *The Protestant Ethic* is often presented as unique and at odds with historiography, it can be mentioned that Weber cited quite a few historians and writers that saw a positive link between Protestantism and capitalism: Macaulay, Thomas Carlyle, W. J. Ashley, Eduard Bernstein, Eberhard Gothein, William Petty, H. T. Buckle, E. T. Rogers, Manley, Temple, Montesquieu, Matthew Arnold, John Keats, Heine, Heinrich Wiskemann, Doyle, Cunningham, and Hermann Levy.[2] To Weber's list one may also add the names of such nineteenth-century economists as Karl Marx and Alfred Marshall (e.g., Marx [1867] 1906:792–93, 825–26; Marshall 1895:36–39).

In referring to the low status of the concept of the spirit of capitalism, I have first of all in mind the fact that the great majority of social scientists do not use this concept (or some identical term). One important reason for this is that they reject the so-called Weber thesis that the spirit of capitalism ignited the Western economy and turned it into modern capitalism, largely as a result of the activities of the ascetic Protestant sects. Mainstream economic historians, in brief, have found no evidence of an important link between Calvinism and similar religions, on the one hand, and a change in economic mentality, on the other. What further adds to the uncertain status of the concept of the spirit of capitalism is Weber's argument that the impact of ascetic Protestantism on capitalist mentality was a onetime affair and of no further historical consequence once religion had been dethroned from its central position in the Western universe. This last point, it should be added, represents to my mind a misreading of Weber, who devotes a full chapter in *The Protestant Ethic and the Spirit of Capitalism* to the nonreligious spirit of capitalism that could be found in eighteenth-century America, as illustrated by the writings of Benjamin Franklin. Nonetheless, the impression that the spirit of capitalism only played an important role in modern capitalism during a very brief historical period still remains.

The U.S. Economy at the Time of Tocqueville's Visit

Let us now turn to Tocqueville and his analysis of the United States. The 26-year-old Tocqueville spent about nine months in the United States, where he arrived on May 10, 1831, and travelled around till February 20, 1832, when he left the country. The first volume of *Democracy in America* was published in 1835 and the second in 1840. Both were primarily based on information that Tocqueville had gathered during his trip to the United States, even though he also added to his knowledge during the years he spent writing his study. Tocqueville, as we know, paints a full picture of life in the United States in *Democracy in America,* and this includes its economy.

Before taking a close look at what Tocqueville has to say about the American economy, I would like to say something about the U.S. economy at the time of Tocqueville's visit, as seen by economic historians. In doing so, I shall primarily rely on a well-known study by Douglass North on the U.S. economy during its formative period, *The Economic Growth of the United States, 1790–1860.* According to North, the years from the end of the eighteenth century to the mid-1800s were absolutely crucial for getting the U.S. economy going in an entrepreneurial direction. The first steps toward the creation of a national market were taken during this period, and to explain this North refers primarily to price differentials. The three main regions of the Republic now slowly began to merge into one huge market. There was, first of all, the South, which mainly produced a few plantation staples for export. Then there was the East, which was the center for manufacturing, banking, and commerce. And finally, there was the West, which supplied the East and the South with food, thanks to its surplus production of grain and livestock. What made the economy so dynamic during this period, according to North, were primarily the cotton trade and the migration westwards. The former brought in income as well as capital from abroad, and migration opened up new land and new opportunities.

The time in the 1830s, when Tocqueville visited the United States, was particularly important in creating an entrepreneurial American economy. North writes: "The twenty years between the trough of the precipitous depression of 1818 and that of the even more severe depression following 1839 were a critical period in American economic growth. *If one were to date the beginning of acceleration in the economy's growth and the years when industrialization began, it would be during this period"* (North 1961:189; emphasis added).

During the nine months in 1831–1832 that Tocqueville toured the United States, there was, according to North, "a surge of economic activity [that] was evident on all sides and in all regions" (North 1961:194). North notes in particular "the quickening pace of economic activity [that] was evident in 1831 and 1832" (*ibid.*).

The American Spirit of Capitalism and Its Defining Features

What role did what Weber termed "the spirit of capitalism" play in these economic events in the United States? North, as is clear from what has just been said, finds no room for concepts of this type, and it is here, I suggest, that we may learn from *Democracy in America*. If we define the spirit of capitalism as the mental propensity of economic actors for dynamic market behavior, we quickly note that Tocqueville has quite a bit to say on this topic. *Democracy in America* contains, in fact, a vivid and detailed picture of the American spirit of capitalism in the early 1800s, which Tocqueville describes as "the restless activity of Americans to make a profit by working hard." Tocqueville, of course, uses his own terminology to describe what may be called the spirit of capitalism in the United States; and to give a precise account of his ideas on this score it is important to use the exact terms that are used in *Democracy in America*. One reason for this is that Tocqueville's terminology differs quite a bit from the terminology that is used in modern economics and social science. Proceeding in this manner also makes it easier to highlight the differences between Tocqueville's type of analysis and that of conventional economic and social science analysis.

Before introducing Tocqueville's views on the spirit of capitalism, it can be noted that his terminology is considerably closer to that of Weber in *The Protestant Ethic* than to mainstream economics and social science. In particular, the Weberian term *spirit* (*Geist*) is frequently used in *Democracy in America,* including when it comes to the economy (*esprit*).[3] Tocqueville speaks, for example, of "the spirit of enterprise" (*l'esprit de l'entreprise*) in the United States (Tocqueville [1835–40] 2000: 154, 364, 388, 390, 394; 1959:75). He writes at one point in his notes for *Democracy in America* that "what distinguishes the

North is the *spirit of enterprise*; what distinguishes the South is the *spirit of chivalry*" (Tocqueville 1959:75). It should also be noted that although the term *spirit*, with its associations to religion, came naturally to Tocqueville in the early 1800s, it already seemed a bit strained to Weber, and it has today an odd and quaint tone. Tocqueville's portrait of the spirit of capitalism in *Democracy in America* differs on certain points from the description of the spirit of capitalism in *The Protestant Ethic,* even if the two are similar enough to be seen as variations of the same species. According to Tocqueville, the Americans (except in the South) are characterized by the following traits in their economic lives: (1) "*restiveness,*" (2) a "*taste for material well-being,*" (3) work regarded as "*honorable*"; and (4) "*audacity*" or "*boldness*" in business (Tocqueville [1835–1840] 2000:384–90, 506–09, 511–14, 525–29, 594–95). Like Weber, Tocqueville sees a direct link between the spirit of capitalism and religion. As opposed to Weber, however, Tocqueville emphasizes the close link between the spirit of capitalism and political behavior.

It is also clear that Weber and Tocqueville view people's attitude to work as part of the spirit of capitalism. One may nonetheless be justified in singling out "*restiveness*" (*inquiétude*) as especially important to Tocqueville's portrait of the American spirit of capitalism, just as the ascetic attitude to work was at the heart of Weber's description of the early European spirit of capitalism. In the United States, Tocqueville says, restiveness takes the expression that people often want to move, that they are about to move, or that they are in the process of moving. Although in an aristocracy everything has a fixed place and no one moves anywhere, in a democracy it is just the opposite. The United States, according to *Democracy in America,* is "a community . . . where all the citizens are on the move" (*ibid.,* p. 596). People are "excited, uncertain, breathless, ready to change will and place" (*ibid.,* p. 616). Some people move in a physical sense and others in a social sense. It is not only immigrants who move on to their final destination, once they have arrived to the United States; those who have been in the country for a generation or more often decide to leave their homes and join the movement Westwards. And those who do not move in a physical sense change their behavior or their ideas. Nothing is stable, everything is fluid; "all that is solid melts into air," as Marx and Engels famously put it in *The Communist Manifesto* (Marx and Engels [1848] 1978:476).

The desire to move and to change things, Tocqueville argues, cannot take much of a political expression in the United States because its political structure is poorly developed and there are few political jobs. In the area of the economy, in contrast, there are plenty of opportunities. "When public offices are few, poorly paid, unstable, and when, on the other hand, industrial careers are numerous and productive," we read in *Democracy in America,* "it is toward industry and not the administration that the new and impatient desires born daily of equality are directed" (*ibid.,* p. 605). The "vast hopes" that appear once aristocratic barriers have been removed, are therefore primarily directed at the economy—at making money and at buying new things (*ibid.,* p. 513). People "dream constantly of the goods they do not have" (*ibid.,* p. 511).

Always ready to tackle new economic tasks and challenges, Americans become impatient and move from one economic activity to another, in the hope of doing better. One of the key passages about the American spirit of capitalism reads as follows:

> In the United States, a man carefully builds a dwelling in which to pass his declining years, and he sells it while the roof is being laid; he plants a garden and he rents it out just as he is going to taste its fruits; he clears a field and he leaves to others the care of harvesting its crops. He embraces a profession and quits it. He settles in a place from which he departs soon after so as to take his changing desires elsewhere. Should his private affairs give him some respite, he immediately plunges into the whirlwind of politics. And when toward the end of a year filled with work some leisure still remains to him, he carries his restive curiosity here and there within the vast limits of the United States. (*ibid.* p. 512)

The aggregate result of all this restiveness is a beehive of economic activity, where something new has barely been finished before it is replaced by something that looks more promising. This leads to a situation that Tocqueville describes as a "secret restiveness," which adds to the general restiveness. This secret restiveness is due to the fact that what people want are material objects and consequently not of lasting value (*ibid.,* p. 512). There is also the fact that infinite dreams and infinite needs can by definition not be satisfied; everybody strives constantly for more, and final consummation therefore eludes them. Both of these phenomena, Tocqueville says, help to explain why there is "a sort of cloud" hanging over the Americans and why they display such a "singular melancholy" (*ibid.,* p. 511, 514). People are "grave and almost sad in their pleasures" (*ibid.,* p. 511). The end result, Tocqueville says, is a "spectacle"—a "useless pursuit of complete felicity" (*ibid.,* p. 512). "This *is* Tocqueville, not Galbraith," as Robert K. Merton points out (Merton 1973:125).

The second defining feature of the American spirit of capitalism, according to *Democracy in America,* is *"the taste for material well-being"* (*le goût du bien-être matériel*), which is described as "the care of satisfying the least needs of the body and of providing the smallest comforts of life" (*ibid.,* p. 506). Tocqueville notes that this taste is "violent" and he also refers to it, perhaps more fittingly, as a "passion for material well-being" (*la passion du bien-être matériel*) and a "love of material enjoyments" (*l'amour des jouissances matérielles; ibid.,* pp. 506, 508). What makes these last expressions interesting is that they explicitly refer to the role of emotions in economic actions, something that is rarely done in mainstream economic thought. In *The Passions and the Interests* (1977), Albert O. Hirschman has classically described how modern economics from its very beginning assumed that emotions and economic analysis do not belong together, and how this meant that an important dimension of economic life was ignored. *Homo economicus* is rational, but has no emotions whatsoever (e.g., Persky 1995).

Tocqueville, who wrote his work on the United States around the time when the idea of *homo economicus* was being formulated, instinctively avoided taking the route of John Stuart Mill in this regard, and this may well be one of the reasons why Tocqueville (but not Mill) gave such a good picture of the economic atmosphere in the United States.[4] To this should be added that through his analysis of the taste for material well-being, Tocqueville also makes an early contribution to the study of consumerism, which he discovered to be an integral part of American economic life. On this last point Tocqueville differs from Weber, who does not see consumerism as part of the spirit of capitalism in *The Protestant Ethic,* but only asceticism and the tendency to reinvest.

The taste or love for material well-being is "universal" in American society, Tocqueville says, and can also be found among the poor (*ibid.,* p. 507). He refers to the role that "imagination [of material comfort]" plays among the poor and how they cast "a glance of hope and longing" at the goods of those who are more fortunate (*ibid.*). Whereas hope for material well-being is characteristic of the poor, the rich fear that they will lose what they have. This has to do with the fact that the rich in the United States have had to make their own fortune and therefore know what it is like to live without material wealth. This also goes for the rich who have inherited their wealth, Tocqueville says; they are well aware of the fact that they may one day lose their riches.

At this point of his discussion of the taste for material well-being, Tocqueville makes a brief comparison between the attitude to well-being that can be found among the elite in an aristocracy and the one that can be found among the rich in a democracy. Aristocrats, he says, do not think very much about wealth or their possessions, which they take for granted. They display "haughty scorn" and "high-minded disdain" for material objects (*ibid.,* pp. 506, 507). To illustrate their attitude in this regard, Tocqueville uses the example of revolutions. Drawing perhaps on information from members of his own family, he notes that "all revolutions that have troubled or destroyed aristocracies have shown with what facility people accustomed to the superfluous can do without the necessary, whereas men who have laboriously arrived at ease can hardly live after having lost it" (*ibid.,* p. 506). Tocqueville's ideas on this topic, it may be added, go well with the observations of Bruno Bettelheim from his stay in a German concentration camp in the 1930s (Bettelheim 1943). The closer that people held on to their material goods and conventional status, Bettelheim says, the harder it was for them to be stripped of these when they entered the world of the concentration camp.

Tocqueville similarly notes that the group that has invested the most of itself in material objects is the middle class: "The passion for material well-being is essentially a middle-class passion; it grows larger and spreads with this class; it becomes preponderant with it. From there it reaches the higher ranks of society and descends within the people" (*ibid.,* p. 507). More generally, Tocqueville regarded the middle class as central to democratic society and its economy already in the 1830s.

But even if the passion for material well-being is universal in a democracy such as the United States, Tocqueville says that it can nonetheless best be described as a "contained passion," which has little in common with the grand passions of the aristocrats (*ibid.,* p. 508). What drove typical Americans in the early 1800s was not a desire for castles or to surround themselves with luxuries, but to create what Tocqueville terms *comfort,* which represented a considerably more modest ambition. Whereas luxury was a symbol for the life of the elite in an aristocracy, comfort was the equivalent for the life of the successful in a democracy (for the invention of the concept of comfort, see Crowley 2003). The difference between luxury and comfort is clearly outlined in the following quote:

[In a democracy] it is not a question of building vast palaces, of vanquishing and outwitting nature, of depleting the universe in order better to satiate the passions of a man; it is about adding a few toises to one's field, planting an orchard, enlarging a residence, making life easier and more comfortable at each instant, preventing inconvenience, and satisfying the least needs without effort and almost without cost. (*ibid.*, p. 509)

Just as Tocqueville saw the restiveness of Americans as having a dark side to it, this was also the case with their taste for well-being. The love or passion with which material objects were being pursued in the United States, he argues, was threatening to slowly undo their concern with the important things in life. "These objects are small," he says, "but the soul clings to them: it considers them every day and from very close; in the end they hide the rest of the world from it, and they sometimes come to place themselves between it and God" (*ibid.*). Consumerism, in other words, was on a collision course with religion—a theme that Tocqueville was to return to in his analysis of the role of religion in American economic life.

The third feature of the American spirit of capitalism is *work,* and here one can find similarities as well as differences between Tocqueville's analysis of the situation in the United States and Weber's analysis of the situation in Europe. In the United States, we read in *Democracy in America,* everybody has to work for a living, and every type of work is considered honorable, including work for profit. Even the U.S. President, Tocqueville notes with raised eyebrows, gets paid for his job. And whereas the work of, say, a servant is considered as totally menial in an aristocracy, it is seen in a much more positive light in a democracy. One reason for this is that the servant knows that one day he or she may become a master and vice versa.

The very special way in which people in a democratic society regard work comes out with the most clarity in *Democracy in America* when it is compared to work in an aristocracy. In a democracy everyone feels compelled to work, and this includes those who can afford not to do so. It is seen as dishonorable *not* to work, and for this reason also the rich feel compelled to work, to get involved with politics or in some other way keep busy. Wealthy Americans who want to do nothing, Tocqueville says, have to go to Europe, which still contains enough "debris of aristocratic societies" to make leisure and inactivity an honorable occupation (*ibid.*).

A very important feature of U.S. society is also that work to make a profit is seen as an honorable activity. "Equality not only rehabilitates the idea of work, it uplifts the idea of working to procure lucre" (*ibid.*, p. 525). Aristocrats, in contrast, despise those who work to make a profit and pretend to be beyond this type of contemptible activity:

In aristocracies, it is not precisely work that is scorned, but work with a view to profit. Work is glorious when ambition of virtue alone makes one undertake it. Under aristocracy, nevertheless, it constantly happens that he who works for honor is not insensitive to the lure of gain. But these two desires meet only in the depth of his soul. He takes much care to conceal from all regard the place where they unite. He willingly hides it from himself. In aristocratic countries there is scarcely a public official who does not claim to serve the state without interest. (*ibid.*)

Although all types of work in a democracy are honorable, people prefer nonetheless to work in certain sectors of the economy rather than in others. Agriculture, for example, is seen as much less promising than do commerce and industry. Only rich people can make a good profit from agriculture, Tocqueville says. To the extent that ordinary Americans do get involved in agriculture, however, they invest it with "industrial passions" and "the spirit of trade" (*ibid.*, p. 529). The result is that the United States has no peasants, only farmers.

Commerce and industry are the two areas where one can most easily make a quick profit, and therefore attract the most people. Tocqueville was full of admiration for the enormous progress of the United States in these two areas. He sums up his view as follows:

In the United States the greatest industrial enterprises are executed without difficulty, because the population as a whole is involved in industry and because the poorest as well as the most opulent citizens willingly unite their efforts in this . . . Americans arrived only yesterday on the soil they inhabit, and they have already overturned the whole order of nature to their profit. They have united the Hudson to the Mississippi and linked the Atlantic Ocean with the Gulf of Mexico across more than five hundred leagues of continent that separate these two seas. The longest railroads that have been made up to our day are in America.

But what strikes me most in the United States is not the extraordinary greatness of a few industrial enterprises, it is the innumerable multitude of small enterprises (*ibid.*, pp. 528–29)

Although Tocqueville has often been criticized for his failure to visit any factories during his trip to the United States, the passage just cited makes clear that he nonetheless was well aware of the importance of industry.[5] The same is clear from his famous statement about the way that industrial development will polarize democratic society in the United States into two antagonistic groups, workers and capitalists. On the one hand, there are the workers who will become ever more ignorant because of the division of labor ("brutes"). On the other hand are the factory owners, who get to plan more and more of economic life thanks to the same division of labor, and who therefore will become increasingly powerful and sophisticated (*ibid.*, p. 530). Tocqueville famously concludes his analysis of workers and capitalists with the statement that "if ever permanent inequality of conditions and aristocracy are introduced anew into the world, one can predict that they will enter by this door" (*ibid.*, p. 532).

Finally we come to the last defining feature of the American spirit of capitalism, namely the attitude of "*audacity*" or "*boldness*" that exists in business (e.g., *ibid.*, pp. 384–90, 594–95). This phenomenon, it deserves to be pointed out, is related to, but not identical to, risk taking. Tocqueville essentially argues that "chance" will always be important in a democratic society and, as a result, business will be seen as a "lottery" (*ibid.*, p. 594). To some extent Tocqueville means by this that democratic societies tend to develop a distinct "opportunity structure," as noted by Robert Merton (e.g., Merton 1995). Tocqueville similarly notes the element of rational calculation and risk taking that is involved.

Tocqueville's argument about the audacity and boldness that is characteristic of American commercial culture goes beyond what we today mean by rational decision making and risk taking, however. There is also, for example, a distinct emotional element involved. "Those who live amid democratic instability," Tocqueville writes, "constantly have the image of chance before their eyes, and in the end they love all undertakings in which chance plays a role" (*ibid.*, p. 528). He concludes: "they are all brought into commerce, not only because of the gain it promises them, but for *love of the emotions* that it gives them" (*ibid.* emphasis added; cf. pp. 270–71). "They love the sensation as much as the gain" (*ibid.*, p. 271).

Tocqueville supplies one detailed example in *Democracy in America* of what accounts for this boldness that is so important to "the commercial greatness of the United States," and this is shipping (*ibid.*, p. 384, cf. 384–90).[6] The Americans sail much faster across the Atlantic than any other people, and this means that they can transport goods at a cheaper price. Tocqueville devotes several pages of his study to possible explanations for this phenomenon, which he regards as an example of the "maritime genius" of the Americans (*ibid.*, p. 385). One possible reason could be that ships are cheaper to build in the United States than in other countries, and Tocqueville notes that this is marginally the case. On the other hand, the wages of the sailors on American ships are higher than the wages on non-American ships. American ships are furthermore not as well constructed as other ships, and they do not last as long. Tocqueville concludes that "one would seek in vain the causes of this superiority [of the Americans] in material advantages; it is due to purely intellectual and moral qualities" (*ibid.*, p. 386).

These intellectual and moral qualities Tocqueville also refers to as "*a sort of heroism in the manner of doing business*" (*ibid.*, p. 387; emphasis added). The real reason Americans can sail faster across the Atlantic than anyone else and keep such low prices is explained as follows:

> The European navigator ventures on the seas only with prudence; he departs only when the weather invites him to; if an unforeseen accident comes upon him, he enters into port at night, he furls a part of his sails, and when he sees the ocean within the approach of land, he slows his course and examines the sun.
>
> The American neglects these precautions and braves these dangers. He departs while the tempest still roars; at night as in day he opens all his sails to the wind; while on the go, he repairs his ship, worn down by the storm, and when he finally approaches the end of his course, he continues to fly toward the shore as if he already perceived the port. (*ibid.*, p. 386)

It deserves to be underlined that what is involved here is not only conventional risk taking but also something else: "the American, in acting [in this way], not only follows calculation, he obeys, above all, his nature" (*ibid.*, p. 387).

Before leaving Tocqueville's description of the American spirit of capitalism, it deserves to be added that he also discusses the attitude to time among the Americans and how this is related to the economy. The past means little to people in a democracy, we are told, as opposed to the situation in an aristocratic society where the past means everything. Democracies similarly tend to discredit the importance of the future, which according to Tocqueville is the realm of religion. What remains is the present; and this is the only dimension that interests the Americans: "they are disposed to act as if they will exist for only a simple day" (*ibid.*, p. 523).

The Role of Religion in the American Spirit of Capitalism

Tocqueville visited the United States during a period of great revival among the Protestant sects, known as the Second Awakening.[7] Similar to Weber,

Tocqueville saw a general and important link between economic life and religion, but there also exist differences between the two. Tocqueville's view of religion in the United States not only was related to his analysis of the crucial role that Puritanism has played in the United States (which will be discussed later), but also had deep roots in his own personal conviction that a life without religion was destructive and ultimately untenable. Although Tocqueville's private relationship to religion is complex and difficult to capture in a few lines, his public attitude, as expressed in his books and political speeches, is quite different (e.g., Goldstein 1968). In private, Tocqueville expressed doubt and sometimes also stated that he was not a believer. In public, on the other hand, he firmly supported religion and especially Catholicism; he also argued that religion had an important moral role to play in society at large.

What Tocqueville says about the relationship between economics and religion in *Democracy in America* draws on his general view of life. Human beings, according to Tocqueville, do not only have to attend to the needs of the body, through material goods, but also to the needs of the soul, through immaterial goods. "The human heart is vaster than one supposes; it can at once contain a taste for the goods of the earth and a love of those of Heaven; sometimes it seems to give itself over frantically to one of the two; but it is never long before it thinks of the other" (*ibid.*, p. 520). What differentiates humans from animals, according to Tocqueville, is not their material desires—these are essentially the same—but the fact that by having a soul, human beings can use reason and not only instinct to provide for themselves. "In men, the angel teaches the beast the art of satisfying itself" (*ibid.*, p. 521).

Human beings are consequently able to provide for needs other than their most primitive ones. This, however, is only the case on condition that they attend properly to their souls; if not, their productive powers will decline, with poverty and destitution as a result. Because democracy tends to encourage materialism, religious countermeasures have to be introduced into democratic countries if the economy is to do well. "Materialism," according to Tocqueville, "is a dangerous malady of the human mind in all nations; but one must dread it particularly in a democratic people because it combines marvellously with the most familiar vice in the heart of these peoples" (*ibid.*, p. 519).

Tocqueville not only establishes a positive link between religious behavior and economic behavior in his study, he also presents the general mechanisms through which they interact with one another. First of all, religion has the capacity to prevent human desires for material goods from being endless.

Religion puts a limit to these desires, which means that they can be satisfied. Thanks to Christianity, we read in *Democracy in America,* "the human spirit never perceives an unlimited field before itself; however bold it may be, from time to time it feels that it ought to halt before insurmountable barriers" (*ibid.,* p. 279). On this point Tocqueville sounds very much like Emile Durkheim, who in *Suicide* discusses "economic anomie" and how people suffer when there are no limits to their economic desires (e.g., Durkheim [1897] 1951:246, 259).

The second mechanism that turns religion into a positive factor in economic life, according to Tocqueville, is that religion teaches individuals to become regular, methodical, and concentrated in their pursuit of various goals, including economic ones. Through religion, Tocqueville explains, individuals learn to ignore the many temptations in everyday life and instead keep their eyes on the much more important awards in the next life. This way of behaving comes in very handy in economic life, Tocqueville explains. "Men are therefore . . . accustomed naturally, and so to speak without wanting it, to consider for a long succession of years an unmoving object towards which they constantly advance, and they learn by insensible progressions to repress a thousand little desires the better to succeed in satisfying the great and permanent desire that torments them" (*ibid.,* p. 522). This mode of behavior is then used for economic matters: "when the same men want to occupy themselves with earthly things, these habits are found again" (*ibid.*). Tocqueville concludes that "this explains why religious peoples have accomplished such lasting things" (*ibid.*).[8]

This view of the relationship between religion and economic life is then applied to the situation in the United States in *Democracy in America.* In general, Tocqueville found Americans to be very religious, and he states that the United States was the most genuinely Christian country that existed in his days (*ibid.,* p. 273). "On my arrival in the United States it was the religious aspect of the country that first struck me" (*ibid.,* p. 282). Tocqueville is also very careful to point out that religion must not be involved in politics, if it is to have a positive impact on the economy and on a country more generally. He considered it a disaster that the Catholic Church had been so closely involved with the king and the aristocracy in France before the Revolution, and felt that this was the main reason why the Catholic Church was not more popular in his home country. Tocqueville was adamant not only that the state must be separated from the church but that the church should keep out of politics.

"I would rather chain priests in the sanctuary than allow them to leave it" (*ibid.,* p. 521). He similarly argued that one of the main reasons for the positive impact of religion on social and economic life in the United States was precisely the fact that the preachers kept out of politics.

The general mechanisms through which religion had this positive impact have already been presented: It sets limits to people's behavior and it introduces regular and methodical habits into people's lives. But Tocqueville also introduces another factor into his analysis of the situation in America that deserves to be highlighted, and that is women. In the United States it is women, Tocqueville says, who are the most religious, and "it is women who make mores" (*ibid.,* p. 279). Women are much less susceptible to materialism than males because they spend more of their time in the home and do not participate in public life and the official economy. The key role that a strong and healthy family life plays in a successful economy, according to Tocqueville, comes out very well in *Democracy in America*: "When . . . the American returns to the bosom of his family, he immediately meets the image of order and peace. There all his pleasures are simple and natural, his joys innocent and tranquil; and as he arrives at happiness through regularity of life, he becomes habituated to regulating his opinions as well as his tastes without difficulty" (*ibid.*).

A final factor that helps to account for the close and positive relationship between religion and economic behavior in the United States, according to Tocqueville, has to do with the special outlook on secular and economic matters that one can find among American priests. Whereas priests in Europe exclusively focus on the rewards in the next world, it is different in the United States, where the priests also promise rewards in this world. They are interested in industry and in general have a positive relationship to the material dimension of modern life:

> In the Middle Ages priests spoke only of the other life; they scarcely worried about proving that a sincere Christian can be a happy man here below. But American preachers constantly come back to earth and only with great trouble can they take their eyes off it. . . . It is often difficult to know when listening to them if the principal object of religion is to procure eternal felicity in the other world or well-being in this one. (*ibid.,* pp. 506–07)

American priests, as Tocqueville puts it in his notes for *Democracy in America,* are "entrepreneurs of a religious industry" (Tocqueville 1959:185).

According to Tocqueville, there exists a set of ideas in the United States on how economic behavior and morality (including religion) belong together, and he refers to this as an "official doctrine," "*the doctrine of self-interest (intérêt) well understood*" (*ibid.*, pp. 500–06). The Americans, Tocqueville says, do not have a public morality that they idealize and call beautiful, in the way that aristocrats do. Instead they pride themselves on having a public morality that is *useful,* along the lines of Benjamin Franklin.[9] It is useful, more precisely, because it helps people to reach their material goals. The key idea in the doctrine of self-interest well understood, in brief, is that Americans are honest, keep promises and so on, because it helps them to accomplish what they want—not because this behavior is virtuous in and by itself. "They therefore do not deny that each man can follow his interest, but they do their best to prove that the interest of each is to be honest" (*ibid.*, p. 501). Religion is part of this way of proceeding, and it is consequently useful for the average persons to be religious.

The doctrine of self-interest well understood is "marvellously accommodated to the weaknesses of men," according to Tocqueville, and the reason for this is that it does not assume that people are driven by lofty ideals but only that they will attempt to realize their interests (*ibid.*, p. 502). The term *intérêt* is usually rendered as "self-interest" in the translation of "*la doctrine de l'intérêt bien entendu,*" but it would perhaps be better to simply translate it as "interest," because this term does not give as strong associations to greed and avarice.[10] This qualification is necessary to be aware of if one, for example, is to understand Tocqueville's statement that "religion [in the United States] makes use of interest to guide people" (*ibid.*, p. 505). Interest, in other words, can be used to connect people's material needs to their religious needs, similar to the way that desires for material goods and the needs of the soul should meet in the human being. That Tocqueville's doctrine of self-interest well understood is not cynical is also clear from his observation that Americans tend to overplay the extent to which they do good because it serves their interests. It is not at all uncommon, Tocqueville says, that Americans perform acts out of pure altruism (*ibid.*, p. 502).

The Role of Politics in the American Spirit of Capitalism

As opposed to Weber in *The Protestant Ethic,* Tocqueville pays considerable attention to the political dimension of the spirit of capitalism or, more precisely, to the political conditions under which the spirit of capitalism can exist as part of a dynamic economy. In presenting Tocqueville's ideas on this topic, it is necessary to first look at the basic conceptual scheme of *Democracy in America* and to establish what role the economy, including the spirit of capitalism, plays in this. Similar to Adam Smith in *The Wealth of Nations* (which Tocqueville knew well), he was careful to point out that the economic sphere has to be independent of the political sphere, but that they nonetheless are closely connected in a capitalist economy.[11]

To understand Tocqueville's way of approaching the relationship between economics and politics, it is convenient to start with the conceptual scheme of *Democracy in America*. This consists of two interrelated ideas: (1) that society is moving away from what Tocqueville terms aristocracy and toward democracy, and (2) that democracy can be either despotic or characterized by freedom (cf. Furet 1981). An aristocracy, Tocqueville states, is a society in which a tiny minority controls all the economic, social, and political resources, whereas a democracy is a society in which this monopoly has been decisively broken and where resources are spread out among different groups and individuals. How to steer society's general evolution toward democracy in a positive political direction constitutes, according to Tocqueville, "*the great political problem of our time*" (ibid., p. 298; emphasis added). Whether this problem is handled in such a way that it will result is despotism or freedom will also have dramatic consequences for the development of economic life. Despotism, in all brevity, leads to a stagnant economy, and a free democratic society to a dynamic economy (see Fig. 2-1).

Tocqueville was convinced that there exists "a tight bond and a necessary relation between these two things: freedom and industry" (*ibid.*, p. 515). He states that "I do not know if one can cite a single manufacturing and commercial people, from the Tyrians to the Florentines to the English, that has not been a free people" (*ibid.*). The mechanisms that would explain how freedom and economic growth are related in detail are unfortunately not made explicit in *Democracy in America*. Tocqueville has, on the other hand, quite a bit to say about the impact that despotism has on the economy in a democratic society. Democracy, he explains, has a natural tendency toward despotism, and if this is not decisively countered, politics and economics will suffer. When a society becomes democratic, according to Tocqueville, this often means that various intermediary aristocratic organizations have been removed, say as a result of a revolution. This means that there are only a huge number of isolated individuals in democratic society, on the one hand, and a centralized power, on the other. And when this is the case, it is easy for some form of

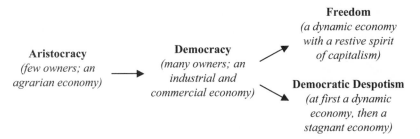

FIGURE 2-1 The Basic Conceptual Scheme of Tocqueville's *Democracy in America*, with Special Emphasis on the Economy

Comment: Whereas a static and agrarian economy characterizes what Tocqueville terms an *aristocracy* in *Democracy in America,* a much more differentiated economy comes into being with the levelling of economic, political, and social conditions of the type that Tocqueville has in mind when he uses the term *democracy.* With freedom in a democracy also come a dynamic economy and a vibrant, restive spirit of capitalism. If the general trend in modern society toward democracy is handled poorly, it will end in despotism ("democratic despotism"), and this, in its turn, will lead to a stagnant economy. Tocqueville speaks of conventional despotism (such as under Louis-Philippe during 1830–48) and mild despotism (of a future kind).

"democratic despotism" to emerge, such as the absolute monarchy that was introduced in France after the July Revolution in 1830. When this happens, the economy will react very positively at first, but then decline and eventually come to a halt. The reason for this is that the state will increasingly interfere in various small details in the economy, something that has a paralyzing effect on economic life. The state will similarly prevent many economic initiatives from being taken, simply by its presence.

Whereas the creation of an absolute monarchy in a democratic society (as in France between 1830 and 1848) shows that society is somewhere between aristocracy and democracy, Tocqueville argues that a pure democratic society (such as the United States) may also be overcome by despotism. In this case, however, despotism will be of a different type: less dependent on force but more intrusive. Tocqueville describes the pure version of democratic despotism in a way that shows some parallels to Foucault: "It is absolute, detailed, regular, far-seeing, and mild. It would resemble paternal power if, like that, it had for its object to prepare men for manhood; but on the contrary, it seeks only to keep them fixed irrevocably in childhood; it likes citizens to enjoy themselves provided that they think only of enjoying themselves" (*ibid.,* p. 663).

People in a democracy, Tocqueville says, are typically fond of order; they have a deep fear of disorder, and freedom typically comes with a certain amount of disorder. There is also the fact that because all individuals in a democracy are isolated from one another, they have great difficulty in accomplishing anything on their own. This has as a consequence, in its turn, that if something is to be done, you have to turn to the state. The process of industrialization means that the state will increasingly interfere in society through various regulations; it will also be in charge of creating a new infrastructure.

There is finally a strong tendency towards "individualism" in democracies (*ibid.*, pp. 485–88). When Tocqueville uses this term in *Democracy in America*, however, it has a different meaning than the conventional one. *Individualism*, we are told, means that the individual decides, in a calm and rational way, that it is more sensible to withdraw to a small circle of family and close friends than to get involved in politics. Individualism, Tocqueville emphasizes, differs from selfishness, which is a passion and has little to do with reason and contemplation. Tocqueville's theory of individualism is an outgrowth of his personal conviction that only a politically active people can take charge of things successfully—including the economy.

According to Tocqueville, it was crucial for a democratic country such as France to opt for freedom and steer free of despotism. This is exactly where his intense interest for the United States came in, because this country had shown one way in which this could be done. The Americans had accomplished this feat primarily by relying on a new type of political system and the creation of so-called secondary powers in between the individual and the state (*ibid.*, pp. 642–50). The free press had played a role as well, and so had the American system of justice with its juries, elected judges, and judicial review.

It is necessary to realize, according to Tocqueville, that no democratic society can operate effectively without a certain amount of political centralization. "Governmental despotism," as he puts it, is necessary to deal with problems that all citizens have in common (*ibid.*, p. 82). It is equally important to realize, however, that the state must not intervene in cases where people can handle the problems themselves by cooperating locally. This situation (which today is referred to as subsidiarity) is termed "administrative centralization" by Tocqueville (*ibid.*, pp.82–93). American federalism, which in the 1800s rested on a foundation of townships, was according to Tocqueville a brilliant example of how "governmental centralization" can exist without "administrative centralization."

The second key element in the successful American solution to the political dilemma of democratic society, as Tocqueville saw it, has often been referred to in the debate about social capital, namely the creation of organizations (e.g., Fukuyama 1995; Skocpol 1996; Skocpol, Ganz, and Munson 2000). Tocqueville's view on organizations in the United States in the 1800s is close to that of Weber on the United States in the early 1900s; "Americans . . . constantly unite" (Tocqueville) and "[America is] the association-land par excellence" (Weber; *ibid.,* p. 489; Weber [1910] 1972:20; cf. Weber [1920] 1946).

What has been discussed less often in the literature on Tocqueville and social capital, however, is the role that economic organizations, as opposed to voluntary organizations, play in democratic society. By being politically active, Tocqueville argues in *Democracy in America,* people in the United States learn how to create organizations for specific purposes, and this knowledge is then used in economic life. Here, as elsewhere, the fact that a number of individuals join together means that they can accomplish far more than single individuals. By filling the gap between the individual and the state, organizations also block the state from unduly interfering in various economic activities—and thereby make it easier for the spirit of capitalism to flourish.

On the Origin of the American Spirit of Capitalism

Weber attributes much importance to the question of the origin of the spirit of capitalism in *The Protestant Ethic,* and this is also true for Tocqueville in *Democracy in America (ibid.,* pp. 18–44, 264–302). "I saw in the origin of the Americans, in what I called their point of departure," Tocqueville says, "the first and the most efficacious of all causes to which the current prosperity in America can be attributed" (*ibid.,* p. 266). He also argues that although it is true that you always have to go back to the origin of a nation to understand its later development, this is often not possible because the lack of historical records. For the formative period of a young nation such as the United States, however, there is plenty of information.

In trying to establish what caused the spirit of capitalism to flourish so strongly in the United States, from Tocqueville's perspective, one may first of all note that aristocracies are inhospitable to this spirit. Aristocratic countries are by definition agrarian economies, in which the spirit of profit making is looked down upon. As commerce and industry begin to develop, however, so does democracy—but not necessarily the spirit of capitalism. If a democracy is despotic, as has already been noted, its economy will soon become stagnant. Democracy, in brief, is a necessary but not a sufficient condition for a vigorous spirit of capitalism.

Tocqueville also discusses the possibility that the American spirit of capitalism might be due to geographic features. He writes in a nearly lyrical way about the rich and wonderful nature of the United States: "It presents, as in the first days of the creation, rivers whose source does not dry up, green and moist solitudes, boundless fields that the plowshare of the laborer has not yet turned" (*ibid.*, p. 268). But Tocqueville also notes that the nature of South America is much richer than that of North America, and South America has failed to develop. From this observation he draws the conclusion that geographic factors cannot be the primary cause of the wealth of the United States. It is a contributing factor, but that is all.

Tocqueville addresses the question of what has made the United States into such a rich country in a central section of *Democracy in America* entitled "That the Laws Serve to Maintain a Democratic Republic in the United States More than Physical Causes, and Mores More than Laws" (*ibid.*, pp. 292–95). Here he states that even though geographic factors have played a role in the emergence of the United States, "physical causes . . . do not influence the destiny of nations as much as one supposes" (*ibid.*, p. 293). Tocqueville similarly rejects the idea that laws or the legal system would be the main cause of its flourishing state, and illustrates this by pointing out that even though Mexico has adopted the same laws as the United States, it has failed to develop in a similar direction. Laws, as Tocqueville puts it, are more important to the way that a country will develop than its geographic conditions—but they are also less important, in their turn, than mores. His general conclusion is as follows: "it is . . . particularly mores that render the Americans of the United States, alone among all Americans, capable of supporting the empire of democracy; and it is again [mores] that make the various Anglo-American democracies more or less regulated and prosperous" (*ibid.*, p. 295).[12]

What Tocqueville means by mores (*moeurs*) in the United States is close to what Weber means by "the spirit of capitalism" in Europe and which Weber also refers to as *Lebensführung/Lebensstil* or approximately lifestyle (e.g., Weber [1904–05] 1958:55, 58–9). Tocqueville gives the following definition of mores: "I understand by this word the sum of the intellectual and moral dispositions (*dispositions*) that men bring to the state of society" (*ibid.*, p. 292, n. 1). Mores include, among other things, "habits", "opinions", "usages," and "beliefs" (*ibid.*, p. 295). Tocqueville also distinguishes between mores that are emotional in character ("*habits of the heart*") and those that are intellectual ("*habits of the mind*"; *ibid.*, p. 275; emphasis added).

What accounts for the dynamic prosperity in the United States, Tocqueville suggests, is precisely the special character of its civilization or mores: "Anglo-American civilization . . . is the product (and this point of departure ought constantly to be present in one's thinking) of two perfectly distinct elements that elsewhere have often made war with each other, but which, in America, they have succeeded in incorporating somehow into one another and combining marvellously. I mean to speak of the *spirit of religion* and the *spirit of freedom*" (*ibid.*, p. 43).

Whereas the first settlers, who went to Virginia, were single men and adventurers looking for quick profits, the settlers in Massachusetts were religious people, driven by religious ideals and not by a desire for material wealth. The settlers also came with their families and were eager to establish order and good morals. "I see the whole destiny of America contained in the first Puritan who landed on its shores, like the whole human race in the first man" (*ibid.*, p. 267).

The first settlers also brought along mores of freedom from England. This made them start their new lives in America in freedom and reject despotism. Furthermore, England did not supervise its colonies in a very strict way, according to Tocqueville, and this allowed freedom to flourish as well. The Americans finally also developed local autonomy in the form of townships, which became a veritable school in freedom for the settlers. By participating in these townships, the settlers acquired independence and freedom as well as political sophistication.

Tocqueville repeatedly notes that what is remarkable about the United States, and what also constitutes the main cause of the spirit of capitalism in this country, is that it has succeeded in uniting a sense of freedom with religion. On the one hand, "religion sees in civil freedom a noble exercise of the faculties of man; in the political world, a field left by the Creator to the efforts of intelligence" (*ibid.*, p. 43). On the other hand, "freedom sees in religion the companion of its struggles and triumphs, the cradle of its infancy, the divine source of its rights" (*ibid.*, pp. 43–44). Tocqueville sums the whole thing up as follows: "*the Americans are a Puritan and a commercial people*" (*ibid.*, p. 465; emphasis added).

Concluding Remarks

It is now time to return to the main concerns of this chapter, which were set out at the beginning. They were (1) to attempt to improve the status of the concept of the spirit of capitalism with the help of Tocqueville; and

(2) to also show that we may add to this concept, by drawing on *Democracy in America*. As to the first concern, I hope to have removed some of the unease that is associated with this concept, by having presented a new and important empirical example of the existence of the spirit of capitalism, namely the United States in the early 1800s. It also deserves to be noted that Tocqueville, just as Weber, pinpoints Puritanism or ascetic Protestantism as one of the key ingredients in this spirit. Tocqueville's American example is also much more straightforward than the example in *The Protestant Ethic*. Finally, the reader may want to recall once more what I said at the outset of this article, namely that in the nineteenth century the idea that there was a close link between Protestantism and capitalism was rather common.

As to the empirical quality of Tocqueville's example, it should first of all be emphasized that Tocqueville was at the very forefront of empirical social science in his time (if we allow ourselves to interpret this time in terms that differ substantially from those in which it preferred to cast itself). Tocqueville's use of interviews, note taking, and printed material for the analysis in *Democracy in America* is exemplary for the early 1800s, and no doubt qualified him as one of the masters of sociological research (cf. Aron 1968).[13] Tocqueville's general conclusion about the U.S. economy in *Democracy in America*—that it can be characterized as a truly dynamic and entrepreneurial economy—has also been confirmed in later research by economic historians, as exemplified by Douglass North's study of economic growth in the United States that was mentioned at the beginning of this paper (North 1961). North emphasizes that it was precisely during the period that Tocqueville visited the United States, as well as the preceding ten to fifteen years (1818–1839), that the American economy started to accelerate and that industrialization began. Tocqueville's analysis helps us to look at other dimensions of economic life than does North's study—the reality that, for example, led to the historical emergence of the two expressions "self-made man" and "businessman" in the 1830s (e.g., Boorstin 1974:115; Huntington 2004:70).

The many shrewd observations on the American spirit of capitalism that one can find in Tocqueville's study must naturally be submitted to empirical tests. It nonetheless seems to me that many of these observations (as well as Tocqueville's explanations and terminology) can add to the current discussion of what accounts for the dynamic economic growth that has characterized the United States since its founding.

It is furthermore my opinion that Tocqueville not only has added another important historical example to the literature on the spirit of capitalism, but that he also has helped to further develop this concept, compared to its formulation in Weber's work. He has done so in primarily two ways: by adding an explicitly political dimension to it, and by suggesting that a dynamic spirit of capitalism is not something exceptional in the history of capitalism, which only existed for a relatively short period and then disappeared forever, but that it can be a *common* (if not continuous) feature of the economy. It should also be mentioned that Tocqueville, as opposed to Weber, made room for consumerism in his concept of the spirit of capitalism, through his ideas about the search for material well-being in the United States.

Tocqueville's addition of an explicit political dimension to the concept of the spirit of capitalism needs little elaboration beyond what has already been said. A dynamic economic atmosphere can only exist for a relatively short period if the state interferes too much in the economy, according to Tocqueville. For economic progress to be continuous, some kind of solution to the problem of how to construct a centralized power—but not a too powerful centralized power—has to be found. One solution to this problem, Tocqueville says, is federalism of the U.S. type, complemented by a system of townships of the type that could be found in Massachusetts.

Second, in *The Protestant Ethic* Weber portrays the spirit of modern capitalism as a unique phenomenon, limited in its existence to a relatively brief period in the history of capitalism and whose invigorating and onetime impact on economic life was soon replaced by a new set of continuously operating institutions. Tocqueville, in contrast, views the spirit of capitalism as a much more ordinary and continuous phenomenon, with its own special place in the structure of the economy, next to what sociologists today would call institutions and organizations. By portraying the spirit of capitalism in this manner Tocqueville, I argue, raises the important question: Should the spirit of capitalism really be understood as subordinate in importance to institutions and organizations, or can it be seen as equally important as these two "structural" features? Or, to phrase the problem at a more general level, have contemporary sociologists perhaps exaggerated the importance of institutions and organizations at the expense of ideas, norms, and everything else that make up the spirit of human undertakings?

References

Aron, Raymond. 1968. *Main Currents in Sociological Thought*. Vol. 1. Garden City, NY: Anchor Books.

Bendix, Reinhard. 1967. "The Protestant Ethic–Revisited." *Comparative Studies in Society and History* 9,3:266–73.

Bettelheim, Bruno. 1943. "Individual and Mass Behavior in Extreme Situations." *Journal of Abnormal and Social Psychology* 38:417–52.

Boesche, Roger. 1987. *The Strange Liberalism of Alexis de Tocqueville*. Ithaca, NY: Cornell University Press.

Boorstin, Daniel. 1974. *The Americans: The Democratic Experience*. New York: Vintage.

Chalcraft, David and Austin Harrington (eds.). 2001. *The Protestant Ethic Debate: Max Weber Replies to his Critics, 1907-1910*. Liverpool: Liverpool University Press.

Crowley, John. 2003. *The Invention of Comfort: Sensibilities and Design in Early Modern Britain and Early America*. Philadelphia: Johns Hopkins University Press.

Drescher, Seymour. 1968. *Dilemmas of Democracy: Tocqueville and Modernization*. Pittsburgh: University of Pittsburgh Press.

Durkheim, Emile. [1897] 1951. *Suicide: A Study in Sociology*. Glencoe, IL: The Free Press.

Fukuyama, Frank. 1995. *Trust: The Social Virtues and the Creation of Prosperity*. London: Penguin.

Furet, François. 1981. "Le Système Conceptuel de la 'Démocratie en Amérique." Pp. 7–49 in vol. 1 of Alexis de Tocqueville, *De la Démocratie en Amérique*. Paris: Flammarion.

Goldstein, Doris. 1968. *Trial of Faith: Religion and Politics in Tocqueville's Thought*. New York: Elsevier.

Hereth, Michael. 1977. "Der Verlust der Freiheit durch Hingabe an die Ökonomie." Pp. 246–59 in *Grundprobleme der Politischen Ökonomie*. Munich: R. Piper & Co. Verlag.

Hirschman, Albert O. 1977. *The Passions and the Interests: Political Arguments for Capitalism Before Its Triumph*. Princeton, NJ: Princeton University Press.

Hirschman, Albert O. 1986. *Rival Views of Market Society*. New York: Viking.

Huntington, Samuel. 2004. *Who Are We?* New York: Simon and Schuster.

Käsler, Dirk. 1988. *Max Weber: An Introduction to His Life and Work*. Cambridge, U.K.: Polity Press.

Marshall, Alfred. 1895. *Principles of Economics*. New York: Macmillan.

Marx, Karl. [1867] 1906. *Capital: A Critique of Political Economy*. New York: Modern Library.

Marx, Karl and Friedrich Engels. [1848] 1978. "Manifesto of the Communist Party." Pp. 473–500 in Robert Tucker (ed.), *The Marx-Engels Reader*. 2nd ed. New York: W.W. Norton & Company.

Merton, Robert K. 1973. *The Sociology of Science*. Chicago: University of Chicago Press.

Merton, Robert K. 1995. "Opportunity Structure: The Emergence, Diffusion, and Differentiation of a Sociological Concept, 1930s-1950s." Pp. 3–78 in Freda Adler and William Laufer (eds.), *The Legacy of Anomie Theory*. Advances in Criminological Theory # 6. New Brunswick, NJ: Transaction Publishers.

Mill, John Stuart. [1848] 1987. *Principles of Political Economy*. Ed. William Ashley. Chicago: Augustus M. Kelley Publishers.

North, Douglass. 1961. *The Economic Growth of the United States, 1790–1860*. Englewood Cliffs, NJ: Prentice-Hall.

Persky, Victor. 1995. "The Ethology of *Homo Economicus.*" *Journal of Economic Perspectives* 9,2:22–31.

Pessen, Edward. 1971. "The Egalitarian Myth and the American Social Reality: Wealth, Mobility and Equality in the 'Era of the Common Man.'" *American Historical Review* 76,4:989–1034.

Pessen, Edward. 1982. "Tocqueville's Misreading of America, America's Misreading of Tocqueville." *The Tocqueville Review* 4,1:5–22.

Schleifer, James. 1980. *The Making of Tocqueville's Democracy in America*. Chapel Hill: University of North Carolina.

Schumpeter, Joseph A. 1954. *History of Economic Analysis*. New York: Oxford University Press.

Skocpol, Theda. 1996. "Unsolved Mysteries: The Tocqueville Files." *American Prospect* 7,25:20–25.

Skocpol, Theda, Marshall Ganz, and Ziad Munson. 2000. "A Nation of Organizers: The Institutional Origins of Civic Voluntarism in the United States." *American Political Science Review* 94,3:527–46.

Sombart, Werner. 1902. *Der Moderne Kapitalismus*. 2 vols. Leipzig: Duncker & Humblot.

Steiner, Philippe. 1998. *Sociologie de la Connaissance économique*. Paris: Presses Universitaires de France.

Tocqueville, Alexis de. [1835–40] 1990. *De la Démocratie en Amérique*. Ed. Eduardo Nolla. 2 vols. Paris: J. Vrin.

Tocqueville, Alexis de. [1835–40] 1945. *Democracy in America*. Trans. Henry Reeve. 2 vols. New York: Knopf.

Tocqueville, Alexis de. [1835–40] 1994. *Democracy in America*. Ed. J. P. Mayer, trans. George Lawrence. London: Fontana Press.

Tocqueville, Alexis de. [1835–40] 2000. *Democracy in America*. Ed. and trans. Harvey Mansfield and Delba Winthrop. Chicago: University of Chicago Press.

Tocqueville, Alexis de. [1835–40] 2004. *Democracy in America*. Trans. Arthur Goldhammar. New York: Library of America.

Tocqueville, Alexis de. [1835] 1997. *Memoir on Pauperism*. Ed. Gertrude Himmelfarb, Trans. Seymour Drescher. London: IEA Health and Welfare Unit.

Tocqueville, Alexis de. 1959. *Journey to America*. Ed. J. P. Mayer, trans. George Lawrence. New Haven: Yale University Press.

Tocqueville, Alexis de. 1985. *Selected Letters on Politics and Society*. Ed. Roger Boesche, trans. James Toupin and Roger Boesche. Berkeley: University of California Press.

Tocqueville, Alexis de. 1995. *Correspondance et Ecrits Locaux*. Vol. 10 of *Oeuvres Complètes*. Paris: Gallimard.

Weber, Max. [1904–05] 1958. *The Protestant Ethic and the Spirit of Capitalism.* Trans. Talcott Parsons. New York: Scribner's.

Weber, Max. [1910] 1972. "Max Weber's Proposal for the Sociological Study of Voluntary Organizations." *Journal of Voluntary Action Research* 1:20–3.

Weber, Max. [1920] 1946. "The Protestant Sects and the Spirit of Capitalism". Pp. 302–22 in Hans Gerth and C. Wright Mills (eds.), *From Max Weber.* New York: Oxford University Press.

Notes to Chapter Two

1. According to what I consider to be the most substantial analysis of Tocqueville's view of the economy, his ideas on this topic are described as a mishmash of internally inconsistent views (Drescher 1968:51-87).

2. Weber several times makes the statement that it was commonplace in his time to see a positive relationship between Protestantism and capitalism (e.g., Weber [1904–1905] 1958:191:23, 280:86; Chalcraft and Harrington 2001:117). From this we may conclude that the burden of proof in Weber's days was rather on *disproving* this link. For a useful discussion of Weber's views on this issue, see especially Bendix 1967 (cf., e.g., Käsler 1988:75). See also Bendix's statement that "my colleague Neil Smelser informs me that similar comments [on the positive relationship between Protestantism and capitalism] occur frequently among English writers of the early nineteenth century who discussed the development of trade and industry" (Bendix 1967:300, 305).

3. The term *spirit of capitalism* is usually attributed to Werner Sombart, who used it in 1902 in *Der Moderne Kapitalismus*. Sombart's use of this term, however, differs from that of Weber, who discussed the spirit of modern rational capitalism and how it has its roots in ascetic Protestantism already in 1897 (Chalcraft and Harrington 2001:62).

4. As an example of John Stuart Mill's failure to understand the significance of the spirit of capitalism in the United States, and how this failure was rooted in his distaste for its entrepreneurial and profit-oriented atmosphere, one may cite *Principles of Political Economy* (1848). Mill here expresses quite a bit of contempt for the "dollar-hunting" of American men and the "breeding [of] dollar-hunters" of American women (Mill [1848] 1987:748, n. 1). According to Mill, it was only in "backward countries" that there is an interest in "increased production"; in advanced countries the main issue is "a better distribution" (*ibid.*, p. 749). Roger Boesche's discussion of "Tocqueville's [aristocratic] distaste for bourgeois society" for its "obsession with wealth" in *The Strange Liberalism of Alexis de Tocqueville* falls in the same category as Mill's comments—and similarly fails to grasp the significance of Tocqueville's description of the American spirit of capitalism (Boesche 1987:85ff.).

5. In writings about the analysis of the economy in *Democracy in America,* it is often pointed out that Tocqueville did not visit the textile factories in Lowell, Massachusetts, and more generally that he did not understand the U.S. economy because he was blind to the process of industrialization (e.g., Drescher 1968:51-87). To this may be

answered that Tocqueville nonetheless succeeded in capturing the spirit of American capitalism, and that this spirit had not yet found a full institutional expression—a bit like the situation in Massachusetts in the 1600s according to *The Protestant Ethic* ("the spirit of capitalism . . . was present [in Massachusetts] *before* the capitalist order," Weber [1904–05] 1958:55; emphasis added). During his trip to England in 1835, which took place before vol. 2 of *Democracy in America* had been completed, Tocqueville nonetheless caught a glimpse of industrialization in action.

6. The Americans' indulgence toward bankruptcy (as compared to that of the Europeans) is perhaps related to commercial boldness and audacity as well (*ibid.,* pp. 587–88, 595).

7. According to Doris Goldstein, who is the author of the standard work on Tocqueville's relationship to religion, Tocqueville failed to understand what was going on in American religious life during his visit. She also notes that authors such as S. M. Lipset, Robert Bellah, and Daniel Boorstin do not share this opinion (Goldstein 1968:19–27).

8. Tocqueville's analysis of how the methodical character of religion is transmitted to economic behavior shows obvious parallels to Weber's argument in *The Protestant Ethic*. This is something that Seymour Drescher misses in his discussion of the relationship between the key argument in *The Protestant Ethic* and *Democracy in America*: "At times Tocqueville in his notes [on the United States] almost glimpsed the Weber thesis on the relationship between Protestantism and capitalism, but his overriding conception of religion as 'spiritual', and economics as 'material' realms of human activity kept his focus on the inhibiting potentials of religious values on economic behavior" (Drescher 1968:69).

9. The reader may recall that Benjamin Franklin is the central figure in Weber's account of the modern spirit of capitalism in chap. 2 of *The Protestant Ethic*. The same idea is present in the statement "Honesty is the best policy," cited by Weber in "The Protestant Sects and the Spirit of Capitalism" (Weber [1920] 1946:313).

10. There currently exist four translations of *Democracy of America* (plus a retranslation of the first translation by Reeve, made by Bowen). George Lawrence and Arthur Goldhammar translate *intérêt bien entendu* as "self-interest properly understood"; Henry Reeve prefers "self-interest rightly understood"; and Harvey Mansfield and Delba Winthrop "self-interest well understood" (Tocqueville [1835–40] 1994:525; Tocqueville [1835–1840] 1945, 2:121; Tocqueville [1835–1840] 2004:610; Tocqueville [1835–1840] 2004:500–506). To this may be added that Albert O. Hirschman suggests "enlightened self-interest" for "*intérêt bien compris,*" and that the term "enlightened self-interest" is often used to characterize the ideal during the Enlightenment (Hirschman 1986:49).

11. Tocqueville studied economics before, during, and after his trip to the United States. Before he completed *Democracy in America* he read Adam Smith and Jean-Baptiste Say and also had conversations with Nassau Senior. Tocqueville, as already noted, was not attracted to the analytical type of economics that would emerge in mid-nineteenth-century England and later overtake economics more generally. For

Tocqueville's knowledge of economics, see in particular Schleifer 1980:283–84, Steiner 1998:162–83.

12. Tocqueville often uses the term *institution* (*institution*) in *Democracy in America* (e.g., *ibid.*, pp. 53, 130, 165, 280-81, 344, 536, 618). The exact meaning of this term, however, is somewhat unclear. My own sense is that Tocqueville sees institutions as the result of the three main forces that account for the evolution of a country, namely (1) geographical conditions, (2) laws, and (3) mores. I base this interpretation on the section that comes after the section entitled "That the Laws Serve to Maintain a Democratic Republic in the United States More than Physical Causes, and Mores More than Laws," which is called "Would Laws and Mores Suffice to Maintain Democratic Institutions Elsewhere than in America?" (*ibid.*, pp. 296–98; cf. pp. 292–95).

13. As an example of how Tocqueville used empirical evidence, one may take the concept of restiveness. At least two of the people whom Tocqueville interviewed mentioned this phenomenon; he also discusses it in an early sketch on the theme of "[The] National Character of the Americans" (Tocqueville 1959, pp. 59, 97, 182).

3   Income Inequality and the Protestant Ethic

Robert H. Frank, Cornell University

M AX WEBER ARGUED THAT CAPITALISM COULDN'T HAVE taken root without the Protestant ethic, but once under way had no further need for it. Here, I argue for the converse of this thesis—that capitalism's launch did not require the Protestant ethic, but its continued survival may depend on our willingness to adopt policies inspired by it. The difficulty is that working hard and abiding by the rules is no longer the reliable formula for success it once was. In recent decades, the real incomes of middle-class adherents to this formula in the United States have been stagnating or declining, even as their debt levels have been rising precipitously.

Following preliminary remarks about the logic of Weber's original argument, I discuss why only those near the top of the economic pyramid have experienced significant income and wealth growth since the early 1970s in the United States. (Although the changes I identify have been most pronounced here, similar movements have been occurring in many other countries.) I then describe how the resulting changes in spending patterns have created new economic burdens for the middle class. I conclude by suggesting why both rich and poor should favor expanded reliance on economic policies inspired by the Protestant ethic.

The Challenge of Traditionalism

The power of traditionalism to inhibit economic development was one of Weber's central concerns in *The Protestant Ethic and the Spirit of Capitalism.*

To succeed, capitalist enterprises needed to lure people away from their traditional modes of living to engage in paid work that was often tedious and demanding. Weber's fear was that, by itself, the carrot of economic reward was simply not up to this task. One problem, as he saw it, was that people from traditional backgrounds often responded perversely to capitalism's material incentives. For instance, in describing how workers reacted to piece-rate pay schemes, he wrote: "But a peculiar difficulty has been met with surprising frequency: raising the piece-rates has often had the result that not more but less has been accomplished in the same time, because the worker reacted to the increase not by increasing but by decreasing the amount of his work."[1]

If material incentives couldn't induce workers to expend the necessary effort, how were capitalist enterprises to survive? Weber's answer was that the Protestant ethic would provide the necessary push. It was the Protestant tradition, he argued, that taught people to experience the actual performance of work as its own intrinsic reward. With access to an ample supply of people acculturated in this tradition, entrepreneurs were thus able simply to sidestep the impotence of monetary rewards.

Another challenge to capitalism's emergence, in Weber's account, was the difficulty of postponing current consumption to finance the new system's enormous appetite for investment capital. But here, too, he argued, the Protestant ethic provided a remedy. Its inculcation of thrift as a virtue predisposed adherents not only to postpone gratification from current consumption, but actually to take pleasure in doing so.

In Weber's theory, then, capitalism's overriding problem was how to get started in the face of traditionalism's constraints. Once launched, he argued, its dynamic was sufficiently powerful to be self-sustaining. At that point, he wrote, further influence from religion is not only unnecessary, but actually counterproductive: "The capitalistic system . . . no longer needs the support of any religious forces, and feels the attempts of religion to influence economic life, in so far as they can still be felt at all, to be as much an unjustified interference as its regulation by the State."[2]

I do not deny that the Protestant ethic helped promote the expansion of market exchange for many of the reasons described by Weber. Yet in hindsight it seems clear that the Protestant ethic was by no means essential for capitalism's emergence. For example, we see myriad cases of people willing to work energetically for pay in parts of the world where Protestantism was never practiced. As for the supposedly irrational responses to piece-rate pay schemes, contemporary economists point out that economic theory never predicted that labor supply would always rise with an increase in the wage rate. Indeed, there is nothing perverse about the goal of attaining a target income, and rational people who pursue that goal will always work fewer hours when the piece rate rises.

What Weber overlooked was that life, even in traditional societies, is graded on the curve. Choice land and other resources that everyone wants have always been scarce, and the question of who gets these resources has always been settled by relative rather than absolute spending power. For example, if everyone wants a house with a view and only 10 percent of houses have one, then views will go to those in the top 10 percent of the income distribution. So if some went to work for pay at the dawn of the capitalist era whereas others didn't, the second group would face growing pressure to match the first group's spending power.

Weber also overstated capitalism's difficulty in financing new investment. Although he was astute to recognize Protestantism's role in promoting the accumulation of capital through personal savings, he failed to appreciate the many other sources of capital on which new business can rely in the absence of personal savings. An enterprise with an unusually attractive product, for example, typically generates large profit margins, which it can use to finance expansion. And even in traditional societies, the wealthy have always had ample capital to lend if the terms were favorable.

In brief, although Weber should get full credit for his insights about numerous specific ways in which the Protestant ethic promoted the early growth of capitalism, it appears that he overstated his case. The Protestant ethic, though undoubtedly helpful, simply was not an essential precondition for capitalism's emergence.

Weber was also insightful to recognize the powerful dynamic that swept capitalist development along once it got started. However, here, too, he may have overreached. I will argue that although the capitalist dynamic is every bit as powerful as Weber believed it to be, it also entails powerful self-destructive tendencies that he did not foresee. The irony is that the system may not survive these tendencies without greater reliance on policies whose roots lie in Weber's own Protestant ethic.

The Growth in Income and Wealth
Inequality in the United States

Income growth from 1949 until the end of 1970s was well described by the famous picket-fence chart shown in Figure 3-1. Incomes grew at about the same

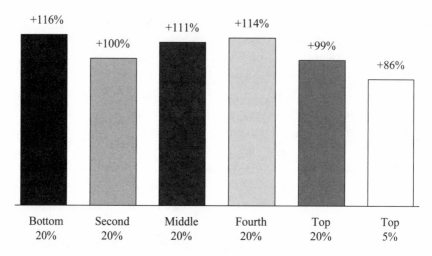

FIGURE 3-1 Changes in Before-Tax Household Incomes, 1949–1979.
SOURCE: http://www.census.gov/hhes/income/histinc/f03.html

rate for all income classes during that period, a little under 3 percent per year. In times of steady income growth, consumption expenditures tend to track incomes closely. Spending was thus also increasing at a fairly uniform rate across the income scale during this period.

That pattern began to change at some point during the 1970s. During the 24-year period shown in Figure 3-2, the real purchasing power of people at the bottom of the income distribution remained essentially unchanged, and gains throughout the middle of the income distribution were extremely small. For example, median family earnings were only 12.6 percent higher at the end of that period than at the beginning. Income gains for families in the top quintile were substantially larger and were larger still for those in the top 5 percent. Yet even for these groups income growth was not as great as during the earlier period. The later period was thus a period of both slower growth and much more uneven growth.

Income inequality has also increased in two important ways not portrayed in Figures 3-1 and 3-2. One is that changes in the income tax structure during the Ronald Reagan presidency significantly shifted real after-tax purchasing power in favor of those atop the socioeconomic ladder. This change was reinforced by additional tax cuts targeted toward high-income families during the first term of George W. Bush. A second change not reflected in Figures 3-1 and 3-2 is the magnitude of the earnings gains recorded by those at the very top.

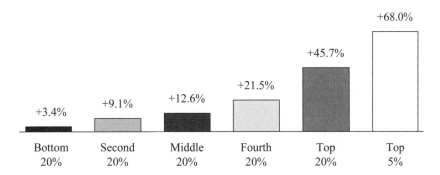

FIGURE 3-2 Changes in Before-Tax Incomes, 1979–2003.
SOURCE: http://www.census.gov/hhes/income/histinc/h03ar.html

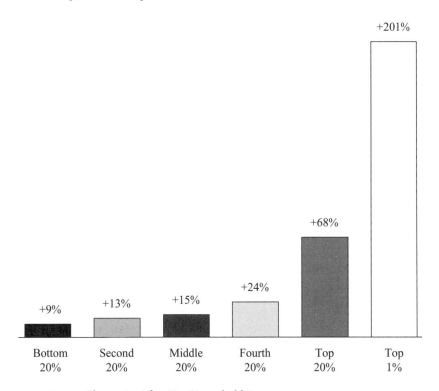

FIGURE 3-3 Change in After-Tax Household Income, 1979–2000
SOURCE: Center on Budget and Policy Priorities, "The New, Definitive CBO Data on Income and Tax Trends," September 23, 2003.

Figure 3-3 portrays some of the results of these two additional effects. Note that the bottom 20 percent of earners (net of both tax and transfer payments) gained slightly more ground than in Figure 3-2, which showed pretax incomes (net of transfer payments). Note also that the gains accruing to the top 1 percent in Figure 3-3 are almost three times as large the corresponding pretax gains experienced by the top 5 percent. For people in the middle quintile, however, growth in after-tax incomes occurred at essentially the same modest pace as growth in pretax incomes.

The pattern of income changes observed in recent years repeats itself in virtually every population subgroup. Thus, if we look at the top quintile of the earnings distribution, earnings growth is relatively small near the bottom of that group and only slightly larger in the middle, but is much larger among the top 1 percent. We see the same pattern again among the top 1 percent. In this group, the lion's share of the income gains have accrued to the top tenth of 1 percent.

Only fragmentary data exist for people that high up in the income distribution, but a few snapshots are available. For more than 25 years, for example, *Business Week* has conducted an annual survey of the earnings of CEOs of the largest U.S. corporations. In 1980, these executives earned 42 times as much as the average American worker, a ratio that is larger than the corresponding ratios seen in countries like Japan and Germany even today. But by 2001, American CEOs were earning 531 times the average worker's salary. There is evidence that the gains have been even more pronounced for those who stand even higher than CEOs on the income ladder.[3]

A similar picture emerges when we look at how the distribution of wealth has changed over time. It has been widely reported than half of all Americans own stocks, the apparent implication being that there was a fairly broad sharing of the huge run-up in asset prices that occurred during the 1990s. In fact, however, asset ownership has become even more heavily concentrated during recent years. As Figure 3-4 shows, for example, the net worth of the median household remained virtually unchanged between 1989 and 1999, a period during which the total net worth of American households nearly doubled.

People in the middle simply don't own much stock. Because their pensions were, for the most part, defined-benefit plans rather than defined-contribution plans, they did not benefit significantly from the stock market boom of the 1990s.

As with income, the real growth in wealth came predominantly at the top. As shown in Figure 3-5, for example, the bottom 40 percent of households actually experienced a significant decline in net worth between 1983 and 1998, a period during which the top 1 percent saw its wealth grow by more than 40 percent.

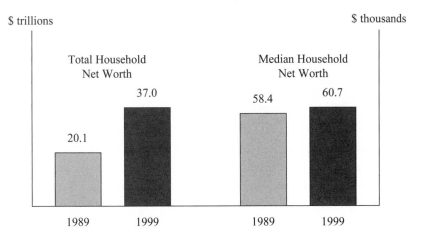

FIGURE 3-4 Changes in Net Worth, 1989–1999.
SOURCE: Edward Wolff, 2002.

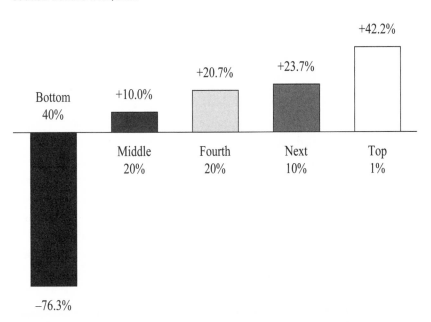

FIGURE 3-5 Changes in Average Household Net Worth, 1983–1998.
SOURCE: Edward Wolff, 2002.

It was within the top 1 percent that the most spectacular changes in net worth occurred. For the past several decades, *Forbes* magazine has published a list of the estimated net worth of the 400 richest Americans. In 1982 there were only 13 billionaires on this list, five of them children of the Texas oil baron H. L. Hunt. By 1996 there were 179 billionaires on the Forbes list, and by 2004 there were 313. Together the Forbes 400 are now worth more than a trillion dollars, nearly one-eighth the national income of China, a country with more than one billion people.

Why Has Inequality Grown?

In the standard economic account, the salary a person commands in the labor market is proportional to his or her stock of human capital—an amalgam of talent, experience, education, training, and other factors that affect productivity. Armed with this perspective, many economists have argued that the recent growth in inequality has been the result of an increase in the rate of return to education and other forms of human capital. Yet we observe essentially the same pattern of inequality growth among college graduates as in the population as a whole. The least prosperous college graduates have struggled to stay even and those in the middle have made only modest gains, whereas those at the top have done spectacularly well. Among college graduates, the return to education has been higher in some fields than in others. For example, the earnings of computer science graduates grew more rapidly during the last two decades than those of English majors. But even among English majors, those at the top have enjoyed spectacular earnings growth.

Others have argued that inequality has increased in the United States because globalization has put unskilled American workers in competition with low-wage workers from other lands. Yet the basic pattern of inequality growth has been the same even among dentists, who are largely immune from foreign competition. Most dentists today earn little more than their counterparts from 1979, but the best paid dentists earn almost three times as much.[4]

The human-capital story directs our attention to the worker rather than the job. Yet a person who embodies a certain level of human capital will realize its full value only if placed in a position with adequate scope and opportunity. For example, whereas the value of having a slightly more talented salesperson may mean little if the task is to sell children's shoes, it will mean a great deal if the task is to sell securities to the world's largest pension funds.

Philip Cook and I have argued that an important contributor to increased inequality has been the spread and intensification of reward structures once confined largely to markets for sports and entertainment.[5] In conventional labor markets, reward is proportional to absolute performance. Thus, in the classic piece-rate scheme, a worker who assembles 101 widgets in a week gets paid 1 percent more than a coworker who assembles only 100. In contrast, we define a winner-take-all market as one in which small differences in performance often translate into enormous differences in economic reward.

The winner-take-all perspective urges us to look first to the nature of the positions people hold, rather than to their personal characteristics. An economist under the influence of the human-capital metaphor might ask: Why not save money by hiring two mediocre people to fill an important position instead of paying the exorbitant salary required to attract someone unusually good? Although that sort of substitution might work with physical capital, it does not necessarily work with human capital. Two average surgeons or CEOs or novelists or quarterbacks are often a poor substitute for a single gifted one.

The result is that for positions for which additional talent has great value to the employer or the marketplace, there is no reason to expect that the market will compensate individuals in proportion to their human capital. For these positions—ones that confer the greatest leverage or "amplification" of human talent—small increments of talent have great value and may be greatly rewarded as a result of the normal competitive market process. This insight lies at the core of our alternative explanation of growing inequality.

Technology has greatly extended the power and reach of the planet's most gifted performers. The printing press let a relatively few gifted storytellers displace millions of village raconteurs. Now that we listen mostly to recorded music, the world's best musicians can literally be everywhere at once. The electronic newswire has allowed a small number of syndicated columnists to displace a host of local journalists. And the proliferation of personal computers enabled a handful of software developers to replace thousands of tax accountants.

For present purposes, a key feature of winner-take-all markets is that participants' rewards depend on relative, not just absolute, performance. Whereas a farmer's pay depends on the absolute amount of wheat he or she produces, and not on how that compares with the amounts produced by other farmers, a software developer's pay depends largely on performance ranking. In the market for personal income tax software, for instance, once the market reached consensus on which among the scores or even hundreds of competing programs was the most comprehensive and user-friendly, the lesser-ranked programs quickly disappeared. Although Intuit's *TurboTax* may have been only slightly better than its nearest rivals, the rewards to its developer were enormously greater.

Of course, the dependence of economic reward on performance ranking is nothing new. What is new is the rapid erosion of the barriers that once prevented the top performers from serving broader markets. In the music industry, the driving force was the arrival of breathtakingly lifelike recorded music. Changes in physical production technologies have been important in other industries as well, but these changes often explain only a small part of the picture.

Of central importance in other cases has been the emergence of the so-called information revolution. In the global village, there is unprecedented market consensus on who the top players are in each arena and unprecedented opportunity to deal with these players. A company that made the best tire in Akron was once assured of being a player in at least the northern Ohio tire market; today's sophisticated consumers, however, increasingly purchase their tires from only a handful of the best tire producers worldwide.

Before there can be large and concentrated rewards in a winner-take-all market, not only must the top performers generate high value, but there must also be effective competition for their services. Yet in many markets, a variety of formal and informal rules traditionally prevented such competition.

Most major sports leagues, for example, once maintained restrictive agreements that prevented team owners from bidding for one another's most talented players. It was Major League Baseball's reserve clause, for example, that made players the exclusive property of the teams that drafted them. Even though the introduction of nationally televised games in the 1950s increased the economic leverage of baseball players enormously, the ensuing decades saw little real growth in their salaries. In the wake of Los Angeles Dodger pitcher Andy Messersmith's successful court challenge to the reserve clause in 1975, however, player salaries began to grow explosively, now averaging almost $3 million per year. Similar salary trajectories have ensued as players have won at least limited free-agency rights in all the major professional team sports.

Unlike the owners of professional sports teams, the owners of businesses were never subject to formal sanctions against bidding for one another's most talented employees. There were often informal norms, however, that seemed to have virtually the same effect. Under these norms, it was once the almost-universal practice to promote business executives from within, which often enabled companies to retain top executives for less than one-tenth of today's salaries.

The antiraiding norms of business have recently begun to unravel, in part perhaps because managerial talent has in fact become more fungible in the new environment. As recently as 1984, the business community arched its collective eyebrow when Apple hired a new chief executive with a background in soft-drink marketing. Since then, interfirm and interindustry boundaries have become increasingly permeable, and business executives are today little different from the free agents of professional sports. Thus, no one expressed surprise when RJR Nabisco's Louis Gerstner left to head up IBM. Firms that fail to pay standout executives their due now stand to lose them to aggressive rivals.

With corporate malfeasance much in the news in recent years, there is little doubt that at least some of the spectacular corporate pay packages were not won on merit. It is a mistake, however, to view corporate malfeasance as the only, or even the most important, cause of rising pay disparity. Despite the well-publicized cases of late, corporate corruption is almost certainly a less important problem today than it was several decades ago. Interlocking directorates, for example, are less common today, and shareholder activists backed by multibillion-dollar pension funds simply did not exist several decades ago. Pay disparities have increased because new technologies have increased the leverage of key players in every arena, and increased competition has translated that additional leverage into higher pay.

Do Growing Pay Disparities Matter?

Technologies that extend the reach of top performers have greatly benefited consumers, but they have also led to increased inequality. Thus, as noted, the incomes of middle-income families are now slightly higher in real absolute terms than they were two decades ago, but substantially lower, in relative terms.

I will consider two possible ways in which this rise in inequality might have made things worse for these families. First, I will examine how the capacity of material goods to deliver satisfaction, in purely psychological terms, depends heavily on the context in which those goods are consumed. I will then discuss a variety of more tangible ways in which a family's economic welfare might be adversely affected by the spending of others.

The Psychological Costs of Inequality

Most of us were taught from an early age not to worry about how our incomes compare with the incomes of others. This sensible advice stems from the observation that because there will always be others with more, focusing closely on income comparisons can't help but generate reasons to feel unhappy.

However, suppose you were faced with a choice between the following hypothetical worlds:

World A: You earn $110,000 per year, others earn $200,000.

World B: You earn $100,000 per year, others earn $85,000.

The income figures represent real purchasing power. Thus, your higher income in World A would enable you to purchase a house that is 10 percent larger than the one you would be able to afford in World B, 10 percent more restaurant meals, and so on. No matter which world you choose, your relative position will not change in the future. Confronting a once-for-all choice between these two worlds, which one would you choose?

Much of neoclassical economic theory rests on the premise that World A is the uniquely correct choice. This theory assumes that people derive satisfaction primarily from the absolute quantity of goods and services they consume. On that measure, World A is better because it offers higher absolute consumption for every citizen. That fact notwithstanding, however, a substantial proportion of people confronted with this choice say they would opt for World B.[6]

Many economists appear reluctant to take seriously the concerns that might lead people to make this choice. On its face, this is a curious position for a profession whose practitioners often warmly endorse Jeremy Bentham's dictum that a taste for poetry is no better than a taste for pushpins. If most people say they would prefer World B, a genuine commitment to consumer sovereignty would appear to rule out any categorical claim that World A is necessarily best for all.

Modern disciples of Adam Smith have nonetheless been extremely reluctant to introduce the purely psychological costs of inequality into discussions of economic policy. Yet as Smith himself recognized, experiencing such costs is a basic component of human nature. Writing more than two centuries ago, he introduced the important idea that local consumption standards influence the goods and services that people consider essential (or "necessaries," as Smith called them). In the following passage, for example, he described the factors that influence the amount an individual must spend on clothing to be able appear in public "without shame."

By necessaries I understand not only the commodities which are indispensably necessary for the support of life, but whatever the custom of the country renders it indecent for creditable people, even of the lowest order, to be without. A linen shirt, for example, is, strictly speaking, not a necessary of life. The Greeks and Romans lived, I suppose, very comfortably though they had no linen. But in the present times, through the greater part of Europe, a creditable day-labourer would be ashamed to appear in public without a linen shirt, the want of which would be supposed to denote that disgraceful degree of poverty which, it is presumed, nobody can well fall into without extreme bad conduct. Custom, in the same manner, has rendered leather shoes a necessary of life in England. The poorest creditable person of either sex would be ashamed to appear in public without them.[7]

The absolute standard of living in the United States today is of course vastly higher than it was in Adam Smith's eighteenth-century Scotland. Yet Smith's observations apply with equal force to contemporary industrial societies. Consider, for instance, *New York Times* correspondent Dirk Johnson's account of the experiences of Wendy Williams, a middle-school student from a low-income family in a highly prosperous community in Illinois.[8] Both of Wendy's parents are employed at low-wage jobs, and the family lives in Chateau Estates, a trailer park at which her school bus picks her up each morning.

Watching classmates strut past in designer clothes, Wendy Williams sat silently on the yellow school bus, wearing a cheap belt and rummage-sale slacks. One boy stopped and yanked his thumb, demanding her seat.

"Move it, trailer girl," he sneered.

It has never been easy to live on the wrong side of the tracks. But in the economically robust 1990s, with sprawling new houses and three-car garages sprouting like cornstalks on the Midwestern prairie, the sting that comes with scarcity gets rubbed with an extra bit of salt.

• • •

To be without money, in so many ways, is to be left out.

"I told this girl: 'That's a really awesome shirt. Where did you get it?'" said Wendy, explaining that she knew it was out of her price range, but that she wanted to join the small talk. "And she looked at me and laughed and said, 'Why would you want to know?'"

A lanky, soft-spoken girl with large brown eyes, Wendy pursed her lips to hide a slight overbite that got her the nickname Rabbit, a humiliation she once begged her mother and father to avoid by sending her to an orthodontist.

For struggling parents, keenly aware that adolescents agonize over the social pecking order, the styles of the moment and the face in the mirror, there is no small sense of failure in telling a child that she cannot have what her classmates take for granted.

"Do you know what it's like?" asked Wendy's mother, Veronica Williams, "to have your daughter come home and say, 'Mom, the kids say my clothes are tacky,' and then walk off with her head hanging low."

An adolescent in eighteenth-century Scotland would not have been much embarrassed by having a slight overbite, because not even the wealthiest members of society wore braces on their teeth then. In the intervening years, however, rising living standards have altered the frame of reference that defines an acceptable standard of cosmetic dentistry. On what ground might we argue that inequality's toll on individuals like Wendy Williams is unimportant because it occurs in psychological rather than explicit monetary terms?

More Tangible Costs of a Widening Income Gap

Increased spending at the top of the income distribution not only has imposed psychological costs on families in the middle, but it has also raised the cost of achieving many basic goals. It has done so by means of a process that I call expenditure cascades.[9] Expenditure cascades have been launched by the large growth in purchasing power at the top of the income ladder.

Consumption generally tracks income. When the incomes of the wealthy rise, they eventually spend more on houses, cars, clothing, and other goods, just as others do. Upon learning that someone at the top has built a 60,000-square-foot house or purchased a new Ferrari Scaglietti, most people in the middle quintile feel no inclination to alter their own spending. Among those just below the top, however, such purchases have an impact. They subtly change the social frame of reference that defines what kinds of houses and cars seem necessary or appropriate. Additional spending by top earners thus leads others just below them to spend more. And when they do so, others just below them are affected in the same way, and so on, all the way down the income ladder.

In short, burgeoning incomes at the top have launched expenditure cascades that have put financial pressure on the middle class. An expenditure cascade in housing, for example, helps explain why the median size of a newly constructed house in the United States, which stood at less than 1,600 square feet in 1980, had grown to more than 2,100 square feet by 2001.[10] During the same period, the median family's real income increased by less than 15 percent—not nearly enough to comfortably finance so much larger a house.

The steep rise in median house prices is one of the most important sources of the middle-class economic squeeze. It is an indirect consequence of the higher incomes and spending of top earners. Although it might seem that a family could escape the squeeze by just buying a smaller house, that option would in fact entail a significant cost. The problem is that there is a strong link between the price of a house and the quality of the corresponding neighborhood school. Failure to buy a house near the median price for the area means having to send one's children to below-average schools, a cost that most parents seem unwilling to bear. The upshot is that despite a modest increase in their incomes, middle-class families must now work longer hours, borrow more, save less, and commute longer distances to continue sending their children to schools of just average quality.

Increased spending at the top has also imposed other costs on those below. Middle-class families who buy a typical 3,000-pound sedan will incur risks that didn't exist in the 1970s, because they must now share the roads with 6,000-pound Lincoln Navigators and 7,500-pound Ford Excursions. In self-defense, they may want to spend more for a heavier vehicle.

Consider, too, how increased spending at the top affects how much one must spend on a professional wardrobe. Placement counselors have always stressed the importance of dressing well for job interviews. Dressing well is a relative concept, however. To look good means to look better than other candidates. Because top earners have more money, they spend more on clothing, which has led those just below them to spend more, and so on. So to look good for a job interview, the median earner must spend more than before. Of course, if one job candidate is clearly much better qualified than others for a given position, the clothing he or she wears during job interviews is unlikely to make any difference. But competition is stiff for jobs that pay well and offer opportunities for advancement, and there are typically many well-qualified candidates for such jobs. Under the circumstances, candidates are prudent to take whatever steps they can to gain an edge.

Even the gifts that middle-income families feel compelled to give have been affected by the greater affluence of top earners. Top earners have been spending a lot more on gifts because they have a lot more money. As in the examples just considered, their extra spending has launched an expenditure cascade. When others spend more for gifts at weddings, anniversaries, birthdays, and other special occasions, the rest of us must follow suit, or else risk being seen as people who just don't care.

The Educational Arms Race: Another Costly Burden for the Middle Class

Because the pay gap between top earners and others has grown sharply in every field, competition is much more intense than before for top positions. The employers that post openings for such positions typically receive résumés from hundreds or even thousands of applicants, more than they can possibly interview. Increasingly, a candidate's educational credentials have become the most important criterion in the screening process. Many employers now limit their interviews to applicants from a small handful of top-ranked schools. As expected, this change has fueled explosive growth in demand for elite educational credentials.

For the sons and daughters of the middle class, it was always more difficult than for the children of the wealthy to gain admission to the nation's leading universities. The growing demand for elite credentials has made access even more difficult. It has also made higher education more expensive and made it less likely that financial aid will be awarded on the basis of need.

In response to the increased demand for elite credentials, a growing number of institutions have moved aggressively to acquire the resources that confer elite academic status. Because elite status is an inherently relative concept, however, the primary effect has been to bid up the prices of these resources. The resulting "positional arms races" help explain why tuitions at both public and private universities have risen sharply.[11] At public universities, for example, tuitions more than tripled between 1980 and 2004 and rose at nearly the same rate in private universities.[12] At some elite private schools, the annual cost of tuition, room, and board now exceeds $45,000.

Even as tuition and other college costs have been rising, the amount of financial aid available to middle-income and poor families has been dwindling. Because the average SAT score of entering freshmen is itself an important index of an institution's academic status, schools aspiring to elite status have little choice but to bid aggressively for top-scoring students—hence, the growing tendency for merit-based financial aid to displace need-based financial aid. The upshot is that for students from middle- and low-income families, the net cost of receiving a college education has risen dramatically.

At the same time, the economic payoff from a college degree has not kept pace. Indeed, the median salary of college degree holders has actually fallen during the last three decades. Among young male wage and salary workers, for example, the median earnings of those holding a bachelor's degree or higher was $52,087 in 1972 but only $48,955 in 2002 (both figures in 2002 dollars).[13]

For the millions of students who have been unable to attend college because of the economic squeeze on the middle class, things are even worse. Although the payoff to a college degree has declined in absolute terms, it has increased relative to the payoff of having only a high school diploma. For those with only a high school diploma, median earnings were $42,630 in 1972 but only $29,647 in 2002 (again, both figures in 2002 dollars).

So even the slight income gains we saw recorded for median earners in Figures 3-2 and 3-3 are illusory in a broader economic sense. The real hourly pay rates for most individuals in this group are lower now than they were 25 years ago. Their small gains in total family income are the result almost entirely of greater labor force participation of married women.

Consequences of the Financial Squeeze

If the real incomes of middle-class families are little larger than before, how have these families financed their higher levels of consumption and larger tuition payments? In part by working longer hours, but mainly by saving less, borrowing more, and doing without things that were once considered essential. American families with at least one credit card, for example, now carry an average of more than $9,000 in credit card debt, and personal bankruptcy filings are occurring at seven times the rate they did in 1980. The national personal savings rate, always low by international standards, has fallen sharply since the 1980s. One in five American families has zero or negative net worth. Bachelor's degree holders graduate today with an average of almost $20,000 in student loans, and those who go on to graduate school emerge with roughly $45,000 in student loans.[14] Some 45 million Americans now have no health insurance, 5 million more than in the early 1990s.[15]

In brief, the data support popular press accounts portraying widespread and genuine economic distress among middle-class families. The difficulties confronting these families are not the result of exploitation by employers with market power. Rather, they stem in large part from the growing inequality in income and wealth that has resulted from ordinary market forces. Modern technology has greatly amplified the economic leverage of the best performers in every domain. By all indications, it will continue to do so. If future income gains continue to be captured disproportionately by top earners, as the winner-take-all perspective suggests, things will get worse. Luxury spending will continue to grow briskly, launching additional expenditure cascades that will raise the price of admission to the middle class still further.

Conclusion

If the capitalist system is to survive, middle-class families who work hard and play by society's rules must be able to make ends meet. Yet millions of such families already cannot afford basic health insurance or a house in a safe neighborhood with decent schools. The middle class in America seems hardly on the verge of open revolt, but beyond some point, further growth in inequality is bound to cause trouble, as it has in other countries.

Neither Protestantism nor any other coherent ethical system insists that a just wage is whatever wage the free market happens to serve up. On the contrary, concerns about fairness have moved virtually every society to take numerous steps to help counter the social costs of market inequality. In the United States, the institutions crafted for this purpose—which include the progressive tax system, the Social Security system, Pell Grants, and other policies for promoting access to education—have come under assault in recent years. All the while, market forces have been serving up unprecedented growth in inequality, making these institutions even more important.

Max Weber invoked the Protestant ethic to help explain capitalism's emergence but felt that it would be no longer necessary—and might even be counterproductive—once capitalism got up a head of steam. I have argued that the Protestant ethic was by no means necessary for capitalism's launch (although it may have helped), but that a revival of the progressive institutions inspired by it may be essential for the system's continued survival. Time will tell.

References

Baum, Sandy and Marie O'Malley. "College on Credit: How Borrowers Perceive their Education Debt. Results of the 2002 National Student Loan Survey." Nellie Mae Corporation, February 6, 2003.

Brobeck, Stephen. "Recent Trends in Bank Credit Card Marketing and Indebtedness." The Consumer Federation of America, 1998.

College Board, "Trends in College Pricing 2004," http://www.collegeboard.com/prod_downloads/press/cost04/041264TrendsPricing2004FINAL.pdf

Draut, Tamara. *Strapped.* New York: Doubleday, 2006, chap. 2.

Frank, Robert H. and Philip Cook. *The Winner-Take-All Society.* New York: The Free Press, 1995.

Frank, Robert H., Bjornulf Ostvik-White, and Adam Levine. "Expenditure Cascades." Cornell University mimeograph, 2005.

Johnson, Dirk. "When Money Is Everything, Except Hers," *New York Times,* October 28, 1998: A1.

Krugman, Paul. "For Richer: How the Permissive Capitalism of the Boom Destroyed American Equality." *New York Times Magazine,* October 20, 2002: 62–142.

Smith, Adam. *The Wealth of Nations.* New York: Random House, 1937.

Solnick, Sara J. and David Hemenway. "Is More Always Better? A Survey on Positional Concerns." 37 *Journal of Economic Behavior and Organization,* 373, 1998.

U.S. Department of Education, National Center for Education Statistics, The Condition of Education 2004, Indicator 14, Table 14-1. http://nces.ed.gov//programs/coed/2004/pdf/14_2004.pdf

Weber, Max. *The Protestant Ethic and the Spirit of Capitalism,* http://xroads.virginia.edu/~HYPER/WEBER/cover.html

Wolff, Edward N. *Top Heavy: A Study of Increasing Inequality of Wealth in America.* New York: The New Press, 2002.

Notes to Chapter Three

1. *The Protestant Ethic and the Spirit of Capitalism,* chap. II.

2. Ibid.

3. See, for example, Krugman, 2002.

4. For a discussion of increased inequality among different groups, see Frank and Cook, 1995, chap. 5.

5. See Frank and Cook, 1995.

6. See, for example, Solnick and Hemenway, 1997.

7. Smith, 1937.

8. Johnson, 1998, p. A1.

9. See Frank et al., 2005.

10. http://www.census.gov/prod/2003pubs/02statab/construct.pdf; http://www.census.gov/hhes/income/histinc/f03.html

11. For a discussion, see Frank and Cook, 1995, chap. 8.

12. College Board, 2004.

13. U.S. Department of Education, 2004.

14. Baum and O'Malley, 2003.

15. http://www.nchc.org/facts/coverage.shtml

II POLITICS, LEGAL-RATIONAL INSTITUTIONS, AND CORRUPTION

4   On Politicized Capitalism

Victor Nee, Cornell University, and
Sonja Opper, Lund University

TRANSFORMATIVE INSTITUTIONAL CHANGE IN DEPARTURES from state socialism relies not only on evolutionary bottom-up processes but also on sustained intervention by the state to build a new institutional framework. The state must simultaneously dismantle the institutions of central planning and put in place the requisite rules of competition and cooperation of a capitalist economy. The shift of control rights is often retarded, however, by mutually reinforcing interests that perpetuate a close relationship between the state and the firm. On the one hand, state actors are rarely willing to institute a new economic system that completely deprives them of direct control rights at the firm level. On the other hand, managers often prefer the continuation of direct state-firm linkages to gain access to resources in a highly insecure and rapidly changing business environment. As a result, "there is still a much different atmosphere of interaction between government and individual economic agents in ex-socialist countries than in countries with a long tradition of free markets" (Murrell 1996:32).

We call this type of institutional order *politicized capitalism,* where state actors set the regulatory framework *and* remain directly involved in guiding transactions at the firm level. In transitions from state socialism, politicized capitalism is a hybrid order comprising recombinant institutional elements, preexisting and emergent organizational forms, and networks oriented to establishing a market economy (Stark 1996; Nee 2005). It is a mixed economy in which market liberalization and ownership reform are unfinished, preserving partial control rights by the state as both a redistributive allocator and an owner of productive assets. Although the new rules of a market economy impose formal limits on state interventions in the firm, the defining feature of politicized capitalism is the overlap of political and economic markets and the absence of clearly defined state-firm boundaries. The central dilemma faced by reformers is to promote market-driven economic growth within the constraints imposed by competing demands of political and economic actors.

Politicized capitalism emerged in China in the 1980s in the course of market transition (Zhou 2000). This chapter examines the structural tensions between state intervention and marketization in the emergence of China's new capitalist economy. Apart from occasional rural markets, the market as a coordinating mechanism of production and distribution was virtually nonexistent before the start of economic reform in 1978. Under Mao, markets and private ownership of productive assets were eliminated and replaced by a vast, multitiered national system of nonmarket bureaucratic allocation. The characteristic feature of the Maoist-era institutional order was a pervasive reliance on political controls in a redistributive economy where the Communist Party and government managed all dimensions of production and distribution (Schurmann 1968; Whyte and Parish 1984; Walder 1986). Market transition is a dynamic transformative process characterized by a diminishing role of central planning and increasing significance of market institutions in economic life. Figure 4-1 provides a conceptual map, with ideal-type institutional orders arrayed by the extent to which market versus planning and private versus state ownership of productive assets enable, motivate, and guide economic activity. Politicized capitalism is a hybrid institutional order in which recombinant elements of central planning and state control combine and interact with emergent markets and private ownership forms. It comprises institutional arrangements patched together in ad hoc improvisations to address the needs and demands arising from rapid market-oriented economic growth.

The question we explore here is whether politicized capitalism embodies a Nash-like equilibrium, the stable institutional order at the culmination of departures from central planning. In this case, the defining feature of politicized capitalism persists in the close overlap of political and economic markets wherein the state is actively involved at the firm level. Alternatively, if politicized capitalism is itself an embodiment of the organizational dynamics of market transition, constructed from recombinant institutional elements to facilitate the rise of a capitalist economy, as Greif (2006) has detailed for

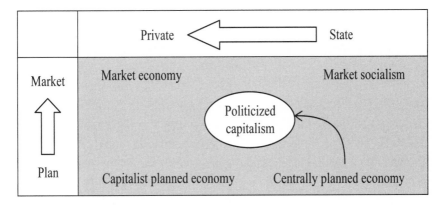

FIGURE 4-1 Politicized Capitalism as a Transformative Economic Order

Europe, we predict that political interference in economic life declines in industrial sectors and regions to the extent that an emergent market economy replaces the centrally planned economy (Nee 1989, 1992). If this alternative scenario holds, it would be confirmed by evidence of decline in the politicized nature of economic decisions in state-firm relations as the role of the state shifts to greater emphasis on building market institutions, i.e., property rights, legal system, market structures.

China's politicized capitalism bears a strong family resemblance to other developmental states in East Asia in its reliance on state intervention to promote transformative economic growth. The goal of the state is to wield state power at the national and local levels to enable, motivate, and guide economic development in order to "catch up" with the advanced industrial economies. In China even more than in the other East Asian developmental states, growth and economic modernization are the basis of state power, providing legitimacy for the continuation of the Chinese Communist Party (CCP) leadership. A strategy of transition has evolved that addresses the interest of reformers in safeguarding the power and privileges of the political elite even while implementing wide-ranging economic reforms that both reduce the scope of state managerial controls over production and distribution and expand the role of the market as a mechanism to motivate and guide economic growth.

Politicized capitalism as a hybrid order permeates the transition economy, but its role in guiding economic action is a variable feature of economic life subject to empirical analysis. The remainder of the chapter is organized as follows: In the following sections we discuss core features of China's politicized capitalism as a distinct type of developmental state and then give an overview of China's growth-promoting macro-policies. We then explore state interventionism at the firm level as a core feature of China's hybrid capitalist system. We focus on discrete empirical studies exploring two types of state interventions: (1) state assistance in the firm's external transactions, such as government assistance in securing loans and (2) state interventionism in corporate governance inside the firm. In conclusion, we offer an outlook on the expected development of China's institutional order of politicized capitalism.

Overall, we report evidence on the persistence of state involvement at the firm level. Our evidence reveals a rather complex situation: On the one hand, direct state involvement in decision-making at the firm level has a negative effect on performance; on the other hand, firms will not openly reject state involvement because they still rely on state actors to ease resource constraints of China's regulated markets. Because market transition creates conditions of decreasing resource dependence on the state, politicized capitalism is inherently in disequilibrium (Nee 1989; Nee and Lian 1994). Where private firms compete in open markets, entrepreneurs prefer to be free of the Communist Party. A tipping point is reached when a critical mass of entrepreneurs no longer depends on state-controlled resources, and growing reliance on tax revenues contributed by private enterprises reinforces incentives for government to make resource allocation decisions based on assessment of their effects on local economic performance and on their prospects for career mobility.

Politicized Capitalism as an Institutional Order

China's economic miracle has riveted attention on the positive role of the state in promoting transformative economic development. As Stiglitz observes, "The contrast between Russia's transition, as engineered by the international economic institutions, and that of China, designed by itself, could not be greater: While in 1990 China's gross domestic product (GDP) was 60 percent that of Russia, by the end of the decade the numbers had been reversed. While Russia saw an unprecedented increase in poverty China saw an unprecedented decrease" (2002:6). Per capita GDP grew from $100 to $944 (constant prices 1995) between 1978 and 2002. The market capitalization of firms listed on China's stock exchanges increased from 1 percent of the GDP in 1992 to 37 percent by 2002. Exports increased from $39 billion in 1978 to $470 billion per annum in 2002 (constant prices 1995). Annual net foreign direct investments grew from $386 million in 1982 to $46.8 billion in 2002 (World Bank

2004). China thus becomes the latest entry in the pantheon of successful developmental states, along with South Korea, Taiwan, and Japan (Stiglitz 2002).

In its core features, China's current economic system of politicized capitalism resembles that in other East Asian societies in the early stages of economic takeoff. Direct state intervention at the firm level is widespread, and the state's guiding hand in promoting national growth remains visible. Two mutually reinforcing institutional changes frame the interactions between the local state bureaucracy and firm-level economic actors: a) modernization of the party and government bureaucracy and b) fiscal decentralization.

Strengthening Bureaucratic Capacity after Mao

Modernization of the state bureaucracy has been the government's priority throughout the reform period. Mao's decade-long Cultural Revolution crippled China's state apparatus. It politicized the structure of bureaucratic career mobility, severely undermining rules and norms of merit-based recruitment and promotion. The predominance of "red" cadres recruited and promoted on the basis of their political activism reduced the state's capability to perform routine administrative tasks. Demoralization and the accompanying breakdown of rational-legal norms and procedures resulted in reliance on personal connections (*guanxi*) in the functioning of public administration. Given widespread local cadre opposition at the outset of economic reform, reform leaders soon realized that restoring the efficacy of the state bureaucracy was essential to success in their ambitious reforms (Nee 2000).

Administrative reforms in the 1980s introduced strict retirement ages for government officials and a one-time buyout strategy to retire old veterans as a means to push out Maoist bureaucrats who were impeding progress in market-oriented economic reforms. Early retirement was aimed at reducing bureaucratic inertia and commitment to the old planning mentality of state socialism (Lipton and Sachs 1990; Murrell 1996). Reformers also sought to build a modernized bureaucracy by implementing merit-based entrance exams and promotion schemes to reinforce incentives to improve local economic development (Li 1998; Li and Lian 1999). College education and technical qualifications became general entrance criteria. Many elite bureaucrats are recruited with engineering and public administration degrees, reflecting the emphasis on technical training and expertise.

As a result of these administrative reforms, government regulations and procedural guidelines have become more and more precise and transparent (Yao 2001). This has increased the predictability of bureaucratic decisions and reduced uncertainty with respect to government policy and regulatory practices. The passage in 2005 of a comprehensive legal code governing civil service culminated this two-decade-long concerted effort by reform leaders to modernize China's state bureaucracy. The new civil service law sets forth strict, rule-governed performance guidelines with respect to appropriate conduct. Public announcement of openings, reliance on scores in civil service examinations to recruit candidates, annual performance reviews, competitive examinations in routine promotions, and monitoring by the personnel department have been institutionalized at all levels of the national bureaucracy.

Notwithstanding national reform measures, the quality of the state bureaucracy varies considerably across regions and localities in China. Progress in building a modern bureaucracy has been uneven and inconsistent. In poor, rural hinterland regions, corruption is an incorrigible feature of local public administration. Predatory behavior on the part of government officials is reflected in the routine use of local state administration to extract surplus from peasants through local levies and taxes, hosting of banquets at the expense of entrepreneurs, requisition of farmland for use by developers without adequate compensation to the farmers, and official tolerance of environmental degradation. Moreover, local bureaucrats routinely intervene as predatory agents under the cover of promoting economic development. Widespread public perception of abuse of power and corruption has contributed to a sharp increase in the frequency and contentiousness of local protests and rebellions. The annual number of mass incidents is on the rise, with around 87,000 registered protests and petitions in 2005 (Li 2006). Despite the national guidelines upholding merit-based recruitment and promotions of government and party bureaucrats, the poor hinterland regions lag far behind the coastal provinces in the formal training and technical competence of civil servants.

Max Weber ([1922] 1978) observed that the rise of market capitalism and the development of modern bureaucracy are closely coupled institutional processes. As in the rise of capitalism in the West, modernization of the civil service in China has made the most rapid progress in the prosperous private enterprise economy of the coastal regions. In the course of two decades of reform, the Yangzi Delta region, an epicenter of Chinese capitalism, has attained a level of bureaucratic efficiency comparable with Western industrialized countries. According to the *World Competitiveness Yearbook,* covering 61 countries and economic regions worldwide, Zhejiang province was ranked 17 in terms of bureaucratic efficiency[1] (score 4.31) in 2006, ahead of the United

States (4.39) and Australia (4.35). Although China's overall score is much lower, ranking 35, it ranks higher than some European industrialized countries including Germany, the United Kingdom, Belgium, and Italy. Corruption and bribe taking are also far less pronounced in Zhejiang province (rank 36; scoring higher than the Czech Republic and Hungary, Europe's successful transition economies) than in China as a whole (rank 46). Recruitment of elite bureaucrats relies on open competitive national searches. Recruiters are even sent to North America to interview Chinese students with postgraduate degrees from U.S. and Canadian universities for specific key positions. Short-term training workshops in the West are increasingly popular and involve the major elite universities.

Though traditional China was the first to institute national civil service examinations in recruiting scholar-officials for the imperial bureaucracy, the spirit of that bureaucracy was shaped by generalists, the elite literati committed to Confucian moral and ethical teaching. It was not until the contemporary era that rational-legal norms and approach to public administration have gained legitimacy as the defining spirit for the government bureaucracy. Rather than generalists, as in the "red" cadres of the Cultural Revolution era, today's elite bureaucrats are recruited for their technical expertise and promoted for their performance as technocrats. Competition in internal bureaucratic promotion is intense and the standards of annual performance reviews are high but transparent, allowing fair evaluations and predictable career paths. Through strict implementation of national rules and standards, the provincial government of Zhejiang province has successfully reestablished the high social status government officials traditionally held in China. With its emphasis on merit-based recruitment and promotion, Hangzhou municipal government has built a modern bureaucracy that uses state-of-the-art knowledge in public administration and related fields, typically favoring indirect means of governance—tax policy, regulatory action—over direct interventions in the firm.

The building blocks of Zhejiang's bureaucratic modernization are promulgated in China's civil service laws and preceding regulations. The particular success may lie in a specific esprit de corps that Zhejiang's government succeeded in establishing. Notwithstanding, Zhejiang's success in building an effective state bureaucracy should not diverge much from other areas of China where private enterprise and markets have gained a critical mass. Overall, the state bureaucracy is undergoing a process of dynamic transformation from a

Maoist-era politicized state apparatus to a technocratic bureaucracy that emphasizes higher education and technical expertise in the recruitment and promotion of bureaucrats. Secure government employment coupled with high social
status and attractive benefits serve as incentive to avoid malfeasance. As this
transformation progresses, politicized capitalism is in disequilibrium as the rise
of a private-enterprise economy and competitive markets rapidly diminishes
the relative industrial output of state-owned enterprises (SOEs) and drives the
Chinese state inexorably toward less direct intervention at the firm-level, and
more emphasis on indirect instruments such as taxation and credit policies.

Fiscal Federalism

The theory of state and local finance has long stressed the disciplining effect
of fiscal decentralization on government activities and the provision of public goods. Qian and Roland (1998) offer a model to analyze the relationships
among the organization of the state, economic policies, and the tightness of
fiscal budget constraints. They identify two main mechanisms that may constrain predatory political interference in the economy. First, under the assumption of factor mobility, a federalist system introduces competition among
local governments, which increases opportunity costs of bailouts and any activities leading to inferior enterprise performance (Weingast 1995). If local
government jurisdictions fail to provide a hospitable business environment,
they face poor chances of attracting resources needed to enhance economic
prosperity. Competition in a federalist system eventually limits discretionary
authority, predatory behavior, and rent-seeking. Second, in federal systems,
fiscal decentralization may harden budget constraints of jurisdictions and
provide incentives for efficiency-oriented local activities. Local governments
compete to build a business environment favorable to private capital.

Indeed, China's policy of fiscal decentralization has constituted a key institutional innovation aimed at strengthening economic incentives of municipal and provincial governments to support market-oriented economic reform.
According to the fiscal revenue-sharing system, lower-level governments have
the obligation to submit a fixed proportion of fiscal revenues to their superior
government unit, while retaining the residual for their own budget. Given that
tax revenues are positively correlated with firm performance, local bureaucrats have an incentive to do what they can to assure that local firms prosper
(Montinola et al. 1995; Li 1998). Fiscal federalism has thus developed into a
major driving force of economic reforms in China. With increasing financial

independence of local governments, revenue-generating reforms have gained in importance, whereas the incentive for local governments to maintain elements of the old socialist command economy has declined.

Increasing financial responsibilities and hardening budget constraints imposed strong pressure on government to privatize the local economies, given low profitability, weak tax revenues, and increasing state subsidies needed to maintain loss-making state industries, and the superior economic performance of private firms over state-owned firms. Local governments developed a strong interest in divesting loss-making state-owned firms. Figure 4-2 depicts the close negative bivariate relation between state-owned production and local revenues and more specifically between state-owned industrial production and corporate tax income at the provincial level between 1995 and 2004. It shows that provinces that have declining industrial production from state-owned enterprises relative to nonstate firms also have higher corporate tax revenues.

Provincial and municipal governments responded to increasing economic pressure by accelerating privatization and divestiture of state-owned assets. Following China's official policy, "zhuada, fangxiao" (grasp the big ones and let the small ones free), the 1990s saw an unprecedented increase in the pace of privatization of these enterprises. Small- and medium-size firms were sold through manager or employee buyouts or auctioned off, whereas big state corporations of the so-called sensible key sectors were partially privatized and corporatized, with many of them being listed at one of China's two stock exchanges. As a consequence, the number of state-owned enterprises was reduced by more than 70 percent from 113,000 to 31,000 and total national employment in them was reduced from 110 million to 64 million between 1996 and 2004, while their total production value was stabilized at around 35 percent of gross industrial output. Within the nonstate economy, private sector development emerged as the most dynamic growth engine of China's economy. By the end of 2004, registered employment in the private sector already reached 96 million with an annual production growth of 40 percent, out-competing all other ownership forms (*China State Statistical Yearbook 2005*).

Figure 4-3 illustrates the close parallel development of waning state-owned industrial production and increasing market liberalization based on pooled provincial-level data covering the period between 1997 and 2003. It confirms that as the market economy expands, the gross industrial output contributed

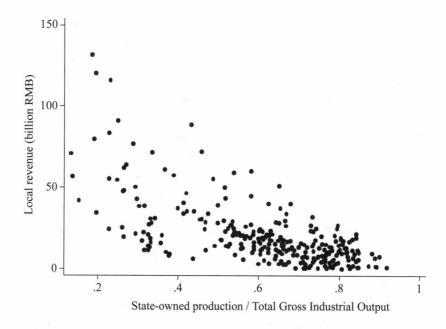

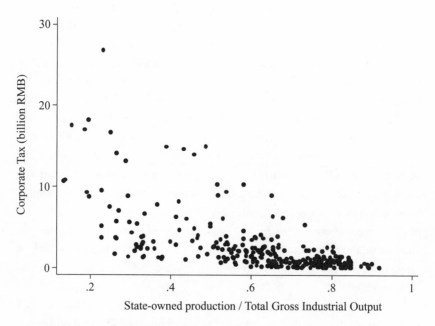

FIGURE 4-2 State-Owned Production and Provincial Revenues,
1995–2004
SOURCE: National Bureau of Statistics of China.

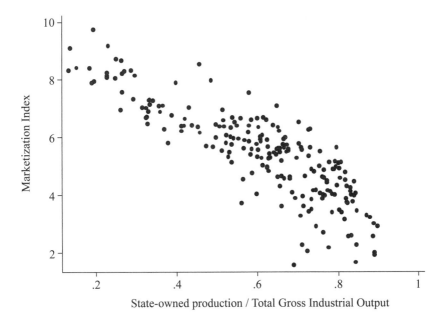

FIGURE 4-3 Bivariate Relation Between Provincial State-Owned
Enterprise-Production/Gross Industrial Output and Marketization
Index, 1997–2003
SOURCE: Data from National Bureau of Statistics of China; Fan and Wang (2003).

by state-owned enterprises declines. In other words, as predicted, in market transitions the greater the size of the market economy, the less state-owned productive assets can compete with private-ownership forms in the production of industrial output (Nee 1992; Naughton 1995). We infer from Figure 4-3 that the state-owned sector is strongest in regions of the transition economy where competitive markets are still subordinate to the state in the allocation of scarce resources.

Overview of Growth Promoting Industrial Policies

The changing relative contribution of state-owned enterprises and private firms drives a dynamic transition in the role of the state towards the custodial and midwife role of the East Asian developmental state. Like Taiwan, South Korea, and Singapore, China has instituted an overall growth strategy of modernization and technological innovation that provides an institutional and political framework for intense collaboration and cooperation between the political and the business elites. The first so-called industrial policy (*chanye zhengce*) guidelines were implemented in 1989,[2] when the government perceived that the old planning apparatus was no longer suitable to steer economic priorities—particularly industrial development—in China's economic development. Since then, the government has frequently revised and reformulated industrial priorities in an effort to single out future winners and losers in the ongoing structural transformation of the economy. The government seeks to create an environment conducive to the growth of large-scale firms that can eventually turn into big, multinational players who establish global brand names. Common instruments such as market entry regulation, taxation, and loan decisions are part of the state's tool kit to influence the direction of structural transformation (Lu 2000). In this sense, China's industrial policy is also actively involved in shaping market structures.

In parallel, the Chinese government developed a science and technology program that relies on the mechanism of central planning and resource allocation. Major institutions in charge of formulating the national science and technology (S&T) plans are the State Science and Technology Commission and the State Economic and Trade Commission. A set of four mutually complementary S&T programs builds the framework of China's national technology policy.[3] Each program supports a close science-business interface to secure innovation activities with good prospects for productivity growth and to maximize the commercialization of research and development (R&D) output. While the individual programs follow a set of distinct core objectives, with specific tools to promote technological development, the planning institutions gradually adjust national priorities and targeted research goals in response to the changing overall state development goals. Concurrent to the structural changes within China's research landscape, the central government has gradually increased the relative role of R&D policies. In 1995, the "Decision on accelerating scientific and technological progress" formulated a target value of 1.5 percent of GDP for national S&T expenditures. Although China has not yet reached its target value, the recent increase of R&D expenditures over the last few years is indeed impressive. Between 1999 and 2003 the annual R&D expenditures increased from 0.8 percent to 1.3 percent, meanwhile surpassing even the average value of the EU-15 countries. The majority of R&D expenditures accrue in the business sector, followed by R&D institutes and universities. In parallel, the proportion of scientists and engineers in the overall S&T population increased significantly from 54 percent to 69 percent between 1999 and 2003 (National Bureau of Statistics of China 2004).

The state's modernization efforts are supported by massive investments in China's system of higher education. Overall educational funds increased from 2.8 percent of GDP in 1991 to 5.2 percent in 2002. Government funding equaled 3.3 percent of GDP in 2002, and the remaining educational funds were generated by tuition fees and nongovernment funding organizations (State Statistical Bureau 2004). In terms of public expenditure of GDP on education, China is comparable with Singapore and ranks only slightly lower than Japan and Korea. Institutions of higher education enjoy special attention and received 23 percent of government appropriations for education in 2002. The annual number of university graduates increased from only 0.16 million in 1978 at the start of the reform period to 2.39 million in 2004. Due to China's centralized system of university entry exams, the structural composition of university graduates is closely aligned with the specific needs of China's economic development. About 35 percent of China's university graduates hold a degree in engineering, 15 percent in business administration, and another 9 percent in natural sciences (National Bureau of Statistics of China 2005). This makes China the biggest producer of engineers worldwide (with about 800,000 graduates in 2004).

In contrast to Japan's technological catching-up process, which basically relied on the country's own development strength, China's reformers have embraced foreign technology to jump-start national economic development. Foreign direct investment (FDI) emerged as a core element of the national reform agenda from the outset of economic reforms in the late 1970s. The state promoted FDI to serve two complementary purposes: First, foreign investments obviously alleviated China's capital constraint; second, the new FDI policies were designed specifically to speed the country's technological catching-up process through channels such as reverse engineering, skilled labor turnovers, and demonstration effects. Special economic zones with generous tax and fiscal incentives not only facilitated the inflow of scarce capital, but also served as entry ports for advanced technologies, Western-style management techniques, and organizational blueprints. Countrywide development of technology parks and development zones facilitated an immense inflow of FDIs across China. Meanwhile, China ranks number one worldwide among FDI recipient countries with an FDI inflow of 153 billion USD in 2004 (State Statistical Bureau 2005). Steered by specific investment incentive schemes,

FDIs gradually shifted from labor-intensive technologies toward capital- and knowledge-intensive technologies. Local content regulations guaranteed that national firms benefited from the growing FDI inflow as suppliers of input factors and machinery. More recently, local content regulations even included R&D activities in order to deepen the technological exchange between multinational companies and local firms.

Politicized Capitalism and the Firm

While the aforementioned programs represent many of the standard features of national policies of developmental states (Evans 1995), state activities in China's politicized capitalism typically go beyond the provision of growth-promoting strategies that indirectly encourage firm development. Due to the overlap of political and economic markets in politicized capitalism, state actors also enjoy opportunities to directly interfere at the firm level. Figure 4-4 highlights the dual role of the party-state and its representatives, as the rule-setting body and as actively involved in firm transactions. In politicized capitalism, the firm not only responds to market signals, but its performance and economic success are also affected by its relations with state representatives and the extent and quality of government involvement within the firm. Due to weak legal and political checks and balances, legal limits to political interference are largely absent. Although China has invested tremendous efforts to bring its business laws and regulations into accordance with Western practices, legal institutions are still weak and provide little protection against state interference. A core feature of China's legal reforms is to build legitimacy for economic reforms and sustain transformative economic growth without affecting the CCP's monopoly on political power. Hence, the legal system is still not independent from the Communist Party, and local courts remain in a subordinate position in relation to the local party committees (Findlay 1999).

One can differentiate between two distinct types of direct state interventions at the firm level:

a) State involvement in market transactions of the firm, particularly to assist and support business deals in state-controlled markets, and b) Direct state involvement in the firm's corporate governance.

State Involvement in Market Transactions

State involvement as a third party in economic transactions is widespread when firms operate in partially liberalized or state-controlled markets. In such

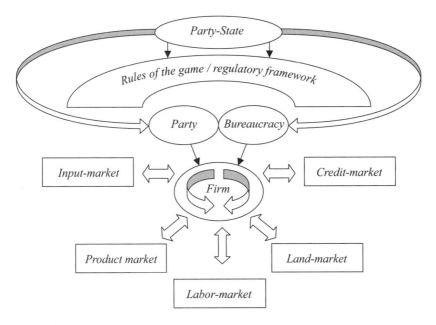

FIGURE 4-4 The Firm in Politicized Capitalism

cases, resource dependence theory predicts a voluntary construction of clientelist ties between firms and government in an effort to alleviate and mitigate resource constraints. Political capital becomes an important asset and may affect a firm's success in securing business deals. Examples of state-controlled or highly regulated markets are those for land-use rights, for public construction projects, for credit and for capital, as well as specific state production monopolies such as tobacco and energy. Outcomes in these markets are not fully determined through market mechanisms bringing supply and demand into equilibrium; instead, business transactions are still heavily regulated and controlled by the state. Hence, political capital embodied in personal relationships between political and economic actors may provide crucial information advantages or provide legitimacy and credibility for entrepreneurs that eventually help to secure a business deal. By contrast, in competitive markets, market outcomes are determined by the price mechanism; hence, the economic benefits of political ties decrease. Market transition theory predicts that the importance of political connections for business success is negatively correlated with the degree of economic liberalization and marketization (Nee 1989; Bian and Logan 1996). Hence, in heavily state-regulated industrial sectors and regions, entrepreneurs must cultivate personal connections with

powerful government bureaucrats to gain reliable access to resources and protect their firms from predatory interventions (Wank 1996; Xin and Pearce
1996; Peng and Luo 2000).

In our field research involving 80 interviews with private entrepreneurs in
the Yangzi Delta in the summer and fall of 2005, we found rich evidence supporting the close connection between the extent of state control and the value
of political capital. Many entrepreneurs whose businesses competed in free
markets told us they do not invest in political capital. The general manager
of a computer company, for instance, clearly rejected the idea of playing the
"game of politics," and explained, "In my sector, the government cannot give
me much, not much tax breaks, and not much government contracts." By contrast, entrepreneurs in state-controlled and highly regulated markets, such as
the construction business, told us they invest considerable efforts to establish
close personal ties with the political elite. Especially for entrepreneurs who
depend on government contracts for their business, having strong political
ties with government is often the decisive factor in business success. One entrepreneur in the water purification business in the Yangzi Delta remarked:
"Competitive bidding is just a form. It doesn't involve the entire process in
terms of results . . . Political connections are still as important as before . . . If
some senior government official gives a signal we will get the project. Sometimes we lose bids, because someone else gets the nod from a senior official."[4]
Government interference and influence in regulated markets often goes well
beyond the legal limits and involves corruption and bribery. A Chinese study
conducted in 2004 reveals that about 80 percent of illegal land-use cases can
be attributed to local government malfeasance (Li 2006).

Resource constraints and the need to secure the "helping hand" of government are particularly important for firms beyond a certain critical size. With
size, firm vulnerability increases, due both to increasing rent-seeking activities of government officials and to resource dependence, so that good government relations become a crucial factor in doing business. As one interviewee
pointed out, "Once you are big, you are in trouble. You must have good relationships with the government then . . . If the party wants you to die, you have
no way to live."[5] Managers and entrepreneurs develop and cultivate political
capital through the informal pursuit of old friendships with government officials in social gatherings and family visits (particularly managers who held
previous positions in the government), and through financial donations to
support government projects. There is also the formal inclusion of government officials on so-called expert committees formed as a consulting body

to provide guidance in important firm decisions. Entrepreneurs in regulated markets tend to make significant financial investments in maintaining political connections. Our interviewees indicated that "social expenditures" of up to 1 percent of the contract value are expected; the investment might be a higher percentage in smaller deals.[6]

Our anecdotal evidence from interviews with entrepreneurs in the Yangzi Delta region is supported by data from the World Bank's Investment Climate Survey of 2,400 firms conducted in 2003 in 18 cities in China. The survey was conducted in two parts: one to be answered by the firm's CEO and the other by the CFO or accountant. Using this World Bank dataset, we compare the state's role in assisting business transactions in both types of market structures. As an example of a state-controlled market, we focus on China's credit market, which represents one of the least-reformed sectors of China's transition economy. For a case study of competitive markets, we chose China's product market, which (with few exceptions, i.e., state monopolies in tobacco and energy) was the first market to be liberalized in China's economic reforms.

To assess the effect of political connections in both market structures we chose to compare the effect of political capital as measured by direct government assistance to the firm and the involvement of a party official in the firm's management. The party and government can best be described as a multiplex principal-agent relationship, with the party being the principal and the government agencies representing diverse agents (Shirk 1992, 1993). The local party committees can therefore offer access to most administrative bureaus at the local level. For instance, the party can provide an indispensable network outside of which bank credit is much more difficult to access. Membership in the CCP is often regarded as a minimum requirement for a career as a professional manager—particularly in state-owned enterprises and in private firms that exceed a certain size and influence. A CEO with active involvement as a party secretary, vice party secretary, or party committee member signals a closer and stronger party affiliation. According to the Investment Climate Survey, more than 42 percent of the surveyed firms actually have a CEO who holds an office in the CCP. Some regional variation can be observed, with more liberalized and reformed areas showing a smaller proportion of politically active CEOs and less-liberalized, economically backward regions showing a higher proportion.

The banking sector is still dominated by four state-owned commercial banks and three political banks. Although the state banks have been joined by 12 joint-equity banks, about 90 regional city banks and private banks like the

Minsheng Bank (founded in 1996), the oligopolist structure of the Chinese banking sector persists. The People's Bank of China controls interest rates for different kinds of deposits, state-owned banks still benefit considerably from their established branch network, and the state commercial banks are still the central provider of financial control. The Chinese government has implemented only partial reform of the commercial banking sector. Recent reforms show a surprising degree of inconsistency. For example, the Commercial Bank Law (effective in 1995) guarantees the formal-legal independence of commercial banks, but the law still emphasizes that loan decisions should be taken under the "guidance of state economic policies" (art. 34). Abundant evidence confirms that China's commercial banks are not independent in their loan decisions (Zhu 1999; Leung and Mok 2000; Lin 2001). Political intervention is still rife despite legal reform of banking to foster formal autonomy in lending decisions. In 2003, private firms and individuals received only about 1 percent of short-term loans of China's state commercial banks, including the four state commercial banks, policy banks, and agencies of postal savings (*China State Statistical Yearbook 2005*: 674). Even the newly founded joint-equity banks are not completely immune from political interventions (Wong 2000).

The importance of political capital for a firm's success in getting a bank loan can be readily inferred from Figure 4-5, which compares credit access across 18 cities for firms that do not receive government assistance (left-hand side) with those that do (right-hand side). Figure 4-6 shows that where the CEO is politically well-connected and active as party secretary, firms have greater success in securing bank loans.

That political ties play an essential role independently of the firm's ownership status is confirmed by Table 4-1. With only two exceptions (listed firms and collective firms with CEOs holding a party office), both government assistance and active party participation of CEOs are associated with greatly improved chances to secure a bank loan. Although bivariate relations are of course technically and methodically not appropriate to establish causal relationships, market transition theory and resource dependence theory both provide strong arguments supporting underlying causalities hinting at a strong interventionism of political capital in China's state-controlled financial market. Our findings are also consistent with an analysis by Li et al. (2005) of a sample of more than 3,000 private firms showing that political connections are helpful in obtaining bank loans and tend to reduce discrimination by state banks.

A closer look at the sectoral distribution of government assistance confirms that political ties are used instrumentally to steer scarce capital into

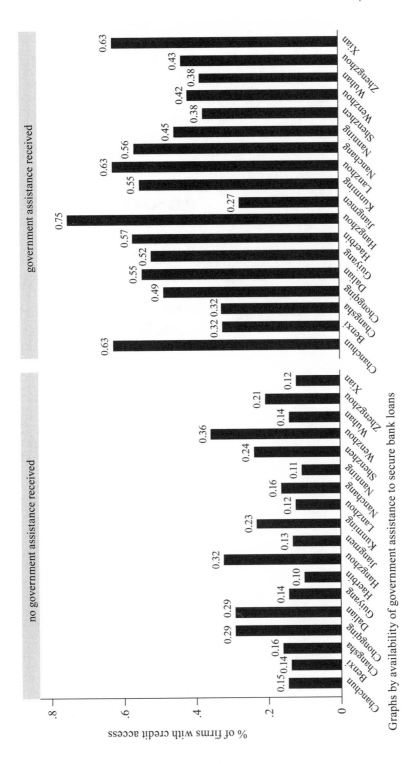

FIGURE 4-5 Effect of Government Assistance on Access to Bank Finance, 2003

SOURCE: Data from World Bank Investment Climate Survey, 2003.

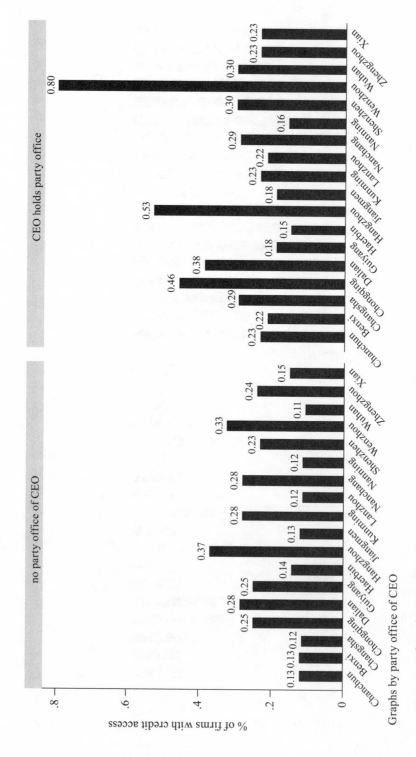

FIGURE 4-6 Effect of Politically Active CEOs on Access to Bank Finance, 2003

SOURCE: Data from World Bank Investment Climate Survey, 2003.

TABLE 4-1 Political Capital and Credit Access by Ownership Form

		SOE	Collectively owned firm	Listed firm	Private firm	100% individual ownership firm
Proportion of firms having a bank loan	Without government assistance	18.30%	12.29%	47.62%	15.33%	15.94%
	With government	44.32%	46.43%	62.96%	42.37%	42.24%
Proportion of firms having a bank loan	CEO without party office	15.97%	14.88%	66.66%	16.99%	16.72%
	CEO with party office	24.83%	14.02%	40.00%	32.17%	32.17%

SOURCE: World Bank Investment Climate Survey 2003.

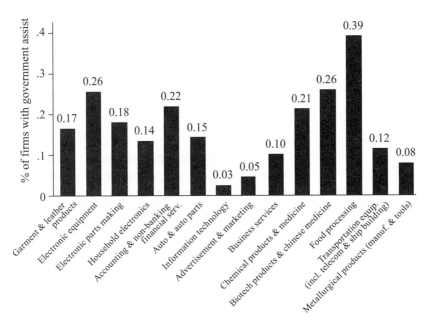

FIGURE 4-7 Sectoral Distribution of Government Assistance
SOURCE: World Bank Investment Climate Survey, 2003.

preferred industrial endeavors. Figure 4-7 provides evidence that government assistance in loan applications is particularly common in China's high-tech sectors such as biotechnology and electronics, which enjoy priority in China's current industrial policy and technology programs. In the high-technology

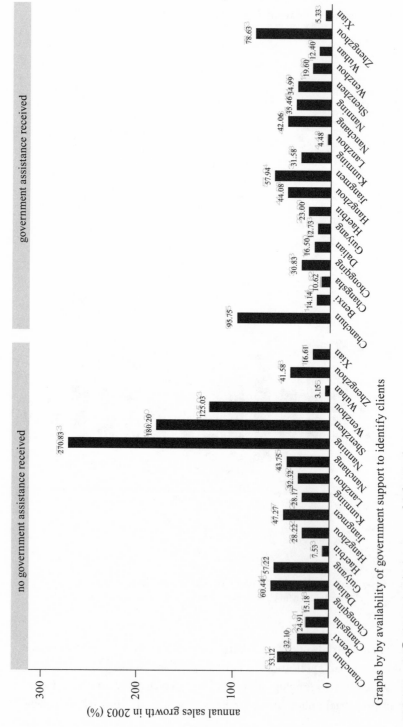

FIGURE 4-8 Government Assistance and Sales Performance

SOURCE: World Bank Investment Climate Survey, 2003.

sector, China's policy is similar to that of other Asian developmental states (Whitley 1999; Kang 2002).

Our analysis of the effect of political capital in product markets—our counterexample of a liberalized market—reveals a completely different picture. Figure 4-8 shows that political ties do not in general improve sales performance, as indicated in the comparison of firms without government assistance in securing clients (left-hand side) and those that enjoy government sponsorship (right-hand side). Only in Benxi and Xian does government assistance appear to be associated with slightly improved performance. In general, government assistance in securing either domestic or international clients does not affect the firm's sales growth. Specifically, as shown in Figure 4-9, political capital embodied in politically active CEOs does not result in stronger performance in the firm's sales.

Table 4-2 confirms our findings for most ownership forms. With the exception of collectively owned firms, political ties and government support are not linked to advantages on the product market. To the contrary, firms generally exhibit stronger growth in sales if they lack political ties in the form of government assistance and politically active CEOs.

Thus, it is clear that economic benefits generated by political capital depend crucially on the extent of market liberalization. Consistent with market transition theory (Nee 1989), positive payoffs of political capital are confined to regulated and state-controlled markets, whereas political capital does not yield any additional benefits in competitive markets. Our results match well with recent work by Li, Meng, and Zhang (2006), who analyzed determinants of party membership of entrepreneurs. Their findings show that the less developed the local market-supporting institutions and the less liberalized the local markets, the more likely entrepreneurs are to enter politics.

State Involvement in Firm Decisions

The implementation of the Company Law promulgated in 1994 has altered both the quality and intensity of state intervention in the firm, depriving the government of its former unchallenged monopoly rights and control over former state-owned enterprises. In the 1990s, state-crafted institutional change established the framework for converting them into public corporations. The objective was to transform loss-making state enterprises into profit-making firms through corporatization and listing on stock exchanges. With the Company Law, the government sought to bring organizational standards in line with Western-style corporate governance (Guthrie 1999), shifting power from

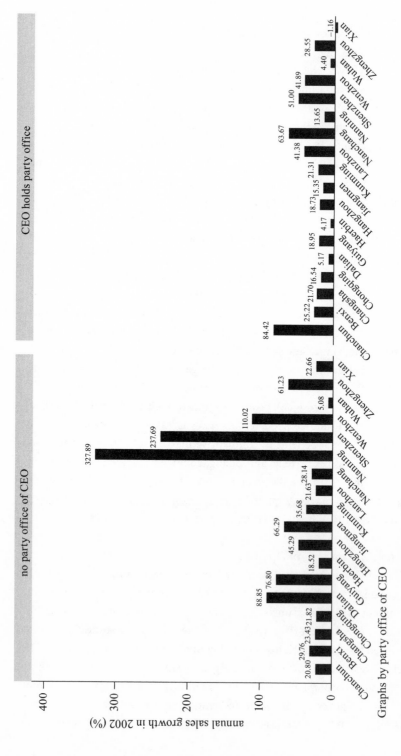

FIGURE 4-9 Politically Active CEOs and Sales Performance

SOURCE: World Bank Investment Climate Survey, 2003.

TABLE 4-2 Political Capital and Sales Growth by Ownership Form

		SOE	Collectively owned firm	Listed firm	Private firm	100% individual ownership firm
Sales growth in %	Without government assistance	27.35%	23.08%	30.09%	76.85%	97.06%
	With government	23.21%	38.17%	33.33%	27.66%	30.43%
Sales growth in %	CEO without party office	39.07%	20.25%	50.42%	75.54%	99.89%
	CEO with party office	22.49%	29.73%	13.30%	23.21%	17.89%

SOURCE: World Bank Investment Climate Survey 2003.

the party and government to the board of directors and the CEO as major decision makers within the firm (Wong, Opper, and Hu 2004). State involvement in firm decision making, however, was not completely abolished. In an effort to not lose all control rights over China's industrial key sectors, specific aspects of established political governance structures were maintained. Not surprisingly, this provided politicians and bureaucrats with opportunities for direct intervention in the firm. The state is particularly interested in maintaining involvement in large-scale modern corporations, business groups, and conglomerates in core industries, either listed or unlisted. Certain giant former state-owned enterprises, such as China National Offshore Oil Corporation (CNOCC) listed on the Shanghai Stock Exchange, are regarded as crucial in leading China's bid as a global economic power. Whether as a private firm that has grown into a major player in its niche or as a former state-owned enterprise, the larger the enterprise, the more the state becomes interested in guiding its future development. Two major channels for direct interference can be identified: state ownership of shares and governance structures within the firm.

State Intervention via the Ownership Channel

Although China has witnessed a major privatization move, reducing the size of the state sector by over 70 percent between 1996 and 2004, the government has often retained partial control rights in large-scale firms. Corporatization and stock exchange listing have reduced the average state shareholding in firms listed on the Shanghai Stock Exchange to about one-third of the firms' total shares. However, another third is held by corporatized state-owned companies.

Thus, on average, 60 percent of company shares are still under either direct or indirect state influence.

Bureaucrats maintain direct ties to such firms through their participation as members of the board of directors representing state-owned shares. As such, they are entitled to represent the state's interests in the firm's strategic decisions, albeit within the framework of an advisory capacity as stipulated by the rules of corporate governance of the Company Law (Gensler and Yang 1995). Thus, while the firm's top executive, the CEO, has full control over its management, the state has a voice—the more so the larger its ownership share in the firm—and votes on strategic decisions.

Such state participation in corporate governance, however, turns out to be problematic. State asset administration is carried out by an institution that serves as a representative of the central government. These so-called state asset management companies usually have weak incentives to perform monitoring activities. First of all, their officials usually do not receive any personal benefits from effective monitoring. Second, state shareholders do not operate under hard budget constraints; even if budgets are admittedly hardened, state shareholders can almost be sure to be bailed out by the state treasury if companies suffer financial distress. Not surprisingly, corporate performance of China's listed companies is negatively related to the proportion of a company's state shares (Xu and Wang 1999; Qi, Wu, and Hua 2000).

Government ownership of course also invites intervention in corporate governance beyond the regular board meetings and shareholder meetings. The continuation of close firm-business relations and informal networks among actors allow for ready interference in almost all types of firm decisions. Government involvement in corporate governance of firms listed on the Shanghai Stock Exchange is particularly pronounced when it comes to decisions affecting financial issues, that is, decisions on mergers, change in shareholding structure, and on share placements and new issues. Overall performance effects of this direct government intervention are negative, however, showing the state's inability to overcome the inherent incentive and information problems of state ownership even after a shift toward greater reliance on market mechanisms (Nee, Opper, and Wong 2007).

State Intervention Through Politicized Governance Structures
State involvement is further exacerbated through the persistence of politicized vertical command structures within the firm. Although the official policy line

was to encourage a complete separation of government and business functions (*zhengqi fenkai*) to support a rationalization of the economic sphere,[7] the reforms in actuality revealed a high degree of ambivalence and inconsistency. In spite of the official propaganda, which claims to constrain the state's role to that of a normal shareholder without any priority rights to interfere in the firm's organization and governance, China's new company legislation reveals a more ambivalent position toward depoliticizing the former state-owned enterprise.

To begin with, Company Law, Article 14, still calls for a supervision of enterprises by the government and social masses. Inevitably, this claim may create conflicts with the intended enterprise independence. Even more serious deficits of the official depoliticization strategy result from the continuing influence of the "three old political committees"—party committee, labor committee, and trade union—placed within the firm. Despite the creation of new organizational and governance structures, such as shareholders' meeting, board of directors, and supervisory committee alongside the position of the CEO, the old political organs were not abolished. Instead, the Company Law guarantees and regulates their future involvement and responsibilities. Although the "old three" lost a large amount of their inherited coordination and control rights, their survival invites a continuation of political involvement in the firm's decisions. Particularly their long tradition as central political bodies within the firm provides fertile grounds for continuing informal involvement (Wu and Du 1998:68). Figure 4-10 sketches the internal structure and persisting links between the three old committees and new decision-making bodies [board of directors, manager, and board of supervisors].

Article 17 of the Company Law specifies "the activities of the local branch units of the CCP in a company shall be carried out in accordance with the Constitution of the CCP," but this constitution provides little additional clarification of the party's scope of involvement. It simply delegates the implementation of higher party decisions to local party committees and grants them the right to "supervise party cadres and any other personnel." More specific was former General Secretary Jiang Zemin's detailed sketch of the party's activities at the enterprise level. According to his guidelines, the party should focus on four functions: (1) implementation of the party line, (2) fulfillment of party-related tasks with special attention to production and management, (3) participation in the most important business decisions, and (4) support for

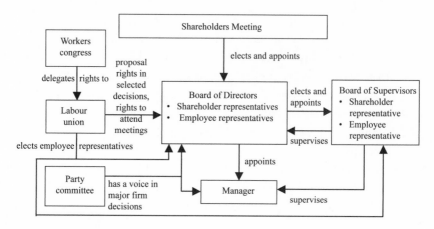

FIGURE 4-10 Corporate Governance of China's Listed Firms (According to Company Law)
SOURCE: Opper (2004).

the board of directors, the supervisory committee, and management (Foreign Broadcasting Information Service 1999).

Survey evidence confirms the active role of party committees. An in-depth study of state involvement in listed corporations finds persisting party interference in almost all domains of the firm's activity, with party committees exercising an even stronger influence in the firm than government bureaus (Nee, Opper and Wong 2007). Local party committees exert the most control in personnel decisions, especially the selection of managers of departments, branches, and subsidiaries, and the selection and dismissal of vice chief executive officers. In essence, party involvement concentrates on personnel issues, which have been a central focus of the *nomenklatura* system for decades of socialist planning (Shirk 1992:61). The fact that local party units tend to have a high level of involvement in decisions assigned de jure to the enterprise manager suggests that they may use the manager's office as their venue for interventionist activities.

Party influence within the firm may be even stronger if the CEO is actively involved in the party and holds a party office. Particularly in large- and medium-size firms, management positions are often filled by politically active members of the CCP. The previously mentioned Investment Climate Survey of 2,400 firms found that more than 40 percent of CEOs concurrently hold party positions. Although politically active CEOs are naturally most common in state-owned enterprises (with more than 70 percent of CEOs holding a party position), political participation of management personnel is also widespread in non-state-owned firms. Fifty-seven percent of CEOs in the surveyed listed firms and 17 percent of CEOs in officially registered private firms held party offices. Recruitments of politically active CEOs are often motivated by an effort to gain information advantages and utilize political capital to mitigate resource constraints, that is, in access to credit markets and markets for land and construction permits.

Conflicts of interests arise easily, as the Company Law lacks mechanisms to align the party committee's interests with the firm's performance. The party committee has neither residual claims nor benefits from local tax revenues. Party members, moreover, are insufficiently insulated from patron-client ties and may easily be "captured" by interest groups or be tempted to maximize their own self-interests. In sum, the party committee presides over a political network in the firm that can be used to mobilize informal opposition to reform policies that threaten vested interests in the firm. Our own interviews revealed conflicts of interests over labor issues as well as in strategic decisions, such as investments beyond the borders of the local locality.

Party intervention in firm decisions can have negative effects on performance. Based on data from 66 listed firms at Shanghai Stock Exchange specifying the extent of party intervention in 63 distinct firm decisions overall, Nee, Opper and Wong (2007) found evidence for such negative effects (on "return on assets" and "return on equity") for party interference, particularly in financial decisions. This contributes to explaining why SOEs are unable to compete effectively with private enterprise. Interventions by the state in listed firms in which the state is a major shareholder have a negative effect on the firms' economic performance at a time when they face increasing market competition from private enterprise.

Conclusion

Our analysis has sought to highlight the structural and organizational features of politicized capitalism as a hybrid institutional order. The focal question is whether China's politicized capitalism is a new type of capitalism that will endure and complement the landscape of capitalist systems. The construction of politicized capitalism by means of ad hoc improvisations responding to the demands of rapid market-driven economic growth is a source of institutional continuity. Given the central role of the state at the outset of reform, path dependence alone would dictate a strong state component in the constitution of the new Chinese capitalism. After all, the same state that managed production and distribution under central planning guides the transition to capitalism.

The dilemma of state involvement in guiding economic life is that, on the one hand, state intervention is associated with negative effects on the firm's performance when state bureaucrats directly influence decision making in the firm. On the other hand, in spite of negative performance effects, firms are not able to completely distance themselves from state actors as long as they depend on access to scarce resources controlled by the state in regulated markets such as the credit market or the market for land-use rights. Hence, politicized capitalism currently rests on lock-in effects in sectors where political and economic markets interact to blur the boundaries between the state and the firm. Large-scale, capital intensive firms dependent on state-controlled resources and firms in sectors characterized by a high dependence on government contracts such as the construction and the real estate business have strong economic reasons to accept and cultivate close state-firm relations. Moreover, partial state ownership in recently privatized state-owned enterprises provides ample opportunities for direct state intervention in corporate governance. If politicized capitalism persists in Nash-like equilibrium, then the structural and organizational interpenetration of political and economic markets will remain as incorrigible features of Chinese capitalism.

Notwithstanding lock-in effects of path dependence, politicized capitalism as a hybrid order itself embodies organizational dynamics of market transition. As evident from the contrast in utility of political capital in product and credit markets, the benefits from close state-firm relations mainly stem from the governments' ability to provide access to scarce resources and on state-owned enterprise. We infer from this that politicized capitalism is to an extent largely bounded within the state regulated and controlled sectors and constrained by the extent and size of the market economy. Small- and medium-scale firms, for example, operating in close-knit local business networks and in competitive markets are often able to distance themselves from the state in securing financial capital. It is estimated that about 30–50 percent of China's total capital investment is allocated outside the banking system (Tsai 2002). Friends, families, private founders and even business partners establish a reliable lending network that provides mutual loan opportunities. Several of our interviewees pointed out that they prefer private lending to bank lending as an efficient and flexible way of getting short-term capital. Moreover, a deepening market transition is under way, partly enforced by commitments to liberalization specified in China's World Trade Organization accession contract. In addition to the growing share of domestic nonstate financial institutions, increasing competition by foreign financial institutions will help to liberalize China's credit market, though progress is expected to be slow and gradual due to the extended branch networks China's state-owned banks can rely on. Hence even in the banking sector, currently the most regulated sector, the trend is clearly in the direction of liberalization.

Overall, we show that China's politicized capitalism is still in dynamic transition. Fiscal decentralization and the continued rapid growth of the industrial output contributed by the private enterprise sector encourage interest in shifting to the custodial and midwife roles characteristic of mature East Asian developmental states (Johnson 1982; Amsden 1989; Wade 1990; Evans 1995). Following the privatization of small- and middle-sized state-owned enterprises in the early 2000s, local governments are less involved in influencing economic decisions within the firm as they attempt to improve the business environment to attract entrepreneurs and investments to their region. It is not too far of a stretch to imagine that reformers might eventually want to include in their ambitious reform agenda a national commitment to constructing a modern polity wherein open electoral politics moves China beyond an outdated Communist Party dictatorship. It would take such a reform for China to move decisively beyond politicized capitalism to emerge as a mature East Asian developmental state, where the state and its bureaucrats operate within the framework of an independent legal system, which guarantees clear and distinct state-firm boundaries, with private actors shielded against arbitrary state interference.

References

Amsden, Alice. 1989. *Asia's Next Giant. South Korea and Late Industrialization.* New York: Oxford University Press.

Bian, Yanjie and John R. Logan. 1996. "Market Transition and the Persistence of Power: The Changing Stratification System in Urban China." *American Sociological Review* 61: 739–758.

Evans, Peter. 1995. *Embedded Autonomy: States and Industrial Transformation.* Princeton, NJ: Princeton University Press.

Fan, Gang and Xiaolu Wang. 2003. "NERI Index of Marketization of China's Provinces," National Economic Research Institute, Beijing.

Findlay, Mark. 1999. "Independence and the Judiciary in the PRC: Expectations for Constitutional Legality in China." Pp. 281–99 in *Law, Capitalism and Power in Asia,* edited by K. Jayasuriya. London: Routledge.

Foreign Broadcasting Information Service. 1999. FBIS-CHI-1999-0817: 9.

Gensler, Howard and Jiliang Yang. 1995. *A Guide to China's Tax & Business Laws.* Hong Kong: FT Law & Tax Asia Pacific.

Greif, Avner. 2006. *Institutions and the Path to the Modern Economy: Lessons from Medieval Trade.* Cambridge, UK: Cambridge University Press.

Guthrie, Douglas. 1999. *Dragon in a Three-Piece Suit.* Princeton, NJ: Princeton University Press.

Johnson, Chalmers. 1982. *MITI and the Japanese Miracle. The Growth of Industrial Policy, 1925-1975.* Stanford: Stanford University Press.

Kang, David C. 2002. "Bad Loans to Good Friends: Money Politics and the Developmental State in South Korea." *International Organization* 56: 177–207.

Leung, Man-Kwong and Vincent Wai-Kwong Mok. 2000. "Commercialization of Banks in China: Institutional Changes and Effects on Listed Enterprises." *Journal of Contemporary China* 9: 41–52.

Li, Cheng. 2006. "Think National, Blame Local: Central-Provincial Dynamics in the Hu Era." *China Leadership Monitor,* 17: 1–24.

Li, David. 1998. "Changing Incentives of the Chinese Bureaucracy." *American Economic Review: Papers and Proceedings* 88: 393–397.

Li, Hongbin, Lingsheng Meng, Qian Wang, and Li-An Zhou. 2005. "Political Connections and Firm Performance: Evidence from Chinese Private Firms." Unpublished working paper, Chinese University of Hong Kong.

Li, Hongbin, Lingsheng Meng, and Junsen Zhang. 2006. "Why Do Entrepreneurs Enter Politics? Evidence from China." *Economic Enquiry,* 44(3): 559–578.

Li, Shuhe and Peng Lian. 1999. "Decentralization and Coordination: China's Credible Commitment to Preserve the Market under Authoritarianism." *China Economic Review,* 10: 161–190.

Lin, Justin Yifu. 2001. "WTO Accession and Financial Reform in China." *Cato Journal,* 21(1): 13–18.

Lipton, David and Jeffrey Sachs. 1990. "Creating a Market Economy in Eastern Europe: The Case of Poland." *Brookings Papers on Economic Activity* 1990(1): 75–147.

Lu, Ding. 2000. "Industrial Policy and Resource Allocation: Implications on China's Participation in Globalization," *China Economic Review* 11: 342–360.

Montinola, Gabrielle, Yingyi Qian, and Barry R. Weingast. 1995. "Federalism, Chinese Style: The Political Basis for Economic Success in China." *World Politics* 48: 50–81.

Murrell, Peter. 1996. "How Far Has the Transition Progressed?" *The Journal of Economic Perspectives* 10: 25–44.

National Bureau of Statistics of China. 2004. *China Statistical Yearbook 2004.* Beijing: China Statistics Press.

National Bureau of Statistics of China. 2005. *China Statistical Yearbook 2004*. Beijing: China Statistics Press.

Naughton, Barry. 1995. *Growing out of the Plan: Chinese Economic Reform 1978–1993*. Cambridge, UK: University of Cambridge Press.

Nee, Victor. 1989. "A Theory of Market Transition: From Redistribution to Markets in State Socialism." *American Sociological Review* 56: 267–282.

Nee, Victor. 1992. "Organizational Dynamics of Market Transition." *Administrative Science Quarterly* 37: 1–27.

Nee, Victor. 2000. "The Role of the State in Making a Market Economy." *Journal of Institutional and Theoretical Economics* 156: 64–88.

Nee, Victor. 2005. "Organizational Dynamics of Institutional Change: Politicized Capitalism in China." Pp. 53–74 in *The Economic Sociology of Capitalism,* edited by Victor Nee and Richard Swedberg. Princeton, NJ: Princeton University Press.

Nee, Victor and Peng Lian. 1994. "Sleeping with the Enemy: A Dynamic Model of Declining Political Commitment in State Socialism." *Theory and Society* 23: 253–296.

Nee, Victor, Sonja Opper, and Sonia M. L. Wong. 2007. "Developmental State and Corporate Governance in China." *Management Organization Review* 3(1): 19–53.

Opper, Sonja. 2004. *Zwischen Political Governance und Corporate Governance: Eine institutionelle Analyse chinesischer Aktiengesellschaften*. Baden-Baden, Germany: Nomos.

Peng, Mike W. and Yadong Luo. 2000. "Managerial Ties and Firm Performance in a Transition Economy: The Nature of a Micro-Macro Link." *Academy of Management Journal* 43(3): 486–501.

Peng, Yusheng. 2001. "Chinese Townships and Villages as Industrial Corporations: Ownership, Governance and Productivity." *American Journal of Sociology* 106:1338–70.

Qi, Daqing, Woody Wu, and Zhang Hua. 2000. "Shareholding Structure and Corporate Performance of Partially Privatized Firms: Evidence from Listed Companies." *Pacific-Basin Finance Journal,* 8: 587–610.

Qian, Yingyi and Gerard Roland. 1998. "Federalism and the Soft Budget Constraint." *American Economic Review* 88: 1143–1162.

Schurmann, Franz. 1968. *Ideology and Organization in Communist China*. Berkeley and Los Angeles: University of California Press.

Shirk, Susan L. 1992. "The Chinese Political System and the Political Strategy of Economic Reform." In *Bureaucracy, Politics, and Decision Making in Post-Mao China,* eds. K. Lieberthal and David Lampton. Berkeley: University of California Press.

Shirk, Susan L. 1993. *The Political Logic of Economic Reform in China*. Berkeley and Los Angeles: University of California Press.

Stark, David. 1996. "Recombinant Property in East European Capitalism." *American Journal of Sociology* 101:993–1027.

Stiglitz, Joseph. 2002. *Globalization and Its Discontents*. New York: Norton.

Tsai, Kellee S. 2002. *Back-Alley Banking: Private Entrepreneurs in China*. Ithaca, NY: Cornell University Press.

Wade, Robert. 1990 *Governing the Market.* Princeton: Princeton University Press.

Walder, Andrew G. 1986. *Communist Neo-Traditionalism.* Berkeley and Los Angeles: University of California Press.

Wank, David. 1996. "The Institutional Prices of Market Clientelism: Guanxi and Private Business in a South China City." *China Quarterly,* No. 147, pp. 820–838.

Weber, Max. [1922] 1978. *Economy and Society: An Outline of Interpretive Sociology,* edited by Guenter Roth and Claus Wittich. Berkeley and Los Angeles: University of California Press.

Weingast, Barry. 1995. "The Economic Role of Political Institutions: Market-preserving Federalism and Economic Development." *Journal of Law, Economics and Organization* 11: 1–31.

Whitley, Richard. 1999. *Divergent Capitalisms. The Social Structuring and Change of Business Systems.* Oxford: Oxford University Press.

Whyte, Martin King and William L. Parish. 1984. *Urban Life in Contemporary China.* Chicago: University of Chicago Press.

Wong, Richard. 2000. "Competition in China's Domestic Banking Industry." Part II, *China Online,* 03.10.2000.

Wong, Sonia M. L., Sonja Opper, and Ruyin Hu. 2004. "Shareholding Structure, Depoliticization and Enterprise Performance: Lessons from China's Listed Companies." *Economics of Transition* 12: 29–66.

World Bank. 2004. World Development Index. Washington, DC.

World Competitiveness Yearbook. 2005. Lausanne: Institute for Management Development.

Wu, Shukun and Yumin Du. 1998. "Jiyu jiankong zhuti de gongsi zhili moshi tantao." *Zhongguo Gongye Jingji* 9:64–68.

Xin, Katherine R. and Jone L. Pearce. 1996. "Guanxi: Connections as Substitutes for Formal Institutional Support." *Academy of Management Journal* 39(6): 1641–1658.

Xinhua New Agency. 2001. "The 10th Five Year Plan". March 17. Beijing: Xinhua News Agency.

Xu, Xiaonian and Yan Wang. 1999. "Ownership Structure and Corporate Governance in Chinese Stock Companies." *China Economics Review* 10: 75–98.

Yao, Yansheng (ed). 2001. *Hangzhou Shouce.* Hangzhou: Hangzhou Chubanshe.

Zhongguo Renmin Daxue Jinrong yu Zhengquan Yanjiusuo, ed. 2000. *Zhongguo Zhengquan Fagui Zonghui.* Beijing: Zhongguo Caizheng Jingji Chubanshe.

Zhou, Xueguang. 2000. "Economic Transition and Income Inequality in Urban China: Evidence from a Panel Data." *American Journal of Sociology* 105:1135

Zhu, Tian. 1999. "China's Corporatization Drive: An Evaluation and Policy Implications." *Contemporary Economic Policy* 17: 530–539.

Notes to Chapter Four

*We wish to acknowledge the support of the John Templeton Foundation, which funded the research for this essay.

1. Respondents are asked to assess whether the bureaucracy hinders business activities.

2. The first industrial policy guideline was the *"Guowuyuan guanyu dangqian chanye zhengce yaodian de jueding,"* released by the State Council on March 15, 1989.

3. The so-called Spark program (since 1986) supports rural development; Program 863 (since 1986) currently emphasizes education in the fields of automatization, computer-aided design, and computer integrated manufacturing systems—technologies, medical apparatus, biotechnology, and material sciences; the Torch Program (since 1988) focuses on the provision of research infrastructure; and the Key Technologies R&D Program provides support for R&D in key industrial sectors.

4. Interview conducted November 11, 2005, in the Yangzi Delta.

5. Interview conducted on November 11, 2005, with the founder of a firm producing building material in the Yangzi Delta.

6. Interview conducted with a supplier of construction material on November 1, 2005, in the Yangzi Delta.

7. This context was mentioned in *"Gufenzhi qiye shidian banfa"* (05/15/1992), Chapter 1, line 1, in *Zhongguo Renmin Daxue Jinrong yu Zhengquan Yanjiusuo* (Eds.), 2000. A statement by Wang Zhongyu, Secretary General of the State Council, further details: "The first (aim) is to accelerate the separation of government functions from enterprise management, make further efforts to change government functions, reform the relationship of administrative subordination between the government and enterprises, comprehensively realize the decision-making power of enterprises, relieve the competent government departments of their relationship of administrative subordination with the economic entities run by them or the enterprise directly managed by them, and thoroughly cut their ties in terms of manpower and financial resources" (Xinhua, February 3, 2001). In this spirit, the tenth 5-year plan specifies, "to complete the establishment of a modern enterprise system under which there will be clearly established ownership, well defined power and responsibility, a separation of enterprise management from government administration, and scientific management" (Xinhua, March 17, 2001).

5 Law, Economy, and Globalization: Max Weber and How International Financial Institutions Understand Law

Bruce G. Carruthers, Northwestern University, and Terence C. Halliday, American Bar Foundation

T HE GLOBAL SPREAD OF NEOLIBERALISM SUGGESTS THAT Adam Smith now reigns supreme in the world of economic ideas. During the 1980s and 1990s, advanced and developing economies alike embraced privatization, deregulation, balanced budgets, and market liberalization, sometimes for domestic political reasons and sometimes at the insistence of international financial institutions (IFIs; Fourcade-Gourinchas and Babb 2002; Stiglitz 2002). Socialism, the historical alternative to capitalism, disappeared as countries in eastern and central Europe, the former Soviet Union, and China shifted to market economies. What remains are a variety of capitalisms (Hall and Soskice 2000) and developing countries, which seek to build capitalist economies. Market principles have been embraced not only by individual countries but also by the major organizations charged with managing the international economy and encouraging economic development. The International Monetary Fund (IMF) and the World Bank, for example, put much more trust in the invisible hand of the market than in the visible hands of the state.

Yet Adam Smith's dominance in shaping economic policy will probably not last, for how neoliberals regard law shows the growing relevance of Max Weber. Market enthusiasts now recognize the importance of the "rule of law" (e.g., Wolf 2004: 61,233). Adam Smith famously celebrated the virtues of markets and noted the importance of government in providing the law and order that markets require (Smith 1976, II: 231–2). Max Weber thought much more deeply about the connections between law and capitalism, and indeed many IFIs have discovered that legal institutions are a critical part of the foundation for markets. In part, they draw on neoinstitutional economists like Douglass North (1981, 1990). The neoliberalism of the IMF is already well-known (see, e.g., Stiglitz 2002), so in this essay we will consider its implicit neo-Weberianism as well. Similarly, by the 1980s the World Bank had concluded that the best strategy for combating world poverty was to encourage market-based economic growth, and it considered which institutions support markets and how law affects market growth. Careful reflection on the connections between law and markets is particularly timely given the global spread of capitalism and the global pursuit of rule of law.

As part of an expanding portfolio of concerns, many IFIs now consider law to be within their policy ambit. Corporate bankruptcy or insolvency law has been of particular interest. As private corporations operating in markets have become the primary engines of economic activity, countries have devised rules to govern what happens when those firms fail. If capitalism means hard budget constraints, bankruptcy law is the legal instrument that gives bite to those constraints. It dissolves or reorganizes corporations, offering a basis for organizational death and transfiguration. Starting in the early 1990s, bankruptcy law has been of interest to many global institutions, including the IMF, the World Bank, the Asian Development Bank (ADB), the European Bank for Reconstruction and Development (EBRD), and the United Nations (UN) Commission on International Trade Law (UNCITRAL). Until 2005 and the UN General Assembly's adoption of UNCITRAL's Legislative Guide on Insolvency, none of these institutions managed to monopolize thinking about bankruptcy law or to pull bankruptcy law within its organizational jurisdiction. Analyses, diagnoses, recommendations, and solutions proliferated as a global conversation about this law unfolded. These reached a climax within the UN, which effectively settled institutional rivalries for the time being.[1]

Here, we follow this policy conversation and use it to trace out implicit and explicit understandings about the connection between law and capitalism. The conversation is not merely academic, to be sure, because of how it shapes policy. The IMF, for example, attaches many strings to the money it lends a troubled country as part its financial rescue package (the "loan conditionalities," see Babb and Buira 2004), and these strings now often include bankruptcy law reform. The World Bank's 2002 *World Development Report* included a chapter-length discussion of judicial systems, and the Bank has become very interested in bolstering the capacity and competence of courts. More generally, however, ideas play a critical role in shaping the kinds of alternatives among which policy makers choose, so it is important to understand their creation and promulgation (Campbell 2002).

We begin by reviewing Weber's arguments about the connection between predictable law and capitalism and the role of experts in legal rationalization. We shall next consider contemporary arguments made by IFIs about the virtues of legal predictability and transparency for capitalist markets. In many respects, these arguments reproduce some of Weber's ideas, although he is not cited. The arguments derive from neoinstitutional economics combined with practical experience. Whatever consensus there is about predictability and transparency, however, there is less agreement on how best to create them, or what the IFIs should do. It is one thing to say that rules should be predictable, and quite another to specify what they should predictably do, or whether predictability can be legislated. In addition, IFIs are considering rules in a multijurisdictional context where, in principle, each country sets its own rules. Legal pluralism complicates the situation because it means that the decision to embrace a particular rule depends not only on whether the rule has beneficial consequences (e.g., leads to more investment and economic growth) but also on whether the rule is perceived to be *legitimate*. A fuller appreciation of Weber would move the policy discussion forward and could give IFIs greater analytical purchase on the problems they face regarding law's relation to markets.

Fortunately, because the IFIs have been very interested in the specific rules that govern corporate bankruptcy, we have more than just abstract principle or philosophy to work with, and so consider the different policy proposals and interventions pursued by IFIs. These recently culminated during an intense deliberative period in which many different ideas about corporate bankruptcy law have been proposed. Although economics as a discipline has come to appreciate the importance of institutions (e.g., North 1981, 1990), the debate was largely ignited by two major events: the 1989/90 wave of transitions from command to market economies and the 1997/98 Asian financial crisis.

Weber on Predictability, Law, and Capitalism

Weber's arguments on this issue are well known in sociology and relatively easy to summarize (Swedberg 1998: 82, 90, 99, 104–5). Modern capitalism has specific institutional presuppositions that include calculable law, rational capital accounting, freedom from irrational limitations, rational technology, free labor, and the commercialization of economic life (Weber 1981: 276–77). Capitalism requires law that can be: ". . . counted upon, like a machine" (Weber 1981: 342–43); it needs a legal system that is ". . . calculable in accordance with rational rules" (Weber 1978: 337). Hence, those who construct legal-commercial relationships (forming a corporation, borrowing money, signing a contract) know with a high degree of certainty what those relationships will entail. Because so much activity in a modern economy consists of the creation and exchange of formal property rights, the legal aspects of market activity are central.

Legal predictability contributes to rationality in that decision makers are able to know what consequences they face, and so can choose the best alternative. Rational capital accounting, the most general of the presuppositions, involves monetary valuation of assets and liabilities to measure the profitability of economic activity (Weber 1978: 91). Similarly, calculable law ensures that the *legal* consequences of economic action are also ascertainable *ex ante*.[2] As an example, Weber discusses England's patent law of 1623, the "first rational patent law" (Weber 1981: 312), and argues that the intellectual property rights it enshrined helped to spur innovation and entrepreneurship. He also notes that since medieval businessmen could not tolerate the magical formalism of Germanic law or the unpredictability of trial-by-ordeal (Weber 1981: 340–41), whenever possible they avoided unpredictable legal systems. This may help explain the origins of the *lex mercatoria,* although it does not account for the general emergence of calculable law (Swedberg 1998: 105).

The long-term trend in the West has been toward formally rational law. This "rationalization" process was neither inevitable nor self-sustaining, however. Most famously, Weber faced a problem in that England was the first capitalist economy even though common law was not very rational in a strictly formal sense (it relied on judge-made law and an unwritten constitution). According to Swedberg (1998: 106), however, Weber distinguished between formal legal rationality and calculability, and although England lacked the former it had no shortage of the latter (see Harris 2000). Weber also argued that economic rationalization led to legal rationalization (e.g., Weber 1978: 883), but the effect was only partial and indirect (Weber 1978: 654–655,892). For Weber, the strongest push for legal rationalization came from the legal specialists and professionals who have shaped law into a set of formal rules that as much as possible are complete, consistent, and logically interconnected

(Weber 1978: 776, 811). Legal rationalization has been propelled primarily by expert legal specialists, with the support of those who favor legal predictability (e.g., capitalists).

The term *presupposition* suggests that calculable law is a necessary but not sufficient condition for modern capitalism. One could have calculable law without capitalism, but not vice versa. Thus, those interested in encouraging capitalist economic growth might draw the neo-Weberian lesson that legal reform is a useful development strategy: Is law in a given country sufficiently "calculable" or "predictable"? If not, then the legal system needs improvement. Weber in effect provides an institutional prescription for calculable law. It includes formal substantive and procedural law, bureaucratically organized courts staffed by autonomous career judges, and a skilled profession. Coincidentally, it is precisely this institutional framework that the IFIs have adopted for insolvency systems, but with one additional element that Weber omitted— out-of-court procedures that operate in the "shadow of the law."

Predictable Bankruptcy Law and Unpredictable Bankruptcy

Corporate bankruptcy is one of the hallmarks of a market economy. Competition among firms means that some succeed whereas others fail, and bankruptcy law provides a way to deal with failure. If incorporation and contract are two key features that a commercial legal system offers to a market economy (Swedberg 1998: 100–102), then bankruptcy calls both the existence of a firm and the sanctity of its contractual obligations into question. Whether liquidated or reorganized, bankrupt firms fail to keep most of their legal promises. This means that bankruptcy injects considerable uncertainty into economic relationships and produces further financial losses. Bankruptcy severs the nexus of contracts at the heart of a firm.

Modern corporate bankruptcy laws typically allow for both liquidation and reorganization, although law can favor one over the other. For example, a country with a "debtor friendly" bankruptcy law will prefer corporate reorganization over liquidation. A bankrupt firm may simply close down, lay off all employees, and distribute the assets to creditors, or the firm can be reorganized so that it can return to profitable operation. Procedurally, corporate bankruptcy law determines when financially troubled companies can seek legal protection from their creditors, who may initiate proceedings, what powers corporate management retain after initiation, how much prior contractual obligations can be altered or negated, who has priority in the distribution of assets, and the procedures for corporate reorganization.

In *liquidation,* the assets of an insolvent firm aren't sufficient to repay all the creditors, so the main problem is to share the shortfall among competing claimants and distribute the assets accordingly. Creditors cannot be sure how much of the money loaned to an insolvent debtor will be recovered, but they all want to see other creditors bear the brunt of the shortfall. For a *reorganization* to work, serious corporate surgery is usually required: Labor and loan contracts need to be renegotiated to reduce wages and debts, unprofitable divisions will be closed down, onerous executory contracts terminated, and so on. The main problem for reorganization is to devise a viable rescue plan, and then put someone competent in charge to execute it (one contentious issue is whether current management should remain). Again, creditors, customers, suppliers, and other stakeholders don't know, *ex ante,* how their relationships to the reorganized firm are going to change. For both liquidation and reorganization, timing matters. In liquidations, proceedings need to begin before too much of the creditors' money is lost, and successful reorganizations need to start before the firm's situation becomes completely hopeless.

Bankruptcy law deals with market failure and its complications in an orderly fashion. Ironically, bankruptcy law is intended to manage, as predictably as possible, one critical, consequential, and inevitable form of economic uncertainty. Thus, the Weberian issue of certainty is at the very heart of bankruptcy law. With the growing importance of markets, the economic and social significance of bankruptcy law can only increase.

Certainty is not the only important issue with which bankruptcy law grapples. The distributional problem that corporate liquidation poses is one that engenders conflict among competing claimants: There isn't enough money, so who is to suffer? Do some claimants deserve more? Corporate reorganization raises politically salient issues such as employment and economic growth: Giving firms a second chance may help preserve jobs and maintain productive capacity, but it risks impairing the contractual claims and property rights of creditors and may give incompetent managers an undeserved second chance. Overly generous reorganization provisions can relax the hard budget constraints that distinguish capitalism from socialism. As we will see, the consensus in favor of certain, predictable law doesn't by itself go very far in settling the other important issues that bankruptcy poses.

Neo-Weberianism and the IFIs

Sociologists are familiar with Weber's analysis, but economists are mostly not, and however much the IFIs use academic research when thinking about law, there is almost no mention of Weber.[3] Yet the use of neo-Weberian language is striking. For instance, consider the World Bank's centerpiece document on insolvency law: "Transparency, accountability and predictability are fundamental to sound credit relationships" (World Bank 2001: 2), and elsewhere, "Effective insolvency systems include rules that are reasonably predictable, transparent and hold all parties duly accountable throughout the process. There is no substitute for clear law. A predictable law promotes stability in commercial transactions, fosters lending and investment at lower risk premiums, and promotes consensual resolutions of disputes . . ." (World Bank 2001: 25). An earlier draft document was even blunter: "What is therefore required is a clear, predictable and transparent insolvency process which affords the creditor a reliable means of calculating the consequences in the event that insolvency actually occurs. The attribute of certainty is a vital one in terms of a creditor's ability to assess and to manage risk" (World Bank 1999: 5).

Following the Asian Financial Crisis, the ADB asserted that there is a "need for certainty or predictability in commercial affairs," and also a "need for transparency" (Asian Development Bank 2000: 26). Such needs could be met by predictable law. The EBRD deals with eastern and central Europe, but it also focuses on insolvency law and has criticized the region on the grounds that "the level of [legal] predictability and transparency across the entire region is woefully low" (Uttamchandani 2004: 455). The IMF asserted that one overall object of insolvency law was "the allocation of risk among participants in a market economy in a predictable, equitable, and transparent manner" (IMF 1999: 5). Following its successful negotiation of a Model Cross-Border Insolvency Law, UNCITRAL underscored the dangers of unpredictable law: "The soundness and credibility of insolvency laws and practices are central to the efforts of Governments and regulators to enhance the operation of the global financial system. Inefficient, antiquated or poorly designed insolvency laws and practices whose outcomes are uncertain, capricious, unfair or parochial threaten the benefits of globalization" (UNCITRAL 1999:2).

International financial institutions now recognize the importance of predictable, calculable law for markets. In some respects, they are revisiting the 1960s law-and-development movement (Tamanaha 1995, Ginsburg 2000), but with lessons drawn from the shift from socialism to capitalism and the Asian Financial Crisis. Both of these experiences forced policymakers to reorient their thinking. In dealing with the transition economies, IFIs had to consider how to get the basic building blocks of a market economy to function effectively. The Asian Crisis served as a stiff reminder that even highly successful market economies (e.g., high growth, high investment, low inflation, etc.) could still get into very serious trouble. Both the short-term diagnosis and treatment (e.g., the bailout loans and conditionalities) and the longer-term analyses put some blame on East Asian legal systems.

Recognition of law still didn't solve the problem of how to create predictable, calculable law. Western advisors to transition economies, for example, soon realized that much more is required than just writing clear, self-evident laws. Furthermore, although contemporary capitalism is global, the commercial laws that undergird it are not. National laws vary from one jurisdiction to another, and the ability to pass their own laws is a prerogative that nations are extremely reluctant to surrender. Even if the IMF or World Bank could devise one "best" bankruptcy law, it would be unrealistic to suppose that other countries would simply adopt it. Developing countries with a colonial past are especially sensitive about importing laws from former colonizers, and so even laws that are "technically" superior may be politically problematic.

Global Institutions and Corporate Insolvency

During the 1990s, IFIs realized that bankruptcy law was important and that unpredictable laws hurt economic development. However, they disagreed over how to proceed from this point of consensus. In addition to differences over the content of law, there were several reform strategies (Halliday and Carruthers 2005). One is to devise abstract principles on which all can agree, and then to allow individual countries to interpret them in a manner suitable to their own situation. This approach makes it easier to get consensus, but will result in more varied outcomes because different jurisdictions make different interpretations. Another strategy is to set standards for different aspects of bankruptcy law and to urge countries to meet those standards. This ensures a minimal degree of quality, but allows jurisdictions to go beyond those standards. Standards are harder to agree upon than abstract principles, but when successfully implemented they produce less legal variability.

Yet another strategy involves a model law. Here the challenge is to negotiate a law on which all can agree. A model law constrains the options available to a country and results in more legal uniformity. Finally, because a number of extant insolvency laws are known to function well, another strategy would be to identify one country's law as the "best" and disseminate it. Obviously, such an option would resolve the issue of whether a particular law "worked," but it raises the problem of whether laws can simply be transplanted from one place to another, as well as the more intractable problem of whose law to transplant. In cases of importation of laws, there is also the issue of whether too much obvious deference by one state to the laws of another will be politically acceptable.

In addition to these possibilities is the important matter of how much to coordinate with the other IFIs in creating predictable law. Along with recognition of the importance of bankruptcy law came the realization that it constituted new and valuable "policy turf" and that it was advantageous to claim that turf. However much cooperation was appropriate, competition always threatened to break out. Finally, the IFIs could stress diagnosis, prescription, or both. That is, they could describe existing situations, or they could offer advice on how to solve problems, or they could do both.

Different organizations went in different directions, and only recently did a *modus vivendi* emerge. The EBRD, for example, made corporate bankruptcy law a priority for transition economies (Bernstein 2002: 3–4). Along with some other areas (e.g., secured transactions, capital markets, corporate governance, etc.), bankruptcy law was identified as having an especially big impact on national investment. In the past, the EBRD regularly conducted a Legal Indicator Survey to rate countries (Uttamchandani 2004: 454). The process of public assessment and benchmarking was intended to let countries know where problems existed. It set up comparisons with other transition economies and let interested parties such as investors know about the problems, all of which created pressure for reform.

The EBRD devised principles (*Core Principles for an Insolvency Law Regime*, see http://www.ebrd.com/country/sector/law/index.htm) about what an Insolvency Law Regime (ILR) should do, for example, "The ILR should at all times promote economy, transparency and speedy resolution." From its Legal Indicator Survey and these general standards, the EBRD derived specific diagnostic standards that it uses to evaluate countries both on their formal insolvency laws and on implementation. These standards are used for private consultations between the Bank and national authorities, and they are integrated into EBRD lending algorithms.

The EBRD publishes country assessments that allow for comparisons across countries and between a country and the general standards, but also underscore the connection between the rule of law and the transition to a market economy. For example, the 2005 assessment of Kazakhstan (http://www.ebrd.com/country/sector/law/cla/kaza.pdf) provides a systematic assessment of Kazakh commercial law, including both its "extensiveness" (the quality of law on the books) and "effectiveness" (how well it is implemented). It includes a chart illustrating the correlation between institutionalization of the rule of law and progress toward a market economy. Similar reports have been done for other countries such as Russia, Croatia, and Azerbaijan.

The EBRD produces summary documents such as *Transition Reports* and *Law in Transition* to report on annual progress so that a country's current status can be judged (e.g., Uttamchandani, Harmer, Cooper, and Ronen-Mevorach 2005). Even countries with deplorable legal systems receive some praise if there is movement in the right direction. The bank also uses its technical assistance program to fund projects supporting the development of legal capacity, predictability, and noncorruption.

Like the EBRD, the ADB is a regional development bank, and after the Asian Financial Crisis it became very interested in corporate insolvency law (ADB 1999: 7). By coincidence, the ADB had just published a study of the role of law in Asian economic development (Pistor and Wellons 1998). This is one of the few IFI documents that directly engages Weber's ideas on law and the economy, but it concludes that there is no simple relationship between the two because so many East Asian economies enjoyed dramatic economic growth even though their legal systems were problematic (Pistor and Wellons 1998: 3, 5, 26). In the rush to respond to the Asian Financial Crisis, the ADB later produced a series of less nuanced analyses, and Weber disappeared from view. But faith in the importance of legal predictability continued.

Under the auspices of the Regional Technical Assistance for Insolvency Law Reform (RETA 5795), the ADB undertook diagnoses and technical assistance in countries whose insolvency legal systems were deemed deficient. The premise behind the program was that Asian insolvency law was out of date and needed more predictability. The ADB commissioned a series of country studies, but also developed general standards: "There are a number of common, almost universal, elements associated with the creation and operation of corporations which suggest that laws concerning their financial stability and viability should be similar or should contain common identifiable basic elements" (ADB 2000: 25). The ADB was sensitive to the charge that it was engendering legal homogeneity, and it recognized that insolvency laws were quite varied (ADB 1999: 9). Nevertheless, it believed there were underlying principles and sought to articulate them.

Consider the first Good Practice Standard: "An insolvency law regime should clearly distinguish between, on the one hand, personal or individual bankruptcy and, on the other, corporate bankruptcy" (ADB 2000: 28). This seems uncontroversial, although the next standard is not: "All corporations, both private and state-owned (with the possible exception of banking and insurance corporations), should be subject to the same insolvency law regime" (ADB 2000: 29). The second suggests that the hard budget constraints enacted through bankruptcy law should be applied generally, possibly excluding only banks and insurance companies. This standard pointedly notes that public ownership per se should not spare a firm from bankruptcy. Its rigorous application would be consequential in countries with many state-owned enterprises.

The ADB lays out a series of Good Practice Standards and then determines each country's compliance with each standard: Countries apply, apply in part, or do not apply a particular standard. No attempt is made to rank standards by importance, and there is no finer-grained classification. The entire exercise obviously helps put legal reform on the agenda by calling attention to insolvency law, and it provides a detailed evaluation for each country about where the problems lie and how that country compares with international standards. The ADB also recognizes some of the unique features that East Asia possesses. First, Asian countries traditionally do not rely on the legal system to help organize the economy (ADB 2000: 75; Pistor and Wellons 1998: 5). Many of the biggest companies are essentially family firms, and so firm governance builds on a nexus of kinship, not on a nexus of contracts. This often means that legal institutions are underdeveloped and unable to play a big role in governing economic relationships. In addition, cultural attitudes in many Asian countries steer away from formal dispute resolution methods (ADB 2000: 78); the preference is to solve problems informally and privately. Because so much of bankruptcy law is about the management of conflict, people are discouraged from using law.

The ADB and EBRD have a regional focus that undoubtedly simplifies the challenges they face. By contrast, the IMF and World Bank must take a global perspective. The World Bank attends to the long-term needs of developing economies, whereas the IMF focuses on the short-term financial situation of its entire membership. Both became very interested in corporate bankruptcy law during the 1990s.

Although it considered bankruptcy law in the context of national financial development (World Bank 1989), the Bank's attention to insolvency law was largely provoked by the Asian Financial Crisis, combined with a growing appreciation of the importance of economic institutions. The Bank quickly sought a leadership role and, led by Gordon Johnson, it pitched its efforts at the highest level. The title of one of the early background documents (1999) reveals these ambitions: *Building Effective Insolvency Systems: Toward Principles and Guidelines.* Two years later, the Bank published its *Principles and Guidelines for Effective Insolvency and Creditor Rights Systems* (2001). The latter lists 35 principles applicable to national insolvency systems, and it repeatedly underscores the virtues of predictability and transparency. It recognizes that the principles will have to be "adapted" to the realities of developing economies, and so there will be some measure of legal variability.

The World Bank goes further than does the ADB by applying the assessment methodology of the World Bank and IMF to insolvency law through the mechanism of Review of Standards and Codes (ROSC). ROSCs are diagnostic instruments that the Bank and Fund use to appraise a country's conformity with global standards. Of a similar level of detail to the EBRD current diagnostic instrument, the World Bank/IMF ROSC goes through each major area of substantive law and institutions and rates whether a country conforms. These appraisals inform both annual Article IV evaluations of country members by the IMF and technical assistance and lending decisions.

Although there is no automatic penalty for failure to comply with the Bank's principles or their specification in the ROSCs, the Bank and Fund still retain the ultimate sanction of loan conditionality for countries in financial crisis. The Bank also relies on market forces to do its work. The Bank's principles argue that emerging market economies without effective insolvency systems will have a harder time attracting investment (World Bank 2001: 17). In other words, the World Bank doesn't need to rely on coercion because, it believes, the world's capital market will function as an enforcer: Capital will naturally flow to countries with superior legal systems. The Bank's principles offer a kind of road map to effective insolvency systems, but in the long run capital mobility will lead countries in the same direction any way.

The Asian Financial Crisis also brought the IMF's attention to bankruptcy law. Over time, the IMF's central mission has evolved to the point where its bailout loans come with a number of different strings attached. These strings (*conditionalities*) reflect IMF understandings of what is needed to solve a country's problems. As Babb and Buira (2004) note, the IMF worried about inflation and balanced budgets in the 1960s. During the 1980s this interest expanded to make sure countries did not default on their external loans, and later to encompass market reforms and other parts of the neoliberal package. Most recently, measures against terrorism have been embraced by the IMF (at the behest of the U.S. Treasury Department). In general, the IMF has gone from insisting on macroeconomic adjustment to structural adjustment and institutional change as a loan condition. Borrowing countries no longer just worry about balanced budgets and inflation: They also have to institute policy changes. After the Asian Financial Crisis, legal reform became part of IMF conditionalities.

In the short run, the IMF's new concern about insolvency law was reflected in its loans to Thailand, South Korea, and Indonesia. The various letters of intent stipulated specific changes in corporate bankruptcy law (e.g., Government of Indonesia 1998), and particularly in the case of Indonesia, the IMF soon learned that the creation of predictable law was not a straightforward matter. After seeing a new and transparent insolvency law adopted by Indonesia, the IMF (and foreign investors) witnessed a number of surprising court rulings that demonstrated that predictable law involves much more than clearly written law on the books (Halliday and Carruthers 2005). Unfortunately, the IMF's orientation and competencies are geared toward short-term problems, and this makes it ill-suited to longer-term tasks like building effective institutions.

In addition to short-term interventions, the IMF also developed an overarching framework within which to put the specific deals it hurriedly negotiated, and this resulted in the so-called Blue Book (IMF 1999). Given that the IMF is in the business of responding to crises, the link to insolvency law lay in the IMF's perception that financial crises are made much worse without effective and predictable insolvency procedures (IMF 1999: 1). In the absence of such procedures, the IMF believes, financial crises are both deeper and harder to fix.

Unlike the World Bank, the IMF did not lay out principles. Rather, it simply articulated the key issues for insolvency law. It did not presume either to describe existing systems or to propose general standards (IMF 1999: 1). For the IMF Legal Department, the objectives of insolvency law are twofold: "the allocation of risk among participants in a market economy in a predictable, equitable, and transparent manner," and "to protect and maximize value for the benefit of all interested parties and the economy in general" (IMF 1999: 5). To achieve these objectives, insolvency systems need a legal framework that sets out various rights and obligations and an institutional framework to implement those rights and obligations effectively. The Blue Book acknowledges the importance of a well-functioning, independent judicial system in supporting both elements, but it says nothing about how to create such a judiciary (IMF 1999: 3, 78). Most of the document consists of discussions of the key issues of substantive bankruptcy law, with summary conclusions about each issue.

The EBRD, ADB, World Bank, and IMF each encountered insolvency law at about the same time. All four had ample technical expertise and experience in financial affairs, but none had obvious jurisdiction over this particular issue. Each organization proceeded in a slightly different direction from the common premise that insolvency law should be predictable and calculable. They have been mindful of one another's efforts, acting at times like rivals and interlocutors. The ADB and EBRD systematically evaluated the laws of their member countries and have offered technical assistance to encourage legal reform. The World Bank and IMF have evaluated closely the laws of a small set of countries who were in severe financial difficulty and have linked their assessments to loan conditionalities. Increasingly they backed up their principles with precise diagnostic instruments, to the extent that all four institutions now have in place detailed mechanisms for appraising a country's insolvency system.

Behind each approach lay a series of conferences, deliberations, and meetings that brought together a small number of international experts, practitioners, and academics. Representatives from the International Bar Association (Committee J) and the International Association of Restructuring, Insolvency and Bankruptcy Professionals (INSOL) usually participated, as well. Although each organization took a distinctive approach, collectively they drew on the same small pool of high-level lawyers and accounting experts.[4] There was very little direct input either from the corporations that go bankrupt, or from the employees or creditors who suffer the consequences of bankruptcy. Nor did politicians or legislators participate. Experts and professionals overwhelmingly dominated the discussions.

The final organization we discuss, UNCITRAL, is the smallest of the group. It has, however, been the most ambitious in trying to fashion something both integrative and concrete. Unlike the others, its strengths are legal rather than financial or economic, and it is the most "democratic" and "legislative" organization among the group. This gives it an important measure of legitimacy that the others do not possess, and it can bestow its legitimacy onto the legal products it creates. Furthermore, UNCITRAL could build upon prior success.

UNCITRAL was founded in 1966 by the UN General Assembly to harmonize laws and reduce barriers to international trade. UNCITRAL shared with others an unquestioned faith in the importance of legal certainty and predictability (UNCITRAL 2000). It is now composed of sixty member states elected by the General Assembly to represent the various regions and economic and legal systems of the world. Formal proceedings are essentially governed by "the sense of the meeting," unlike governance in the IMF or World Bank (where countries have votes weighted by the size of their financial contribution, thus empowering rich countries). Starting in 1999, in response to an Australian proposal that built on UNCITRAL's successful negotiation of a Model Cross-Border Insolvency Law, UNCITRAL's Working Group on Insolvency was revived to develop a legislative guide. A guide presents legislators with a set of broad principles to govern insolvency law and then proceeds through the main substantive topics of a national bankruptcy law, in each case laying out the goals, discussing the merits of major alternatives, and proposing recommendations. The legislative guide offers much more flexibility than do model laws because it lowers the bar of agreement from a single model standard to alternative recommendations. These are offered at differing levels of specificity, depending on the consensus reached in the working group and Commission. Although a legislative guide will not produce the degree of legal standardization of a multilateral treaty or a model law, it does harmonize legal systems around common principles and a limited number of alternatives.

Over several years, the UNCITRAL working group successfully negotiated a *Legislative Guide on Insolvency Law*. It was adopted in 2004 and is intended to help countries write new insolvency laws. It is not intended specifically for countries undergoing a financial crisis, and it does not distinguish between developed or developing economies, or between market and transition economies. The model law is available for all: "The Legislative Guide does not provide a single set of model solutions to address the issues central to an effective and efficient insolvency law, but assists the reader to evaluate different approaches available and to choose the one most suitable in the national or local context" (UNCITRAL 2005: 2). The *Guide* presents a menu of legal alternatives and invites the country to choose what seems best. Besides the official States members of the Commission, the meetings were attended by observers from other countries and organizations. The latter included the IMF, World Bank, ADB, EBRD, INSOL, the International Bar Association, the American Bar Association, and the International Insolvency Institute, who were active participants in both the formal sessions and some of the expert sessions held between working group meetings. Thus, in addition to creating their own products, the IMF, World Bank, ADB, and EBRD participated in the UNCITRAL process.

Like the others, UNCITRAL underscored the importance of legal certainty: "An insolvency law should be transparent and predictable . . . Unpredictable application of the insolvency law has the potential to undermine not only the confidence of all participants in insolvency proceedings, but also their willingness to make credit and other investment decisions prior to insolvency" (UNCITRAL 2005: 13). Among other things, uncertain law lowers investment and raises interest rates. The *Guide* argues for countries to protect insolvency proceedings from domestic political or social influences and suggests that whatever priorities and distributions the insolvency process enshrines should preserve foremost the sanctity of prebankruptcy contracts (UNCITRAL 2005: 13). Insolvency should be a legal process that unfolds in an independent court system. In addition to detailed recommendations, alternatives, and accompanying commentary, the *Guide* acknowledges the importance of a supporting institutional framework for the proper implementation of laws. It also notes that extralegal institutions are really beyond the purview of UNCITRAL, whatever their importance.

It seems surprising that UNCITRAL was able to involve the IMF, World Bank, ADB, and EBRD, which all had their own approach to bankruptcy law and still create consensus around a global standard. In fact, the involvement of international organizations in the UNCITRAL effort depended on legitimacy (Halliday and Carruthers 2005). Although the IFIs could justify their efforts through their own pragmatic expertise and that of their expert panels and consultations, the IMF and World Bank in particular had a legitimation problem. On the one hand, both organizations are manifestly unrepresentative in their decision making because the wealthy countries contribute more money and consequently get more voting rights. Similarly, they rely on experts recruited disproportionately from advanced countries. On the other hand, because the World Bank and IMF have used coercion, via conditionalities, to compel domestic reform, they engender a domestic political backlash. Global standards promulgated by these organizations are almost always resisted by national legislators. Regional banks, such as the EBRD and ADB, attract less opprobrium, but their scope is only regional.

The IFIs recognized the value of UNCITRAL as an authoritative venue that combined representation with expertise and in which deals could be negotiated. As a creation of the UN General Assembly, UNCITRAL had a mandate and legitimacy that none of the others could match. The voting system gave each country, rich or poor, one vote, and UNCITRAL did not use financial leverage to give countries unwelcome advice. For these reasons, the others found it useful to work through UNCITRAL, knowing that the consent of individual countries would be necessary anyway because they were the ones that would have to alter their own insolvency systems.

In fact, the convergence of the world's norm-making institutions on insolvency yielded more than even UNCITRAL initially anticipated. Whereas the IFIs gained the legitimacy of a UN deliberative body, UNCITRAL gained IFI financial leverage and the capacity to monitor the world's legal systems. UNCITRAL has, in effect, negotiated with the World Bank and the IMF to incorporate the principal recommendations of the *Legislative Guide* into the ROSCs that are used by the IFIs to evaluate national insolvency systems. In this way UNCITRAL gains a significant mechanism for enforcement of its global norms.

Neo-Weberianism and IFIs

Thus far we have shown unquestioned agreement among the major IFIs that certain, predictable law is necessary for a modern market economy. The sudden interest in law may seem surprising coming from organizations that hitherto focused overwhelmingly on financial and economic affairs, but events of the 1990s forced them to broaden their horizons and consider the legal framework for markets. We have also explained how this overall understanding has been applied to the particular case of corporate insolvency law.

Ideas about legal predictability came from different sources. World Bank thinking reflected somewhat the influence of neoinstitutional economists like Douglass North, who stress the importance of predictable property rights for long-term economic growth (North 1981). A review of the World Bank's annual *World Development Report* shows no sign of Weber's influence, however, and very little of North throughout the 1980s (he isn't even in the bibliography). The 1989 report did cite North and the law-and-economics scholar Richard Posner in a discussion of national financial systems where the Bank stressed the need for "clear legal rules" (World Bank 1989: 85). North is discussed again in several of the reports published after the Asian Financial Crisis, although Posner is not. Evidently, the World Bank became aware of North's arguments starting in the late 1980s, but it was the Financial Crisis that forced the Bank to engage his ideas more thoroughly.[5] By contrast, the IMF seems not to have drawn upon neoinstitutional economics or other scholarly literatures, but instead learned about law from the practical experiences of lawyers and bankers. Their informants reported that unpredictable law was a problem in East Asia, and the IMF quickly incorporated that claim into its postcrisis diagnosis and prescription.

One ADB-sponsored study (Pistor and Wellons 1998) mentioned Weber's work, but almost immediately after publication the crisis hit and Weber disappeared from view. Postcrisis ADB literature doesn't cite North, either. The EBRD's *Law in Transition* publication began in 1992. No social science scholarship on law was discussed in the early years of the journal, although the focus was very much on commercial law in transition economies. Even the Autumn/Winter 1996 edition of *Law in Transition,* which highlighted the impact of law on investment (and analyzed the new Czech bankruptcy law), said nothing about why the EBRD believed calculable law to be important (EBRD 1996: 1–2).

Whatever the sources of these ideas, the evidence suggests the real limits of the neo-Weberian consensus. Agreement that predictable law is good does not by itself create predictable law, and the problem of how to enact such law has clearly been a challenge. Coordination in a multicountry, multiorganizational issue area would by itself be difficult even if all agreed on how to proceed. Furthermore, "predictability" is not a characteristic that distinguishes one particular law, for there are many predictable insolvency laws. Which version of predictable law to choose raises numerous political issues that straightforward insistence on predictability per se cannot resolve.

The inadvertent rediscovery of Weber's discussion of legal predictability necessarily leaves out important portions of his analysis. Were the IFIs to undertake a thoroughgoing exposition of his work,[6] two aspects of Weber's historical analysis of law and capitalism would seem especially relevant. First, predictable law is largely the handiwork of legal professionals and specialists. The production of formally rational law both reflects and reinforces their expertise. Second, such expert production is supported by a separate social group, capitalists, who benefit from the predictability that such law offers. These two points raise issues that have not been fully considered by today's IFIs even as they focus on insolvency law.

The first point suggests that the creation of predictable law must involve the domestic courts and legal profession, that is, legal specialists. It is not something that can be produced by fiat through a bilateral agreement between an international organization and a national government. Although new law on the books is a tangible and public result that pleases politicians and can satisfy loan conditionalities, law and society scholars have long appreciated the difference between formal law and law-in-action. Legal predictability resides in law-in-action, not legal texts per se. Predictability in implementation necessarily depends on those who implement law, that is, the lawyers, judges, and other participants within a country's legal system. The failure to create such a system, or opposition from key professions, can render reforms ineffective (Halliday and Carruthers 2004; Halliday and Carruthers 2002). Moreover, different professions may disagree over what insolvency system best serves their own interests. Jurisdictional conflicts between lawyers and accountants, for instance, can occur not only within countries (Carruthers and Halliday 1998) but in global norm-making. IFIs understandably relied on international legal experts to produce standards and models for corporate insolvency law. This was only a first step, however, and if the IFIs want national laws to function predictably, then they will have to consider legal institutions as well as legal texts.

Several IFIs have shown some reluctance to add legal institutions to their list of responsibilities. Although the UNCITRAL, IMF, and ADB standards all acknowledge the importance of institutions, it is only the World Bank's *Principles* that elaborated them in any detail. In practice, the IMF, World Bank, and ADB have been actively involved in institution building as an element of technical assistance or as a component of their structural adjustment programs, but those attempts have been recent and not always successful.[7] Pushing reform from the outside risks impugning national sovereignty. Hence, working through UNCITRAL seemed an attractive route: Through a quasi-legislative process, the *Legislative Guide* could earn the support of individual member countries. In addition, because it was still up to nations whether to adopt the model law, they were not being "forced" to do so by foreign organizations—at least not directly. Indirectly, it is likely that the IMF and World Bank will point countries to the *Legislative Guide* in order to remedy problems that the

ROSCs reveal. Even if a country does adopt the law, however, the formal text still has to be interpreted and implemented by a domestic legal system, and this can be done creatively and variably. Whether legal reform comes through adoption of the UNCITRAL *Guide,* or on the basis of some other organization's principles or standards, the interests and capacities of domestic legal systems will determine how predictable new insolvency law can be.

The second point is perhaps more fundamental, for it raises the issue of who seeks predictability in the first place and whether predictability can be obtained through legal means. What constituency favors predictable law? In the IFI argument, it is stated as a bald and simple fact that investors (capitalists) require predictable law. But Weber's historical discussion raises doubts about such a simple assertion. Predictability is useful for some groups, under particular conditions. It may not be necessary or even desirable under all circumstances. For example, it is clear that although in 1997 and 1998 the IMF and World Bank discovered the inadequate state of East Asian insolvency laws, foreign investors had nevertheless poured money into the region for decades. Either investors were astonishingly ignorant of the true state of East Asian law, or they were able to tolerate more legal unpredictability than the IFIs gave them credit for. The ongoing inflow of capital into China, despite the manifest shortcomings of its commercial laws, again casts doubt on the idea that investors *require* legal certainty (Carothers 2003: 6, Huang 2003). Investors may, under certain circumstances, find legal uncertainty tolerable or unproblematic. Perhaps they can live with it if the rates of return are sufficiently high, or it may be that they are able to devise functional substitutes and work around unpredictable law (Macaulay 1963).

Investors' need for legal predictability should be a matter for empirical investigation rather than assumption. It is also important to consider who benefits from legal *uncertainty.* A legal system that truly operates like a machine is one that affords little discretion or importance to lawyers and judges. They act like cogs and transmission belts and derive neither prestige nor power from their position. If their professional judgments are to matter, then legal rules cannot be completely deterministic or predictable. The legal profession itself may not wish to make law too certain.

Legal predictability can also pit locals against foreigners. Unpredictable law often means that extralegal considerations (politics, patronage, family ties, etc.) affect legal outcomes, and these are usually better understood by local elites than by international investors. Foreigners are more apt to miss or overlook the informal social networks that can shape implementation and are certainly less likely to be embedded in such networks. Legal predictability, understood as a situation where the literal meaning of legal text determines how law in action unfolds, puts foreign investors and domestic actors on the same basis and doesn't privilege local knowledge or social networks. Thus, domestic interests can oppose calculable law because it undermines one of their advantages.

Locals and foreigners may also differ over how much importance to give law in the first place. The ADB proposed a cultural argument in recognizing that business elites in East Asia generally avoided the formal legal system as a way to solve problems. Asian culture values informal methods and quiet diplomacy. Because corporate insolvency necessarily involves many overt conflicts, there may be widespread resistance to IFI attempts to ensure that the restructuring or closure of troubled corporations happens in the courts.

Conclusion

It is now clear how much Max Weber can add to Adam Smith. The neoliberal agenda strongly dominates international policy making, and those who embrace it have learned that markets are not self-sustaining. Markets require institutional supports, and here IFIs recognize the importance of law. Their conception of law is too simplistic, however, consisting of a mantra-like repetition of the idea that markets require calculable law.

The process of bankruptcy is an inevitable part of a competitive market economy. Some firms do well and others poorly, and eventually the poor performers fail outright. At this point, corporate bankruptcy law disposes of the failed firm. Bankruptcy adds uncertainty to the economy because it means that economic actors can disappear or be radically transformed. Whether a firm is liquidated or reorganized, bankruptcy also means that the contractual relationships that firms enter into can be severed, violated, or transformed.

Bankruptcy law deals with the economic uncertainty that corporate failure creates. Perhaps that is why organizations so wedded to the idea that capitalism requires certainty stressed the importance of predictable bankruptcy law. Even if bankruptcy inevitably created additional market uncertainty, then at least the law that enacted bankruptcy should be predictable. Yet this conviction still leaves matters very incomplete, for it is still not clear how to create legal predictability and who will help to create such predictability. Weber is convenient if one wants to cite briefly a famous sociologist on the importance of legal predictability, but he can be positively illuminating if used more fully to consider these unresolved questions about predictability.

References

Asian Development Bank. 1999. *Law and Development at the Asian Development Bank*. Manila, Philippines: ADB.

Asian Development Bank. 2000. *Law and Policy Reform at the Asian Development Bank*, Vol 1. Manila, Philippines: ADB.

Babb, Sarah L. and Ariel Buira. 2004. "Mission Creep, Mission Push and Discretion in Sociological Perspective: The Case of IMF Conditionality," Paper presented at the XVIII G24 Technical Group Meeting, Geneva, Switzerland.

Bernstein, David . 2002. "Process Drives Success: Key Lessons from a Decade of Legal Reform," *Law in Transition,* Autumn 2002: 2–13.

Campbell, John L. 2002. "Ideas, Politics, and Public Policy," *Annual Review of Sociology* 28: 21–38.

Carothers, Thomas. 2003. "Promoting the Rule of Law Abroad: The Problem of Knowledge," *Carnegie Endowment for International Peace Working Paper No. 34.*

Carruthers, Bruce G. and Terence C. Halliday. 1998. *Rescuing Business: The Making of Corporate Bankruptcy Law in England and the United States.* Oxford: Oxford University Press.

European Bank for Reconstruction and Development. 1996. *Law in Transition,* Autumn/Winter.

European Bank for Reconstruction and Development. N.d. *Core Principles for an Insolvency Law Regime.* London: EBRD. Accessed at http://www.ebrd.com/country/sector/law/insolve/core/principle.pdf, December 26, 2006

Fourcade-Gourinchas, Marion and Sarah L. Babb. 2002. "The Rebirth of the Liberal Creed: Paths to Neoliberalism in Four Countries," *American Journal of Sociology* 108(3): 533–579.

Ginsburg, Tom. 2000. "Does Law Matter for Economic Development? Evidence from East Asia," *Law and Society Review* 34(3): 829–856.

Government of Indonesia. 1998. "Memorandum of Economic and Financial Policies to IMF," April 10, 1998, Accessed at http://www.imf.org/external/np/loi/041098.HTM, December 26, 2006.

Hall, Peter A. and David Soskice. 2000. "An Introduction to Varieties of Capitalism," in *Varieties of Capitalism: The Institutional Foundations of Comparative Advantage,* ed. Peter A. Hall and David Soskice. New York: Oxford University Press.

Halliday, Terence C., and Bruce G. Carruthers. 2002. "Conformity, Contestation and Culture in the Globalization of Insolvency Regimes: International Institutions and Law-Making in Indonesia and China." American Bar Foundation Working Paper 2214.

Halliday, Terence C., and Bruce G. Carruthers. 2004. "Epistemological Conflicts and Institutional Impediments: The Rocky Road to Corporate Bankruptcy Reforms in Korea." *Law Reform in Korea,* ed. Tom Ginsburg. New York: RoutledgeCurzon.

Halliday, Terence C., and Bruce G. Carruthers. 2007. "The Recursivity of Law: Global Norm-Making and National Law-Making in the Globalization of Corporate Insolvency Regimes." American Bar Foundation Working Paper. *American Journal of Sociology* (in press).

Harris, Ron. 2000. *Industrializing English Law: Entrepreneurship and Business Organization, 1720–1844.* Cambridge, UK: Cambridge University Press.

Huang, Yasheng. 2003. *Selling China: Foreign Direct Investment during the Reform Era.* Cambridge, UK: Cambridge University Press.

International Monetary Fund. 1999. *Orderly and Effective Insolvency Procedures: Key Issues.* Washington, D.C.: IMF.

Macaulay, Stewart. 1963. "Non-Contractual Relations in Business," *American Sociological Review* 28: 55–69.

North, Douglass C. 1981. *Structure and Change in Economic History.* New York: Norton.

North, Douglass C. 1990. *Institutions, Institutional Change and Economic Performance.* Cambridge, UK: Cambridge University Press.

Pistor, Katharina and Philip A. Wellons. 1998. *The Role of Law and Legal Institutions in Asian Economic Development 1960–1995.* Oxford: Oxford University Press.

Smith, Adam. 1976 [1789]. *An Inquiry into the Nature and Causes of the Wealth of Nations.* Chicago: University of Chicago Press.

Stiglitz, Joseph E. 2002. *Globalization and Its Discontents.* New York: Norton.

Swedberg, Richard. 1998. *Max Weber and the Idea of Economic Sociology.* Princeton: Princeton University Press.

Tamanaha, Brian Z. 1995. "The Lessons of Law-and-Development Studies," *American Journal of International Law* 89: 470–486.

UNCITRAL. 1999. "United Nations Commission on International Trade Law, 32nd session, Vienna, 17 May–4 June 1999," A/CN.9/462/Add.1; 13 April 1999. New York: United Nations.

UNCITRAL. 2000. "United Nations Commission on International Trade Law, 33rd session, New York, 12 June–7 July 2000," A/CN.9/469; 6 Jan 2000. New York: United Nations.

UNCITRAL. 2005. *Legislative Guide on Insolvency Law.* New York: United Nations.

Uttamchandani, Mahesh. 2004 "Insolvency Law and Practice in Europe's Transition Economies," *Butterworth's Journal of International Banking and Financial Law,* December 2004.

Uttamchandani, Mahesh, Ronald Harmer, Neil Cooper, and Irit Ronen-Mevorach. 2005. "What Consumers of Insolvency Law Regimes Need to Know," *Law in Transition,* 2005.

Weber, Max. 1978. *Economy and Society,* ed. Guenther Roth and Claus Wittich. Berkeley: University of California Press.

Weber, Max. 1981. *General Economic History,* tr. Frank Knight. New Brunswick N.J.: Transaction Books.

Wolf, Martin. 2004. *Why Globalization Works.* New Haven: Yale University Press.

World Bank. 1989. *World Development Report.* Washington, D.C.: World Bank.

World Bank. 1999. *Building Effective Insolvency Systems: Toward Principles and Guidelines.* World Bank Draft Background Paper. Washington, D.C.: World Bank.

World Bank. 2001. *Principles and Guidelines for Effective Insolvency and Creditor Rights Systems,* Washington, D.C.: World Bank.

World Bank. 2002. *World Development Report.* Washington D.C.: World Bank.

Notes to Chapter Five

1. This paper is based on (a) extensive fieldwork within each of the institutions discussed here, most notably UNCITRAL; (b) hundreds of interviews with leaders in the global movement to develop a universal standard for insolvency law; and (c) public and private documents from all institutions.

2. Legal norms ". . . convey to an individual certain calculable chances of having economic goods available or of acquiring them under certain conditions in the future" (Weber 1978: 315).

3. Pistor and Wellons's (1998) ADB-sponsored survey is very much the exception.

4. For example, of the six consultants for the IMF Blue Book, Manfred Balz is now General Counsel of Deutsche Telekom. He was a principal architect of the Russian insolvency law, a principal drafter of the new German insolvency law, and a former chairman of the Group on Bankruptcy of the European Union Council. Balz was also a member of the World Bank's Task Force on the Insolvency Initiative and consulted with the IMF on the Cambodian and Korean reforms. Jay Westbrook, Professor of Law at the University of Texas, was on the World Bank Task Force and was the Reporter on the American Law Institute's cross-border insolvency laws for the North American Free Trade Agreement. Ronald Harmer, an Australian lawyer and former president of INSOL, is a delegate to the UNCITRAL Working Group and a consultant who developed, with Neil Cooper, another former INSOL president and active member of the UNCITRAL Working Group, the diagnostic instrument of the EBRD.

5. North is a primary source for neoinstitutional economics (1981) and seems unaware of Weber's arguments about legal predictability.

6. Consider that one of the top IMF officials centrally involved in creating the Blue Book admitted to the authors of never having even heard of Max Weber.

7. For example, IMF Legal Department traditionally did the Fund's legal work but did not advise on things like development policy or structural adjustment loans until the mid-1990s.

6   The Social Construction of Corruption

Mark Granovetter, Stanford University

IN THIS CHAPTER I SKETCH SOME SOCIOLOGICAL ARGUMENTS about corruption. Recent literature is dominated by economic treatments that focus on identifying structures of incentives that make corruption more likely and on assessing the impact of corruption on economic efficiency. Such arguments are usually framed in terms of agency theory, where a corrupt individual is an agent betraying a principal who has vested fiduciary obligations in him. In such treatments, the relationship between agent and principal is defined by how incentives are arranged, and the actors are otherwise indistinguishable or "representative" individuals. I argue here that although such models may be reasonable, other things equal, in practice they underdetermine outcomes because they abstract away from the social aspects of how incentives come to be arranged as they are and how they come to be endowed with the value and the meaning that they ultimately have for actors. These important questions lie largely outside an economic frame of reference and require analysis of social, cultural, and historical elements.

The second edition of the Oxford English Dictionary defines *corruption* as "Perversion or destruction of integrity in the discharge of public duties by bribery or favour." Note the several elements in this typical definition. One refers to "public" duties, which limits the concept to individuals acting on behalf of the public, normally government officials at some level. Although this is no doubt the most common usage, it is not unusual to hear the term extended to describe private individuals as "corrupt," such as a professor who accepts money or other favors in return for higher grades. The term *duties* implies that corruption entails abuse of the trust and formal responsibility someone has undertaken by virtue of a position held in some organization. The rules of such organizations thus become relevant.

The exact meaning of these and other elements of this definition are open to discussion and depend upon social constructions. *Integrity* in the discharge of public or other duties is defined by social and professional norms that vary by time and place, and the meaning of *bribery* is negotiable and elastic. In the typical two-person case, the concept of bribery assumes that A conveys a payment, gift, or favor to B, and B makes some decision, provides some service, or takes some action that improves A's welfare, and can do so because he occupies some organizational position. Imputation of bribery further assumes (a) that the two sets of events are causally related—there is some *quid pro quo*—they are not simply independent of one another, and (b) that this give and take is inappropriate by legal or by commonly accepted local moral standards, or both. Whether either of these two conditions is actually met is often the subject of contention.

Moreover, corrupt exchanges can be further coded as to whether they mainly represent *bribery* or *extortion*. Where a public official dispenses to a citizen something valued, that he controls by virtue of his bureaucratic position, this distinction refers to which of the pair initiates the corrupt exchange: It is bribery if initiated by the citizen and extortion if by the official. This apparently straightforward distinction can be hard to make in practice. In systems where it is generally understood that a side payment is required to process what is in principle available without one, for example, a driver's license, officials do not need to request the payment. Yet the applicant has not really initiated the exchange, and may well experience the situation as extortion. Where the need for a payment is ambiguous, officials may simply make its necessity clear by conspicuous foot-dragging, whose meaning is hard to mistake.[1]

A slightly broader conception of corruption involves not an exchange between two identified individuals, but a situation where a single individual, using a position of trust, appropriates an organization's goods or services that he does not deserve. Embezzlement is a typical case. A recent example would be corporate managers who erected elaborate accounting frauds for their own enrichment, at the expense of shareholders. Note that a crucial element here is the local conception of who in an organization "deserves" what under which circumstances.

Judgments of corruption always assume that a moral violation has occurred, whether or not an actual law has been broken.[2] This assumption is sometimes widely accepted (as, e.g., with the infamous Montesinos bribes in Peru, captured on videotape, which brought down the Fujimori government in 2000; see McMillan and Zoido 2004). But many actions do not reach the radar screen of corruption monitors because parties effectively neutralize or preempt the taint of moral defect. That is, individuals aware of the actions in question accept what I call some "principle of neutralization": an account that acknowledges the causal connection between a payment and a service, or that items have been appropriated as the result of a position held, but implies that given the particular circumstances, no moral violation has occurred.[3] Measures of corruption that depend on perceived infractions (such as, e.g., those collected by Transparency International—see www. transparency.org) are insensitive to activity that is neutralized in this way.

Aspects of Corruption in Exchange Within Dyads and Between Individuals and Organizations

Much familiar corruption involves exchange between two individuals. The theoretical issue is what determines the legitimacy of an exchange, by locally and globally accepted standards (which may conflict, as I discuss later). Exchange theory has paid considerable attention to individuals' perceptions of justice and fairness in exchange (see, e.g., Cook and Rice 2003, 59–61), but legitimacy is a different issue because it refers to a larger audience than the dyad alone and is not attuned only to whether each party gets a fair return, but rather whether the return is appropriate by some standard that originates outside the dyad.

Meanings and norms thus matter a lot, as we can see by observing that many behaviorally identical actions may be interpreted very differently depending on circumstances. To say that an exchange involves a "gift," "favor," or "loan" is morally neutral. But if we code the same exchanges as "bribery" or "extortion," this is quite different and implies condemnation. We need to explore what social principles govern our interpretations of given exchanges.

Gifts and favors are regulated by a norm of reciprocity, which operates in more than one dimension. One aspect is that return gifts or favors should be in a similar modality as the original. It is hard to say precisely what this means, but some instances are obvious to nearly everyone, such as that one should not reciprocate an invitation to dinner at someone's home with a cash payment. There is also an etiquette about the timing of reciprocation, for example, invitations to dinner should not be reciprocated the very next day. As La Rochefoucauld reminds us in his Maxims (1665: Maxim #226), "excessive eagerness to discharge an obligation is a form of ingratitude."

The norm of reciprocity also specifies that return gifts and favors should be roughly in proportion to the original offering. If a gift or favor falls far short, the attribution of ingratitude inhibits further exchange. But if it is excessive, either when originally given or in reciprocation, recipients may suspect that the giver expects something more in return than is appropriate.

Judgments of what is excessive and appropriate are finely tuned to local culture and circumstance. For example, Darr, in his study of upstate New York electronics salesmen, reports that they often took customers to lunch, and that this was considered appropriate in an ongoing relationship. Offering lunch to *prospective* buyers, however, was considered a bribe because it was excessive, that is, not called for given the lack of a previous relationship in which reciprocity was expected. This inappropriateness conferred a moral stigma on such an offer, which therefore was rarely made. This shows that not only the current situation or organizational rules, but also the particular history of an exchange relation, determine what is considered appropriate.

These cases refer to dyadic exchange. Another case where corruption may be imputed is where individuals take resources from organizations to which they are not formally entitled. In such cases, a judgment of corruption may be neutralized in various ways. So Darr (2003) reports that engineers who spent too much company money on dinner were excused by the CEO because they had gotten so many good sales leads. The principle of neutralization here is one of distributive justice. Such a principle extends even to cases when employees remove goods or use services of their employers without authorization and in clear violation of company policy. These would seem straightforward cases of corrupt behavior, but not if a local consensus assumes that employees deserved what they got.

There are two main contexts in which this occurs. In one, employers knowingly pay lower wages than they or the employees think reasonable, assuming that some pilferage will take place that makes up the difference. This is a widespread past and present practice (see, e.g., Liebow 1967, 38–39; Ditton 1977) distinguishable from theft when employers, though aware of the pilferage, "wink" at what is going on (Ditton 1977: 48), in effect framing the items taken as "perks" rather than unauthorized appropriations. Employers have some incentive to continue this situation because it gives them leeway to discipline or fire employees not to their liking for violating a formal if typically unenforced rule.

Management often considers employees who do not understand such arrangements to be bumblers and fools. Dalton (1959) describes, for example, a department store chain where lunch counter employees were informally expected to take some food home at the end of the day, and the turmoil that ensued when one store's lunch counter manager locked up the refrigerator at day's close, preventing this rule violation. Her counter naturally showed higher profits than others, but morale sank and management implied that her unusual results must reflect incorrect bookkeeping. Her indignant resignation restored the *status quo ante*.

Dalton (1959) also suggests a more complicated role for such perks, proposing that they often constitute a system of informal rewards essential for the smooth functioning of the organization. These are targeted for those who have made important contributions, but of a kind that are difficult to give official recognition, such as supporting the boss in a conflict with another unit. Though such informal rewards could get out of hand if appropriated by those who had not made important contributions, Dalton suggests that social control often intervenes to prevent excess. In one case, an employee wanted the house paint that he saw others taking. Most thought, however, that his contributions did not warrant this perk. Thus, he was given a supply of paint which, however, omitted the crucial drying fluid. Dalton reports that the employee excitedly painted his house, but the work was ruined by the ensuing accumulation of dust and insects. He could hardly complain, however, since the paint was officially forbidden to be taken. Instead, he became "a laughingstock without recourse" (Dalton 1959, 202n).

The Role of Relative Social Status in Corruption

The relative social status of parties to social exchange matters a great deal in understanding corruption. I noted earlier that it is considered inappropriate to reciprocate a dinner invitation too hastily, or in the wrong modality (e.g., by cash payment). Although most normally socialized individuals know this, it is interesting to analyze more closely why these actions offend. Both cases, in fact, turn on the same issue: Gestures such as dinner invitations entail a claim to status equality and intend to be part of continuing social relations and exchange of favors. Reciprocation that is overly hasty or conveyed in cash implies rejection of such an ongoing, equal-status relationship.[4]

This leads us to some general arguments about the circumstances under which exchanges are considered corrupt. Anthropologist Larissa Lomnitz writes about the highly refined system of exchanges of favors among the Chilean middle class in the mid-twentieth century (Lomnitz 1971, 1988). Rules of reciprocity were complex and subtle, but it was clear that there were some limits on how favors should be repaid or returned. So, for example, "sexual advances made by a man as the result of granting a favor to a woman would be regarded as extremely gross behavior," and reciprocity "does not include tangible presents, and definitely excludes money." The reason is that "offering these would be regarded as a personal offense between social equals" (1971: 96).

She elaborates, developing an important theme: "Material payment in return for favors is graft. It means the absence of any possibility of personal relationship or having friends in common. Accepting a bribe is an acknowledgement of social inferiority, like accepting a tip or gratuity" (Lomnitz 1988: 44). If a favor is done in the hope of supporting some claim of status similarity, then the preferred reciprocation is gratitude, social approval, gifts, or the promise of future assistance in return; a monetary tip is a status insult. A gift implies the likelihood of an ongoing social relationship in which gifts and favors will continue to be exchanged, whereas a tip is a one-time event which precludes further exchange. It follows that to the extent people in a society are socially equal, the exchange of money for favors, which is typically defined as corrupt, will be very much reduced, as the goals otherwise served by bribes can be accomplished by exchange of favors among equals.[5,6]

If accepting a bribe is to acknowledge social inferiority, then one factor affecting the extent of corruption is the pattern of status differentials between groups whose exchanges are typically implicated in corruption, for example, government officials and private economic actors. These patterns vary widely depending on historical and political circumstances. In the mid-century Chilean setting that Lomnitz describes, business was dominated by a socially defined upper class, and the government bureaucracy by a middle class that for complex historical reasons had lost their previously important position as industrialists. The social distance between business interests and bureaucracy facilitated graft as a form of well-understood market exchange, in which bureaucrats willingly accepted cash or material payments in return for favors to businessmen, since the social inferiority that this implied was already well understood (Lomnitz 1971: 194; 1988: 46).

In such a setting, bribes that flow from business to government comport with the pre-existing status structure. But then the reverse flow would be diffi-
. cult: If government officials needed to pay businessmen for services that could not be properly or legally bought, such payments would meet resistance based on the social status difference. A good example of this may be the case of Peru, where Vladimiro Montesinos, as director of the Peruvian intelligence service, systematically bribed judges, politicians, and media owners to provide decisions, votes, and information favorable to the Fujimori regime. The regime's undoing resulted from the failure to bribe the owners of one small yet influential newspaper controlled since 1898 by a single prominent, high-status family (McMillan and Zoido 2004: 84), who also owned a cable television channel. In most situations, successful bribes to the majority of relevant businesses would be sufficient, as it was for judges and politicians. However, a single television channel can wield enormous influence if, as occurred in this case, it repeatedly publicizes incontrovertible evidence of high-level corruption (in the form of videos of the actual corrupt transactions, secretly made by Vladimiro Montesinos himself, and subsequently widely known as "vladivideos"; McMillan and Zoido 2004: 89).

This is not to say that bribes cannot take place between equals or flow from those socially inferior to those socially superior. But for this to occur goes against the grain of normal social interaction and is more complicated, requiring extensive management and buffering, at much higher cost and complexity, and requiring far more skill, than simple monetary payments. Thus Lomnitz notes that when equal-status individuals in Mexico need to bribe one another, which is normally socially proscribed, the exchange is conducted through intermediaries called coyotes. This spares both partners in the exchange the need to meet personally (Lomnitz 1988: 46).

In contrast to Chile are cultures where government bureaucrats are of higher social status than businesspeople, as has been the case historically in China—a pattern that persists during the recent wave of market reforms. This does not prevent those in business from arranging favors from government officials, which is common (see Wank 2000) and may indeed be absolutely necessary in order to conduct business (Lin 2001). But the direction of status difference means that a simple exchange of favors for money becomes unlikely. Instead, elaborate systems of gift giving, banquets, entertainment, and favors keyed to the highly particular needs of officials are developed. Whereas a cash payment to the official would be considered an insult, the banquets and special favors can be thought of as a form of deference, which the higher-status person can imagine is owed to him. This may explain the long-term elaboration of such gift giving in the Chinese economy.

An interesting example is that of "Boss Lai," the central figure in an enormous corruption scandal in the Chinese city of Xiamen that exploded in 1998—in which customs revenue of around ten billion US dollars had been evaded by his business interests. Lai Changxing was of much lower social background than most of the officials whose cooperation he needed, and therefore developed many techniques to offset the likely reluctance of such officials to accept bribes. One is that he "always took care to maintain the appearance of proffering gifts out of personal concern for the needs of an official rather than as a *quid pro quo* exchange" (Wank 2002: 14). Faced with rejection of gifts or bribes by officials who considered him socially inferior, Lai used intermediaries to avoid face-to-face interaction (as in Mexico) and made especially good use of a seven-story mansion that he opulently decorated, which included a dance hall, karaoke lounge, movie theater, sauna, footbath facilities, and five luxurious suites "all attended to by a staff of attractive young women who reportedly provided sexual services" (Wank 2002: 19). Officials who would not take money from the socially inferior Boss Lai were less reluctant to indulge in the pleasures of his "Red Mansion," where Lai was nowhere to be seen (though his video cameras were secretly taping officials' illicit activities).

My arguments about corruption and social status differentials have referred to bribes. Extortion, in which the payment is demanded rather than offered, is different, but symmetrical arguments apply. Suppose a government official is socially inferior to a businessman from whom he attempts to extort payments in order to act favorably. In the case of a bribe, the exchange is unproblematic, because the lower status of the official makes it easier for him to accept a bribe. Conversely, this lower status makes it more difficult for him to demand a payment from a higher-status business counterpart, because this is implicitly an attempt to counterbalance the status differential by leveraging one's official position. For this to be acceptable requires the extortion to be disguised and conveyed politely, just as bribes from inferiors to superiors must be managed subtly. Extortion by those socially superior from those of lower status, however, is likely to be accepted routinely. James Scott observes that in developing nations where civil servants have higher status than most citizens, corruption (by which he means extortion) will thrive (1972: 15).

Note that the distinction between bribery and extortion is necessary to understand under what circumstances funds are likely to flow between those of different social status. Whereas a lower-status businessman may find his bribe refused by a higher-status civil servant, the latter has no problem taking the payment if he extorted it. The reason is that it cannot be an insult if he is the one who solicited it to begin with, as this transaction is then aligned with, rather than contrary to, the direction of status differential. Thus, a purely behavioristic view that simply noted the direction of a monetary transfer is insufficient to identify probability of flows, which depends on the direction of initiative and the social meanings associated with this direction.

The lesson here is that the configuration of social networks and social status differences between those who need favors and those in a position to provide them in an economy may strongly shape the modalities, the costs, and the likelihood of such favors being provided. To study such processes in the absence of understanding these forces omits one of the most important causal determinants.

Patron-Client Relations, Corruption, and Loyalty

The businessperson who bribes an official of lower social status usually conducts this activity as if it were a market-type relationship, more or less impersonal and without expectation of continuing relations. In Peru, Vladimiro Montesinos even used the artifice of written contracts, specifying the obligations of those bribed, despite the obvious lack of legal standing for such documents (McMillan and Zoido, 2004). Exchange of favors among equals, by contrast, typically is embedded in expectations of a continuing relation, and this is one reason the exchange of favors can be carried out without definite expectations of the timing and nature of reciprocity. This affords considerable flexibility to the exchange process. (For a similar analysis of exchanges among venture capitalists in Silicon Valley, see Ferrary 2003).

There is one situation in which resources and favors do flow from those of higher status to those of lower status *and* there is an expectation of continuing relationship: This is the important realm of patron-client relationships. Depending on the nature of what flows back from lower to higher status individuals and on local social constructions, the resulting exchanges may or may not be coded as corrupt. A typical case is politicians, usually of middle-status origins, and their lower-social-status supporters. Some such cases include simple market transactions such as buying votes. This is often one-shot, as in the familiar image of money being handed out in Chicago bars on election night. In many settings, however, politicians engage in longer-term relations with constituents, and different kinds of favors flow down, including employment, public works, and other items that those in government may control, and loyalty, political support, and votes flow up. Such political figures may build up long-term cadres of supporters that they use to gain and maintain positions of influence and power. The nature of the exchange is such that the less powerful and lower-status individual cannot reciprocate with favors or cash, and therefore balances the account by providing loyalty and subordination (cf. Lomnitz 1988: 47). When employment is provided, such patronage builds up cliques of individuals in public administration who remain loyal to their patron whether the patron is in or out of power. Such collections of patrons and their coteries are familiar in most political systems and may typically be the basis for coordinated action that can be more efficient than when administrators have to build relations with a previously unknown network of subordinates. However, they also facilitate corrupt activity such as covert financial operations that depend on secrecy and trust (cf. Lomnitz on Mexico, 1988: 48).

A crucial issue in the vast literature on patron-client relations is whether clients are merely utility-maximizing actors responding to incentives provided by patrons, feigning loyalty while awaiting an opportunity to defect once their market position permits it; or are actually loyal, meaning that their solidarity with patrons exceeds what incentives prescribe and is less likely to shift as the incentive situation does (see the analysis by Eisenstadt and Roniger 1984: 261, of contrasting cases and their account of the sources of the difference).

Market vs. Network Corruption, Conflicts of Interest, and the Role of Ideology

James Scott (1972) distinguishes between market and nonmarket corruption. By *market corruption,* he means the "selling of government goods and services to the highest bidder" (1972: 12). As an ideal type, such corruption is impersonal, in the way that ideal-type markets are: The identity of buyers and sellers is irrelevant because the transaction is more or less anonymous. Scott gives as an example the sale of offices, monopolies, franchises, and taxation powers. He does note, however, that in premodern times, such practices were often perfectly legal, as in early Stuart England (1972: Chapter 3).[7]

Scott calls *nonmarket corruption* situations where people honor obligations to others they know, in ways that are considered illegal, improper, or corrupt by legal or other standards. I would call this *network corruption,* and it is useful to inquire as to its sources and extent.

The question is under what circumstances people holding positions of public trust will consider their private obligations to others to supersede legal or political mandates that in principle should guide their behavior. One possibility is that societies vary in the extent of these obligations. Where social networks are narrowly defined, obligations are unlikely to interfere with the performance of public duty. No systematic comparative study of variation in the extent of obligation networks across societies exists, and daunting theoretical and methodological obstacles are easy to imagine. But this does not mean that variations are insignificant or that comparative research would not be of great interest.

Olivier de Sardan, for example, argues that there are far more extensive solidarity networks in Africa than in Europe and that African families are "widely extended and replete with pressures and solicitations which can hardly be ignored. Links created within peer groups (primary school, secondary school, and college friends) last until retirement" (1999: 40), as do solidarities that arise from associations, churches, and parties. All these relations "include an almost general obligation of mutual assistance. One cannot refuse a service, a favour, a bit of string-pulling or compliance to a relative, neighbor, party comrade or friends . . . The circle of individuals to whom one feels obliged to render services is thus astonishingly wide" (1999: 40). The loss of reputation from failing to adhere to such obligations is severe. In postcolonial settings where states arbitrarily assembled by colonial powers still command little loyalty and bureaucracies work poorly, loss of reputation may mean the inability to acquire services that the government is supposed to provide. Those in this situation are reduced to bribery, instead of "acting like everyone else, through an exchange of favors" (1999:41). In this setting, market corruption is epiphenomenal, a "mere symptom of the lack of an activatable network, a temporary deficit in 'social capital'" (1999:41). Widespread corruption in Africa, by this account, is predictable from the vast reach of network obligations in comparison to the power of civic ones.

In some settings, the habit of exchanging major favors through social networks may have developed in particular social circumstances that offered few viable alternatives. The often noted extensive development of a second economy through informal networks under state socialism is a good example. As Scheppele notes, under state socialism, there was an understood bargain that citizens would refrain from public protests, and that in return, the regimes "allowed ordinary citizens to convert public property to private use, as a sort of payment for acquiescing in a regime that people would otherwise not have supported" (1999: 516). This bargain resembles those I alluded to earlier in which people were expected to appropriate goods from their firms in compensation for their low salaries. But because under state socialism this activity was not isolated, and instead involved elaborate networks of exchange whose purpose was to produce or exchange goods for the black market, we can see it as an elaborate system of exchanging favors. These exchanges were economically necessary because the officially condoned activity as regulated by central planning was too rigid and unrealistic to provide goods and services that citizens considered necessary.[8]

Scheppele suggests that the strong normative system that sustained such exchange remained in place under transition. In a difficult economic situation, where wages fell and work was highly insecure, people stayed with the pattern of protecting their friends. In such a situation, however, "strangers are at risk. The strangers/foreigners who come into these changing economies are quite likely to be victims . . . and to believe . . . that corruption is everywhere" (1999: 520). She goes on to observe that the "impersonal universalistic norms that allow people to turn their backs on friends to give a contract to the highest bidder or to take a chance on a stranger are not in place . . . What looks like corruption are the survival skills of people who are still living in uncertain times, and who have learned to be suspicious of universalistic ideologies" (1999: 522). Western advisors assume that when people are strangers to each other, their interactions will be more trustworthy, but much of the world doubts this (1999: 529). Indeed, corruption is "about violations of duties that people actually feel themselves to be bound by. Duties of friendship, loyalty and integrity within one's networks matter a lot in the former Soviet world . . . So corruption can be seen . . . as occurring when people do not put their friends and family before others" (1999: 530). Correspondingly, bribery is not necessary unless you are an outsider. Bribery is "where money substitutes for friendship networks" (1999:531). "Corruption," Scheppele observes, "cannot be a failure

of duty where no duty is felt . . . Insofar as Westerners come to the East expect-
ing transactions among strangers to provide the moral model for doing deals,
they are bound to be disappointed" (1999: 532).

Competing ideologies, in this case, pit reformers and Westerners against
long-time participants in the economic system. It is conceivable that this
conflict will decline and standards converge insofar as the economic crisis of
transition moderates. There may be societies, however, where conflicts of ideology are even more deeply ingrained because of long-term conflicts of interest. For the Chilean case that Lomnitz describes, the favors that middle-class
individuals employed in the bureaucracy did for one another sometimes violated formal regulations that prescribed impersonal relationships. Aware that
such favors might be at the expense of those without good connections, those
engaging in such exchange were ambivalent. But on the whole they neutralized imputations of corruption by appeal to an "ideology of class solidarity
based on friendship and reciprocity" (Lomnitz 1971: 99).

This ideology clearly contradicts that of liberal free enterprise, which pre-
scribes advancement on merit alone and proscribes tampering with the operation of free markets.[9] Lomnitz observes, however, that these liberal views,
though enshrined in Latin American legal systems, are widely seen as expressing the "values of the elite." The middle class, "while outwardly respectful of
the law, has little use for those values." Instead, competition "is viewed as a
necessary evil, caused by the scarcity of resources; it is not valued as a proving-
ground for individual worth"; and "Chileans abroad tend to be critical of competitive middle-class values in industrial societies, which they view as creating a friendless, dull, herdlike existence" (1971: 100). Further, the ideology of
friendship and solidarity provides an advantage for middle-class Chileans to
compete and succeed in Chile, in relation to members of the upper or lower
classes (Lomnitz 1971: 105).

Thus, the ideology that effectively neutralizes perceptions or imputations
of corrupt behavior contrasts explicitly to another that would condemn and
restrain reciprocity of this type as illegitimate and corrupt. This conflict of
ideologies is not socially random, but reflects real conflicts of interest between
well-defined social groups in a society highly stratified along class and social-
status lines. Another interesting example of this is suggested by Richard
Hofstadter, in *The Age of Reform* (1955). Hofstadter analyzes the Progressive
movement in turn-of-the twentieth-century American cities, which combated
urban political machines. He proposes that the machines and the immigrants

to whom they provided patronage were symbiotic and that both patrons and clients were satisfied. However, to the Progressives, he argues, drawn from among those members of the middle class who were losing their social status and leadership positions to immigrants and newly rising industrialists alike, the machines seemed the embodiment of evil. The ideology of clean government developed out of their status anxiety and gives another example of how conflicts among status groups are refracted in ideology, one of whose most effective tools is to persuade the general public that its way of defining corruption is correct.[10] In Progressive America, this attempt had considerable success. By contrast, in early Stuart England, when the sale of offices to wealthy merchants with no other entrée to the political system was legal, aristocrats strongly objected that such sale was corrupt and inappropriate. But since the practice benefited a wealthy status group rather than immigrant newcomers (as in America), and moreover stabilized the Stuart monarchy by buying off a new wealth-based elite, the attempt to define the practice as corrupt did not succeed (Scott 1972: chap. 3). Scott also suggests that the success of eighteenth-century French aristocrats in blocking the selling of offices turned many bourgeois against the Bourbon regime and made revolution more likely (1972: 47). Thus, what is considered corrupt may result from the balance of power among groups struggling to define the dominant view, and this definition may then in turn affect these power relations.

A different type of neutralization that arises from ideology and the conflict of interest that it expresses occurs in center-periphery political and fiscal relations. When a central political authority extracts resources from component elements in a federal system, resistance to such extraction may take various forms. If local officials withhold demanded revenues, the center views this as corrupt action; but this may be coded locally as legitimate resistance to excessive and illegitimate demands. Such coding may be formulated into ideologies and potent slogans such as "no taxation without representation," as in colonial America. Indeed, when parties disagree sharply on the legitimacy of extraction, as did Americans and British in 1776, there may not be any peaceful way to resolve the issue.

Such disputes may lead to political explosions like the American Revolutionary War. On a smaller scale, they may also be exploited by local entrepreneurs. Thus, in the corruption scandal in Xiamen, China, which I mentioned earlier, it is especially interesting that the enormous scale of import tax evasion by Boss Lai was only possible with the extensive cooperation of local authorities. Indeed, that cooperation was so extensive that Lai was sometimes referred to as "underground director" of the Xiamen Customs House, and the routine bureaucratic operations of the local government's customs officers were integrated into those of his business. In effect, the Customs House became "a profit center for [Boss Lai's] Yuanhua Corporation" (Wank 2002: 22). There are a number of reasons why this was possible, including Lai's consummate skill at manipulating complex networks of officials and their subordinates. But one necessary condition for these events was that the revenue siphoned off in the illicit activity was locally earned (by the enormous trade activity in Xiamen's busy port) yet destined for the most part to support Beijing's central government functions. Because the main victims of the scheme could be interpreted as making excessive demands on local revenues, moral scruples about the activity were substantially neutralized.

As with most principles of neutralization, whether one thinks that this was merely a rationalization for corrupt behavior that should be strongly condemned, or the expression of an appropriate local autonomy, depends on one's view of the legitimacy of the extraction that was being resisted. Boss Lai skillfully built on feelings of local autonomy by using large amounts of his proceeds to become a local benefactor; among many other expenditures, he bought the city's soccer team and gave ill-equipped police squads new motorcycles, jeeps, and cell phones and built new training facilities. His funding substantially rebuilt his home village, a couple of hours' drive from Xiamen, where he and his family became local heroes (Beech 2002). Thus, he provided for the local area in ways that would not have occurred had the revenues been directed properly to Beijing. Had he merely pocketed his gains, local citizens would have been much less likely to cooperate, because it would have been harder for them to frame the activity as resistance to central extraction in support of local activity.

Discussion

Because defining behavior as "corrupt" inevitably entails a judgment about what behavior is legitimate and appropriate, there is an irreducible sociological component that has been given surprisingly little attention. Judgments about legitimacy are part of larger normative frameworks that people produce in all known social structures. Norms do not come from above, nor do they arise in most cases from some evolutionary process that selects for efficiency. Instead, they are enacted, reproduced, or changed in the course of each group's everyday social activity. Norms may be in part a reflex of changes in practical realities, as when increasing women's participation in the workforce makes sexist conceptions appear quaint and outdated. Yet they have some life of their own and can predate and influence as well as emerge from social change, as Gunnar Myrdal noted in his 1944 study, *An American Dilemma,* which in effect predicted a civil rights movement from the disjunction between common American ideals and actual behavior.

Norms are not easy to manipulate, yet it is common in human history that groups with conflicting interests present different sets of standards for what behavior is appropriate, and label behavior that benefits competing groups as illegitimate or more specifically "corrupt." This device, which can only have much effect over some medium to long term, has certainly been successful at times. Competition occurs along several dimensions, and as postmodern scholars remind us, groups that can impose a hegemonic discourse that shapes peoples' understanding gain a powerful advantage.

But understanding the judgment of corruption entails more than knowing which abstract norm applies to a particular situation. Which norm applies, and how it is to be interpreted for a particular case, typically involves knowledge and assessment of the relationship between exchanging parties—their status differential, past obligations accumulated, and the general social milieu surrounding their transactions. This observation is the more apt, to the extent that network corruption is at issue. By contrast, market corruption, in which services are corruptly but impersonally sold to the highest bidder, may be well described by economic models in which parties to exchange are merely representative individuals (for an excellent summary, see Bardhan 1997). Techniques of neutralization, as described in the present paper, are more likely to apply to network than to market exchange. The literature on corruption gives little insight as to the balance between market and network varieties. We should be cautious, however, about assuming too sharp a line between them. One reason is that, as a number of scholars have observed, many actors prefer to achieve their goals through networks of obligation and turn to bribes or extortion only when these networks fail or are absent.[11] Thus, there is an intimate relation between the two types. But even in corruption that begins as a purely "market" phenomenon, the need for secrecy, which is a central element of such corruption (cf. Shleifer and Vishny 1993), makes it highly likely that repeat offenders will cultivate appropriate personal ties for their own protection, thus endowing market corruption with important network elements.

Given space limitations, in this paper I have mainly considered the small-scale exchange aspects of corruption. But as these comments about how market and network corruption relate to one another may suggest, there is much more to say about the social network structure of corruption. One aspect of this, that I mention just briefly, but that bears quite a lot of analysis, is that the ability to effectively corrupt the administration of some substantial activity requires "corruption entrepreneurs" who are masters of social network manipulation. It is never automatic that such masters will arise and succeed, so in order to have the right balance of explanation between structure and agency, more is needed than an understanding of incentives, though that is certainly a necessary starting point. The general principles that govern success should be similar to those that have been proposed for network entrepreneurs of all kinds (cf. Burt 1992; Padgett and Ansell 1993 and Granovetter 2002), but with some specific wrinkles that apply more to corruption than elsewhere. One such wrinkle results from the need for secrecy, so that once you have succeeded in persuading someone to engage in what is defined as corrupt activity, it is hard for that person to stop, because the threat of exposure effectively deters backsliding. Thus, able corruption entrepreneurs assiduously collect blackmail materials, such as the videotapes made by Montesinos in Peru or Boss Lai in Xiamen.

One crucial element of skill for corruption entrepreneurs is knowing whom to recruit. High-level members of formal organizations can be effective insofar as their subordinates fall into line in corrupt activity, by virtue of their acceptance of orders in the hierarchy. But bureaucratic hierarchies do not engender the automatic obedience that some transaction cost theorists imagine, and in particular, there may be reluctance of lower-level employees to follow clearly illegal orders. This limitation prompted Boss Lai to engage in what Wank calls a "dual-track" strategy, of recruiting both high-level and low-level staff of the Xiamen Customs House to his scheme. Thus the low-level staff had incentives to comply and their superiors to look the other way or indeed routinize and legitimate the new procedures (Wank 2002: 21).

Knowing whom to recruit in the quest for corruption means more than knowing what their organizational capacities are. Because those recruited to corruption may in turn recruit their own formal and informal network to this activity, the corruption entrepreneur must have a good sense of whose network reaches where, so as to choose strategic targets centrally located in networks that reach into those informal structures and formal organizations that can best serve his goals. This technique is what Wank calls "delegation" (2002: 17), and requires the corruption entrepreneur to have a strong intuition about what the overall network structure looks like, so that his recruits will most effectively leverage his efforts.

Such comments only scratch the surface of what could be learned about the network structure of corruption, or for that matter other proscribed activity, including the operation of organized crime or terrorism. In this, as in the arguments on legitimation, neutralization, and social definition of appropriate exchange, there is much work left to do. I hope here to have suggested the potential rewards of these efforts.

References

Bardhan, Pranab. 1997. "Corruption and Development: A Review of Issues." *Journal of Economic Literature* 35 (September): 1320–1346.

Beech, Hannah. 2002. "Smuggler's Blues." TIME Asia, 160(14): October 7.

Brinkley, Alan. 1985. "Richard Hofstadter's *The Age of Reform*: A Reconsideration." *Reviews in American History* 13(3): 462–480.

Burt, Ronald. 1992. *Structural Holes*. Cambridge, MA: Harvard University Press.

Cook, Karen and Eric R. W. Rice. 2003. "Social Exchange Theory." In *Handbook of Social Psychology*, ed. John Delamater, chap. 3. New York: Kluwer/Plenum.

Dalton, Melville. 1959. *Men Who Manage*. New York: Wiley.

Darr, Asaf. 2003. "Gifting Practices and Interorganizational Relations: Constructing Obligation Networks in the Electronic Sector." *Sociological Forum* 18(1): 31–51.

Ditton, Jason. 1977. "Perks, Pilferage and the Fiddle: The Historical Structure of Invisible Wages." *Theory and Society* 4(1): 39–71.

Eisenstadt, S. N. and L. Roniger. 1984. *Patrons, Clients and Friends: Interpersonal Relations and the Structure of Trust in Society*. Cambridge, UK: Cambridge University Press.

Ferrary, Michel. 2003. "The Gift Exchange in the Social Networks of Silicon Valley." *California Management Review* 45(4): 120–138.

Granovetter, Mark. 1995. *Getting a Job: A Study of Contacts and Careers*. 2nd ed. Chicago: University of Chicago Press.

Granovetter, Mark. 2002. "A Theoretical Agenda for Economic Sociology." Pp. 35–59 in *The New Economic Sociology: Developments in an Emerging Field*, ed. Mauro F. Guillen, Randall Collins, Paula England, and Marshall Meyer. New York: Russell Sage Foundation.

Gupta, Akhil. 1995. "Blurred Boundaries: The Discourse of Corruption, the Culture of Politics and the Imagined State." *American Ethnologist* 22(2, May): 375–402.

Hofstadter, Richard. 1955. *The Age of Reform: From Bryan to FDR*. New York: Random House.

La Rochefoucauld, Francois duc de. 1665. *Maximes*. Paris.

Lewis, Sinclair. 1922. *Babbitt*. New York: Harcourt Brace.

Liebow, Elliot. 1967. *Tally's Corner*. Boston: Little Brown.

Lin, Yi-min. 2001. *Between Politics and Markets: Firms, Competition and Institutional Change in Post-Mao China*. Cambridge, UK: Cambridge University Press.

Lomnitz, Larissa. 1971. "Reciprocity of Favors in the Urban Middle Class of Chile." Pp. 93–106 in *Studies in Economic Anthropology*, ed. George Dalton. Washington, DC: American Anthropological Association.

Lomnitz, Larissa. 1988. "Informal Exchange Networks in Formal Systems: A Theoretical Model." *American Anthropologist*, NS vol. 90(1): 42–55.

Mayer, Adrian. 1960. *Caste and Kinship in Central India*. Berkeley: University of California Press.

McMillan, John and Pablo Zoido. 2004. "How to Subvert Democracy: Montesinos in Peru." *Journal of Economic Perspectives* 18(4, Fall): 69–92.

Myrdal, Gunnar. 1944. *An American Dilemma: The Negro Problem and Modern Democracy*. New York: Harper and Brothers.

Olivier de Sardan, J. P. 1999. "A Moral Economy of Corruption in Africa?" *The Journal of Modern African Studies* 1: 25–52.

Padgett, John F. and Christopher Ansell. 1993 "Robust Action and the Rise of the Medici: 1400–1434." *American Journal of Sociology* 98:1259–1319

Scheppele, Kim 1999. "The Inevitable Corruption of Transition." *Connecticut Journal of International Law* 14: 509–532.

Scott, James. 1972. *Comparative Political Corruption*. Englewood Cliffs, NJ: Prentice-Hall.

Shleifer, Andrei and Robert Vishny. 1993. "Corruption." *Quarterly Journal of Economics* (August): 599–617.

Stark, David. 1986. "Rethinking Internal Labor Markets: New Insights from a Comparative Perspective." *American Sociological Review* 51 (4, August): 492–504.

Sykes, Gresham and David Matza. 1957. "Techniques of Neutralization: A Theory of Delinquency." *American Sociological Review* 22(6): 664–670.

Wank, David. 2000. *Commodifying Communism*. New York: Cambridge University Press.

Wank, David. 2002. "Evolving Business-State Clientelism in China: The Institutional Process of a Smuggling Operation." Presented at the American Political Science Association's Annual Meeting, 2002. Sophia University, Tokyo, Japan.

You, Jong-sung and Sanjeev Khagram. 2005. "A Comparative Study of Inequality and Corruption." *American Sociological Review* 70(February): 136–157.

Notes to Chapter Six

1. At times, a great deal of social skill and local knowledge may be required to understand that a payment is required and what that payment is. See Gupta's account

of a failed attempt by naïve farmers in an Indian village to offer the appropriate bribe (1995:379–381). One reason for the failure is that for the local officials, "a great deal of importance was attached to not naming a sum" (381).

2. It does not necessarily follow that this moral violation is to be unconditionally condemned. Bardhan gives the counterexample of bribing a policeman not to torture a suspect (1997: 1321).

3. I take the idea of "neutralization" from the work of Sykes and Matza (1957) on "techniques of neutralization," in which they show how juvenile delinquents admit their crimes yet hold values similar to law-abiding citizens, arguing that for various reasons, their victims deserved what befell them.

4. Eating together signifies status equality across a wide spectrum of cultures. One way to sort through the exquisitely elaborated status distinctions of Indian caste, for example, is to study which groups may eat what kinds of foods with which other groups (see the detailed treatment in Mayer, 1960). The classic literary account of rejection of the status equality implied by a dinner invitation is Sinclair Lewis's painful depiction of a dinner thrown by George Babbitt, in a failed attempt at upward social mobility (*Babbitt*, chap.15).

5. You and Khagram (2005) provide empirical evidence across countries that the level of income inequality is positively related to the extent of perceived corruption.

6. But this argument, which is culturally congruent to most Western cultures, may not be universally valid. Thus, Olivier de Sardan (1999) argues that in many African societies, unlike European ones, everyday forms of sociability have been monetized, so that one gives "taxi fare" to visitors, coins to children of friends, even a "bank-note to your step-mother when running into her on the street." Whereas in Europe, money dealings are condemned in most social domains, in Africa there is no domain, including marriage, in which "money does not play a permanent role" (1999: 46). It follows that exchanges viewed in the West as corrupt would be more common because, other things equal, money changes hands more readily in such a culture.

7. He thus refers to such practices as "proto-corruption." This designation is anachronistic, however, because it makes sense only in view of the knowledge that the activity will be considered corrupt at some future time.

8. For a detailed account of how elaborate these cooperative networks could become, see Stark (1986) on informal networks in Hungarian factories under state socialism.

9. Indeed, it seems likely that the nearly universal adherence to such liberal or neoliberal views among economists is one reason for their recent enthusiasm for showing that corruption leads to inefficiency. Such a view is not inevitable for an economist, however, because under some circumstances it is displaced by a Panglossian view that any existing institutional practice must be serving some efficiency purpose, otherwise it would have been competed away. The reigning aphorism for this view is that you "won't find dollar bills lying in the street": Inefficient institutions present an opportunity for profit for those who could do things better, and all opportunities for profit are taken. Lenient antitrust views of some transaction cost economists are

one example of this position in action. Because both views are compatible with some aspects of economic thought, it can be hard to predict economists' positions on public policy. Thus, in the Microsoft antitrust case, economists and economics-oriented legal scholars found themselves expressing strong views on both sides, often independent of their position on the political spectrum.

10. Generations of revisionist historians have disputed many elements of Hofstadter's interpretations, but his arguments about Progressives have generally fared better than those about Populism. For a detailed and nuanced review, see Brinkley 1985.

11. In this regard, preferences are similar to those in job seeking, where the use of impersonal sources generally implies inability to tap personal networks (see Granovetter 1995).

III RELIGION

7   The Role of Spiritual Capital in Economic Behavior

Barnaby Marsh, Oxford University

I N HIS LANDMARK WORK *THE PROTESTANT ETHIC AND THE Spirit of Capitalism,* one of Max Weber's central arguments is that beliefs and spiritual outlook make a decisive difference in accounting for the evolution of certain social and economic structures. Although various scholars have pointed to exceptions and weaknesses of Weber's central thesis on Protestantism and the creation of wealth, his contention that immaterial and "spiritual" factors can have effects as important as those of material considerations was brilliant and has come to be the dominant assumption throughout the social sciences. Intangibles such as outlooks, ideals, and beliefs (held either individually or collectively) have now become fundamental considerations in branches of study as diverse as racial and gender inequality, entrepreneurial wealth creation, and economic statecraft.

However, this key insight has yet to be incorporated in any serious and systematic way in fields that look at the behavioral and motivational roots of complex social processes, such as economics, psychology, and evolutionary biology. Essentially, this may be because these fields have focused primarily on finding and testing basic-level building blocks of behavior (using currencies such as subjective utility, reinforcement value, and reproductive fitness, respectively), rather than on considering effects of emergent reality found as individual choices are aggregated and as they are made with respect to context, custom, and culture. Thus, although the adoption of simple currencies has been a powerful tool in allowing social scientists to construct, test, and refine elegant and generally workable theories, it has also resulted in neglect of important considerations at work in real, complex contexts. The limitations of these sterilized approaches can be seen when they are used in applied situations. Often, they are unable to offer precise, reliable predictions of both individual and collective behavior.

This issue tends to be addressed in several ways. The most common from the perspective of single-currency approaches is to conclude that the information that the model/prediction was based upon is incomplete and that more information would need to be collected to make a better prediction. More information may indeed result in better predictions, but the predictive power of models may continue to fall short, especially if emergent forces that are actually driving the behavior are neglected. By illustrative analogy, trying to understand complex processes such as social behavior and economic progress only in terms of basic units can be like trying to understand a forest ecosystem merely by collecting and aggregating the interactions between the plants and animals that it contains or, to give another example, trying to understand what a human being is by collecting and aggregating the basic functions of all the cells in the human body. Although either of these enterprises is possible in principle, the gap between the consideration of the fundamental parts and the emergent whole remains large. What is needed is the ability to consider different kinds of knowledge and information in relation to different levels of understanding and to understand how processes at different levels affect processes at other levels, considering both top-down and bottom-up causality (see Ellis, 2005).

For behavior, this means taking time to consider a broader range of forces that are acting on various *levels* on the motivational state and behavior of the individual and in aggregations of individuals. Indeed, we can do this at the most basic level by looking at different kinds of currencies that can be used to understand individual choice (such as fitness, subjective utility, and reinforcement value). At a more complex level, we can look at the processes via which behavior is deployed to maximize return in terms of these currencies. This includes consideration of how different kinds of advantage (such as use of various kinds of *capital*) are selectively and strategically employed to solve problems relating to access to resources.

My intention in this chapter is to explicitly recognize forces shaping economic behavior by incorporating and integrating the two different levels of analysis previously outlined, and particularly, to recognize the contributions made by sociologists (beginning with Weber and Durkheim) regarding the role of individually subjective beliefs, outlooks, and ideals in the context of social organization and competition. These contributions have importance both at the individual and collective levels of behavior in ways that are still not fully appreciated or recognized in formal models of individual and collective action throughout the social sciences. For instance, little progress has been made in determining the source of some kinds of subjective beliefs and outlooks and why individuals persist in holding these beliefs (such as believing in fairness and in a "just world," having optimism in cases where the odds would suggest otherwise, or having passion for activities that seem to yield little in terms of tangible payoffs). Similarly, gaps occur at the level of how different kinds of capital factor into competitive success. In modern discussions of economic behavior and competitive success, much has been written about the importance of human capital and social capital (see Becker 1964, 1976; Granovetter 1985; Loury 1977, 1987; Cohen and Prusak 2001; Putnam 2000; Bourdieu 1980, 1988; etc.). Here I will argue why the notion of yet another form of capital, spiritual capital, is crucially important. By *spiritual capital,* I mean a kind of capital that consists of the outlooks, ideals, and subjective beliefs held by the individual. Thus, I use *spirit* in the sense used by Max Weber; that is, broadly in terms of individual belief and outlook, in contrast to a usage restricted to religious beliefs.[1]

Species of Capital

Because resources are scarce and not evenly distributed, allocation processes typically entail competition between individuals and natural selection. Variation between individuals will create asymmetries in how individuals behave, with each individual making use of strengths such as physical strength, knowledge, social connections, and other resources. These strengths can be used in combination and at strategic points of opportunity to allow for competitive advantage.

A way of understanding competitive strength is in terms of *capital,* which is anything that can be accumulated, stored, transferred to others, and transformed into competitive advantage. Capital in this broad sense can take many different forms. In banking and commerce contexts, capital is most commonly understood in terms of financial instruments and flows (thus an example of "financial capital"). Marx ([1867] 1905) understood capital as the physical means and modes of production, stressing the control of means and modes of production (labor, factories, machinery; thus, the "physical capital" stock)

in addition to the underlying finance. The naming of other forms of capital—
human, social, and spiritual—acknowledges further forms of wealth potential that are physically intangible but which can have a formidable impact on
competitive advantage (e.g., see Coleman 1990). For instance, individuals may
accumulate knowledge and understanding via education ("human capital";
see Schultz 1961; Becker 1964, 1976; Davenport 1999), develop social skills and
relationships ("social capital"; see Granovetter 1973; Loury 1977, 1987; Lin
1982, 1988; Cohen and Prusak 2001; Putnam 2000; Bourdieu 1980, 1988; etc.),
or hold and be known for certain beliefs or ideals ("spiritual capital") that can
provide advantages in competitive contexts (see Table 7-1).

Most models of behavior will consider *capital* only in a specific context and
with a single meaning, rather than to consider the more difficult and complex
possibility of different kinds of capital being deployed concurrently. This traditional approach is sometimes useful, but too often simplistic. One place to
see various forms of capital at work is in real competition, where individuals
employ capital strategically. In competitive contexts as diverse as winning a
ball game, winning a war, building a competitive business, or running an effective government, a lot more than financial and physical capital is needed
to secure competitive advantage. One also needs know how to use appropriate social relationships (social capital) and skills (human capital) and have
confidence, motivation, and vision (spiritual capital). These forms of capital
don't come automatically with physical and financial capital and usually can't
be quickly "bought" (Bourdieu 1986). Yet they are all necessary for successful
competition.

Why Is "Spiritual Capital" So Important?

As stated earlier, one of the goals of this chapter it to specially recognize the
importance of the work of early sociologists in connection with forces that are

TABLE 7-1 Kinds of Capital

Type of Capital	Advantage-Granting Substance	Sample Reference
Cultural	Customs, ways of doing things	Bourdieu 1986
Human	Education, skills	Becker 1964
Social	Social connections	Coleman 1988
Financial	Money	Smith [1776] 1877
Physical	Buildings, machines, equipment	Marx [1867] 1905
Spiritual	Inspiration, motivation, belief	Weber 1904

important in economic behavior. Unlike Marx, Weber did not believe that material conditions are the sole determinants of history. Instead, he argued that social evolution and economic progress were influenced by the ideas, ideals, and beliefs of individuals. Weber's idea is captured in the notion of spiritual capital, because spiritual capital consists of the subjective beliefs, outlooks, and ideals that guide individual choice and action. At the crux of spiritual capital is the realization that a very small difference in perspective in the minds of individuals can have profound social, political, and economic effects.

Spiritual Capital from a Standpoint of Ecological Competitive Fitness

Before further considering spiritual capital and ways that it can make a difference in competition, it is important to first review the relationship between problem representation and the structure of the external environment, because it is this relationship that influences, shapes, and guides all behavior and that serves as an arbitrator of competitive success. Essentially, we are confronted with a picture in which each individual must navigate through a world characterized by uncertainty, opportunity and danger. This situation can be represented simply in terms of:

1. Agents with interests, needs, and goals
2. Resources and resource distribution
3. Structures that channel the linkage of (1) and (2) (such as culture, laws, norms, institutions).

When we observe behavior, we are seeing the product of an interplay between agents seeking to survive and prosper in the context of ever-changing environmental structures. One way of conceptualizing this situation is to imagine two worlds that interact with each other—a world that exists as represented in the mind of the agent and a world outside and independently of the mind of the agent (see Figure 7-1). This conceptualization assumes "fit" between individual interests and resources at two levels: that of the agent as perceived by the agent, and that of the agent in relation to other agents and relative to the changing ecology of the payoff environment. The world as represented in the mind of the agent is subjective and based on experience and the art of interpretation; it consists of how the agent subjectively recognizes and understands features of the world, its opportunities, and its dangers. It is subjectively constructed and may have features that don't actually exist

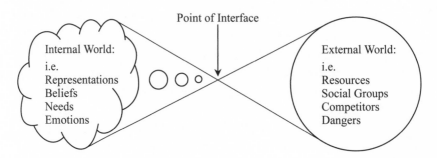

FIGURE 7-1 Internal World/External World

externally. For instance, it will have subjective features that come to have value in relation to the agent's immediate physical state and emotional and motivational needs. In contrast, the world outside the mind of the agent is more "real" in that it consists of the actual resources needed for survival and the concrete realities that emerge when multiple agents are in competition. Individuals must accurately anticipate the actions of others and real changes in the competitive environment (see Van Valen 1973). Different resource-capture strategies can be observed, and individuals may self-organize to reduce uncertainty, the costs of acquiring new information, and generally, to facilitate the distribution of resources (for discussion, see North 2005, pp. 48–59).

It would seem at first glance that the study of the external environment is to focus on what matters, because it is the reality of how individuals behave in relation to resource distribution that ultimately matters. Indeed, what I have described as behavior in relation to the external world has been the primary focus of economics and biology, and even much of psychology. However, for the purposes of understanding behavior and realities that emerge from it, how the world evolves and is represented inside the mind of the agent is as important (if not more important) as the external structure of the environment. How the world is apprehended shapes behavior, and this can not only influence competitive success, but also change the nature of the world itself.

For example, individuals holding optimistic outlooks may approach risks and uncertainty very differently than individuals which are more pessimistic. The individual who carries an optimistic outlook may be more likely to take risk, to explore and test the unknown, to encounter danger and trouble, to gain new information, and possibly, to find creative solutions (for a review and discussion, see Fredrickson 2001; also see Lucas et al. 2000). Conversely, one that lacks such an outlook may be better at avoiding risk and the associated dangers. Even if there is only one external world, it does not necessarily follow that outlooks and strategies will converge, because different kinds of experiences will provide domain-specific expertise. Individuals with different world outlooks will "see" different worlds, and as a result, will live different lives.

Outlooks as Potentially Self-Fulfilling

It is important to consider further that outlooks may not necessarily be independent of outcomes. It is reasonable to assume that individuals who believe deeply in a goal or idea may be more likely to invest heavily in it. Via passion and persistence, they may be more likely to see what seems to be an unlikely vision transformed into reality (see Vallarand et al. 2003). Thus, the outlook and beliefs of the individual may play a role in increasing the chance of the expected outcome becoming self-fulfilling (Merton 1968). Attributes of outlook or belief might also be socially validated as a by-product of information gathering in social contexts. In social situations, individuals are sensitive to behavioral cues given off by other individuals. When individuals who witness others acting with high levels of determination, confidence, and decisiveness, they may change their behavior on the basis of this information (see Marsh 1999 for examples and discussion). Further, in experimental manipulations of subjective value, internal representations of value have been directly linked to changes in competitive success in a model study animal (Marsh 1999). This result was found despite asymmetries in other dimensions such as fighting ability, size, experience, and social position in an established dominance hierarchy. This suggests strongly that outlooks can have fitness consequences.

Lastly, there is the question of how beliefs and outlooks may come to have effects and efficacy when aggregated across populations of many individuals. It is clear, for instance, that advanced modern economies function as they do to a large extent because of collectively held outlooks and beliefs. One common example is the widespread belief in the value of fiat currencies. People use currencies because they represent an abstract store of value that is widely recognized and accepted. The currencies are convenient to use. Currencies have value largely because people believe that they have value and that this value will remain stable at least in the near term. Another example is that systems of law and order will be applied fairly and that violators will have a good chance of finding justice. In either of these cases a critical mass of belief creates new forms of reality. No longer do people need to continually question the soundness of certain stores of value or live in a state of ongoing vigilance to evaluate the intentions of strangers and to police cheaters of any and every kind. They believe in a system and buy into a system that promises to provide certain safeguards, and this greatly reduces transaction costs.

These beliefs create new kinds of reality for as long as enough people have confidence in them. However, as powerful or stable as any of these realities may seem, they may vanish whenever the ideal or belief that grants them their validity is undermined. Examples of such breakdowns can be seen through history, especially in the context of perceived strength of government/political power, currency, and economic credit. Some of the most colorful examples of the power and fall of mass beliefs relate to speculation in the context of capital markets (see LeBon 1960; Mackay 1980; Kindleberger 2001). Here, investors of all types navigate in a climate characterized by expectations, hopes, and fears. Examples such as the Dutch tulip mania, the publicly traded shares of experimental "virtual companies" of the late 1990s, or today's art auctions illustrate how individuals can put tremendous trust in the value of symbolic objects simply because a few others share that trust. This trust is not necessarily irrational (for those who participate, it can even be quite profitable), but it is dependent on the stability and continuation of a collectively held set of outlooks and beliefs. In sum, outlook can have several kinds of downstream social effects. These include:

- The effects that beliefs have on the individual's behavior, which transforms the nature of competitive landscapes;
- The effects that outlooks have on social relations and outcomes of social interactions, including the construction of new norms and formal institutional structures;
- The transformative effects that may occur when similar beliefs are shared and aggregated in populations.

Ways these issues work in social contexts will be discussed later at more length. For the time being, however, the important summary point is that individual beliefs and outlooks can matter to economic behavior and fitness in significant ways and can be used to provide competitive advantages. This can be understood as spiritual capital.

The Power of One: How Spiritual Capital
Can Arise via Heroic Examples

At the group and societal levels, spiritual capital is often closely linked to the power of ideas and ideals. These typically originate from sources that are wholly intangible, but which nonetheless may be related to real needs, wants, and desires, both social and material. These wants and desires themselves may be socially constructed, thus rooted in time and place, in culture, and in the construction of new forms of social identity. The question remains, however: Where does the basic idea or ideal come from, and how does it catch hold?

We know that ideas and ideals must find resonance in the context of hope, desires, and expectations of individuals. For them to catch hold, it is necessary for the idea to seem at least somewhat realistic and worth believing in. This becomes more likely when there is some sort of proof of concept, that is, that the idea or ideal is demonstrated as being feasible, even if it is illustrated via narrative. More often, the proof of an idea or ideals begins with examples set by especially passionate, driven individuals, sometimes only a single individual. When such individuals succeed, they can serve as an example and inspiration for others. They become role models.

One of the most commonly used examples is the need of appropriate role models in disadvantaged social groups. In this case, it has been postulated that individuals look for examples to emulate (e.g., Lockwood, Jordan, and Kunda, 2002). In this narrative, qualities of the role model become centrally important in terms of the possibilities of personal aspiration and social identity. Returning to the topic of spiritual capital, ideals and related social pressure may result in a focus on individuals who hold attributes that are seen to align with success as it is socially defined, and this can be self-perpetuating. For example, a population in which people believe in upward mobility through hard work and persistence may come to have more entrepreneurial dynamism than will a population with few prospects for upward mobility and in which the prevailing sentiment is of hopelessness and despair. Taking this one step further, to the aggregate societal level, the belief in something as simple as everyone having a fair chance of success can make an essential part of the difference between general depression and prosperity (see Landes 2000). In this case, believing in the possibility of success itself is a form of spiritual capital.

Ideas and ideals are so powerful that they can create completely new social, political, and economic realities (see Rabinbach 1990; Berlin 2001).[2]

Consider democracy, communism, and massive efforts to assist victims of major catastrophes, to name only a few examples; in each case, the scale and scope of social and economic organization far exceeds what might be predicted using models where individual competition is the primary goal. Although the consideration of class and political interests accounts for these movements in a more satisfactory way, it still fails to account for the scale and degree of mass buy-in, sacrifice, and investment, which seem very much to be oriented at the pursuit of an idea or ideal, rather than direct and immediate individual economic interest. I would thus assert that when the ideal fails, these movements are subject to fail as well, irrespective of class and political interest, for lack of critical spiritual capital. On the other hand, plentiful examples of ideas, ideals, and outlooks persist even in the absence of direct political and economic support. The section that follows considers how outlooks, ideas, and ideals can persist despite economic, political, and biological costs that would suggest otherwise. As an example, we will examine one of the most universal and persistent cultural carriers of beliefs and ideals to be found, the one which Max Weber made a focus of early sociology: religion.

The Power of Otherworldly Ideals

Most models of economic and social behavior focus on competition and on the primacy of maximizing material well-being and access to scarce resources as a criterion of success. Indeed, most agents, both in the laboratory and in the field, seem to behave generally in accordance with standard postulated frameworks, especially in the absence of study designs that implicate moral considerations such as fairness.[3] Yet, some of the most successful and robust systems of ideals focus on values and goals that would seem to be in direct conflict with what these models presuppose, and often advocate incurring costs to care for others over pure self-interest. Ideas such as belief in an afterlife and in divine judgment of life works, for instance, *can completely reorder or even invert an individual's utility structures, priorities and values.* Thus, conventional, empirically derived material notions of individual welfare and return-maximizing may be turned inside out, as the power of an otherworldly idea or an ideal transforms individual outlook. Indeed, many religions and sects specifically revere qualities such as asceticism as a life ideal, as opposed to the implicit goal of maximum resource accrual that is assumed as the ideal endpoint of most competitive situations (see Weber 1927; Smith 1991).

Practiced within a group or on a large scale, such an outlook can change the nature of social reality, with results that are counterintuitive. For instance, Weber (1904) argued that "outlook" qualities such as persistence, frugality, and diligence were important in explaining why some groups enjoyed more competitive success than did other groups in developing capitalist exchange structures. Indeed, within a group, ideals such as working hard, living simply, and being generous may be highly costly and lead to competitive disadvantages to individuals in the short term. However, the practice of these same ideals of reliability and generosity may possibly give competitive advantage in the longer term as a result of efficiencies that are gained from higher levels of trustworthiness (including cooperation, fairness, and repayment of social indebtedness), sharing resources in times of need and hardship, and less of a need for in-group policing (because believers in an all-knowing deity and ultimate judgment have this as an additional concern). As is the case in any complex social and economic systems, there well might be other considerations at play, in addition to religious beliefs.

One of the most likely considerations relates to the importance of not overlooking the reality that for any good or service, individual utility value and market value (price) are seldom the same. Fixed-price markets don't capture this reality, but instead return a value of goods and services that relates to the dynamics of supply and demand. This value can be misleading because it captures the behavior of only those individuals that are active buyers and sellers in the market. Not all individuals have the benefit of such access. For instance, a poor person might not be able to buy food, shelter, or medicine at the market price, even though his utility value placed on those items is subjectively very high. In contrast, a wealthy person may increase stocks of these same items even if his marginal utility is presently very low. In either case, the utility of the goods to the individual concerned may vary over time; fortunes may change, and items that had a high utility to an individual at one time may have a much lower utility at another, and vice versa, even though the market price may remain constant. Because the marginal utility for most consumption goods diminishes as consumption increases, this necessarily provides an arbitrage opportunity for those who are wealthier to assist with those who are not, because goods bought at market price may be in turn shared in a context of utility. This buys not only goodwill, but also helps to establish a form of social interdependence that arguably strengthens group solidarity. Still, knowing the real costs and benefits from this situation remains difficult to calculate, because actions carry clear negative value on some dimensions and positive values on others, and these values may be realized across many dimensions over long periods.

Further, one could make arguments of subjective value gained on other dimensions, including the satisfaction of fulfilling an ideal, such as "doing one's share." Ideals may not seem to be so important at first glace, but people are often willing to make significant sacrifices simply to assert ideals. These sacrifices can be especially high in cases when individual pride or honor is at stake, in cases of standing up for political idealism (as in the case of entering a protest or going to war), or in devotion to a religious cause. Why do people make such great sacrifices, instead of backing down and taking a path that arguably would reduce negative impacts to their individual biological and economic fitness?

Spiritual Capital in Competition

In terms of competitive success, spiritual capital seems to be as important as other forms of capital in building advantage and securing victory. As we have seen previously, this can be the case for a number of reasons, including confidence and the effects that it will have on competitive effort and on the behavior of others, and as a factor in the emergence of norms that facilitate trust, efficiency, survival, and possibly prosperity.

For individual competitive behavior, links between subjective outlook (and particularly, positive outlook) and outcome are found commonly in various literatures that examine factors related to competitive success, ranging from sports psychology to business strategy (for overviews see Waitley 1979; Covey et al. 1994; Tracy 1994 [especially pp. 38–53]; Wind et al. 2005). The argument made again and again is that belief in abilities or a cause and the confidence that it gives provides increases advantage. Evidence suggests that in contests where other factors are roughly equally, that spiritual capital factors such as outlook, belief in one's own abilities, and the worth of a goal can make a decisive difference.

There is much progress to be made in understanding these forces in more depth, especially with regard to emergent properties to which such forces give rise when ideals and outlooks are aggregated. For the most part, these forces have been neglected in standard economic models, perhaps because of their complex, multicausal nature. However, as we have seen, although basic structural and material considerations may be sufficient to account for some kinds of economic action, they might not tell the whole story. Individuals find ulti-mate fulfillment in being able to identify with, to strive toward, and to reach ideals.[4] It is essential that individuals have opportunities to invest themselves (and sometimes pay necessary costs) in pursuing what they *believe* to be real-istic and valuable dreams. How they do this is partially rooted in the kinds of beliefs that they hold about themselves and about the world. This is spiritual capital, and it can be a critical factor in understanding economic behavior, growth, and prosperity.

References

Becker, G. 1964. *Human Capital.* New York: Columbia University Press.

Becker, G. 1976. *The Economic Approach to Human Behavior.* Chicago: University of Chicago Press.

Berlin, I. 2001. *The Power of Ideas.* Princeton, NJ: Princeton University Press.

Bourdieu, P. 1980. "Le Capital Social. Notes Provisaires." *Actes de la Recherche en Sciences Sociales* 3: 2–3.

Bourdieu, P. 1986. "The Form of Capital." Pp. 241–258 in *Handbook of Theory and Research in Education,* ed. John Richardson. Westport, CT: Greenwood Press.

Bourdieu, P. 1988. *Homo Academicus.* Stanford, CA: Stanford University Press.

Cohen, D. and L. Prusak. 2001. *How Social Capital Makes Organizations Work.* Cambridge, MA: Harvard Business School Press.

Coleman, J. S. 1988. "Social Capital in the Creation of Human Capital." *American Journal of Sociology,* 94: S95–S120.

Coleman, J.S. 1990. *Foundations of Social Theory.* Cambridge, MA: The Belknap Press of Harvard University Press.

Covey, S. R., A. R. Merrill, and R. R. Merrill. 1994. *First Things First.* New York: Simon and Schuster.

Davenport, T. O. 1999. *Human Capital: What It Is and Why People Invest in It.* San Francisco: Jossey-Bass.

Ellis, G. F. R. (2005). "Physics, Complexity, and Causality." *Nature,* vol. 435, 743.

Fredrickson, B. 2001. "The Role of Positive Emotions in Positive Psychology." *American Psychologist* 56(3): 218–226.

Granovetter, M.S. 1973. The Strength of Weak Ties, *Amer. J. of Sociology,* Vol. 78, Issue 6, 1360-80

Granovetter, M. 1985. Economic Action and Social Structure: The Problem of Embeddedness. *American Journal of Sociology* 91: 481–510.

Güth, W., S. Rolf, and B. Schwarze 1982. "An Experimental Analysis of Ultimatum Bargaining," *Journal of Economic Behavior and Organization* 3(4), 367–388.

Henrich, J., R. Boyd, S. Bowles, C. Camerer, E. Fehr, and H. Gintis. 2004. *Foundations of Human Sociality: Economic Experiments and Ethnographic Evidence from Fifteen Small-Scale Societies.* Oxford, UK: Oxford University Press

Kahneman, D., P. Slovic, and A. Tversky. 1982. *Judgment under Uncertainty: Heuristics and Biases.* Cambridge, UK: Cambridge University Press.

Kindleberger, C. 2001. *Manias, Panics and Crashes: A History of Financial Crises.* (4th ed.). London: Macmillan.

Landes, D. 2000. "Culture Makes Almost All the Difference." Pp. 2–13 in *Culture Matters: How Values Shape Human Progress*, eds. L. E. Harrison and S. P. Huntington. New York: Basic Books.

LeBon, G. [1895] 1960. *The Crowd: A Study of the Popular Mind.* New York: Viking Press.

Lin, N. 1982. "Social Resources and Instrumental Action." Pp. 131–145 in *Social Structure and Network Analysis,* eds. P. Marsden and N. Lin. Beverly Hills, CA: Sage Publications.

Lin, N. 1988. "Social Resources and Social Mobility: A Structural Theory of Status Attainment." In *Social Mobility And Social Structure,* ed. R. L. Breiger. Cambridge, UK: Cambridge University Press.

Lockwood, P., C. H. Jordan, and Z. Kunda. 2002. "Motivation by Positive or Negative Role Models: Regulatory Focus Determines Who Will Best Inspire Us." *Journal of Personality and Social Psychology.* 83(4): 854–64.

Loury, G. 1977. "A Dynamic Theory of Racial Income Differences." Chap. 8 in *Women, Minorities, and Income Discrimination,* ed. P.A. Wallace and A. Le Mund. Lexington, MA: Lexington Books.

Loury, G. 1987. "Why Should We Care about Group Inequality?" *Social Philosophy and Policy* 5: 249–271.

Lucas R.E., E. Diener, A. Grob, E. M. Suh, and L. Shao. 2000. "Cross-Cultural Evidence for the Fundamental Features of Extraversion. *Journal of Personality and Social Psychology.* 79(3): 452–68.

Mackay, Charles. [1841] 1980. *Extraordinary Popular Delusions and the Madness in Crowds.* New York: Harmony Books.

Marsh, B. 1999. *Making the Best Choice: Judgment and Strategic Decision Making Under Conditions of Risk and Uncertainty.* Doctoral dissertation, University of Oxford.

Marx, K. [1867] 1905. *Capital: A Critique of Political Economy.* New York: Modern Library.

Maslow, A. 1970. *Motivation and Personality* (2nd ed.), New York: Harper & Row.

Mauss, M. 1954 [1925]. *The Gift. The Form and Reason for Exchange in Archaic Societies.* New York: Norton.

Merton, R. 1968. *Social Theory and Social Structure* (enlarged ed.). New York: Free Press.

North, D. 2005. *Understanding the Process of Economic Change.* Princeton, NJ: Princeton University Press.

Putnam, R. 2000. *Bowling Alone: The Collapse and Revival of the American Community.* New York, Touchstone Press.

Putnam, R. D., R. Leonardi, and R. Y. Nanetti. 2003. *Making Democracy Work: Civic Traditions in Modern Italy.* Princeton, NJ: Princeton University Press.

Rabinbach, A. 1990. *The Human Motor: Energy, Fatigue, and the Origins of Modernity.* New York: Basic Books.

Schultz, T. 1961. "Investment in Human Capital." *American Economic Review.* 51: 1–17.

Smith, A. [1776] 1877. *An Inquiry into the Nature and Causes of the Wealth of Nations.* New York: Putnam.

Smith, H. 1991. *The World's Religions.* San Francisco: Harper SanFrancisco.

Tracy, B. 1994. *Maximum Achievement.* New York: Fireside Books.

Vallarand, R. J., G. A. Mageau, C. Ratelle, M. Leonard, C. Blanchard, R. Koestner, M. Gagne, and J. Marsolis (2003). "Les Passions de l'Ame: On Obsessive and Harmonious Passion." *Journal of Personality and Social Psychology* 85(4): 756–767.

Van Valen, L. (1973). "A New Evolutionary Law," *Evolutionary Theory* 1, 1–30.

Verter, B. 2002. "Spiritual Capital: Theorizing Religion with Bourdieu Against Bourdieu." *Sociological Theory* 21(2): 150–174.

Waitley, D. 1979. *The Psychology of Winning.* New York: Berkley Books.

Weber, M. [1904] 1958. *The Protestant Ethic and the Spirit of Capitalism.* New York: Scribner's.

Weber, M. [1915] 1946. "The Psychology of the World's Religions." Pp. 267–301 in *From Max Weber,* ed. H. Gerth and C. W. Mills. New York: Oxford University Press.

Weber, M. 1927. *General Economic History.* Trans. F. Knight. New York: Greenberg.

Wind, Y., C. Crook, and R. Gunther. 2005. *The Power of Impossible Thinking.* Philadelphia: Wharton School Publishing.

Notes to Chapter Seven

1. As the term has been used by Verter, 2002.

2. As Weber notes: "Not ideas, but material and ideal interests, directly govern men's conduct. Yet very frequently, the world images that have been created by ideas have, like switchmen, determined the tracks along which action has been pushed by the dynamic of interest" ([1915] 1946:280).

3. Evidence from experimental economics suggests that people will insist on "fairness" even when they don't need to and will even go out of their way and incur personal cost to sanction those who defect (see Güth, Rolf, and Schwarze 1982; Henrich et al. 2004).

4. Abraham Maslow's empirically derived "hierarchy of needs" (Maslow 1970) provides a useful taxonomy for the purposes of thinking about this passage from fulfilling material needs to "higher" needs.

8 Political Economy and Religion in the Spirit of Max Weber

Robert J. Barro, Harvard University, and
Rachel M. McCleary, Harvard University

THE ECONOMICS OF RELIGION IS A GROWING ENTERPRISE, with principal origins going back to Adam Smith (1791) and Max Weber (1930). Modern research applies the Smith–Weber framework theoretically and empirically to the two-way interaction between religion and political economy. With religion viewed as a dependent variable, a central question is how economic development and political institutions affect religious participation and beliefs. With religion as an independent variable, a key issue is how religiosity affects individual characteristics, such as work ethic, honesty, and thrift, and thereby influences economic performance. In this paper, we sketch previous studies of this two-way interaction but focus on our ongoing quantitative research with international data.

Believing, Belonging, and Economics

Theories of religion as a dependent variable break down into demand-side and supply-side models, though economists naturally combine the two approaches. An influential demand-side analysis is the secularization model. In this model, economic development reduces individual participation in formal religious services and personal prayer, decreases religious beliefs, and diminishes the influence of organized religion on politics and governance. Some of these ideas go back to Wesley's (1951) eighteenth-century essay "The Use of Money" and Weber (1930) and appear in more recent forms in Berger (1967) and Wilson (1966). Extreme versions of the secularization hypothesis are in Hume (1757) and Freud (1927), who viewed religious beliefs as mainly reflections of fear and ignorance. Thus, they predicted that religion would decline in response to advances in education and science and to movements away from the vicissitudes of agriculture and toward the greater economic security of advanced, urbanized economies. In Marx's (1913) analysis, the decline of religion is one manifestation of a broader trend toward "modernization."

Azzi and Ehrenberg (1975) pioneered the application of the rational-choice approach to the demand for religion. A key feature is a link between religiosity and the probability of salvation. As we discuss in the next section, this link might reflect perceived effects of religious participation and beliefs—more generally, "good works"—on the chance of being saved. Alternatively, along Calvinesque lines, it might be that economic success and religious faith provide signals that a person has been chosen for salvation. Azzi and Ehrenberg weigh the benefits from religiousness against the time and other costs of greater participation. Hence, they predict—consistent with the secularization view—that an increase in real wage rates reduces participation in religious activities. (The assumption is that the higher productivity signaled by a higher real wage rate does not translate into correspondingly greater productivity for time spent on religion.) The model implies that time devoted to formal religious services and personal prayer will be high among persons with low value of time, such as women not in the labor force and retired persons. In addition, older people will spend more time on religion if the probability of salvation depends on something like the present value of lifetime religious "outlays"—especially if past sins can be eradicated through the Catholic confession or other mechanisms for redemption.[1]

The religion-market model, developed by Finke and Stark (1992), Finke and Iannaccone (1993), Iannaccone and Stark (1994), and Iannaccone (1991), focuses on supply-side factors. Following Smith (1791), this literature argues that government regulation and subsidy influence competition among religion providers and, thereby, affect the nature of the religion product. When governments impose state religions and limit entry, the quality and variety of services are predicted to suffer. In response, people participate less in formal religion, although the effects on religious beliefs may be minor. Thus, in Davie's (1994) analysis of modern Britain, societies can have low attendance at formal religious services while still maintaining high religious beliefs— believing may be high relative to belonging.

The United States is an example of a country with a free religion market and a great variety of religious offerings. In this pluralistic setting, remarked on by Tocqueville (1835), competition generates religion "products" that are high in quality and well aligned with individual preferences about degrees of strictness and other characteristics. Hence, participation in formal religious services—and perhaps also levels of religious belief—are predicted to be high.

Weber's (1930) main analysis viewed religiosity as an independent variable that could influence economic outcomes.[2] Religious beliefs affect the economy by fostering traits such as work ethic, honesty (and, hence, trust), thrift, hospitality to strangers, and so on. By enhancing these traits, greater religiosity could spur investment and economic growth.

A key point in the Weberian framework is that religious beliefs—not, per se, participation in organized religion and personal prayer—are what matters for economic outcomes. Religious services and instruction and personal prayer are productive only to the extent that they instill greater beliefs or, perhaps, shift attention toward types of beliefs that reinforce productive economic behavior. For given beliefs, more time and other resources spent on organized or individual religion would be an economic drag, at least for measured market output (gross domestic product [GDP]).

Weber's approach contrasts with a social-capital perspective, in which the networking associated with attendance at religious services could itself be growth promoting. Weber did not view houses of worship as merely forms of social clubs: The special feature of religion is its potential influence on individual traits and values.

Salvation and Economic Incentives in the World Religions

Beliefs about salvation in the major world religions—Hinduism, Buddhism, Christianity, and Islam—provide different economic incentives. A key concept is salvific merit, that is, the connection between the perceived probability of salvation and a person's lifetime activities. Calvinist Protestantism has low or no salvific merit, in the sense that an individual is viewed as predestined to be saved or not. Therefore, individual action has no impact on the probability of salvation. At the other end, Buddhism has high salvific merit, in the sense that following a designated path of lifetime behavior leads with a great deal of assurance to salvation in the sense of enlightenment and knowledge. Catholicism, Hinduism, and Islam have medium salvific merit, in that individuals have some but not necessarily decisive influence on salvation.

Each of the major religions has some mechanism for promoting work effort and wealth accumulation, which contribute to economic success.[3] However, the incentive to acquire and accumulate property is limited in Buddhism, with its high salvific merit, because the sharing of wealth tends to be stressed. One reason for this emphasis is to ensure the survival of the community. By spiritually rewarding networks of mutual aid and charitable acts, a religion lowers the uncertainties of daily life. That is, charity is a form of communal insurance, which can be efficient if the society has a lot of uncertainty, such as that associated with agriculture. Private charity supported by religion would be particularly useful if the society lacks formal structures, such as insurance markets and government welfare programs, to deal with individual uncertainties (see Gill and Lundsgaarde 2004 and Scheve and Stasavage 2005). Buddhism also helps to ensure its own survival by linking salvific merit to particular acts—giving financial aid to the religious class, praying communally, and constructing religious edifices.

Although Buddhism and Hinduism do not have heaven and hell in the Judeo-Christian sense, the believers who perform their obligations are effectively reincarnated into heavenly intermediate stages. Those who fail to perform their obligations are reincarnated into intermediate, transitory stages of purgatory. Supererogatory acts of merit help a person move into a higher stage of heaven by earning salvific merit and can shorten a person's stay in purgatory. Reincarnation is a process that enables a person to get rid of bad karma and move toward perfection or *moksa*. In short, Buddhism and Hinduism are belief systems about how to attain perfection, which can be interpreted as a form of salvation.

At the other end, Calvinist Protestantism, with its emphasis on predestination, would seem at first glance to be weak on economic incentives. After all, according to Calvin, a person is either one of the elect or not, and no "good works" or other worldly acts can do anything about it. However, the uncertainty about salvation is also stressed, as is the motivation to gain some kind of sign that one has been chosen. In the Reformed Churches, which closely follow Calvin's theology, spiritual assurance is an outward sign (social interpretation) not a feeling or psychological state (individual interpretation). As a consequence, human activity that results in material success is the clearest signal that God has chosen the person as one of the elect who will be saved. Economic success is therefore highly valued, but charitable acts are downplayed if not, at times, condemned as going against God's will, for example, by promoting idleness.

Some Protestant religions, such as Pietism and Pentecostalism, posit an inward or personal sign of assurance of salvation. In Pietism, the doctrine of perfection (continuing to mature in faith after receiving salvific assurance) interprets good works as a spiritual sign and part of the process of perfecting one's faith. Such personal assurance motivates the believer to continue to become more perfect in his or her relationship to God. This motivation promotes continued hard work.

Islam and Catholicism interpret hell as having transitory levels with an ultimate permanent state. Heaven, like hell, has provisional states but is ultimately a permanent situation. Those who end up in hell do so as a result of their own volition and not as the result of a vengeful God. In some levels of hell, individuals who have the possibility of being saved, yet have committed serious moral wrongs, will temporarily suffer until an intermediary (angel, prophet, a believer) intercedes on the person's behalf.

Our analysis of international survey data, discussed in the next section, shows that beliefs in hell and an afterlife are highest among Muslims and other Christians, a group that includes many Evangelicals. Next highest is Catholic (and Orthodox), followed by mainline Protestants and then Hindus, who do not tend to identify with Judeo-Christian concepts of heaven and hell. (We lack sufficient data on Buddhists to separate the effects from those of other Eastern religions.)

A possible explanation for some of these findings is that Christianity, particularly mainline Protestantism, places emphasis on individual responsibility for one's religious obligations. In contrast, Islam is legalistic, stressing the fulfillment of laws that are communally enforced. The laxness of communal enforcement of religious beliefs in mainline Protestantism creates an individualistic approach to religious living, a focus on the inward, personal relationship with God. Communal enforcement in Islam stresses outward expressions of one's religiosity and accountability for one's actions to others. Therefore, in Islam, beliefs in heaven and hell are reinforced through a communally shared understanding of life-after-death. Evangelical Protestantism may be similar in this respect, with Catholicism at an intermediate position.

Another point is that, whereas Christianity posits the survival of the soul after death, Islam believes in a physical as well as spiritual survival. The

Qur'añ gives graphic and explicit details of physical sufferings in hell as well as sensual pleasures in paradise. The New Testament, by contrast, provides little detail of immortal survival in heaven and hell. Thus, the physical survival after death in Islam coupled with the knowledge provided by the Qur'añ of what after-death survival will be like, makes heaven and hell quite real for the believer.

Quantitative Analysis of International Data

Our quantitative, cross-country research, applied previously in Barro and McCleary (2003, 2006), uses modern data to test the various theories of religion as a dependent and independent variable. We want to understand how religious participation and beliefs respond to economic development and to government influences on the religion market. We seek, in turn, to see how differing degrees of religiosity and different religion types matter for economic growth and other economic and political variables.

To relate our research program to Weber's, we can note two conflicting assessments that we have received. One is that, if Weber were alive today and had access to modern data and statistical tools, he would be carrying out the type of cross-country empirical work that we have been pursuing. The other is that Weber thought that religion—notably the contrast between Protestantism and Catholicism—was important for economic development only at a particular stage of history involving the assimilation of workers into the factory system. He thought that the religious underpinnings of individual productivity were replaced later by secular institutions and, hence, that differences in religion no longer mattered much for differences in economic outcomes. Thus, Weber did not view religious differences as central in nineteenth-century Europe, and he presumably would not have expected to find important economic effects of religion in the twentieth century. So, in this view, Weber would not find so interesting our quantitative work on modern international data.

International Data on Religiosity

Our empirical research began with a previously constructed broad cross-country data set. The data include national-accounts variables and an array of other economic, political, and social indicators. Principal sources of data are Heston, Summers, and Aten (2002); the World Bank's *World Development Indicators* (2005); Barro and Lee (2001); Freedom House, and *International Country Risk Guide.*

We have expanded the data set to include measures of religiosity. The most useful sources of international data on participation in formal religious services and personal prayer and on religious beliefs are seven cross-country surveys carried out from 1981 to 2003. The four waves of the World Values Survey (WVS) are for 1981–84 (henceforth called 1981), 1990–93 (called 1990), 1995–97 (called 1995), and 1999–2003 (called 2000). There are also two reports on religion from the International Social Survey Program (ISSP): 1990–93, called 1991, and 1998–2000, called 1998. Finally, we have the Gallup Millennium Survey (1999). In this paper, we use the individual data (typically 1,000–2,000 participants in each more or less representative national survey) only to form country averages of data. This perspective accords with our focus on countrywide aspects of religion, notably the links among religiosity, economic growth, and government policies.

We used Barrett's (1982, 2001) *World Christian Encyclopedia*—henceforth, referred to as Barrett—to gauge religion adherence in 1970 and 2000. The underlying data come from censuses and surveys in which people are asked to state the religion, if any, to which they adhere. We grouped adherence into 11 categories: Catholic, Protestant (including Anglican), other Christian (independent Christian churches, unaffiliated Christians, and marginal Christians such as Mormons and Jehovah's Witnesses), Orthodox, Muslim,[4] Hindu (including Jains and Sikhs), Buddhist (including Shinto for Japan), other Eastern religions, Jewish, other religions, and nonreligion (including atheists). These data allow us to construct a measure of religious pluralism, calculated as one minus the Herfindahl index (sum of squares of adherence shares) among persons who adhere to some religion. This measure gives the probability that two persons selected randomly among persons who adhere to some religion belong to different religions.

For assessing the impact of government, we use two dummy variables: one for the existence of an official state religion and another for the presence of state regulation of the religion market. For state religion, we took an all-or-nothing perspective, based on the classifications in Barrett (1982, pp. 800–801; 2001, pp. 834–835).[5] Although the designations are influenced by legal provisions, including statements about religion in constitutions, the concept employed is ultimately *de facto.* The classifications are clearer in some cases than others. In many situations, the constitution designates an official state religion and restricts or prohibits other forms. However, even without these designations or prohibitions, governments sometimes favor a designated religion through subsidies and tax collections or through the mandatory teaching of religion in public schools. These considerations caused Barrett to classify some countries as having a "state religion," despite the absence of an official designation in the constitution. Although we disagree with the classifications in some cases, we thought it problematic to substitute our subjective judgment for Barrett's. Therefore, except in cases of obvious error, we accepted the Barrett designations.[6]

For regulation of religion, we relied on Barrett's narratives for the 1970s for each country, supplemented in some cases by individual country reports. We used one of the concepts suggested by Chaves and Cann (1992)—whether the government appoints or approves the domestic leaders of religions. One advantage of this concept is that it allows us to classify nearly all countries on a reasonably consistent basis. Note that regulation in this sense is not the same as having an official religion—some countries with state religions do not regulate in this way, whereas some countries without official religions do regulate.

Putting the various sources of religion data together, and considering the availability of data on other variables, we can carry out statistical analysis for up to 81 countries, with a maximum number of country–time observations of 258. The exact sample size depends on the measure of religiosity. For example, the Gallup Millennium Survey lacks data on most measures of religious belief, and questions on personal prayer appear in only two of the WVS waves and the two ISSP waves.

Table 8-1 shows the eighty-one countries included and the values of religion variables around 1970. Until recently, Muslim countries were underrepresented in the surveys. However, the 2000 WVS wave added a substantial number of predominantly Muslim countries. In terms of most popular religions (not necessarily a majority of those adhering to some religion), the full sample has thirty-two Catholic countries, fourteen Muslim, eleven Orthodox, ten Protestant, six Eastern religions (including Buddhist), four other religions (mainly in Africa), two other Christian (one of which is the United States), one Hindu, and one Jewish.

The sample has a lot of representation among Communist countries—twenty-two that were Communist in 1970, of which only two (China and Vietnam) are still classed as Communist in 2000. Thus, the sample is useful for assessing the effects on religiosity from current and past Communism. (We do not classify Communism as itself a form of religion.) The countries

TABLE 8-1 Religion Data for Countries in the Sample

Country	State religion (1970)	State regulation (1970s)	Pluralism index (1970)	Largest religions (1970)
Albania	0	1	0.37	Muslim
Algeria	1	0	0.02	Muslim
Argentina	1	1	0.13	Catholic
Armenia	0	1	0.22	Orthodox
Australia	0	0	0.65	Protestant/Catholic/Other Christian
Austria	0	0	0.17	Catholic
Azerbaijan	0	1	0.15	Muslim
Bangladesh	1	1	0.30	Muslim
Belarus	0	1	0.29	Orthodox
Belgium	0	0	0.09	Catholic
Brazil	0	0	0.25	Catholic
Bulgaria	0	0	0.28	Orthodox
Cameroon	0	0	0.77	Other religions/Catholic/Muslim
Canada	0	0	0.67	Catholic/Protestant/Other Christian
Chile	0	0	0.32	Catholic
China	0	1	0.43	Eastern religions
Colombia	1	0	0.07	Catholic
Croatia	0	0	0.22	Catholic
Cyprus	0	0	0.40	Orthodox
Czech Republic	0	1	0.43	Catholic
Denmark	1	0	0.04	Protestant
Dominican Republic	1	0	0.27	Catholic
Egypt	1	0	0.31	Muslim
El Salvador	1	0	0.15	Catholic
Estonia	0	1	0.54	Protestant/Orthodox
Finland	1	1	0.05	Protestant
France	0	1	0.14	Catholic
Germany (West)	0	0	0.59	Catholic/Protestant
Ghana	0	0	0.76	Other religions/Other Christian
Greece	1	1	0.11	Orthodox
Hungary	0	1	0.44	Catholic
Iceland	1	0	0.17	Protestant
India	0	0	0.30	Hindu
Indonesia	0	0	0.65	Muslim/Eastern religions
Iran	1	1	0.04	Muslim
Ireland	1	0	0.17	Catholic
Israel	1	0	0.25	Jewish
Italy	1	1	0.08	Catholic
Japan	0	0	0.40	Buddhist (Shinto)
Jordan	1	0	0.10	Muslim
Kazakhstan	0	1	0.54	Muslim/Orthodox
Korea (South)	0	0	0.74	Other religions/Eastern religions
Latvia	0	1	0.70	Orthodox/Protestant/Catholic
Lithuania	0	1	0.14	Catholic

TABLE 8-1 Continued

Country	State religion (1970)	State regulation (1970s)	Pluralism index (1970)	Largest religions (1970)
Luxembourg	1	1	0.17	Catholic
Macedonia	0	0	0.26	Orthodox
Malaysia	1	0	0.67	Muslim/Eastern religions
Malta	1	0	0.03	Catholic
Mexico	0	0	0.13	Catholic
Moldova	0	1	0.19	Orthodox
Morocco	1	1	0.02	Muslim
Netherlands	0	0	0.61	Catholic/Protestant
New Zealand	0	0	0.53	Protestant
Nigeria	0	1	0.72	Muslim/Other Christian
Norway	1	1	0.03	Protestant
Pakistan	1	0	0.06	Muslim
Peru	1	1	0.08	Catholic
Philippines	0	0	0.40	Catholic
Poland	0	0	0.06	Catholic
Portugal	1	0	0.10	Catholic
Romania	0	0	0.31	Orthodox
Russia	0	1	0.60	Orthodox
Singapore	0	0	0.63	Eastern religions
Slovak Republic	0	1	0.33	Catholic
Slovenia	0	0	0.09	Catholic
Spain	1	0	0.02	Catholic
Sweden	1	1	0.06	Protestant
Switzerland	0	0	0.57	Catholic/Protestant
South Africa	0	0	0.71	Protestant/Other Christian
Taiwan	0	0	0.56	Eastern religions/Buddhist
Tanzania	0	0	0.74	Other religions/Muslim/Catholic
Thailand	1	1	0.14	Buddhist
Turkey	0	1	0.02	Muslim
Uganda	0	1	0.76	Catholic/Other religions/Other Christian
Ukraine	0	1	0.37	Orthodox
United Kingdom	1	1	0.45	Protestant (Anglican)
Uruguay	0	0	0.16	Catholic
United States	0	0	0.69	Other Christian/Protestant/Catholic
Venezuela	1	1	0.16	Catholic
Vietnam	0	0	0.52	Buddhist
Zimbabwe	0	0	0.68	Other Christian/Other religions

NOTES: The presence of a state religion (Value 1 for the dummy variable) refers to the situation around 1970, as designated by Barrett, Kurian, and Johnson (2001, pp. 834–35). State regulation (Value 1) refers to a situation in which the state appoints or approves religious leaders. This designation comes from discussions in Barrett and elsewhere and applies during the 1970s. The pluralism index is one minus the Herfindahl index based on the fractions of adherents in 1970 to ten major religion groups, among persons expressing adherence to some religion. The religions are Buddhist, Catholic, Hindu, Jewish, Muslim, Orthodox, other Christian, other Eastern religions, Protestant, and other religions. These data are from Barrett, Kurian, and Johnson (2001). The countries shown are the ones included in the subsequent statistical analysis (as dictated by data availability).

included are richer than the world average, although poor countries have been increasingly represented over time in the WVS. For example, the full sample includes seven countries in sub-Saharan Africa.

The religiosity questions that we use concern frequency of attendance at formal religious services and personal prayer and yes-or-no answers about beliefs in hell, heaven, an afterlife, and god in some form. We also use a question that is less subject to theological differences across religions—whether the respondent self-identifies as a religious person.

Our analysis of the determinants of religiosity uses panels in which the dependent variables are country averages of answers to religiosity questions. In these panels, we include observations from different surveys at different points in time (allowing for different intercepts for the three sources: WVS, ISSP, and Gallup). In our later analysis of economic growth, to generate as many observations as possible, we assume as an approximation that a single answer to each religiosity question can be used for a given country for every period for which growth rates and the other explanatory variables were observed. In these cases, we started by defining each religiosity variable to be the value from the 1990 WVS if this observation were available. Then we filled in missing values by using, in sequence, the 1981 WVS, 1991 ISSP, 1995 WVS, 1998 ISSP, 1999 Gallup, and 2000 WVS.[7]

The first part of Table 8-2 shows the averages (unweighted across countries) of the religiosity responses for the countries with data. Average attendance at formal services at least weekly is 31%, monthly is 41%, and participation in personal prayer at least weekly is 57%. Average beliefs were 43% for hell, 59% for heaven and an afterlife, and 82% for the existence of god in some sense. 69% of persons said that they were at least somewhat religious.

The remainder of Table 8-2 shows means and standard deviations in 1970 and 2000 for the other variables used in the analysis. Thirty-six percent of the countries had state religions in 1970, compared to 44% in 2000; this increase reflected mainly the 13 previously Communist countries, such as Bulgaria and Ukraine, that implemented state religions between 1990 and 2001.[8] Forty-one percent of countries regulated religion (in the sense described before) in the 1970s. Averages for the religious pluralism indicator (one minus the Herfindahl index for the ten religion categories noted before) were 33% in 1970 and 37% in 2000.

The fraction of the overall population designated as nonreligious, according to Barrett, averaged 11% in 1970 and 10% in 2000, with the small decline

TABLE 8-2 Means and Standard Deviations of Variables

Cells show unweighted averages across countries; standard deviations in parentheses

These variables are averaged over different surveys, with levels geared to 1990

Weekly or more attendance at formal services	0.31 (0.25)	
Monthly or more attendance at formal services	0.41 (0.25)	
Pray at least weekly	0.57 (0.24)	
Belief in hell	0.43 (0.27)	
Belief in heaven	0.59 (0.26)	
Belief in afterlife	0.59 (0.22)	
Belief in god	0.82 (0.18)	
Religious person	0.69 (0.19)	
	1970	**2000**
Log(real per capita GDP)	8.455 (0.959)	8.982 (0.962)
Years of schooling	4.93 (2.54)	7.60 (2.49)
Urbanization rate	0.52 (0.24)	0.63 (0.21)
Life expectancy at age one	67.4 (7.2)	72.2 (7.8)
Population share >65	0.068 (0.039)	0.092 (0.049)
Population share <15	0.342 (0.096)	0.275 (0.096)
State religion	0.36 (0.48)	0.44 (0.50)
State regulation of religion (1970s)	0.41 (0.49)	—
Religious pluralism	0.33 (0.24)	0.37 (0.24)
Communist	0.27 (0.44)	0.025 (0.157)
Nonreligion	0.110 (0.176)	0.096 (0.112)

These variables are relative to the population with adherence to some religion

Buddhist	0.041 (0.156)	0.038 (0.142)
Catholic	0.359 (0.401)	0.355 (0.388)
Hindu	0.015 (0.094)	0.015 (0.089)
Jewish	0.015 (0.096)	0.013 (0.090)
Muslim	0.165 (0.309)	0.176 (0.310)
Orthodox	0.125 (0.274)	0.112 (0.249)
Other Christian religions	0.063 (0.098)	0.089 (0.116)
Other Eastern religions	0.039 (0.130)	0.036 (0.123)
Other religions	0.033 (0.084)	0.027 (0.062)
Protestant	0.146 (0.262)	0.140 (0.241)

NOTES: The columns show the (unweighted) means and standard deviations of the variables used in Table 8-3, along with some other variables. The sample for most variables is the set of observations for which data are available for participation in formal religious services and for the explanatory variables used in Table 8-3. The maximum sample size is 81. For the religious belief variables, the samples are smaller. The religious participation and belief variables come from the various international surveys. Each country with data on these religiosity variables appears only once in computing these averages. The value entered is for WVS 1990, if available. Otherwise, values from the other surveys are used in the sequence WVS 1981, ISSP 1991, WVS 1995, ISSP 1998, Gallup 1999, and WVS 2000. Values from surveys other than 1990 WVS are adjusted based on comparisons across the sets of overlapping observations, for example, between WVS 1990 and WVS 1981. The religion fractions, aside from nonreligious, are relative to the population of adherents to some religion. The nonreligion fraction is relative to the total population.

attributable to the ending of Communism in many countries. For 59 never-Communist countries, the average for nonreligion rose from 3% in 1970 to 6% in 2000. Note that these averages are unweighted across countries. In particular, the averages for Communist countries do not give a large weight to the unusually high nonreligion fractions in China, 64% in 1970 and 50% in 2000.

The bottom part of the table shows the breakdown of religion adherence by type among persons adhering to some religion. Note again that the countries are equally weighted in these averages. In 2000, Catholic is the largest (36%), followed by Muslim (18%), Protestant (14%), Orthodox (11%), and other Christian (9%).

Determinants of Religiosity

Table 8-3 shows panel estimates of systems in which the dependent variables are survey responses about monthly participation in formal religious services, weekly personal prayer, belief in hell and an afterlife, and whether people self-identify as religious.[9] These panels combine data from up to seven survey waves. (The Gallup data are available only for participation, and the prayer question comes from only four waves.) The last column, for the fraction of the population designated as having some religious adherence, is based on Barrett's census/survey information for 1970 and 2000.

The explanatory variables include a single indicator of economic development (the log of real per capita GDP), dummy variables for state religion and state regulation of religion, dummies for contemporaneous and lagged Communism, adherence shares for eight religion groups (where Buddhist and other Eastern religions were combined), and the measure of religious pluralism (computed from the adherence shares for ten groups). The adherence shares are relative to persons identifying with some religion and have Catholic as the left-out category.[10] The samples comprise up to 81 countries and 258 observations for monthly attendance in column 1. Fewer observations are available for the other systems.

Estimation (by three-stage least-squares) allows for correlation of the error terms across surveys for a given country and treats the log of per capita GDP as potentially endogenous with respect to religiosity. Hence, the instrument lists exclude the log of per capita GDP but include two arguably exogenous determinants of economic development: absolute degrees latitude (which relates to climate and, hence, to health and agricultural productivity) and a dummy for land-locked status (which affects transport).[11] The idea is to isolate effects of economic development on religiosity, rather than the reverse.

The other explanatory variables are treated as exogenous and are, therefore, included in the instrument lists. For the measures of religion adherence (among persons adhering to some religion), a possible problem would be reverse influences of religiosity on conversion into particular faiths. Probably a more serious concern involves reverse effects of religiosity on the interplay between state and religion, specifically, on the tendency to have state religion and to regulate religion.

In another study (Barro and McCleary [2005]), we took a political-economy approach to the determination of state religion. Key factors were concentration of persons in the main religion, country size, present and past Communism, and a country's long ago history of state religion. Some role was played by colonial and legal origins that had an impact on religious freedoms. However, we did not find important effects on the probability of state religion from per capita GDP or the composition of religion adherence. These results leave open the possibility that other sources of differences in religiosity could influence the probability of state religion and of state regulation of religion.

One striking result from Table 8-3 is that per capita GDP has a significantly negative effect on all of the religiosity indicators.[12] This finding supports the secularization view as well as the rational-choice perspective of Azzi and Ehrenberg (1975). An irony in this finding is that the proponents of secularization have been in retreat over the last couple decades; for example, Berger (1996) recanted his previous stance.

One observation that boosted the nonsecularists in the social-science literature is that the rich United States has maintained high levels of religiosity over time—Table 8-4 shows that the United States is a substantial outlier in the systems estimated in Table 8-3. Another consideration is that secularists, such as Hume, were unreasonably extreme, arguing counterfactually that religion would rapidly disappear as a significant social force. More accurately, secularization can be seen as a gradual tendency.[13] An additional reason for the success of the nonsecularists is that the highly religious Muslim countries have received increased attention by scholars and nonscholars.

In contrast to the intellectual triumph of the nonsecularists, the overall international evidence reveals a strong negative effect of economic development on religiosity in its various manifestations. For example, starting at sample means in 2000, consider a one-standard-deviation increase in the log of per capita GDP (by 0.96), so that GDP per capita rises from $7,940 to $20,700. This change is estimated to lower monthly attendance by 0.17 (from 0.41 to 0.24),

TABLE 8-3 Determinants of Religious Participation and Beliefs

(Cells show estimated coefficients with standard errors in parentheses)

Explanatory variable	(1) Monthly attendance at formal services	(2) Weekly personal prayer	(3) Belief in hell
Log of per capita GDP	−0.797 (0.093)**	−0.992 (0.147)**	−0.727 (0.114)**
State religion	0.48 (0.15)**	0.14 (0.25)	0.68 (0.19)**
Regulation of religion	−0.52 (0.11)**	−0.49 (0.16)**	−0.42 (0.13)**
Religious pluralism	0.93 (0.36)*	-0.17 (0.57)	0.18 (0.46)
Communist	−1.36 (0.20)**	−1.52 (0.26)**	−0.90 (0.22)**
Ex-Communist (1995)	−1.27 (0.20)**	—	−0.68 (0.24)**
Ex-Communist (1998–2001)	−1.06 (0.16)**	−1.21 (0.23)**	−0.50 (0.20)*
ISSP data	−0.154 (0.088)	−0.32 (0.13)*	0.32 (0.09)**
Gallup data	−0.038 (0.076)	—	—
Eastern religion fraction†	−2.23 (0.26)**	−2.13 (0.42)**	0.26 (0.36)
Hindu fraction	−1.41 (0.53)**	−2.09 (0.68)**	−1.40 (0.61)*
Jewish fraction	−2.13 (0.52)**	−1.79 (0.57)**	−0.64 (0.44)
Muslim fraction	−0.73 (0.22)**	−0.09 (0.39)	2.37 (0.29)**
Orthodox fraction	−1.26 (0.23)**	−0.76 (0.30)*	−0.22 (0.28)
Other Christian fraction	0.52 (0.68)	1.01 (0.97)	2.64 (0.79)**
Other religion fraction	−2.03 (1.10)	−3.10 (2.61)	−1.54 (1.24)
Protestant fraction	−1.93 (0.20)**	−1.03 (0.30)**	−1.48 (0.24)**
Sources	WV81, WV90, IS91,WV95, IS98, GA99, WV00	WV90, IS91, IS98, WV00	WV81, WV90, IS91,WV95, IS98, WV00
Number of countries and total observations	81, 258	63, 127	76, 197
Number of observations for each equation	22, 37, 21, 39, 27, 48, 64	31, 15, 29, 52	21, 34, 15, 37, 29, 61
R-squared for each equation	.80, .57, .68, .73, .68, .69, .69	.61, .71, .58, .65	.66, .46, .63, .63, .60, .74

*$p < 0.05$, **$p < 0.01$.

†Buddhist plus other Eastern religions.

††WV = World Values Survey, IS = ISSP survey, GA = Gallup Millennium Survey.

NOTES: In columns 1–5, each system has 4 to 7 equations, corresponding to observations on the dependent variables at 4 to 7 points in time: 1981–84, called 1981 (World Values Survey data mostly for 1981, supplemented by information from Gallup surveys for a few countries); 1990–93, called 1990 (WVS data mostly for 1990, plus observations on some variables for Greece in 1987 from *Eurodim*); 1990–93, called 1991 (ISSP data mostly for 1991); 1995–97, called 1995 (WVS data mostly for 1995 or 1996); 1998–2000, called 1998 (ISSP data mostly for 1998); 1999 (Gallup Millennium Survey); and 1999–2003, called 2000 (WVS data). The Gallup data cover only for participation in formal religious services. The prayer question is from 1990 and 2000 WVS and 1991 and 1998 ISSP. The dependent variables are population averages for countries of (1) attendance at least monthly at formal religious services, (2) personal prayer at least weekly; (3) belief in hell, (4) belief in an afterlife, and (5) self-identification as religious. The measured value is the fraction of people participating, the fraction who hold the belief, or the fraction who consider themselves religious. The form of each dependent variable is $\log[x/(1.02-x)]$, where x is the fraction of persons participating or believing or considering themselves religious. In column 6, the dependent variable is computed from the fraction of persons adhering to some religion, according to Barrett, Kurian, and Johnson (2001).

TABLE 8-3 Continued

(Cells show estimated coefficients with standard errors in parentheses)

Explanatory variable	(4) Belief in afterlife	(5) Consider self as religious person	(6) Religious fraction of population
Log of per capita GDP	−0.417 (0.093)**	−0.481 (0.120)**	−0.505 (0.077)**
State religion	0.46 (0.16)**	0.18 (0.17)	0.58 (0.16)**
Regulation of religion	−0.46 (0.11)**	−0.37 (0.12)**	−0.58 (0.14)**
Religious pluralism	−0.26 (0.38)	−0.20 (0.44)	—
Communist	−1.02 (0.18)**	−1.03 (0.21)**	−2.12 (0.29)**
Ex-Communist (1995)	−0.93 (0.22)**	−0.53 (0.22)*	—
Ex-Communist (1998-2001)	−0.63 (0.17)**	−0.51 (0.19)**	−1.08 (0.17)**
ISSP data	0.19 (0.08)*	−0.63 (0.11)**	—
Eastern religion fraction†	−0.20 (0.26)	−1.92 (0.30)**	—
Hindu fraction	−1.90 (0.46)**	−0.95 (0.66)	—
Jewish fraction	−1.19 (0.36)**	−1.53 (0.56)**	—
Muslim fraction	1.43 (0.25)**	0.55 (0.25)*	—
Orthodox fraction	−0.30 (0.24)	0.00 (0.26)	—
Other Christian fraction	2.04 (0.64)**	1.13 (0.81)	—
Other religion fraction	−1.80 (1.05)	−0.42 (1.92)	—
Protestant fraction	−0.52 (0.21)*	−0.90 (0.21)**	—
Dummy for 2000 equation	—	—	−0.19 (0.08)*
Sources††	WV81, WV90, IS91, WV95, IS98, WV00	WV81, WV90, IS91, WV95, IS98, WV00	Barrett for 1970 and 2000
Number of countries and total observations	77, 202	74, 202	81, 142
Number of observations for for each equation	26, 34, 15, 37, 29, 61	21, 39, 14 38, 29, 61	62, 80
R-squared for each equation	.66, .51, .68, .36, .43, .62	.61, .47, .52, .44, .47, .56	.49, .61

The log of real per capita GDP, from Heston, Summers, and Aten (2002), is for 1980 in the 1981 equation, 1990 in the equations for 1990 and 1991, and 1995 in the equations for 1995–2000. The religious adherence shares and the indicator of religious pluralism (discussed in the notes to Table 8-1) are for 1970 in the 1981 equations and for 2000 in the other equations. The dummy variable for state religion is for 1970, and that for state regulation of religion is for the 1970s (see the notes to Table 8-1). The dummy for the presence of a Communist regime applies to the pre-1990 period. The coefficients in the 1995 equation and the 1998–2000 equations are different from those in the earlier equations; thereby, we can compute effects from ex-Communism. The dummy for the use of ISSP data applies to the 1991 and 1998 equations, and that for Gallup applies to the 1999 equation (entering only for attendance at religious services).

Each system is estimated by three-stage least-squares. See the text for a discussion of instruments. This procedure does not weight countries differentially for size or other characteristics. Constant terms, not shown, are included for each system. The constants vary by system but not across the equations within a system.

TABLE 8-4 Actual and Fitted Values of Religiosity
(Selected Countries from WVS 2000)

Country	Monthly	Fitted	Weekly	Fitted	Belief	Fitted
Canada	0.36	0.40	0.56	0.47	0.50	0.34
Chile	0.45	0.66	0.66	0.79	0.65	0.56
China	0.03	0.15	—	—	—	—
Czech Republic	0.12	0.23	0.18	0.32	0.13	0.31
Denmark	0.12	0.13	0.20	0.34	0.10	0.16
Egypt	0.45	0.70	—	—	1.00	0.97
Finland	0.14	0.11	0.40	0.30	0.31	0.14
France	0.12	0.29	0.20	0.44	0.20	0.25
Greece	0.34	0.22	0.55	0.44	0.41	0.39
Hungary	0.18	0.18	0.38	0.30	0.20	0.18
India	0.51	0.61	0.74	0.71	0.68	0.50
Indonesia	0.76	0.59	—	—	1.00	0.80
Iran	0.47	0.47	0.73	0.77	0.98	0.94
Ireland	0.68	0.57	0.69	0.66	0.53	0.50
Italy	0.54	0.38	0.62	0.49	0.49	0.34
Japan	0.12	0.09	0.22	0.13	0.30	0.33
Korea (South)	0.46	0.47	0.49	0.32	—	—
Lithuania	0.32	0.25	0.40	0.44	0.68	0.26
Mexico	0.75	0.61	0.80	0.81	0.75	0.47
Nigeria	0.95	0.79	—	—	0.94	0.89
Pakistan	0.91	0.78	—	—	1.00	0.99
Poland	0.78	0.34	0.78	0.53	0.66	0.33
Russia	0.09	0.13	0.26	0.27	0.36	0.30
Singapore	0.44	0.17	0.51	0.20	0.79	0.41
Slovak Republic	0.50	0.20	0.54	0.32	0.46	0.21
South Africa	0.68	0.58	0.82	0.74	0.60	0.62
Spain	0.36	0.54	0.39	0.66	0.36	0.46
Turkey	0.40	0.31	0.89	0.73	0.94	0.87
United Kingdom	0.20	0.25	0.30	0.37	0.36	0.30
United States	0.60	0.38	0.78	0.50	0.75	0.46
Vietnam	0.13	0.28	0.12	0.40	0.17	0.64

NOTES: The table lists selected countries from the 2000 World Values Survey. The fitted values for monthly attendance at religious services, weekly personal prayer, and belief in heaven come from the systems in columns 1-3 of Table 8-3.

weekly prayer by 0.23 (from 0.57 to 0.34), and belief in hell by 0.16 (from 0.43 to 0.27).

Another finding from Table 8-3 is that state religion is positively related to attendance at formal religious services and with beliefs in hell and an afterlife (columns 1, 3, 4). These results apply for a given regulatory setup and a given degree of religious pluralism. Our interpretation is that the subsidy element from state religion motivates more participation, which, in turn, instills greater beliefs. State religion is, however, not significantly related to the extent of personal prayer (column 2). That is, organized religion does not show up as a clear substitute or complement for individual prayer. Given the positive coefficients for beliefs, it is surprising that state religion is unrelated to the extent to which people self-identify as religious (column 5). However, state religion is positively related in column 6 to the fraction of the population that Barrett classifies as adhering to some religion.

For a given status of state religion, Table 8-3 shows that government regulation of the religion market is negatively related to all of the religiosity indicators. This pattern applies even to personal prayer, which was not significantly related to the presence of state religion.

Some of the patterns found for the state religion and regulation variables could reflect reverse causation from religiosity to governmental institutions and policies. However, it is unclear why these reverse effects would produce positive coefficients for state religion and negative ones for state regulation. We find it more plausible that the coefficients reveal effects of the government variables on religiosity—which are plausibly positive for state religion and negative for regulation.

Table 8-3 shows that the extent of religious pluralism (based on patterns of adherence among persons adhering to some religion) is positively related to monthly attendance at formal religious services (column 1). One interpretation, consistent with the religion-market model, is that a greater variety of religions engenders more competition (as suggested by Smith) and results, thereby, in a religion product that appeals more to the typical consumer. However, we find no significant effects of religious pluralism on personal prayer, religious beliefs, or religiousness (columns 2–5).

Contemporaneous Communism has a sharp negative effect on all of the religiosity indicators—thus, at least as gauged by survey responses, these regimes were successful at suppressing various dimensions of religion. The ex-Communism variables, applying either to the 1995 WVS wave or to survey waves for 1998–2000, show how the influence of past Communism changed during the 1990s. The results show a considerable rebound in religiosity, though more in beliefs (columns 3, 4) and religiousness (column 5) than in participation in formal services or prayer (columns 1, 2). Eventually, the anti-religion policies of Communist governments may prove to be only temporary. We reached similar conclusions about the negative effects of Communism on state religion in Barro and McCleary (2005). Communist governments almost never had contemporaneous state religions of the usual sort (except for Somalia around 1970), and many countries reinstituted official state religions between 1990 and 2001, after the fall of Communism.

For patterns of religion adherence, recall that each coefficient in Table 8-3 should be interpreted as relative to the left-out category of Catholic. The mainly negative coefficients show that adherents to other religions are typically less religious in terms of attendance at formal services, personal prayer, and beliefs (columns 1–4). Notable exceptions are Muslims and other Christians (which particularly includes Evangelicals). These groups are remarkably high on beliefs in hell and an afterlife (columns 3, 4), though not significantly higher than Catholic in attendance and prayer (columns 1, 2).

To get an idea of what the model explains and fails to explain, Table 8-4 shows actual and fitted values for selected countries from the 2000 WVS wave. The table considers monthly attendance, personal prayer, and belief in hell—corresponding to the systems in columns 1–3 of Table 8-3.

As already noted, the United States has high religiosity—and much of this behavior is not captured by the model. Monthly attendance at formal services is 60%, compared to the fitted value of 38%—corresponding values are 78% and 50% for weekly prayer and 75% and 46% for belief in hell.

The United States is not the only positive outlier in the model. Two others are Singapore (44% attendance versus fitted of 17% and 79% belief in hell versus fitted of 41%) and Poland (78% attendance versus fitted of 34% and 66% belief in hell versus fitted of 33%). Among former Communist countries, Poland is unusual in being extremely religious during the Communist period and then having mild declines in religiosity after the end of Communism. The only contemporaneous Communist countries in Table 8-4 are China (with the lowest monthly attendance, 3%) and Vietnam (also with low attendance, 13%).

Many places in western Europe have low religiosity, and much of this behavior is explained by the model. Denmark and Finland (and also Sweden, which is not shown) have less than 15% monthly attendance rates. However, Finland is much higher in religious belief than in attendance—31% for belief in hell, not well explained by the model. This pattern of high believing relative to belonging was observed by Davie (1994) to apply in modern Britain. We see something of this pattern in Table 8-4—in the United Kingdom, monthly attendance at services is 20%, whereas belief in hell is 36%.

On the other end, the most religious country in western Europe is Ireland (68% attendance and 53% belief in hell, pretty well explained by the model). Italy and Spain are less religious than Ireland but more religious than the United Kingdom, France, and Scandinavia.

Predominantly Muslim countries exhibit strikingly high levels of belief in hell—98% in Iran, 100% in Indonesia, 100% in Pakistan, and 94% in Turkey. Heavily Muslim Nigeria (about 44% of the population) also had 94% belief. However, the Muslim countries report more varied experiences with respect to participation in formal religious services—only 40% in Turkey and 47% in Iran but 91% in Pakistan.

The results on participation in religious services in Muslim countries seem to reflect differences in interpretations by survey takers and respondents in the WVS of the term "formal religious services." In some countries, women do not attend services at mosques. However, we have learned that, in some of the surveys, a yes answer to participation in formal religious services required mosque attendance, whereas, in others, participation in other types of services by women also counted as formal participation. Hence, we get puzzling patterns of differences by gender among ten predominantly Muslim countries in the 2000 WVS. Five countries (Algeria, Jordan, Morocco, Turkey, and Saudi Arabia) show much greater participation in formal services by men than women. Another five (Bangladesh, Egypt, Indonesia, Iran, and Pakistan) exhibit similar participation rates by gender. India, with a large number of Muslims in an absolute sense, is similar to the latter group in showing only a small excess of male participation over female among the Muslim population. We think that these cross-country differences reflect more about survey procedures than about reality, but we are still investigating. One important inference is that the reported participation numbers from the WVS likely understate the time devoted by the overall population of Muslims to formal religious activities.

Religious Influences on Economic Growth

Table 8-5 shows regressions in which religiosity variables are included as determinants of economic growth. The forms of these systems are analogous to those used in previous cross-country growth studies, such as Barro and Sala-i-Martin (2004, chap. 12). The dependent variable, the growth rate of real per capita GDP, is observed over three ten-year periods: 1965–75, 1975–85, and 1985–95. Explanatory variables aside from religiosity measures are the log of

TABLE 8-5 Regressions for Economic Growth
1965–1975, 1975–1985, 1985–1995

Explanatory variable†	(1) Coefficient (se)	(2) Coefficient (se)	(3) Coefficient (se)	(4) Coefficient (se)
Belief in hell	0.0036* (0.0015)	0.0049* (0.0020)	0.0121** (0.0043)	0.0123** (0.0043)
Monthly attendance	−0.0052** (0.0019)	−0.0052** (0.0020)	−0.0127** (0.0043)	−0.0121** (0.0043)
Religious laws	—	−0.0079 (0.0052)	—	−0.0014 (0.0061)
p value for attendance and belief jointly	0.003	0.006	0.005	0.007
Eastern religion share††	—	—	−0.009 (0.012)	−0.008 (0.0012)
Hindu share	—	—	−0.020 (0.013)	−0.017 (0.013)
Jewish share	—	—	0.001 (0.013)	0.002 (0.013)
Muslim share	—	—	−0.035* (0.015)	−0.036* (0.015)
Other Christian share	—	—	−0.017 (0.019)	−0.020 (0.020)
Orthodox share	—	—	−0.006 (0.010)	−0.004 (0.012)
Other religion share	—	—	0.015 (0.023)	0.013 (0.023)
Protestant share	—	—	−0.016* (0.008)	−0.015 (0.008)
p value for religion shares jointly	—	—	0.004	0.012
Number of countries and total observations	53, 153	52, 151	53, 153	52, 151
Number of observations for each period	48, 53, 52	47, 52, 52	48, 53, 52	47, 52, 52
R-squared for each period	.58, .61, .37	.61, .58, .44	.60, .63, .46	.62, .63, .47

*$p < .05$, **$p < .01$.

† Other explanatory variables were included but coefficients are not shown.

††Buddhist plus other Eastern religions.

NOTES: The dependent variables are the growth rates of real per capita GDP over 1965–1975, 1975–1985, and 1985–1995. The explanatory variables not shown are the log of per capita GDP in 1965, 1975, and 1985; years of male secondary and higher school attainment in 1965, 1975, and 1985; reciprocals of life expectancy at age one in 1960, 1970, and 1980; average ratios over each period of investment to GDP; the log of the total fertility rate in 1960, 1970, and 1980; average ratios for each period of exports plus imports to GDP, filtered for the usual relation of this ratio to the logs of population and area; the growth rate of the terms of trade over each period, interacted with the average ratio of exports plus imports to GDP; the average of the *Political Risk Services* indicator of the rule of law (the value for 1982 or 1985 appears in the first two equations); and the average for each period of the Freedom House measure of democracy (electoral rights) and its square. Columns 3 and 4 include the adherence shares for 1970 (among persons adhering to some religion) for the eight religion groups shown. The Catholic share is the omitted category. Separate constants are included for each period. For data sources, see the text. Estimation is by three-stage least squares, using beginning-of-period or lagged values as instruments. The instrument lists exclude the variables for attendance at religious services and belief in hell but include the dummy variables for state religion and state regulation of religion (described in the notes to Table 8-1), the eight religion adherence shares for 1970, and the pluralism indicator for religious adherence in 1970.

per capita GDP at the start of each period, initial values of life expectancy and years of school attainment, a measure of international openness, the growth rate of the terms of trade, indicators of rule of law and democracy, the log of the fertility rate, and the ratio of investment to GDP.

The religiosity variables are those for monthly attendance at formal religious services and belief in hell.[14] Results are similar if weekly attendance is used instead of monthly attendance and if belief in heaven or an afterlife is substituted for belief in hell.[15] Some of the systems add an eight-way breakdown of religion adherence among people adhering to some religion.

Estimation is by instrumental variables (three-stage least-squares), where the religiosity variables are treated as endogenous and are, therefore, excluded from the instrument lists. These lists include arguably exogenous variables that were found before to influence religiosity: the dummy variables for state religion and state regulation of religion, the religious pluralism indicator, and the religion adherence shares (among persons adhering to some religion). The other instruments are lags of the explanatory variables (except for contemporaneous values of the openness indicator and the terms of trade).

Because the religion adherence shares turn out to be jointly highly significant, we focus on the results that include these shares—Table 8-5, column 3. (The table shows only the coefficients on the religion variables.) The central finding is that belief in hell (or, alternatively, in heaven or an afterlife) has a significantly positive coefficient, 0.012 (se = 0.004), whereas monthly attendance has a significantly negative coefficient, –0.013 (0.004).[16] Thus, higher believing relative to belonging encourages economic growth. To put it another way, growth is enhanced when the religion sector is unusually productive in the sense that output (belief related to an afterlife) is high compared to input (attendance). Given beliefs, more time and resources spent on formal religion can be viewed as a drain on resources, which detracts from market output (GDP).

Figures 8-1 and 8-2 depict graphically the estimated relations between economic growth and the two religiosity variables. The first figure shows the partial relation between growth and the belief-in-hell variable. This graph holds constant the other explanatory variables, most importantly, monthly participation in formal religious services. Thus, the positive relation shown applies when belief increases for given participation. The second figure shows the partial relation of growth to monthly participation in formal religious services. In this case, the negative relation applies for given belief in hell.

The results do not imply that participation in formal religious services is necessarily negative in a full sense for economic growth. This relation

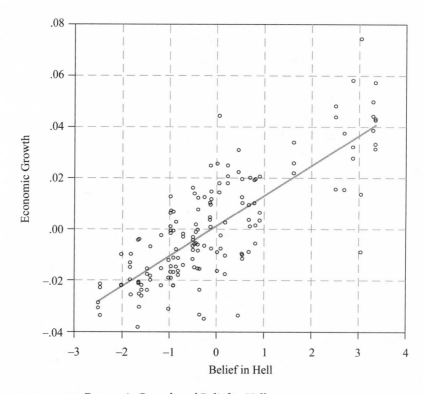

FIGURE 8-1 Economic Growth and Belief in Hell

NOTE: The graph shows the partial effect of belief in hell on the growth rate of real per capita GDP, based on the system in Table 8-5, column 3. The horizontal axis has $\log[x/(1.02-x)]$, where x is the fraction of persons who believe in hell. The average value along the vertical axis was normalized to zero.

depends on the extent to which greater attendance at services instills higher beliefs, that is, on a "religion production function," which we have not yet estimated. However, if we consider overall differences in religiosity—cross-country variations in belief and attendance when we assume the typical positive relation between these two highly correlated variables—the relation with growth turns out to be weak.

The results accord with Weber's emphasis on religion as an influence on beliefs and thereby on individual traits and values. In particular, religion does not operate as a social organization that enhances productive social capital and networking. In that scenario, we would anticipate a positive relation between growth and participation in formal services, rather than the negative relation found in the data. Thus, the special aspect of religion is belief formation.

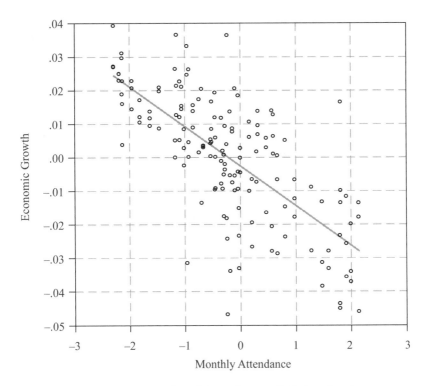

FIGURE 8-2 Economic Growth and Attendance at Religious Services

NOTE: The graph shows the partial effect of monthly attendance at formal religious services on the growth rate of real per capita GDP, based on the system in Table 8-5, column 3. The horizontal axis has $\log[x/(1.02-x)]$, where x is the fraction of persons who attend services at least monthly. The average value along the vertical axis was normalized to zero.

As discussed before, the influences of afterlife beliefs and religious participation may affect economic growth differently depending on the underlying theology. For example, differences across religions involve the meaning of *hell* and *afterlife* (as well as *god*), the connections between beliefs and "good behavior," and the roles of formal religious services. We tried to assess whether the belief and participation variables affected growth differentially between Muslim and other religions and between a broad Eastern group (Buddhist, Hindu, and other Eastern religions) and other religions. These efforts failed to find significant differences, but the limited data may account for this failure.

In Table 8-5, column 3, the eight religion adherence shares are jointly highly significant—the p value for joint significance is 0.004. Among the individual variables, the most striking result is the significantly negative coefficient on Muslim adherence.[17]

One possible channel for a negative effect of Muslim adherence on growth is that governments of predominantly Muslim countries tend to employ legal and regulatory systems that deter economic activity. Kuran (2004) emphasizes this possibility, particularly because of legal structures that restrict contracts, credit, insurance, and corporate ownership. We attempted to assess this channel by using variables from Fox and Sandler (2003) concerning the interplay between religion and state. Unfortunately, the data do not cover directly the concepts stressed by Kuran; the closest measure is a dummy variable for whether religion has a substantial effect on a country's laws and regulations.[18] We used the earliest date available, around 1990. When we add this variable (included also in the instrument lists) in column 4, we get a coefficient that differs insignificantly from zero, and the coefficient of the Muslim adherence variable is virtually unchanged. In column 2, which excludes the religion adherence shares, the coefficient on the religious laws variable is more negative but still not significantly different from zero. Thus, the results fail to confirm the conjecture that the negative estimated effect of Muslim adherence on economic growth operates through legal and regulatory practices. However, the results may be weak because the available data do not adequately capture cross-country differences in the legal-regulatory influences from religion.

Another possibility, mentioned before, is that, because of gender differences in practices and survey procedures, the WVS measures of participation in formal religious services understate the time spent on religious activity in Muslim countries. We have tried to correct for these problems by using information on male participation only, by considering the incidence of very high attendance (more than once per week), and by using information on time spent at personal prayer (available, however, for only about half the Muslim countries). These efforts have been unsuccessful.

We have preliminary results aimed at evaluating the idea that religious beliefs enhance economic growth by shaping individual traits and values. We used the WVS waves for 2000 and 1995 to get responses to three questions related to traits stressed by Weber: work ethic, honesty, and thrift. For work ethic, we used the fraction of persons indicating that they thought that valuing hard work was an important trait for children to learn at home. For honesty, we used the "trust" question used in previous studies.[19] Our assumption is that a person trusts other people when they are, in fact, more honest. For thrift, we used the fraction of persons indicating that "thrift, saving money and things" was an important trait for children to learn at home.

A cross-sectional regression for seventy-eight countries with the work-ethic indicator (from 2000 or 1995 WVS) as the dependent variable is, with standard errors in parentheses:

work ethic = 1.20 + 0.200*(belief in hell) – 0.091*log(per capita GDP)
    (0.28) (0.098)   (0.027)
        + 0.307*ex-Communist, R^2 = 0.55.
        (0.052)

This regression gives some indication that greater belief in hell instills (or goes along with) stronger work ethic.[20] Also interesting is that work ethic declines significantly with the log of per capita GDP but is significantly higher (for given per capita GDP and religiosity) in former Communist countries.

These kinds of results are much weaker for the other two traits considered. For trust, the only significant coefficient is a positive one for the log of per capita GDP, and the R^2 is only 0.21. For thrift, the only significant coefficient is a positive one for ex-Communism, and the R^2 is only 0.13. Thus, Weber may have been right in emphasizing the religion link with work ethic.

Concluding Observations

We focused on macroeconomic aspects of the interplay between religion and political economy. Thus, our empirical work relied on survey information aggregated to the country level on attendance at formal religious services, participation in personal prayer, beliefs in hell and an afterlife, and religiousness. These data derive from seven international surveys conducted between 1981 and 2003.

We found that the various measures of religiosity tended to decline as an indicator of economic development—per capita GDP—increased. Moreover, the instrumental estimation suggests that this linkage represents causation from economic development to religiosity, rather than the reverse.

The presence of a state religion tended to raise attendance at religious services and religious beliefs. We think that these effects reflect the subsidies that typically flow to the established religions. Religiosity tended to decline in response to government regulation of the religion market and with the presence of a Communist government. The elimination of many Communist regimes led to a recovery of religiosity in most of these countries during the 1990s.

Greater religious pluralism, measured by the diversity of adherence among the major religions, tended to raise attendance at formal services but was not significantly related to the other indicators of religiosity. For most religions— Protestant, Orthodox, Hindu, Jewish, and Eastern religions (including Buddhist)—attendance at formal religious services and the other religiosity indicators were lower than was Catholic. The main exceptions were Muslim and other Christian religions (which particularly picks up Evangelicals). Muslim and other Christian religions were particularly high on beliefs in hell and an afterlife.

Future research could usefully extend our findings in a number of directions. One extension would be to use Fox and Sandler's (2003) data to sort out the effects on organized religion from various governmental regulations, subsidies, and prohibitions. Other work we have been pursuing (Barro and McCleary 2005) analyzes the presence or absence of state religions. It would also be valuable to assess the relationships between religiosity and political and social indicators, including measures of electoral rights and civil liberties.

References

Arruñada, Benito (2004). "Catholic Confession of Sins as Third-Party Moral Enforcement," unpublished, Universitat Pompeu Fabra, January.

Azzi, Corry, and Ronald Ehrenberg (1975). "Household Allocation of Time and Church Attendance," *Journal of Political Economy*, February, 27–56.

Barrett, David B. (1982). *World Christian Encyclopedia*. 1st ed., Oxford, Oxford University Press.

Barrett, David B., George T. Kurian, and Todd M. Johnson (2001). *World Christian Encyclopedia*, 2nd ed., Oxford, Oxford University Press.

Barro, Robert J. and Jong Wha Lee (2001). "International Data on Educational Attainment: Updates and Implications," *Oxford Economic Papers*, 541–563.

Barro, Robert J. and Rachel M. McCleary (2003). "Religion and Economic Growth," *American Sociological Review*, October.

Barro, Robert J. and Rachel M. McCleary (2005). "Which Countries Have State Religions?" *Quarterly Journal of Economics*, November, 1331-1370.

Barro, Robert J. and Rachel M. McCleary (2006). "Religion and Political Economy in an International Panel," *Journal for the Scientific Study of Religion*, June, 149-175.

Barro, Robert J. and Xavier Sala-i-Martin (2004). *Economic Growth*, 2nd ed., Cambridge MA, MIT Press.

Berger, Peter L. (1967). *The Sacred Canopy: Elements of a Sociological Theory of Religion*, Garden City NJ, Doubleday.

Berger, Peter L. (1996). "Secularism in Retreat," *National Interest*, Winter, 3–12.

Chaves, Mark and David E. Cann (1992). "Regulation, Pluralism, and Religious Market Structure," *Rationality and Society*, July, 272–290.

Davie, Grace (1994). *Religion in Britain since 1945: Believing without Belonging*, Oxford, Blackwell.

Finke, Roger and Laurence R. Iannaccone (1993). "Supply-Side Explanations for Religious Change," *The Annals of the American Academy of Political and Social Sciences*, May, 27–39.

Finke, Roger and Rodney Stark (1992). *The Churching of America 1776–1990*, New Brunswick NJ, Rutgers University Press.

Fox, Jonathan and Shmuel Sandler (2003). "Separation of Religion and State in the 21st Century: Comparing the Middle East and Western Democracies," presented at the International Studies Association conference, Portland OR, February.

Freud, Sigmund (1927). *The Future of an Illusion*, New York, Norton.

Gill, Anthony and Erik Lundsgaarde (2004). "State Welfare Spending and Religiosity: A Cross-National Analysis," unpublished, University of Washington, January.

Glaeser, Edward E., David I. Laibson, Jose Scheinkman, and Christine L. Soutter (2000). "Measuring Trust," *Quarterly Journal of Economics*, August, 811–846.

Heston, Alan, Robert Summers, and Bettina Aten (2002). *Penn World Tables Version 6.1* Center for International Comparisons at the University of Pennsylvania (CICUP), October.

Hume, David (1757). *The Natural History of Religion*, edited by J. C. A. Gaskin, Oxford, Oxford University Press, 1993.

Iannaccone, Laurence R. (1991). "The Consequences of Religious Market Structures: Adam Smith and the Economics of Religion," *Rationality and Society*, April, 156–177.

Iannaccone, Laurence R. (2003). "Looking Backward: A Cross-National Study of Religious Trends," George Mason University, July.

Iannaccone, Laurence R. and Rodney Stark (1994). "A Supply-Side Reinterpretation of the 'Secularization' of Europe," *Journal for the Scientific Study of Religion*, March, 76–88.

Inglehart, Ronald and Wayne E. Baker (2000). "Modernization, Cultural Change, and the Persistence of Traditional Values," *American Sociological Review*, February, 19–51.

Kuran, Timur (2004). "Why the Middle East Is Economically Underdeveloped," *Journal of Economic Perspectives*, summer, 71–90.

Marx, Karl (1913). *A Contribution to the Critique of Political Economy*, Chicago, Kerr.

McCleary, Rachel M. (2007). "Salvation, Damnation, and Economic Incentives," *Journal of Contemporary Religion*, January.

Scheve, Kenneth and David Stasavage (2005). "Religion and Preferences for Social Insurance," unpublished, University of Michigan, March.

Smith, Adam (1791). *An Inquiry into the Nature and Causes of the Wealth of Nations*, 6th ed., London, Strahan.

Tocqueville, Alexis de (1835). *Democracy in America,* London, Saunders and Otley.

Weber, Max. (1930). *The Protestant Ethic and the Spirit of Capitalism,* London, Allen & Unwin.

Wesley, John (1951). *Standard Sermons,* edited by Edward H. Sugden, London, Epworth.

Wilson, Bryan (1966). *Religion in Secular Society: A Sociological Comment,* London, Watts.

World Bank (2005). *World Development Indicators 2005,* The World Bank, Washington DC

Notes to Chapter Eight

1. See Arruñada (2004) for a discussion of the demand for Confession.

2. The views of Wesley (1951), the founder of Methodism, on religion and economy fit with Weber in some respects. Wesley urged his congregants to "gain all you can, save all you can, give all you can." However, Wesley regretted that he had been more successful in promoting the first two tenets than the third. But the first two—akin to Weber's work ethic and thrift—are probably more important than charity as underpinnings of a productive economy. Wesley also regretted that, as his congregants became richer, they became less devout—thus giving an early empirical expression of the secularization hypothesis.

3. For a detailed discussion of the relationship between religious beliefs and economic incentives, see McCleary (2007).

4. We have a rough breakdown from other sources into Sunni, Shiite, and other types but do not use this breakdown in the present analysis. For a discussion in the context of state religions, see Barro and McCleary (2005).

5. See Barro and McCleary (2005) for a fuller discussion of the state-religion variable. This classification misses the important senses in which, for example, the state religions of England and Iran are not the same. Fox and Sandler (2003) are assembling a Religion and State data base in which they classify the relation between religion and state into four broad groupings: separation of religion and state, discrimination against minority religions, restrictions on majority religions, and religious legislation. Although each individual measure is a (0,1) dummy variable, indexes based on the large number of separate components would be nearly continuous. Unfortunately, the Fox-Sandler data are available only since 1990.

6. Barrett classifies some governments as favoring multiple religions or religion in general, although not maintaining a single religion. We classified these cases as lacking a state religion.

7. We adjusted for differences in average levels of responses from the different surveys and periods by comparing the overlapping observations for each pair of surveys, for example, 1990 WVS and 1981 WVS. This procedure means that, in some cases, the religiosity questions postdate the growth-rate observations. However, the instruments used apply to earlier points in time.

8. For the much broader sample of countries considered in Barro and McCleary (2005), the averages for state religion in 1970 and 2000 were about the same and both were much lower than the average for 1900.

9. The functional forms are logistic in the responses, thereby constraining the fitted values to lie in the interval (0,1). See the notes to Table 3.

10. Separate intercepts are allowed for the ISSP and Gallup sources, but the other coefficients are constrained to be the same for all surveys. We have tested for whether there are trends in the religiosity indicators (for given values of per capita GDP and the other explanatory variables). These tests are based on comparisons across the four WVS waves and between the two ISSP waves. The only statistically significant trend is for belief in hell, which is *increasing* over time (for given per capita GDP, etc.).

11. In a very long-term context, land-locked status may be endogenous. Our results are not sensitive to the exclusion of this instrument.

12. Inglehart and Baker (2000) report negative effects of per capita GDP on religiosity, though in systems without instrumental variables.

13. Iannaccone (2003) uses ISSP retrospective information to construct time series back to the 1920s on participation in formal religious services for 30 countries. He argues that a steady pattern of diminished participation—secularization in this sense—applies only to a few countries, such as Britain, France, and Germany.

14. These variables are entered in the logistic forms used in Table 8-3.

15. However, we get insignificant coefficients if we replace belief in hell by belief in god or by whether people self-identify as religious. Thus, afterlife-related beliefs appear to be crucial.

16. We also get this pattern in column 1, which excludes the religion adherence shares. However, these coefficients have smaller magnitudes and are less statistically significant.

17. The only other individually significant coefficient is the marginally significant, negative one for Protestant, −0.016 (se = 0.008). This result is surprising and might disturb Weber, but the coefficient has to be interpreted as a partial effect when religious beliefs and participation are held constant.

18. We also considered the Fox-Sandler indicators for religious mandates on business closings and for mandatory religious education in public schools. These variables lack any explanatory power for economic growth.

19. See, for example, Glaeser et al. (2000). The question is "generally speaking, would you say that most people can be trusted or that you needed to be very careful in dealing with people."

20. The results are a little weaker if belief in hell is replaced by belief in heaven or an afterlife.

9   Beyond Weber

Michael Novak, American Enterprise Institute*

The Strength of Weber's Thesis
in *The Protestant Ethic*

One of Max Weber's great strengths as a theoretician is his ability to grasp
what it was about his own experience that both unfitted him for grasping
certain conceptions the way other peoples did (e.g., that profit seeking is un-
dignified) and simultaneously made it possible for him to grasp realities in
a way that those same others could not (e.g., that religious imagination and
belief can affect economic attitudes and habits).[1] He had a kind of genius for
putting himself in other people's shoes and then adjusting his vision until its
trajectory matched theirs. At that point, he was in position to step forward to
explain to us what we need to do to see matters as others do.

For instance, Weber felt his way back into the point of view of those who
regarded profit-making as morally suspect, ethically inferior, corrupting of
moral character—at bottom a *pudendum* that was to be tolerated only because
of the unalterable necessities of life in this world.[2] He then asked himself,
"What needs to occur to make some among such people come to think of
profit-making as a moral *duty*, an obligation, a good very much to be wished
for? And why has this extra something been so rare in economic history?" As
Richard Swedberg explains in his magisterial book, this point is very near to
the heart of Weber's insight into the role of the Calvinist ethic in lifting economic motivations into a new mode.[3]

Weber was extraordinary in teasing out from raw data the slight shifts in how humans view the human story, in ways that dramatically alter human economic actions. Or if I may put it this way, he was a master of the dramatic story they believe themselves to be acting out with their lives; that is to say, of the background narrative imagination that individuals bring to their actions. In addition, Weber showed how this internalized narrative came to be lived out by many individual economic agents, whose actions slowly wove a growing social system quite different from other economic systems and cultural narratives around the world. Weber's erudition swept across many centuries of history for these comparisons.[4]

Moreover, Weber had a family experience that hit him in the face with this particular problem.[5] His grandfather, Karl Weber, was a linen merchant who took a relaxed view of business, rarely seeking to increase his profits or improve his productivity. He was content to make enough to get by, to live (as it were) on his sinecure. Karl Weber had four sons, the eldest of whom, Karl David, inherited the family business. To the dismay of the family, Karl David, Max Weber's uncle, somehow caught the "capitalist spirit." Uncle Karl worked long and hard to rationalize, modernize, and improve the business. He methodically and systematically recruited ambitious peasants, sought out new buyers, and introduced innovative, more efficient means of mechanical production.[6] By contrast, his brother Max, the famous sociologist's father, studied the law and entered politics, first as a magistrate and later as a parliamentarian. Max Weber, Sr., lacked his brother's drive and ambition, and sought instead to imitate the more comfortable, leisurely lifestyle of his father.

For the young Max Weber, these different modalities of economic action became a puzzle he wished to understand better. As a youngster, he had received Benjamin Franklin's *Necessary Hints to Those That Would Be Rich* and *Advice to a Young Tradesman* as Christmas presents. Franklin's attitude toward work and wealth was starkly different from Weber's father's attitude, but not so entirely different from his uncle's. How do differences and likenesses such as that come to be? How did it come to pass, for example, that Benjamin Franklin—situated in "the back-woods small bourgeois circumstances of Pennsylvania . . . where business threatened for simple lack of money to fall into barter"—could have a better sense of the capitalist spirit than did the great financiers of fourteenth- and fifteenth-century Florence, "the money market of all the great political Powers"?[7]

When I first encountered this anecdote about Weber's early home life, and the puzzle it posed for him, I was greatly relieved. I myself faced a not dissimilar puzzle. Neither a social scientist nor an economist nor an economic historian, I had nonetheless been struck by rather graphic differences among people that I had met in my early years. People really do imagine the world around them in starkly diverse ways, as shown sometimes by their actions, sometimes by their words. Many in my environment were anticapitalist and anticorporation and even hostile to the Protestant ethic (such as they imagined it). I don't only mean some of my Catholic teachers, but also some of my quite secular professors in the university. Yet, whatever anybody said, it seemed unarguable to me that the opportunities provided by the American way of life to poor immigrants such as my family were quite beneficial. As a young and green professor, despite a pronounced leftish tendency myself, I eventually found myself writing an essay on capitalism entitled, "An Underpraised and Undervalued System."[8] In a word, I began trying to learn to see things through the lens of the Protestant ethic (following in Weber's shoes). How could I make sense of the economic actors I saw around me? What motivated them? Why are they different from people I had met in Italy in 1956–1958?[9] Why are my uncles and cousins quite unlike the descriptions of ordinary Americans, immigrants, and workers in so many sociological articles and books, especially by Europeans?[10] Why did Spanish colonial America, with its abundance of gold, silver, and other precious metals, become so poor, especially compared to relatively hardscrabble British colonial America, with its hard-earned tobacco, furs, and timber?[11]

Doubts about the Thesis

Let me confess at the outset that I found some of Max Weber's comments about Catholics and Catholic cultures distorted by a distinctive Protestant sense of superiority, a sense of superiority quite prevalent in Weber's circles.[12] Nonetheless, I was determined to suspend reflexive resistance and simply take in all I could from him, before weighing the evidence and passing judgment.

Weber especially impressed me in the way he raised two questions. First, as Adam Smith and others had noted long before Weber, there are many areas of the world in which people—even dedicated, persistent, industrious people—would, if paid at piece rate, work only to a target they set for themselves, then stop.[13] When Weber noticed that some groups were gripped by what he perceived as a new and different work ethic, such that they felt a kind of duty to earn as much as they could and to go constantly beyond their earlier gains, he wondered how that transformation of values had occurred. Second, I was fascinated by Weber's diagnosis of the psychological dynamics of this new duty to increase one's store and to better one's condition.[14]

Weber's investigation of these questions obliged him to differentiate among the economic effects of major varieties of Protestant theology: Calvinism, Pietism, Methodism, and the Baptist sects.[15] (He also devoted considerable, if intermittent, attention to Roman Catholicism and Lutheranism.) Yet he was careful to point out that, if the decisive factor was religious—or, more precisely, born of pastoral advice intended to bring theological tenets down to practice—over time that factor might well become secularized and in that form could persist for many generations in quite thoroughly secular forms. He made this clear even in the man he chose as his prototypical exemplar of the new ethos, Benjamin Franklin, who was no pious evangelical but a worldly-wise, eudaemonistic, cheerful pragmatist.[16]

Four decades ago, when I was studying the history and philosophy of religion at Harvard, the influence of Weber's American patron, the distinguished Talcott Parsons, was very much present, not least through his student Robert N. Bellah and some of *his* students, such as David Little and Ralph Potter. Most of my classes were held at the Harvard Divinity School, whose atmosphere in those days was anything but procapitalist. Nearly all the theologians there were intensely hostile to capitalism; Paul Tillich repeatedly proclaimed that any serious Christian had to be a socialist.[17] The theological faculty deeply resented Weber's identification of capitalism with Calvinism. Nearly all of them rejected that hypothesis out of hand; indeed, some of them seemed to hate the very suggestion of it. Invariably they would complain that Weber totally misunderstood Reformed theology. They would then point out that for the crucial details of his thesis Weber relied not on creedal statements or formal treatises, but rather on the pastoral writings of ministers like Richard Baxter, better known for his down-to-earth concerns than for heavy theorizing. My colleagues would point out passages in Calvin's *Institutes* that demonstrated his (quite sincere) conviction that the ultimate purpose of human life is not tireless devotion to an earthly calling, but rather faith in the revelation of Christ. Any suggestion of an innate affinity between Protestant theology and capitalism could therefore be dismissed: Weber simply distorted the theology.

In later years, I came to see that my own hostility to capitalism occluded my ability to read certain evidence fairly. Something similar may have affected my fellow theologians. In their haste to fault Weber for misreading Calvin, they themselves ended up misreading Weber. What Weber tries to demonstrate is *not* that the capitalist spirit was born of Calvinist theology purely and directly, but rather from pastoral difficulties that Calvinist theological commitments tended to trigger.[18] Calvin insisted that the absolute sovereignty of God demanded acknowledgment of the doctrine of predestination: God not only foreknows, but actively wills the salvation of some and the damnation of others. Calvin's effort to stress the sheer unmeritedness of the gift of friendship with God for all eternity is admirable. Problems emerged, however, when his teaching was promulgated in pastoral settings among ordinary people. In preaching the doctrine, Reformed clergy sometimes found that their congregations became quite anxious over the state of their souls and began seeking signs by which they might reassure themselves.

> The question, "Am I one of the elect?" must sooner or later have arisen for every believer and have forced all other questions into the background. And how can I be sure of this state of grace? For Calvin himself this was not a problem. He felt himself to be a chosen agent of the Lord, and was certain of his own salvation ... Quite naturally, this attitude was impossible for his followers as early as [Theodore] Beza, and, above all, for the broad mass of ordinary men.[19]

Thus, Weber saw in the doctrine of predestination an extreme inhumanity that caused a feeling of unprecedented inner loneliness and was thus responsible for enormous suffering among the faithful.[20]

As a result, Reformed ministers close to ordinary people began to advise dedicated effort in one's calling as a way to overcome normal anxieties about one's election. Even if such advice consisted solely of such words as, "Just continue being conscientious in your work, and do the best you can," it was quite enough to launch a huge psychological thrust toward economic success.

> So far as predestination was not reinterpreted, toned down, or fundamentally abandoned, two principal, mutually connected, types of pastoral advice appear. On the one hand it is held to be an absolute duty to consider oneself chosen ... On the other hand, in order to attain that self-confidence intense worldly activity is recommended as the most suitable means. It and it alone disperses religious doubts and gives the certainty of grace.[21]

Here, in other words, is a classic and powerful instance of the Law of Unintended Consequences. A formal doctrine whose original intention was to remove all concern with works-righteousness ended up propelling its adherents toward an unprecedented, almost painful, obsession with their works.

To be truthful, I did not find Weber's exposition entirely convincing; he imagined a much too expressly theoretical turn of thought, as in the preceding quote. I find it hard to believe that any person actually thought or felt that way. Still, as I have tried to express in my own sentences, I can imagine down-to-earth equivalents of something like the mechanism he described. In sum, what I really loved in Weber was not so much how plausible or implausible his analysis might be but, rather, the doubly ironic turn of his thought. First, he showed that the doctrine of predestination had totally unforeseen psychological consequences. Then he showed that these seemingly negative consequences had extremely beneficial economic effects—in fact, economically revolutionary effects.

Going beyond Weber

For such reasons, the thesis of Max Weber has remained alive in my consciousness these many years, always less precise than I would have wished it to be, always as fertile and provocative as I first found it, raising as many questions as it seemed to settle. Of course, I encountered many scholars who found plenty to argue against in Weber's thesis and in some or all of the evidence he had adduced in its favor.[22] Indeed, it was often quite fashionable to hold that Weber, despite making an enormous, creative, and fertile contribution to the whole field of economic sociology and history, was wrong in major lines of his argument.

For instance, Weber seemed to understand capitalism more in terms of duty, asceticism, and self-denial and seemed to focus on a calculation of gain and increase and on a purely formal, mechanical idea of logic and reason. Examples of this conception abound in *Protestant Ethic,* but a few passages should illustrate what I mean:

> And, as a rule, it has been neither dare-devil and unscrupulous speculators, economic adventurers such as we meet at all periods of economic history, nor simply great financiers who have carried through this change, outwardly so conspicuous, but nevertheless so decisive for the penetration of economic life

with the new spirit. On the contrary, they were men who had grown up in the hard school of life, calculating and daring at the same time, above all temperate and reliable, shrewd and completely devoted to their business, with strictly bourgeois opinions and principles.[23]

Waste of time is thus the first and in principle the deadliest of sins. The span of human life is infinitely short and precious to make sure of one's own election. Loss of time through sociability, idle talk, luxury, even more sleep than is necessary for health, six to at most eight hours, is worthy of absolute moral condemnation.[24]

Let us now try to clarify the points in which the Puritan idea of the calling and the premium it placed upon ascetic conduct was bound directly to influence the development of a capitalistic way of life. As we have seen, this asceticism turned with all its force against one thing: the spontaneous enjoyment of life and all it had to offer.[25]

The religious valuation of restless, continuous, systematic work in a worldly calling, as the highest means to asceticism, and at the same time the surest and most evident proof of rebirth and genuine faith, must have been the most powerful conceivable lever for the expansion of that attitude toward life which we have here called the spirit of capitalism.[26]

This last selection, in particular, points to a crucial tendency of Weber's thought. Once capitalism became divorced from its original religious impulses, it would turn into what Weber described as *ein stahlartes Gehause* (roughly, a steel-sheathed house), famously rendered by Parsons as "an iron cage." If the Puritan *wanted* to work in a calling, Weber concludes, *we* "are forced to do so." The "inexorable power" of the capitalist ethic, shorn of its religious origins, rests upon "mechanized foundations." Weber discerns in this atheistic, secular system a "mechanical petrification." He describes the modern man of 1900 in terms quite as bleak as those of such poets Matthew Arnold, T. S. Eliot (in *The Wasteland*), and Ezra Pound. Weber even alludes to Goethe in describing modern men as "Specialists without spirit, sensualists without heart; this nullity imagines that it has attained a level of civilization never before achieved."[27] Weber's description, say, of the America I knew seemed to me a rather gloomy, excessively static, and imprisoning vision of a system that, on the contrary, is often marked by the joy of discovery, serendipity, surprise, novelty, a positive vision of the future, optimism, happiness, fulfillment, and gratitude. Weber stressed asceticism and grind; the heart of the system is actually creativity.

I alluded to this duality in the title of one of my books (an introduction to religious studies): Religion consists not only in an arduous, ascetical *ascent of the mountain,* but also in the grace, joy, freedom of the *flight of the dove.*[28] If it is a Protestant tendency to keep applying moral pressure in the direction of a restless perfectionism, it is a Catholic tendency to take restful pleasure in joy and gratitude.[29] When in ecumenical work we put both these tendencies together, we fuse the complementarities of restless concern and restful rejoicing.

In more practical economic terms, the Protestant ethic delights in hard work, asceticism, an always unsatisfied striving for yet more; the Catholic ethic, in insight, initiative, creativity, discovery, the Don Quixote factor. Put theologically, the Protestant ethic tends to emphasize the factors involved in conversion and change of life, that is to say, the changes wrought by redemption. The Catholic ethic has historically worked also to honor the goodness of creation—admittedly wounded, but nonetheless good. The impact of Protestant striving has given a dynamism to economic life. The impact of Catholic delight in the goodness of creation has, by comparison, sometimes encouraged less energy for change and for economic (but not for artistic) creativity.

Monastic Creativity, Lay Creativity

Weber was no doubt correct to call Latin monasticism the first "systematic method of rational conduct with the purpose of overcoming the *status naturae,* to free man of his irrational impulses and his dependence on the world and on nature."[30] But Weber erred in assuming that the Benedictine ideal of worldly withdrawal remained the exclusive mode of Catholic asceticism. Indeed, as early as the eleventh century, the regular canons of towns and villages throughout Europe began to adopt the Rule of St. Augustine and live the monastic life while ministering to the growing urban populations. Western monasticism moved still closer to the life of the laity with Robert of Molesme and the establishment of the Order of Citeaux in 1098. Indeed, as Randall Collins has shown, one of the primary economic drivers in the great revival of European commerce in the twelfth century was the rise of Cistercian monasteries:

> These monasteries were the most economically effective units that had ever existed in Europe, and perhaps in the world, before that time. The community

of monks typically operated a factory. There would be a complex of mills, usually hydraulically powered, for grinding corn as well as for other purposes.
In iron-producing regions, they operated forges with water-powered trip-
hammers; after 1250 the Cistercians dominated iron production in central
France. Iron was produced for their own use but also for sale. In England, the
entire monastic economy was geared toward producing wool for the export
market. The Cistercians were the cutting edge of medieval economic growth.
They pioneered in machinery because of their continuing concern to find la-
bor-saving devices. Their mills were not only used by the surrounding populace
(at a fee) for grinding corn but were widely imitated. The spread of Cistercian
monasteries around Europe was probably the catalyst for much other economic
development, including imitation of its cutthroat investment practices.[31]

In brief, Weber is wrong to separate the ethic of the monks too severely from
the ethic of lay persons who come under their influence. Lay Catholics, too,
felt a vocation of their own, a sense of holiness in their daily work, and a desire to perform it perfectly for God. The decisive moment for Catholic lay asceticism occurred not with the monks (as Weber would have it) but with the
mendicants. The Dominicans and the Franciscans introduced lay Catholics
to the rhythms of the *vita apostolica*. From them especially, the Catholic laity
learned to cherish the holiness in their daily work and a desire to perform it
perfectly for God. Yet I do concur with Weber that the Protestant Reformation
unleashed a special dynamic energy. I would only add that this dynamic was
in evidence not only among Calvinists, but also among freethinkers, Catholics, and Jews, as Trevor-Roper and many others have pointed out.[32]

Creativity in America

In addition, the new form of economy developed in America provided ever
clearer evidence of factors about which Weber gave too impoverished an account. In unexpected ways, which would not, however, have surprised Tocqueville, the distinctive experience of economic life in America falls as much
within the Catholic way of looking at things as within the Protestant ethic described by Weber. The joy of discovery, the delight in novelty, the love of risk
and surprise, the frequently experienced disproportion between effort and rewards—all these Tocqueville points out in considerable detail in his account
of economic life in America. The typical American, Tocqueville observed,

lives in a land of wonders; everything around him is in constant movement, and every movement seems an advance. Consequently, in his mind the idea of newness is closely linked with that of improvement. Nowhere does he see any limit placed by nature to human endeavor; in his eyes something which does not exist is just something that has not been tried yet . . . Choose any American at random, and he should be a man with burning desires, enterprising, adventurous, and, above all, an innovator.[33]

Although Americans retained a strong notion of human imperfection and the need for checks and balances—in other words, a nonutopian understanding of human nature—they also took an almost Catholic delight in the goodness and possibilities and wonders of creation. "Chance," Tocqueville notes,

> is an element always present to the mind of those who live in the unstable conditions of a democracy, and in the end they come to love enterprises in which chance plays a part. This draws them to trade not only for the sake of promised gain, but also because they love the emotions it provides.[34]

It is rather surprising how absent these notes are in Weber, unless one recalls the somber side of his account of the Protestant ethic. Weber, it seems to me, was not a little pessimistic regarding the Protestant ascendancy in modern life. He had a sense of foreboding about modern bourgeois economic culture, and he sometimes longed, by way of contrast, for the romance, danger, and vigor of the long-ago life of the Teutonic Knights.[35]

The Transformation of Values

Many scholars have remarked that, although Weber gave an explanation for the sudden burst of entrepreneurial activity among certain Calvinists in the wake of the Protestant Reformation, he himself was the first to admit that once that break with the economic past had been made, even secularized motives sufficed. In other words, religious passion may have been necessary for the breakout from the fierce inertia of the past, but much cooler (even secular) passions would afterwards suffice. There is, of course, the rival hypothesis of Adam Smith, which has the advantage of being formulated upon a much more generic basis. Smith argued that during the eighteenth century a great many human beings from many different cultural backgrounds were discovering two "natural desires" implanted in the human breast, to which earlier scholars (not being much interested in economic matters) had paid too little attention. One of these was the natural desire "to truck, barter, and exchange,"[36] and the other was the natural desire "of bettering our condition."[37] In societies in which no economic growth is visible, or in which a cycle of prosperity is followed swiftly and inexorably by a cycle of decline, the second of these two natural desires may be beaten down by hard experience and in a fashion repressed.

Hannah Arendt, however, notes that the example of the steady overcoming of poverty in America, even among the poorest and commonest people, awakened "*Das Sozial Problem.*" For the first time, people could see that poverty was not a necessary natural condition. At least, a modest universal prosperity had been attained on one new continent, and so, by inference, the prison of poverty could be broken through universally, if only the right sort of system were put in place. This insight into the fact of economic growth on one continent inspired the belief both that it could be imitated on other continents and that, if it *could* be achieved, there arose a *moral imperative* to reach it. In other words, given the stunting of human possibility inflicted by immemorial poverty, if the chains of poverty could be systematically broken, they ought to be broken.

In this fashion there did, indeed, occur "a transformation of values." For centuries, people had held almost universally that "ye have the poor always with you" (Matthew 26:11). But, in fact, a new conviction was already replacing the old; viz, that it is a moral obligation of societies as well as of individuals to overcome poverty, at least gradually and steadily, perhaps even by revolutionary action. This transformation might also be stated in another way: Whereas earlier poverty had been taken to be the natural condition of most human beings everywhere, later it came to be considered as counter to nature, immoral, the result of inadequate social systems. In America, the process of moving up out of poverty, generation by generation, came to be called "fulfilling the American dream."

Trevor-Roper and many other scholars noted that many early outbursts of enterprise, hard work, and stunning economic growth had become manifest not only among Weber's Calvinists, but in a diverse array of social and cultural contexts, notably in certain Catholic cities in northern Italy and in Catholic quarters of cities of France such as Liège, as well as in cities where the first entrepreneurs were predominantly skeptics and freethinkers and from a wide variety of other religious backgrounds. What all seemed to hold in common, not necessarily in the same spirit, was a strong sense of enterprise (of insight, discovery, and invention especially) as well as a talent for organization and practical execution—plus, to touch on Weber's main point, participation in the new moral sensibility that there are new worlds to create and new wealth to bring into existence.

Many spiritual impulses fed this new sensibility, not only the ironic outcomes of the Calvinist doctrine of predestination. One among them was the sense of new possibilities launched into history by the romantic stories emanating from the New World in America, South and North. The sheer *newness* of America fueled the European imagination; here was native soil, barely trod by human feet, full of wonders, bounding with untapped potential. Nobody describes this encounter better than Tocqueville:

> It was then that North America was discovered, as if God had held it in reserve and it had only just arisen above the waters of the flood. There, there are still, as on the first days of creation, rivers whose founts never run dry, green and watery solitudes, and limitless fields never yet turned by the ploughshare. In this condition it offers itself not to the isolated, ignorant, and barbarous man of the first ages, but to man who has already mastered the most important secrets of nature, united to his fellows, and taught by the experience of fifty centuries.[38]

Upon such a stage, men might dare to dream the impossible. This continent opened new vistas, offering wholly new perspectives. It invited its inhabitants to participate in creation as they never had before, to delight in discovering the workings of nature. No less an authority than Lincoln saw this tendency among his countrymen:

> In anciently inhabited countries, the dust of ages—a real, downright old-fogyism—seems to settle upon, and smother the intellects and energies of man. It is in this view that I have mentioned the discovery of America as an event greatly favoring and facilitating useful discoveries and inventions.

Columbus's achievement was, to Lincoln's mind, "most favorable—almost necessary—to the immancipation [sic] of thought, and the consequent advancement of civilization and the arts."[39] It is this element of discovery—so natural, indeed so central, to the American experience—that is manifestly missing from Weber.

The Global Transformation

In the century since 1904, the world has seen more than a hundred nations undergoing massive economic and political transformation. Such transformations have put Weber's thesis to the test. Toward the end of the last century, particularly, several scholars were struck by the number of disparate nations in which something at least very *like* Weber's thesis seemed to be being vindicated: an enormous transformation of attitudes toward work and wealth, preceded by or accompanied by something like a profound religious conversion.[40] Scholars today have a wealth of data to collect and reflect upon from the new so-called economic miracles since, say, the end of World War II. Nation after nation, sometimes region after region, has entered upon the journey of rapid economic growth and political transformation. Since 1980, in a story very largely still untold, China and India have between them raised more than half a billion of their citizens out of poverty in their rapid adoption of economies of enterprise, relatively free markets, low taxation, and global trade. In a fascinating study of (and *apologia* for) emerging globalization, Jagdish Bhagwati observes that "according to the Asian Development Bank, poverty declined from an estimated 28 percent in 1978 to 9 percent in 1998 in China. Official Indian estimates report that poverty fell from 51 percent in 1977–78 to 26 percent in 1999–2000."[41]

There is no doubt about Weber's identification of moral and spiritual factors that are crucial in such eras of rapid social transformation. Again, it is probably true that in most cases, if not all, some fairly close analogues of the Protestant ethic turned out to be in evidence. Yet it can hardly be maintained that the version of Calvinism identified by Weber is or needs to be present. Although his thesis requires a broader, more generalized restatement, his identification of a spiritual and moral component necessary for successful economic activity has turned out to be more useful than ever. Countries that neglect the moral dimension in their efforts to secure economic growth are likely to pay a very heavy price in economic breakdowns of many kinds.

In short, despite the materialistic assumptions and prejudices of the twentieth century, it turns out that success in economics is very largely dependent on the spiritual and moral qualities embodied in the practice of economic agents. Moral and spiritual flaws have economic consequences. In economic transactions, failures in insight, determination, perseverance, honesty, respect for law, cooperativeness with one's fellows, fairness in one's dealings, and other breakdowns of the human spirit are self-punishing. Even certain worldviews are self-punishing, for instance, the view that economic innovation violates divine taboos or that the pursuit of economic growth is morally inferior to stasis. Max Weber pioneered in drawing the attention of economists (and others) to this crucial dimension of economic behavior, and that is the solid rock under just one of his several claims to scholarly immortality.

References

Barro, Richard J. and Rachel M. McCleary. 2003. "Religion and Economic Growth across Countries." *American Sociological Review* 68: 760–81.

Bhagwati, Jagdish. 2004. *In Defense of Globalization.* New York: Oxford University Press.

Collins, Randall. 1986. *Weberian Sociological Theory.* New York: Cambridge University Press.

Crowe, Frederick E., S.J. 1959. "Complacency and Concern in the Thought of St. Thomas Aquinas." *Theological Studies* 20: 1–39.

Eisenstadt, S. N., ed. 1968. *The Protestant Ethic and Modernization.* New York: Basic Books.

Lee, Felicia R. 2004. "Faith Can Enrich More than the Soul." *New York Times,* January 31: B7.

Lincoln, Abraham. 1989. "Lecture on Discoveries and Inventions." Jacksonville, Illinois, February 11, 1859. *Speeches and Writings: 1859–1865.* Washington, DC: Library of America.

Little, David. 1969. *Religion, Order, and Law.* New York: Harper & Row.

Mitzman, Arthur. 1970. *The Iron Cage: An Historical Interpretation of Max Weber.* New York: Knopf.

Novak, Michael. July/August 1977. "An Underpraised and Undervalued System." *Worldview* 9–12.

Novak, Michael. 1978. *Ascent of the Mountain, Flight of the Dove: An Invitation to Religious Studies.* New York: Harper & Row.

Novak, Michael. March 1982. "Why Latin America Is Poor." *The Atlantic Monthly* pp. 66–75.

Novak, Michael. 1989. *Catholic Social Thought and Liberal Institutions: Freedom with Justice.* New Brunswick, NJ: Transaction.

Novak, Michael. 1991. *The Spirit of Democratic Capitalism.* New York: Simon & Schuster.

Novak, Michael. 1993. *The Catholic Ethic and the Spirit of Capitalism.* New York: Free Press.

Novak, Michael. 1997. *The Fire of Invention.* Lanham, MD: Rowman & Littlefield.

Novak, Michael. April 1999. "Controversial Engagements." *First Things.*

Parisi, Faustino. June 2004. "Lo spirito del capitalismo con M. Weber ed oltre M. Weber." *Studia Moralia* 42:1.

Samuelson, Kurt. 1964. *Religion and Economic Action,* trans. E. G. French. New York: Harper & Row.

Smith, Adam. [1776] 1981. *An Inquiry into the Nature and Causes of the Wealth of Nations.* Indianapolis: Liberty Classics.

Swedberg, Richard. 1998. *Max Weber and the Idea of Economic Sociology.* Princeton, NJ: Princeton University Press.

Tillich, Paul. 1970. *Political Expectation,* ed. J. L. Adams. New York: Harper and Row.

Tocqueville, Alexis de. 1969. *Democracy in America,* ed. J. P. Mayer, trans. G. Lawrence. New York: Doubleday.

Trevor-Roper, H. R. 1969. "Religion, the Reformation, and Social Change." *The European Witch-Craze of the Sixteenth and Seventeenth Centuries and Other Essays.* New York: Harper & Row.

Viner, Jacob. 1978. *Religious Thought and Economic Society.* Durham, NC: Duke University Press.

Weber, Max. 1958. *The Protestant Ethic and the Spirit of Capitalism,* trans. Talcott Parsons. New York: Charles Scribner's Sons.

Weber, Max. 1966. *General Economic History,* trans. Frank H. Knight. New York: Collier.

Wogaman, J. Philip. 1977. *The Great Economic Debate.* Philadelphia: Westminster.

Notes to Chapter Nine

*The author is indebted to Christopher Levenick, W. H. Brady Doctoral Fellow in the Humanities at the American Enterprise Institute, for his assistance in preparing this manuscript.

1. For a sampling of my earlier writings on Max Weber, see *The Spirit of Democratic Capitalism* (Lanham: Madison, [1982] 1991), esp. pp. 36–39, 40–48, 371–72; *Catholic Social Thought and Liberal Institutions: Freedom with Justice* (New Brunswick, NJ: Transaction, [1984] 1989), esp. pp. 9, 12, 66–70; *The Catholic Ethic and the Spirit of Capitalism* (New York: Free Press, 1993), esp. pp. 1–10, 229–32. A remarkably good critique of my work on Weber can be found in Faustino Parisi, "Lo spirito del capitalismo con M. Weber ed oltre M. Weber," *Studia Moralia* 42:1 (June, 2004): 117–148.

2. Max Weber, *The Protestant Ethic and the Spirit of Capitalism* [hereafter *Protestant Ethic*], trans. Talcott Parsons (New York: Charles Scribner's Sons, 1958): p. 73.

3. "What is central to modern capitalism, [Weber] says, is the tendency to view work (including money-making) as a vocation or an end in itself, and it is the origin of *this* attitude that needs to be established. It is not possible, Weber argues, that this specific approach to work is somehow the invention of a single individual; it has to originate in the collective lifestyle of a group of people." Richard Swedberg, *Max Weber and the Idea of Economic Sociology* [hereafter *Max Weber*] (Princeton: Princeton University Press, 1998), p. 120.

4. Weber offers a more comprehensive account of the rise of capitalism in his *General Economic History,* trans. Frank H. Knight (New York: Collier, 1966). Swedberg correctly notes that "modern rational capitalism, as Weber repeatedly states in *General Economic History,* is the result of a number of events that took place before as well as after the creation of a new capitalist spirit. Among the events that took place before this event is the birth of the Western city and modern (Roman) law; and among

those that came after is the factory system and the systematic use of science in production." Swedberg, *Max Weber,* p. 129

5. I am indebted to Arthur Mitzman's *The Iron Cage: An Historical Interpretation of Max Weber* [hereafter *Iron Cage*] (New York: Knopf, 1970) for most of the biographical details that follow.

6. The pronounced parallels between Karl David and the (anonymous) "first innovator" who turns the "idyllic state" of precapitalist business into a "bitter competitive struggle" are hardly accidental. Cf. Mitzman, *Iron Cage,* p. 16, with the following passage from *Protestant Ethic*: "Now at some time this leisureliness [of traditional businessmen] was suddenly destroyed, and often entirely without any essential change in the form of organization, such as the transition to a unified factory, to mechanical weaving, etc. What happened was, on the contrary, often no more than this: some young man from one of the putting-out families went out into the country, carefully chose weavers for his employ, greatly increased the rigour of his supervision of their work, and thus turned them from peasants into labourers. On the other hand, he would begin to change his marketing methods by so far as possible going directly to the final customer, would take the details into his own hands, would personally solicit customers, visiting them every year, and above all would adapt the quality of the product directly to their needs and wishes. At the same time, he began to introduce the principle of low prices and large turnover." Weber, pp. 67–68.

7. Weber, *Protestant Ethic,* p. 74.

8. Michael Novak, "An Underpraised and Undervalued System." *Worldview,* July/August 1977: 9–12.

9. See, for example, the anecdotes presented in Michael Novak, *The Catholic Ethic and the Spirit of Capitalism* (New York: Free Press, 1993): pp. 17–35.

10. "I need to say a word about my Uncle Emil. He was my father's oldest half-brother, by an earlier marriage to my grandfather. He was a big, rough, hearty man who was missing one whole finger and part of another from accidents in the steel mill, and his language was goodhearted, loud, punctuated by laughter, and not at all suited for Sunday school . . . Somewhere along the line at Harvard, I got the idea of submitting every generalization I heard about 'the Americans' to a test: Did that sentence fit my Uncle Emil? For instance, in 1968 newspaper reports that 'Catholic ethnics support Wallace.' I could agree that Emil might have admired the guts of George Wallace in his presidential run in 1968, when Wallace took on 'pointy-headed liberals'. But I am certain that the Wallace crack about 'running over protestors' would have disgusted Emil; and compared to Wallace, Hubert Humphrey was the proven union man. Humphrey was Emil's kind of Democrat. Many political writers and sociologists, in those days, seemed not to know of Uncle Emil. They confused him with the migrants from the South who migrated north into the mills, and did support Wallace. Ethnicity confused them." Michael Novak, "Controversial Engagements." *First Things,* April 1999.

11. "In the plenty of good land the English colonies of North America, though, no doubt, very abundantly provided, are, however, inferior to those of the Spanish and Portugeze [sic], and not superior to those possessed by the French before the late war

[i.e., the Seven Years' War, known in the colonies as the French and Indian War]. But the political institutions of the English colonies have been more favorable to the improvement and cultivation of this land, than those of any of the other three nations." Adam Smith, *An Inquiry into the Nature and Causes of the Wealth of Nations* [hereafter *Wealth of Nations*] (Indianapolis: Liberty Classics, [1776] 1981), p. 572. See also Michael Novak, "Why Latin America Is Poor," *The Atlantic Monthly* (March 1982), pp. 66–75 and *The Spirit of Democratic Capitalism*, pp. 298–314.

12. Weber speaks, for example, of "the undoubted superiority of Calvinism in social organization" (*Protestant Ethic*, p. 108). See also Mitzman, *Iron Cage*, pp. 68–71.

13. "A man does not 'by nature' wish to earn more and more money, but simply to live as he is accustomed to live and to earn as much as is necessary for that purpose. Wherever modern capitalism has begun its work of increasing the productivity of human labour by increasing its intensity, it has encountered the immensely stubborn resistance of this leading trait of pre-capitalistic labour." Weber, *Protestant Ethic*, p. 60.

14. See, for example, Swedberg, *Max Weber*, pp. 119–24.

15. Weber, *Protestant Ethic*, pp. 95–154.

16. "One of the fundamental elements of the spirit of modern capitalism, and not only of that but of all modern culture: rational conduct on the basis of the idea of the calling was born—that is what this discussion has sought to demonstrate—from the spirit of Christian asceticism. One has only to re-read the passage from Franklin, quoted at the beginning of this essay, in order to see that the essential elements of this attitude which was there called the spirit of capitalism are the same as what we have just shown to be the content of the Puritan worldly asceticism, only without the religious basis, which by Franklin's time had died away" Weber, *Protestant Ethic*, p. 180. The earlier passage of Franklin's that Weber refers to here runs over two pages, but includes such famous moral maxims as "Remember, that *time* is money" and "The sound of your hammer at five in the morning, or eight at night, heard by a creditor, makes him easy six months longer; but if he sees you at a billiard-table, or hears your voice in a tavern, when you should be at work, he sends for his money the next day," Weber, *Protestant Ethic*, pp. 48–50.

17. Once, following a lecture to his students, Paul Tillich was asked whether he still supported socialism. The eminent theologian's answer came quickly: "That is the only possible economic system from the Christian point of view." This exchange took place in 1957. J. Philip Wogaman, *The Great Economic Debate* (Philadelphia: Westminster, 1977), p. 133. See also the writings of Tillich himself: "Religious socialism calls the capitalistic system demonic, on the one hand, because of the union of creative and destructive powers present in it; on the other, because of the inevitability of the class struggle independent of subjective morality and piety. The effect of the capitalist system upon society and upon every individual in it takes the typical form of 'possession', that is, of being 'possessed'; its character is demonic." Paul Tillich, *Political Expectation*, ed. J. L. Adams (New York: Harper and Row, 1970), p. 50.

18. In fairness, Weber does attribute part of the Protestant ethic to specifically Protestant theological principles: "It seems at first a mystery how the undoubted superiority of Calvinism in social organization can be connected with this tendency to

tear the individual away from the closed ties with which he is bound to this world . . . In the first place it follows dogmatically . . . Brotherly love, since it may only be practiced for the glory of God and not in the service of the flesh, is expressed in the first place in the fulfillment of the daily tasks given by the *lex naturae*; and in the process this fulfillment assumes a peculiarly objective and impersonal character, that of service in the interest of the rational organization of our social environment" (Weber, *Protestant Ethic,* pp. 108–09). However, as I explain at length below, Weber maintains that anxiety over salvation is what *really* impels the faithful Calvinist to devote himself entirely to worldly asceticism.

19. Weber, *Protestant Ethic,* p. 110.

20. Weber, *Protestant Ethic,* pp. 104, 110.

21. Weber, *Protestant Ethic,* pp. 111–12.

22. Useful samples of this bibliography may be conveniently found in S. N. Eisenstadt, ed., *The Protestant Ethic and Modernization* (New York: Basic Books, 1968), pp. 385–400; David Little, *Religion, Order, and Law* (New York: Harper & Row, 1969), pp. 226–237. See also the introductions to various editions of Weber's work, especially R. H. Tawney's foreword to *The Protestant Ethic and the Spirit of Capitalism* (New York: Charles Scribner's Sons, 1958) and Anthony Giddens's introduction to *The Protestant Ethic and the Spirit of Capitalism* (New York: Charles Scribner's Sons, 1976). Among the strongest critics of Weber's thesis are Kurt Samuelson, *Religion and Economic Action,* trans. E. G. French (New York: Harper & Row, 1964), and Jacob Viner, *Religious Thought and Economic Society* (Durham, NC: Duke University Press, 1978). The best single essay on the subject, in my view, is H. R. Trevor-Roper, "Religion, the Reformation, and Social Change," in *The European Witch-Craze of the Sixteenth and Seventeenth Centuries and Other Essays* (New York: Harper & Row, 1969): pp. 1–45.

23. Weber, *Protestant Ethic,* p. 69.

24. Weber, *Protestant Ethic,* pp. 157–58.

25. Weber, *Protestant Ethic,* p. 166.

26. Weber, *Protestant Ethic,* p. 172.

27. Weber, *Protestant Ethic,* pp. 181–82.

28. Michael Novak, *Ascent of the Mountain, Flight of the Dove: An Invitation to Religious Studies.* Revised edition (New York: Harper & Row, 1978).

29. See, for example, Frederick E. Crowe, S.J., "Complacency and Concern in the Thought of St. Thomas Aquinas," *Theological Studies* 20 (1959): 1–39.

30. Weber, *Protestant Ethic,* pp. 118–19. In a substantially less perceptive manner, Weber denigrates the Greek and Syriac monasticism ("that of the Orient")—the disciples of the Great Cappadoccians, most notably Basil of Caesarea—as "planless otherworldliness and irrational self-torture" (p.118).

31. Randall Collins, *Weberian Sociological Theory* (New York: Cambridge University Press, 1986), pp. 53–54.

32. Trevor-Roper expressed the same reaction I had: "This belief in the positive value of the lay calling was seized upon by Weber as the essence of the 'Protestant ethic', the necessary condition of industrial capitalism. In keeping with his view of a new, revolutionary idea in the sixteenth century, Weber ascribed it, in its verbal form, to Luther

and, in its real significance, to Calvin. But in fact, although Weber was no doubt right to see in the idea of 'the calling' an essential ingredient in the creation of capitalism, he was undoubtedly wrong in assuming that this idea was a purely Protestant idea. His philological reasoning is known to be wrong. And, in fact, the idea was a commonplace before Protestantism." "Religion, the Reformation and Social Change," p. 25.

33. Alexis de Tocqueville, *Democracy in America,* ed. J. P. Mayer, trans. G. Lawrence (New York: Doubleday, 1969), p. 404.

34. Ibid, p. 553. See also Tocqueville's comment that when the American's "setbacks teach him that no one has discovered absolute good; his successes inspire him to seek it without slackening. Thus, searching always, falling, picking himself up again, often disappointed, never discouraged, he is ever striving toward that immense grandeur glimpsed indistinctly at the end of the long track humanity must follow" (p. 453). This persistence implies a high degree of faith, hope, and trust in things unseen. In less open and favorable environments, the frequent frustration of such hopes has resulted, instead, in cynicism.

35. This note of longing is even present in *Protestant Ethic,* when Weber wonders whether "at the end of this tremendous development [i.e., the rise of capitalism] entirely new prophets will arise, or there will be a great rebirth of old ideas and ideals" (p. 182). Mitzman masterfully relates this turn in Weber's thought to the pathos of his own life. See especially *Iron Cage,* pp. 148–296, esp. pp. 181–91.

36. "It is the necessary, though very slow and gradual consequence of a certain propensity in human nature which has in view no such utility; the propensity to truck, barter, and exchange one thing for another." Adam Smith, *Wealth of Nations,* p. 25.

37. "But the principle which prompts us to save, is the desire of bettering our condition, a desire which, though generally calm and dispassionate, comes with us from the womb, and never leaves us till we go into the grave." Adam Smith, *Wealth of Nations,* p. 341.

38. Tocqueville, *Democracy in America,* p. 280.

39. Abraham Lincoln, "Lecture on Discoveries and Inventions," Jacksonville, Illinois, February 11, 1859, in *Speeches and Writings: 1859–1865* (Washington, DC: Library of America, 1989), p. 10. See also my treatment of Lincoln's lecture in *The Fire of Invention* (Lanham, MD: Rowman & Littlefield), pp. 53–59.

40. On the relation of religious commitment to economic prosperity, rigorous, systematic work has been compiled by Richard J. Barro and Rachel M. McCleary, who report a strong empirical correlation between religious belief and economic performance: "Our central perspective is that religion affects economic outcomes mainly by fostering religious beliefs that influence individual traits such as honesty, work ethic, thrift, and openness to strangers." See "Religion and Economic Growth across Countries," *American Sociological Review* 68 (October, 2003): pp. 760–81. A more approachable introduction to their work may be found in Felicia R. Lee, "Faith Can Enrich More than the Soul," *New York Times,* January 31, 2004: Section B, Page 7, Column 3.

41. Jagdish Bhagwati, *InDefense of Globalization* (New York: Oxford University Press, 2004): p. 65.

IV METHODOLOGICAL AND CONCEPTUAL ISSUES

10 The Collective Dynamics of Belief

Duncan J. Watts, Columbia University

O NE OF THE THEMES THAT DOMINATES THE *PROTESTANT Ethic* is that belief precedes rationality; that the values by which one economic order can be judged superior to another are neither universal nor exogenous, but arise endogenously within a specific historical and social context. Although this line of thought has been enormously influential in sociology, it has attracted considerable criticism as well, in particular from advocates of rational choice theory, for whom social outcomes necessarily reflect the attempts of individuals to optimally satisfy their preferences, which are in turn assumed to be stable, exogenous, and, if not universal, then at least very generally shared. How is it then, that people, collectively, come to believe the things that they do? In this chapter, I first review briefly the debate between what I call "rationalist" and "historicist" views of human behavior and argue that both perspectives suffer from different versions of the same problem— that of explaining collective behavior in terms of a representative individual. I then motivate and describe a very simple class of decision-making models, from which I conclude that rules that are simple, intuitive, and even rational from an individual's perspective can generate collective dynamics that are complex, unpredictable, and counterintuitive. As a result, collective outcomes are ambiguously related both to individual preferences and contextual variables, and causality in historical processes is rendered elusive. I conclude by describing how thinking about collective belief formation may shed light on some phenomena of contemporary capitalism.[1]

Introduction

In the *Protestant Ethic and the Spirit of Capitalism,* Weber (1958) famously argued that the origins of modern Western capitalism lie not in the inherent economic superiority of the system over its natural alternatives, but in the religious zealotry of a certain branch of Protestantism—in particular, its belief that wealth accumulation (but not consumption) was material evidence of spiritual purity. Had Protestantism not taken the turn that it did, capitalism would not have developed as we know it today. Thus, in a certain sense, capitalism—or more particularly the laissez-faire style of capitalism practiced in, for example, the United States—was an accident of history. It was, however, an accident that subsequently embedded itself into the very core of the cultures that formed around it, via a process of rationalization in terms of economic principles that came—after the fact—to be regarded as universal. Thus, the accident is not viewed today as an accident at all; rather it is seen as part of an inevitable, deterministic convergence toward rational enlightenment. Weber concluded, therefore, that although its origins may have been unpredictable, its future was not: The Protestant West had been locked into the "iron cage" of capitalism from which it would not escape.[2]

Subsequently, Weber's argument has been adopted as a central pillar of the sociological critique of economic rationality.[3] Attitudes, norms, and rules that are often justified as "rational," "efficient," and "optimal" frequently turn out to have arisen via historically and culturally specific adoption processes that, on closer inspection, seem to be driven not by rationality at all, but by explicit or implicit pressures to conform with some emerging institutional or social norm (Meyer and Rowan 1977; DiMaggio and Powell 1983). Only after such a norm is established as dominant in a particular place and time does its rational superiority with respect to what previously might have been regarded as legitimate competitors come to seem not only self-evident, but also universal. According to this argument, it is then the perceived "rationality" of such institutional arrangements that enables them to extend well beyond the specific historical-cultural circumstances in which they are established.

Needless to say, not everyone is persuaded by this style of argument. One can assert, as Weber appears to do in the *Protestant Ethic,* that beliefs precede rationality, and one can usually tell a story, as Weber does, that is consistent with the argument that these beliefs, and thus their subsequent rationalization, are culturally and historically contingent. One could just as easily assert, however, that the causal arrows points in the opposite direction. All forces, after all, even timeless and universal forces, must manifest themselves in specific places at specific times. Thus, one could interpret the relationship between Protestantism and early modern capitalism as simply the particular historical and cultural circumstances under which a universally superior economic system won out. Certain ultimately irrelevant specifics of those beliefs may be idiosyncratic and contextually dependent, but their important details reflect universal principles. It might *seem,* in other words, as if certain specific features get institutionalized for nonrational reasons and then are subsequently rationalized in terms of universal principles. But in fact the opposite process is occurring: Rationality precedes beliefs, which are therefore merely a means to an end.

On account of the contentious nature of Weber's explicitly historical account of capitalism, the *Protestant Ethic* has come to occupy an important place not only in the development of what would later become economic sociology (Swedberg 1998), but also in the long running debate over causality in historical, social process (Boudon 1998; Calhoun 1998; Goldstone 1998) that has taken place among sociologists, particularly in the last twenty years.[4] At the risk of oversimplifying what has become an increasingly differentiated and sophisticated discussion, I wish to divide the debaters into two camps, which I will label (again risking some violence) *rationalists* and *historicists.* Rationalists, on the one hand, contend that historical outcomes can only be understood when they are derived from instrumental models of individual action that are based on consistent and timeless human traits and preferences (Kiser and Hechter 1998; Goldthorpe 2000). Historicists, by contrast, contend that no such traits and preferences exist; that all action is historically contingent; and that only by examining the basis of what is considered "rational" in any particular and necessarily historical context, can one understand historical processes (Somers 1998).

The remainder of this chapter proceeds as follows. In the next section, I want to describe briefly the pros and cons of these two stylized positions before suggesting that, in fact, they have more in common than at first seems the case. Both, I shall argue, make the same fundamental error of substituting individual for collective behavior; thus both reach conclusions about causality that are ultimately unsustainable. In subsequent sections, I outline an extremely simply model of collective belief formation that helps illuminate the difference between individual and collective dynamics, then discuss some of its implications for understanding collective causality—especially the relation between beliefs and rationality. Finally, I attempt to relate this rather abstract discussion of causality to more concrete examples of contemporary capitalism.

Rationality, History, and Causality

One way to frame the argument between rationalists and historicists is that it is about the process by which people, organizations, institutions, and even societies come to place value on certain things and not others. Rationalists tend to be of the mindset that there is no such process: People always value the same things in all times and all places, and we can know what those things are simply by reflecting for a moment. Usually, rationalists conclude that people value time, goods, and money, and that all three are more-or-less interchangeable. Historicists respond that people do not, in fact, value the same things at all times and in all places, nor does the historical record suggest monotonic convergence toward universal agreement—disagreement, in fact is remarkably persistent, even within cultures (Huckfeldt, Johnson, and Sprague 2004). Furthermore, preferences, values, and beliefs do not simply vary exogenously across temporal, spatial, and social context—at least some of these variations are generated endogenously by the actions of the participants themselves, who are then subsequently subject to the "new rules."

Sewell (1996a), for example, discusses the storming of the Bastille as an event that only became an "event" in the historical sense several days after the fact, and only by virtue of the interpretation given to it by several groups of actors, most of whom were not actually involved in the storming itself.[5] As Sewell points out, the actual occurrences of July 14, 1789, were not inevitably transformative, and had the National Assembly and the King simply ignored them, we quite likely would not have heard of the Bastille today. Probably some kind of revolution would still have occurred, but the manner of its occurring and the particular mechanisms by which the sociopolitical order was overturned may have been quite different. However, the National Assembly did pay attention, elevating what could have been construed as straightforward mob violence to the lofty act of a people recovering their sovereignty. Subsequently the King paid attention as well, withdrawing his soldiers to the provinces and traveling to Paris in contrition. It was these subsequent acts, following from active decisions made by nonparticipants, that generated the real impact of the Bastille. The Bastille itself was nothing—just another random blip in a chaotic series of events of which no one was in charge—but the *story* of the Bastille was everything, uniting a nation around a new set of assumptions, beliefs, and perceptions about what was possible, acceptable, and indeed rational.

Sewell's account of the Bastille suggests that narratives are more than simply records of events; in a very real sense they *are* the events. They are not, however, events like a riot or an attack on a fort, which are merely a sequence of actions. Rather, they are events that transform the values and beliefs of actors in such a way that an action that may not previously have maximized some notion of expected utility, and hence would not have been considered "rational," now does. Or as Sewell remarks elsewhere, "Humans, unlike planets, galaxies, or subatomic particles, are capable of assessing the structures in which they exist, and acting—with imperfectly predictable consequences—in ways that change them." (Sewell 1996b, p. 251). This process, by which the nonrational becomes rational, without ever changing the interpretation of "rational" itself, lies at the heart of the historicist mindset.

Another way to think about the rationalist-historicist argument, therefore, is not simply in terms of universal rationality versus historical contingency, but in terms of the relation between two different kinds of beliefs. First are what might be called *ordinary beliefs*: beliefs that one thing is better than another; that some things are right and others wrong; or that some statements are true, whereas others are false. Ordinary beliefs are the kind we most often associate with the word *belief,* in part because they don't require any particular knowledge or reason to justify them—we simply hold them, even if we haven't thought about why. However, if we do think about why, we immediately encounter the second set of beliefs, which are beliefs about universal, or at least general, principles according to which our ordinary beliefs can be justified. For example, we may believe that the *Mona Lisa* is a great work of art, period. Such a belief is an ordinary belief, because it doesn't require us to know anything about what makes a work of art great or even care about not knowing. However, we may also believe that our ordinary belief is justified by our understanding, obtained possibly through study and experience, of the general principles of art, according to which the quality of particular works can be judged systematically. Because these latter beliefs are, in effect, beliefs about beliefs, I will call them *meta-beliefs.*

In a nutshell, the argument can then be boiled down to the question of whether ordinary beliefs derive from meta-beliefs, or the other way around. According to the rationalist perspective, meta-beliefs are simply the recognition (possibly in temporally specific language) of general, and possibly universal, principles. The key to the rationalist argument is that even if these principles have to be discovered or learned in some historically specific manner, they are not in any sense arbitrary; rather they are fixed benchmarks according to which our ordinary beliefs are either confirmed or rejected. Thus, although the process of establishing a stable set of beliefs about the world may take some time and may exhibit the appearance of chance and contingency, the end result is predetermined by the necessity of converging to unchanging principles. By analogy, it may have been an accident of history that Newton was the first person to write down the universal law of gravitation, but the mathematical form of the law itself was inevitable.

The historicist perspective, quite to the contrary, claims that ordinary beliefs simply emerge out of a cauldron of various nonrational forces and historical accidents. Once one set of beliefs has come to dominate another, it is fixed in place by a process of collective rationalization, in which meta-beliefs are actively constructed to coincide with what we already think is right (Berger and Luckman 1966). Thus, a rationalist would claim that "A is better than B because A conforms more closely than does B to the standards of some general class of things X, to which both A and B belong." A historicist, mean-while, would respond that the very standards of X that are being used to judge A and B were inferred, over time, as generalizations of specific cases, includ-ing A, around which a consensus of value or quality had already arisen. The rationalist argument, in other words, is inextricably self-referential, claiming, in effect, that "A is better than B because A is more like A than B is." As silly as this critique may sound when written down in this formal way, it is remark-ably consistent with many explanations of why certain artifacts, individuals, or even social movements have been successful, where many others that might once have been considered comparable, or even better, failed.

Why, for example, is the *Mona Lisa* far and away the most famous painting in the world? The rationalist explanation is simple: It is so famous, because it is the best. As the art historian Kenneth Clark put it, the *Mona Lisa* is "the su-preme example of perfection," which causes viewers to "forget all our misgiv-ings in admiration of perfect mastery" (Clark 1973). Sassoon (2001), however, argues that statements of this grandiose nature do not stand up to scrutiny. In-deed, there are thousands of great works of art that the *Mona Lisa*, on intrinsic merit alone, would be hard pressed to exceed. Even within the Louvre itself are hundreds of masterpieces, more than a few of which, at various stages in history, have been considered equal or superior to the *Mona Lisa*. Even Leonardo himself painted other masterful portraits, two of which hang in the very next room, which very few nonexperts could identify or even name. Was it therefore the mysterious identity of the subject? Or the intriguing smile? Maybe, but once again there are plenty of other examples of acknowledged masterpieces created in less than perfectly documented circumstances, and no one seems to have even noticed the smile until the mid-nineteenth century.

In other words, whatever characteristics we come up with to justify the known outcome, these characteristics then turn out to be shared by numerous other paintings that no one outside of the art history world has even heard of. So why is the *Mona Lisa* famous, and not a whole class of paintings that share certain highly prized characteristics? Of course, it is possible to keep adding characteristics to the list—"it's the *combination* of the smile, the use of light, the famous artist, the prestigious location," and so on, such that ultimately only one painting—the one we now know is the winner—satisfies the description. Now, however, we encounter the circular reasoning: the *Mona Lisa* is the most famous painting in the world because it is more like the *Mona Lisa* than is anything else.

The historicist critique of rationality as ultimately self-referential is therefore a hard one for rationalists to get around (as opposed to simply dismissing it as postmodernist rubbish). Unfortunately, historicists face an equally serious problem. It *may* always be the case that the very standards by which one thing is judged to be better than another are themselves the outcomes of a collective social process, and that our belief in their objectivity and universality is therefore neither objective nor universal. It *may*, in fact, be the case that we decide first what we like, and only then do we define the relevant standards such that what we already know we like turns out to be better. However, as with theories of cognitive dissonance (Festinger 1957) and social construction (Berger and Luckman 1966), the problem with this argument is that in emphasizing our tendency to rationalize what we already believe, the argument fails to account for why we believe it in the first place. This omission is important because if it turns out that our ordinary beliefs do, in fact, reflect timeless, rational principles—whether as a consequence of internal deliberation, or of some external selection process—then rationalist explanations are effectively correct, if not literally so.[6]

Historicists, in other words, can no more verify their claim that rationality is constructed in some nonpreordained manner than can rationalists verify theirs that "A won because A is the best". One way to resolve this logical im-passe, and a way on which both sides might agree, would be to conduct ex-periments. In the same way that we do for professional team sports, where the best team is judged not by its victory in a single game, but by its record of wins and losses over a playoff series, or an entire season (Lieberson 1997b), we could perhaps agree that if the *Mona Lisa* really deserves to be the most famous painting of all, then if we were to rerun history—possibly many times over—it would always, or at least most of time, prove to be the winner. Furthermore, one might invoke such a hypothetical competition to assess the relative merit not only of competing cultural artifacts, but religious ideas, social norms, and economic institutions as well.

Unfortunately, although in certain special cases it may be possible to con-duct precisely this kind of experiment (Salganik, Dodds, and Watts 2006), real historical processes only ever get run once; thus, we are not in a position to demonstrate that in some other version of the universe, the *Mona Lisa* is just another painting in the Louvre. The problem, moreover, is much worse for general historical processes like the emergence of capitalism, the course of the French Revolution, or the war on terror, than it is for cultural arti-facts. Whether or not they become popular, artifacts at least persist; thus we can measure, for example, how much better known is the Mona Lisa than Géricault's *Raft of the Medusa*; compare their respective attributes; and specu-late on why the former, not the latter, is more famous. We may not be able to experience a world in which their relative positions are reversed, but we can at least consider it. In general historical processes, however, once a decision is made to do one thing and not another, we quickly lose all ability even to imagine what other, counterfactual worlds might have looked like; thus we cannot make any sensible comparisons at all. Experimental history, therefore, is at best impracticable and at worst inconceivable.

Comparative studies, of the kind proposed by Weber and subsequently de-veloped by historical sociologists therefore seem like a reasonable compromise. We cannot rerun history, but we can consider, as Weber did, some (usually small) number of cases—for example, countries that did or did not develop a particular version of Western capitalism—and determine which of many possi-ble *ex ante* variables were consistently (a) the same across countries experienc-ing similar outcomes and (b) different across countries experiencing different outcomes. If we can identify one such variable, or combination of variables—say the presence or absence of Protestantism—we may conclude that Protestantism was the cause of modern capitalism, just as if we had run multiple experiments over and over again, and discovered the same correspondence.

"Small-N" across-case comparisons of this kind, however, have been criticized for succumbing to a linear, deterministic view of reality (Lieberson 1991; Lieberson 1994), meaning that (a) the statement "A causes B" implies that the presence of A always results in B, and A's absence always results in B's absence; (b) changes in the outcome variable are proportional to changes in the input (causal) variables; and (c) the input variables exert effects that are independent of one another. Not everyone agrees with this characterization of small-N research, and arguments abound over what methods comparative-historical sociologists really employ (Steinmetz 2004) as well as to what extent those methods really do assume a deterministic model of the world (Goldstone 1998). Nevertheless, most sociologists these days advocate a stochastic view of causality, treating their dependent variables as random functions of the independent variables.[7] The stochastic view of causality also has problems, however. To begin with, conclusions must now be probabilistic in nature; thus many more cases are required in order to reject a null hypothesis with any confidence. This "large-N" requirement alone may be sufficient to render probabilistic approaches to historical processes impractical—simply because enough cases may not exist. But even when sample size is not a limitation, causal explanations based on across-case comparisons (whether small- or large-N) face a more serious difficulty than stochasticity—namely that of non-linearity (Aminzade 1992; Griffin 1992; Quadagno and Knapp 1992).

Because they can be decomposed easily into their constituent parts, and therefore can be represented meaningfully in terms of component-level characteristics, linear systems are tremendously appealing both intuitively and analytically. Unfortunately, for the same reason, they are extremely poor representations of historical processes. In linear systems, for example, large effects can result only from large causes, similar initial states lead to similar end states, and changes in the dependent variable can be reversed by reversing the corresponding change in the independent variable. In actual historical processes, by contrast, fluctuations in timing or location that would appear trivial under most circumstances can occasionally have monumental consequences. Thus, states of the world that seemed indistinguishable at some point in time can end up looking very different at some later point; conversely, very different initial states may result in very similar-seeming outcomes. Finally, once certain critical events have transpired, it is typically impossible to return to some early state simply by reversing the values of the relevant parameters (in physical systems, this property is called *hysteresis*). Historical processes, in other words, are inextricably *non*linear.

In an attempt to get away from the implausible implications of what Abbott (1988) calls "general linear reality," some historical sociologists have therefore rejected across-case comparisons altogether in favor of either informal within-case analysis or formal descriptive methods such as sequence analysis (Abbott 2000) and narrative networks (Bearman, Faris, and Moody 1999). By incorporating the details of individual cases, rather than simply representing them as parameters (as comparative methods do), descriptive methods can begin to tease out the importance of narrative in shaping history. They also have the advantage of resituating action in the hands of individuals, rather than in aggregate variables or abstract social forces.

Unfortunately, as Abbott himself has acknowledged (Abbott 1998), it is extremely difficult to turn descriptive accounts into causal arguments. At a very minimum, the statement "X caused Y" implies that the occurrence of X is followed by some outcome Y sufficiently often that it could not be explained by chance alone. So if we knew, for example, that going on a particular diet (X) results in weight loss (Y) only about as frequently as people lose weight normally, then even if we observe some instance of a friend, say, who went on the diet and lost weight, we could not claim that the diet actually "caused" the weight loss—*even in that particular case.* Therefore, if all we have available to our analysis is a description of that one case in which X occurred and then Y occurred, we really can say nothing, one way or the other, regarding causality. To establish causality, in other words, we not only need to know about the sequence of events that actually occurred—we also need to know about all the sequences that could have occurred but didn't.

In a nonlinear, stochastic world, therefore, not only are true experiments (in most cases) impossible to conduct, but neither within-case descriptive nor across-case comparative methods can serve as substitutes (Lieberson 1997a). The inability of empirical methods to identify causality in historical processes, however, should not necessarily be construed as good news for rationalists either. As discussed earlier, in fact, the rationalist attempt to instead locate causality within universal "covering laws" of individual action is typically viewed by historicists as simply missing the point (Abbott 1998; Somers 1998). Individuals may indeed behave rationally, or at least reasonably, in the sense that given what they know, and where they are, they try to obtain the best outcome for themselves that they can imagine. However, to paraphrase Marx, they can only do so under the circumstances in which they find themselves. Thus, it is the circumstances—the "boundary conditions"—that determine not only what options individual actors face but even what preferences they have, and thus what they will perceive as "rational" in the first place. The essence of causality, in other words, lies in the construction of an agent's utility function, not in the algorithm by which the agent maximizes the function itself.

There is much to recommend the historicist critique, which in some sense is clearly correct: Anything that changes the rules by which the game is played will result in the actors behaving differently, even if at all times they are behaving rationally. But where does it lead us except back to our starting point? Historicists point out, correctly, that context matters, but in lacking plausible, action-oriented models of generative processes, they have no compelling account of how the context got to be the way it was. Rationalists meanwhile claim, also correctly, that the outcomes that persist are those that coincide with our notions of rationality, but they cannot account for the emergence of these notions without assuming the existence of the very boundary conditions that the historicists wish to explain. Is there a way to break the cycle?

I want to argue that the disagreement between the rationalist and historicist views stems not from any fundamental incompatibility between covering laws (even rational choice covering laws) and historical contingency, but rather from a common misunderstanding of the relationship between micro- (individual) and macro- (collective) behavior. Rational choice models are invariably specified in terms of the behavior of individual actors, where an "actor" can be an individual person, but can also be some aggregate entity, such as a firm or a government, of whose actions one can speak in the singular. Yet the outcomes of interest in history, including the decisions of firms, governments, and so on, are inherently the products of collectives of individuals. The mistake that the rationalist perspective makes is to treat collectives as though they were simply very large people—a convenient fiction that in economics is known as the "representative individual" assumption (Kirman 1992).

Historicists, meanwhile, make a different version of the same mistake. Although they focus on external context over internal rationality, and on contingency over optimization, they still treat the collective as an individual actor responding to its environment.[8] Often this treatment is disguised by an emphasis on aggregate or structural variables in place of explicitly identifiable actors, but regardless of the labels attached to the variables (which in some cases refer to the characteristics of individuals and in others to characteristics of populations), the causal logic requires the assumption of a representative agent.[9] It is the assumption of the representative agent itself, along with the required logical conflation of individual and collective units of analysis, wherein the fundamental error lies.

To illuminate the problem of the representative agent, I want to focus on the micro-macro aggregation process; that is, the business of how individual actors making individual decisions—about what to do, what to buy, or what to believe—manage to generate the collective outcomes—such as social movements, market demand, and religious fervor—that the historian actually observes. To make some progress, I consider only a very special class of micro-macro aggregation phenomena, namely binary decision-making problems. Within that class, I want to argue that under reasonably general conditions, individuals—even individuals exhibiting a fair degree of rationality—will make decisions based in part on the decisions of others. Although this point is neither new nor particularly surprising (at least to most sociologists), its implications for macro-sociological phenomena remain poorly understood.

The Collective Dynamics of Beliefs

The key point to make with respect to the formation of collective beliefs is that individuals do not form their beliefs independently. In this sense, beliefs are part of a much larger class of decisions which, as Schelling (1969; 1973; 1978), Granovetter (1978), and others (Katz and Lazarsfeld 1955; Hedstrom 1998; Watts 2003), including a growing number of economists (Leibenstein 1950; Young 1993; Bernheim 1994; Young 1996; Morris 2000; Brock and Durlauf 2001; Durlauf 2001; Blume and Durlauf 2003), have pointed out, exhibit what might be called *decision externalities,* meaning that the likelihood of choosing some particular alternative depends in some manner on the choices of others. Fashions, fads, and manias—whether in regard to modes of dress (Simmel 1957; Blumer 1969), norms of behavior (Mackay 1932; Aguirre, Quarantelli, and Mendoza 1988), or styles of thought (Sperber 1990), are perhaps the most obvious examples of decisions made on the basis of other people's behavior (Meyersohn and Katz 1957). But even adoption decisions of an apparently more objective nature, including those related to farming techniques (Ryan and Gross 1943), medical drugs (Coleman, Katz, and Menzel 1957), contractual arrangements (Young and Burke 2001), and organizational strategies (Becker 1970; DiMaggio and Powell 1983; Davis 1991) exhibit similar characteristics.

Although decision externalities appear to be widespread, their precise origins remain a matter of some speculation. Experiments in social psychology beginning with Sherif (1937) and Asch (1953) have demonstrated the importance of group pressure in determining the choices of individuals—effects that appear relevant to a range of social behavior, including the expression of political opinions (Noelle-Neumann 1993), participation in criminal activity (Glaeser, Sacerdote, and Scheinkman 1996; Kahan 1997), and tacit conformity to perceived group norms (Bicchieri and Fukui 1999; Cialdini and Goldstein 2004). Individuals may also pay attention to the actions of others in order to learn from them, assuming, in effect, that those others know something that the individual does not. Thus, people infer from one another's observable behavior information as diverse as the likelihood that an incipient revolution will succeed (Lohmann 1994), that a particular technology is superior to its alternative (Arthur and Lane 1993; Lane 1997), or that a particular restaurant (Banerjee 1992; Bikhchandani, Hirshleifer, and Welch 1992) or movie (De Vany and Walls 1996) is worth attending.

Finally, decision externalities may arise out of what economists call *network effects,* meaning that the utility of an object is a function not only of its intrinsic characteristics, but also of the number of other people possessing compatible or complementary devices (Katz and Shapiro 1985; Economides 1996; Liebowitz and Margolis 1998). For example, a fax machine is effectively useless when no one else has one, but becomes increasingly valuable as the size of the relevant "network" grows. By analogy, the value of watching a particular reality TV show, for example, may be enhanced by the enjoyment derived from discussing it with friends and coworkers. Although similar to conformity, such cultural coordination problems are somewhat distinct in that individuals are acting out of a desire to benefit from group participation—"joining the network"—rather than out of fear of sanctioning.

Thus, individuals may be influenced by others for a variety of reasons: out of a desire for conformity; in order to imitate those considered more socially desirable than oneself; as means of reducing the complexity of the decision-making process; as a way of inferring otherwise inaccessible information about the world; or to reap the benefits of coordinated action. Although psychologically distinct, all these mechanisms, along with possibly many others that I have not considered, have the effect of generating decision externalities, in that each decision maker affects the preferences of others and is affected by them.

To make some concrete progress, I want to restrict my attention to the class of binary decisions, meaning that each individual faces a choice between only two alternatives, A and B, which we may also think of as states (e.g., "active" vs. "inactive" or "adopt" vs. "refrain"), one of which, say B, is treated as a default state. This restriction appears severe, in that many decisions of interest including, for example, decisions about which works of art to pay attention to, involve choices between many alternatives simultaneously. As Schelling (1978) and Granovetter (1978) have both argued, however, a binary-decision framework may be much more general than it at first appears, in part because many decisions *are* binary in nature (adopting vs. not adopting some innovation) and in part because many multifaceted decisions can be effectively reduced to sequences of binary decisions (Borghesi and Bouchaud 2006).

The benefit of considering only binary decisions is that we can now take the dramatically simplifying step of writing down the decision rule of an individual i in terms of what we might call an *influence response function* $p_i(\phi_i)$, where $p_i(\phi_i)$ is the probability that an individual i will choose action A as a function of the fraction ϕ_i of i's neighbor choosing A.[10] Influence response functions of this general type are often simply postulated as plausible heuristics (Granovetter 1978; Kuran 1991; Watts 2002). However, recent work (Lopez-Pintado and Watts 2007) demonstrates that under quite reasonable assumptions, they can also be derived as best responses to certain classes of strategic games and social-learning scenarios. In other words, although falling short of "full rationality," influence response functions are entirely consistent with a rational choice view of the world.

Arguably the simplest type of influence response function, and the one that has received by far the most attention in the social contagion literature (Schelling 1973; Granovetter 1978; Morris 2000; Watts 2002), is a *deterministic threshold function,* according to which individual i adopts A with probability 1 if at least some critical fraction ϕ_i^* of i's neighbors has adopted A; otherwise i remains in the default state B. Deterministic threshold functions are particularly convenient because they capture the entire function in a single parameter ϕ_i^*; thus heterogeneity in individual preferences, say, can be captured easily by drawing thresholds from some specified distribution $f(\phi)$. However, there is no obstacle, in principle, to constructing more complicated and realistic influence response functions (Dodds and Watts 2004; Dodds and Watts 2005; Lopez-Pintado and Watts 2007). Regardless of their form, the main question of interest is how these individual-level response functions, once specified, aggregate to produce collective decisions.

The first major insight into this question, dating back to Schelling (1973) and Granovetter (1978), is that collective outcomes are only weakly determined by the characteristics of the population itself. Granovetter in particular emphasized this point, using the example of a hypothetical crowd poised on the brink of a riot. Because all involved are uncertain about the costs and benefits associated with rioting, each member of the crowd is influenced by his peers, such that each of them can be characterized by some threshold rule: "I will join a riot only when sufficiently many others do; otherwise I will refrain." Granovetter observed that if the distribution of thresholds is precisely uniform—that is, one person will riot spontaneously, one person will join in when he observes one other rioter, another will join when he observes two rioters, and so on—the entire crowd will end up in the riot.

This result, however, is exceedingly fragile with respect to perturbations in the distribution of thresholds. If, for example, no one has a threshold of three, and instead two individuals have a threshold of four, then the cascade will terminate after only three people have joined in. The modification is trivial, but to an observer, the result could not be more different: Rather than witnessing an all-out riot, she would see just three trouble makers jostling an otherwise orderly crowd. If presented with these alternative outcomes in different parts of a city or on different days, such an observer might very well conclude that she was witnessing either very different crowds or similar crowds under very different conditions. Yet we know from the construction of the model that both the crowds and the contexts are, by all reasonable measures, indistinguishable.[11]

Although idealized in a number of important respects, Granovetter's example has profound implications for both the aforementioned rationalist and historicist perspectives. If everyone chooses to adopt A instead of B, then a rationalist (i.e., representative agent) model of the world would imply (1) that A is intrinsically better than B; and (2) that we would expect A to win out in any roughly similar population and situation. What Granovetter's crowd demonstrates, however, is that when individual decision rules are determined, even in part, by the decisions of others, neither conclusion holds. The historicist view, meanwhile, fares better in that it at least allows for contingent outcomes; however, the source of the contingency is rather different. Whereas historicists locate the contingency in the social environment, the historical context, or some other feature of the world that is exogenous to the process under consideration, in Granovetter's model, the contingency is endogenous, arising out of the nonlinearity of the process itself. Thus, we may conclude that when individual choices are made interdependently, collective behavior is fundamentally *ambiguous,* meaning that in the presence of even the slightest imprecision regarding the characteristics of the individuals themselves (i.e., considered in isolation of one another), the outcome cannot be predicted, even approximately.

Granovetter's model is clearly simplistic—too simplistic to be an accurate representation of real social processes. However, the ambiguity clouding the relation between individual characteristics and collective behavior grows only stronger and more pervasive for more realistic models of belief formation. For example, Granovetter assumed that each individual observes and weights equally the decisions of all other individuals in the population—an assumption that is almost certainly not valid for most real-life decisions, where typically we receive or solicit information from only a tiny fraction of the total population. Social influence in the real world, therefore, propagates not from everyone to everyone else directly, but indirectly via sparse networks of influence relations. Recent work on such network models of influence, however, suggests that the dynamics of the corresponding collective decisions are even more unpredictable and counterintuitive than in Granovetter's model (Watts 2002; Watts 2003; Watts and Dodds 2007). In sparse networks, for example, even identical distributions of thresholds can display wildly different behavior from realization to realization, without changing the characteristics of the influence network or the relevant boundary conditions.

Under fairly broad conditions, therefore, it is possible to show that when individuals make decisions in response to the decisions of other people, the relationship between individual preferences and collective decisions breaks down. There need not, for example, be any measurable *ex ante* differences, either in the ideas themselves or in the environment through which they spread, between ideas that "succeed" and those that do not. What are we to say about causality in such circumstances?

Individualistic Logic and Collective Dynamics

At the level of individual actors, there is nothing terribly complicated about cause and effect in threshold models. It takes only a moment's reflection to accept that each of us is influenced, to some extent or another, by the attitudes, actions, and decisions of the relatively small group of people to whom we pay close attention, with whom we communicate often, or whose opinions we respect for one reason or another. Thus, the notion that individuals are influenced by their local network neighborhood is relatively intuitive.

What is harder to understand, and therefore to incorporate into our mental models of social processes, is that those very same people are just as much affected by the attitudes, actions, and decisions of their neighbors as we are ourselves. Thus, every member of our "influence neighborhood" has his or her own influence neighborhood, which may or may not overlap to some extent with our own. The same statement is true for every member of our neighbors' neighbors, and again for our neighbors' neighbors' neighbors, and so on. The collective outcome therefore, is determined not by the decision of any representative agent, but by interacting chains of sequential decisions, where any one individual is aware of, and therefore can react to, only part of a larger sequence of decisions that is extended both spatially and temporally. In other words, it is in the aggregation process itself, not in the specification of individual action, that all the ambiguity arises.

Ambiguity, it should be emphasized, does not imply that *anything* can happen—it is still the case that some *kinds* of beliefs may be more likely than others to emerge as dominant. For example, supernatural belief systems like religion seem to serve many socially useful purposes, not least of which is the alleviation of existentialist angst; thus one might reasonably expect that all human cultures will invent, borrow, or adapt some manifestation of supernatural beliefs. Likewise, it is reasonable to suppose that no book on nonlinear differential equations will ever become an international best seller—simply because not enough people could read it even if they were so inclined. In other words, even when people are highly dependent on one another for information about what to prefer, they still have preferences; thus, some general class of beliefs, artifacts, or ideas, in any given time and place, is probably more likely to succeed than others.

As with the example of the *Mona Lisa*, however, this class of viable candidates can be surprisingly broad, and which particular one of them wins out is not just unpredictable—it is effectively arbitrary.[12] Thus, although some form of capitalism might have arisen in any history of the world, to say that American capitalism adopted its current form *either* because it satisfies the needs of people better than its alternatives, as a rationalist might claim, *or* because it came about as a natural, if unanticipated consequence of some preexisting religious philosophy, as an historicist might argue, is to commit the fallacy of attributing individualistic logic to collective behavior. When collective behavior is generated from individual behavior via a nonlinear, stochastic aggregation process, it simply is not "explainable" in the usual way of "A caused B."

When faced with such nonintuitive phenomena, it is not surprising that we look for ways to reinsert simple notions of cause and effect. Conveniently, once any particular outcome has been observed, some story can always be told that traces a path from some initial state A to some final state B, and thus *sounds* like a causal story. It is in this *ex post* sense-making process, during which the formation of our ordinary beliefs is described and accounted for, that our meta-beliefs are formed, and it is our meta-beliefs that allow us to invoke the individualistic framework. The explanation that "we prefer A to B because of some random, distributed sequence of individual-level decisions that nobody really understands" is simply not as appealing an argument as "we prefer A to B because A is better according to the following principles; thus, our decision represents a collective choice of better over worse." It is not even as good as "we prefer A to B because at some earlier time *t*, a certain group of influential people chose A, and everyone else followed them; thus, our decision represents an historical accident that subsequently got locked in." These alternative explanations invoke meta-beliefs in different ways, but they are the same in that they describe a collective process as if only a single entity were making decisions.

Meta-beliefs, however, do more than generate plausible-sounding causal stories—they also have consequences for subsequent decisions. Once we have decided that not only do we prefer A to B, but that we also have a principled basis for doing so, we may subsequently be predisposed to prefer things "like A" to things "like B," in which case our ordinary beliefs will effectively be governed by our meta-beliefs, just if the latter had in fact been "discovered" in the manner of universal principles. Simple threshold models like the one discussed previously are not capable of representing the importance of meta-beliefs, but one might imagine the thresholds themselves changing as a consequence of new beliefs that become widely adopted. Ideally, such a model could account both for the formation of ordinary beliefs and also for their eventual rationalization in terms of meta-beliefs—as instantiated, for example, in collective memory (Olick 1999) or organizational culture (Dobbin 1994)—which then, in turn, set the conditions for subsequent rounds of contestation between existing beliefs and new competitors. A great deal of work remains to be done on formal models of collective behavior if they are to include important features like meta-beliefs, as well as higher-level "actors" like organizations, which are both individual entities, capable of making decisions, and also aggregations of lower-level entities (Abell 2001). I would argue, however, that the fundamental ambiguity clouding individualistic notions of cause and effect will, if anything, only be exacerbated by the introduction of these additional complexities.

Lessons for Modern Capitalism?

So far in this chapter, I have argued that discussions of causality in historical processes—whether of the rationalist or historicist persuasion—have largely overlooked an essential distinction between the individual and the collective. In this sense both rationalists and historicists make the same error, substituting a fictitious individual—the representative agent—for the collective. Although the two perspectives differ on how much of this hypothetical individual's behavior can be attributed to internal rationality and how much to external context, both are equally guilty of applying individualistic logic to what are invariably instances of collective behavior. This being a book about capitalism, however, I want to conclude by relating this somewhat abstract claim to the behavior of markets.

Without question, one of the truly notable events of the last decade has been the phenomenal increase (in the late 1990s) and subsequent decrease in the aggregate value of the U.S. stock market. There are many reasons to think so: some individuals became fabulously wealthy; new industries were spawned (and in some cases subsequently abandoned); and Americans became much more conscious of the stock market than at any other time in history. Given all the attention directed at the stock market, however, one question has received surprisingly little comment: How is it that an entire market can expand and then contract again so dramatically? Some of the variation can no doubt be explained in terms of companies entering and leaving the market, but most of it is due to the dramatic changes in the valuations of companies already present. So how should one properly assign value to these firms?

The economist's (i.e., rationalist) standard answer is that a firm's value reflects the risk-adjusted, time-discounted cash flow generated by its stock. Future revenue, however, can only be estimated by making some assumptions about future performance, risk, and other factors. Therefore, even leaving aside questions about whether or not real people actually evaluate firms the way they are supposed to, the answer still requires the potential investor to form some beliefs regarding the firm's prospects for generating revenues and profits in the long term. Furthermore, because the value of any commodity in a market is only what someone will pay for it, investors must form these beliefs in the context of other investors doing the same thing—what Keynes called a "beauty contest" (Keynes 1936).

Even more confusing, market prices only reflect current beliefs about value to the extent that a trade taking place at the going price doesn't change the price itself. Thus, given what people collectively believe about a firm, the value of a single share is well defined in equilibrium, because selling one share isn't going to make any measurable difference to the price. However, selling *all* the shares of that firm, or even a substantial fraction of them, renders equilibrium prices meaningless. If, for example, everyone who owns shares that are valued at some particular price wants to sell simultaneously, then clearly the price is too high; and potential buyers, knowing this, will only agree to pay less. In such situations, however, when existing beliefs suddenly give way, then until some new, stable set of beliefs takes its place, it is unclear just how much less one should pay. As a result, the price can plummet in a way that is wildly disproportionate to the importance of the information about the economy, say, or the company itself, that triggered the shift in beliefs. Thus sudden and dramatic changes in collective beliefs can raise or lower the measured value of a firm by orders of magnitude, even though very little about the firm itself may have changed.

For example, when 3Com spun off Palm Inc. (the maker of the then popular Palm Pilot) as a subsidiary in March 2000, the subsidiary was valued at more than twice what the parent company had been worth *before* the spin-off (Norris 2003). In the same month, Cisco Systems—a maker of Internet switching equipment—became the most valuable company in the world, with a market capitalization exceeding that of General Motors, Citigroup, and Wal-Mart combined (Berenson and Gaither 2001). At the time, a great many sensible and informed people, including professional analysts and fund managers, apparently believed that the prices they were paying were justified. Yet one year later, Cisco had "lost" 80% of that value, magically wiping out $400 billion dollars of wealth. And two years after that, Palm's market capitalization had fallen from $50 billion to $500 million—a staggering 99% loss in just three years (Norris 2003).

Advocates of rationality might respond that eventually people always figure out the truth, and that if they don't, their views get weeded out through some process of selection (Friedman 1953). Thus, crazy fluctuations like those of Palm and Cisco are dismissed as "irrational" deviations from the otherwise orderly performance of a largely rational market. Over those same three years, however, much the same phenomenon occurred at the scale of the entire stock market. As long as everyone believed in the endless promise of technology companies, prices continued to rise, portfolios become "worth" more, and everyone who owned technology stocks became richer simultaneously. When everyone stopped believing, the opposite occurred. In this manner trillions of dollars in wealth were created, then lost again, simply by everyone deciding collectively that they preferred, then disdained, technology. Everyone literally got richer—and then poorer—at the same time, with all the consequences for consumption, investment, tax revenues, and government policy that follow from macro-changes in wealth.

As with the prior discussion of rationalist versus historicist perspectives, therefore, the characterization of financial markets as rational or irrational is not so much right or wrong, as simply missing the point. The point is that "the market" is not some single entity that typically behaves rationally and just has occasional, albeit unpredictable, bouts of irrationality; rather, it comprises large numbers of individual actors, each of whom is behaving more-or-less sensibly, and each of whom is forming opinions about what is reasonable in response to his or her observations about what other people are doing. And it is in the aggregation process that displays of collective irrationality, or for that matter, rationality, arise. Individuals, in other words, may or may not behave rationally—it may not actually matter. The point is that they do not behave *independently,* and that the interdependencies are every bit as responsible for shaping collective behavior as the preferences of the individuals themselves.

Similar observations apply to consumer markets, which although less volatile than the stock market, are susceptible to the same social forces. In 2003, for example, after many years of consumers flirting with Dr. Robert Atkins's low-carbohydrate diets, demand for "low-carb" foods suddenly exploded, generating thousands of new products on supermarket shelves and accounting for tens or even hundreds of millions of dollars of revenue (Warner 2004). Hundreds of firms participated in this market, researching, producing, distributing, and marketing either modified or entirely new products. The surge even resulted in a number of entirely new firms being created specifically for the purpose of supplying consumer demand for low-carb everything. Then, just as suddenly, the market collapsed, leaving many of the same firms in deep trouble (Warner 2004). How does an idea, which had actually been around for decades, suddenly become so popular that an entire industry is motivated to respond to it, only to evaporate again just as rapidly?

There is, of course, a story—or rather many stories. Perhaps it was that growing public awareness of national obesity trends finally crossed a threshold. Perhaps it was changing lifestyles that led people to prefer ready-to-eat meals over those made from basic ingredients. Perhaps it was the death of Dr. Atkins in 2003 and his company's subsequent decision to branch into food products as well as diet books. Or perhaps it was the success of another low-carb, high-protein diet: *The South Beach Diet.* Conversely, once sufficiently many people actually tried to lose weight with low-carb products, they discovered that the diets didn't work; so that's when the craze ended. All these explanations sound plausible, but once again, in speaking of "the market," or even "people," as a single entity with an individual's desires, preferences, and learning capabilities, they obscure, rather than illuminate, the mechanics of the process by which collectives come to exert demand for some products and not others.

Finally, nowhere are the consequences of collective beliefs more apparent than in cultural markets such as those for books, movies, music, and sport, as well as for the individuals who produce them. One of the most striking features of these cultural markets is what is called the "winner-take-all" (Frank and Cook 1995) or "superstar" (Rosen 1981) effect, according to which market leaders are dramatically more successful (either in terms of market share or compensation) than are runners-up, even when the differences between them are slight. The standard explanation for the effect is that market demand (and hence revenue) is "convex," meaning that at the top end, small increases in quality correspond to large increases in demand (Rosen 1981). In the case of cultural markets, reproduction technology allows each potential consumer to purchase "the best" product for the same price as the next-best; thus because lesser quality is generally a poor substitute for higher quality, a single product—the "superstar"—may experience thousands of times the demand of an average product. From this observation, it quickly follows that the difference in compensation between "the best" artists, writers, actors, and musicians, and even the second-best, ought to be considerable.

Although evidently correct at some level, the convexity argument omits more than it explains. Clearly, when the most popular product is many times more popular than the next most popular product, then as long as the technology can allow for relative costless reproduction, demand will be convex. But how does everybody agree about what they like in the first place? It may be the case, in other words, that roughly 50 million people "wanted" each of the first six volumes of J. K. Rowling's *Harry Potter* series, and that without modern printing and distribution technology, it may not have been possible for them all to buy the same books. But why did so many people want them? And what does the unprecedented success of the series reveal about the qualities of Rowling's writing, the reading preferences of modern children, or the difficulty that even experts have in picking winners?[13] The standard view, as espoused by Tucker (1999), concludes that although there is nothing particularly outstanding about Rowling's writing, and although the length, tone, and characters of her stories appear, if anything, to fly in the face of what experts thought children wanted, it *must* have been what they wanted, else why would they have bought it?

Success, in this view, is its own explanation, after which analysis is reduced to the mere documentation of whatever features the work in question exhibits. Once again, in other words, we end up with self-referential reasoning along the lines of "A succeeded because people wanted something with the qualities of A." However, now we can understand the source of the self-referentiality. The problem is that "the people" are being treated as a single entity that is capable of "wanting" something as an individual might. In truth, there is no such entity—only many individuals making individual-level decisions—but we create one anyway in our narrative explanations, because we don't know how else to explain anything. Unfortunately, in doing so, we eliminate from our consideration the very aggregation process by which a large population of individuals comes to behave like a coherent collective. Once again, both rationalists and historicists are equally guilty of this misattribution of individual logic to collective behavior. The emphasis of their explanations may differ—in the rationalist version, the individual makes something happen, whereas in the historicist version, something happens to the individual—and the nature of the individual may differ as well, sometimes played by a person, and at other times by a collective. In all cases, however, the explanation requires cause and effect to operate at the same scale.

Conclusion

What I have attempted to demonstrate in this chapter is that when dynamics is taking place at more than one scale (here, I have used just two scales, individual and collective, but more are possible), and where the aggregation process between the two is nonlinear and stochastic, causal statements that are meaningful with respect to individual behavior are largely irrelevant to the behavior of the collective, and causality at the level of collectives is rendered deeply ambiguous. Put another way, there is no unique, as in one-to-one, mapping between any compact description of the "before" state and its subsequent unfolding. Rather, the mapping is "many-to-many": many possible sets of initial conditions and exogenous parameters may correspond to any one outcome, and any one set of initial conditions and parameters may correspond to many possible outcomes. In such situations, we may still extract orderly descriptions that help us to understand the behavior of the system, but these descriptions are necessarily probabilistic in nature, comprising, for example, the shapes of probability distributions, rather than the ordering of particular outcomes. Thus, although we may hope to understand better the processes by which collective outcomes are generated, even a perfect understanding of those processes will not correspond to a causal explanation of why *one particular* outcome pertains and not another. Indeed, no such explanation is possible.

For many people, this conclusion may be hard to take seriously, if only because contrary to the claim that much of social reality cannot be explained in the traditional sense, we live awash in explanations. Very little of note happens in a modern society that is not subsequently reported on, dissected, analyzed, and digested. Entire professions, including our own, exist in whole or in part to "make sense" of history as it unfolds. Thus, to say that explanations are not possible is to defy not only everyday experience, but common sense. I would argue, however, that in this case, common sense is wrong and that the apparent success of our explanations derives not from their ability to actually identify cause and effect, but from our desire to believe in the narratives we construct. It may not, after all, matter to us all that much whether these narratives reveal anything about how a particular outcome actually came to be—what matters is that we think they do, and thus reassured we are able to get on with our lives.

That may be fine for most people; however, policy makers, if they wish to be effective, cannot afford the luxury of trusting their common sense, especially when it tells them that outcomes that they failed utterly to anticipate appear in hindsight to make perfect sense. As financial, commodity, and cultural markets become increasingly global and the costs of communication, information, and trade continue to drop precipitously, the social processes by which collectives determine their beliefs about the world will become ever more consequential. In part, these changes are driving down the barriers between historically segregated populations; thus the potential size of collectives is increasing; And in part, they are increasing the speed at which social influence can propagate, and thus social change can potentially manifest itself. In each case, however, the qualifier "potentially" is important. Greater access to previously inaccessible influence can lead to boring homogeneity, but it can also lead to balkanization and conflict, or even to vibrant diversity. Likewise, faster communications and lower transaction costs can lead either to more, or to less, stability in the face of change; to better adaptability, or to worse. Nothing, in other words, is certain in the social world—not even change itself—but whatever kind of policy one is trying to implement—whether it concerns the regulation of capital markets, the development of legal institutions, or the improvement of public health—its impact will be mitigated, enhanced, or subverted by the collective beliefs of the relevant population. Thus if policy makers wish to do more than simply wake up in the morning and see what happens, they have an obligation to understand how it is that people, whether it be themselves, their constituents, or the intended targets of their interventions, come to believe the things they do. Common sense is not much use in this regard, and philosophical debate, having swirled around the topic for decades without result, has exhausted itself. Formal modeling of the kind I have described here may not ultimately yield the answers either, but it does at least have the advantage of illuminating the distinction between the individual and the collective. Clearly there is much to be done to develop the primitive, overly simplistic models discussed here. And even then, the end result will likely not be prescriptive in the way that we have come to expect of models in the physical and engineering sciences, either because social phenomena are simply too complex, or because, unlike physical phenomenon, the very act of understanding human-social behavior, or even just building theories of it, has a way of changing the phenomena themselves. Nevertheless, formal models of social processes can help in the same way that they have helped in every other field of science—by extending our understanding of the world beyond where ordinary intuition can reach.

References

Abbott, Andrew D. 1988. "Transcending General Linear Reality." *Sociological Theory* 6:169–186.

———. 1998. "The Causal Devolution." *Sociological Methods and Research* 27:148–181.

———. 2000. "Sequence Analysis and Optimal Matching Methods in Sociology: Review and Prospect." *Sociological Methods & Research* 29:3–33.

———. 2001. "Time Matters: On Theory and Method." Chicago: University of Chicago Press.

Abell, Peter. 2001. "Causality and Low-Frequency Complex Events: The Role of Comparative Narratives." *Sociological Methods and Research* 30:57–80.

Adams, Julia, Elisabeth Clemens, and Ann S. Orloff. 2005. "Remaking Modernity: Politics, History, and Sociology." Durham, NC: Duke University Press.

Aguirre, B. E., E. L. Quarantelli, and Jorge L. Mendoza. 1988. "The Collective Behavior of Fads: The Characteristics, Effects, and Career of Streaking." *American Sociological Review* 53:569–584.

Aminzade, Ronald. 1992. "Historical Sociology and Time." *Sociological Methods & Research* 20:456–480.

Arthur, W. Brian, and David Lane. 1993. "Information contagion." *Structural Change and Economic Dynamics* 4:81–104.

Asch, Solomon E. 1953. "Effects of group pressure upon the modification and distortion of judgments." Pp. 151–162 in *Group Dynamics: Research and Theory*, edited by D. Cartwright and A. Zander. Evanston, IL: Row, Peterson and Co.

Banerjee, Abhijit V. 1992. "A Simple Model of Herd Behavior." *The Quarterly Journal of Economics* 107:797–817.

Bearman, Peter S., Robert Faris, and James Moody. 1999. "Blocking the future: New solutions for old problems in historical social science." *Social Science History* 23:501–533.

Becker, Marshall H. 1970. "Sociometric Location and Innovativeness: Reformulation and Extension of the Diffusion Model." *American Sociological Review* 35:267–282.

Berenson, Alex, and Chris Gaither. 2001. "Warning by Cisco, an Internet titan." in *New York Times*. New York, April 17.

Berger, Peter L., and Thomas Luckman. 1966. *The Social Construction of Reality*. New York: Anchor Books.

Bernheim, B. Douglas. 1994. "A Theory of Conformity." *Journal of Political Economy* 102:841–877.

Bicchieri, Christina, and Yoshitaka Fukui. 1999. "The Great Illusion: Ignorance, Informational Cascades and the Persistence of Unpopular Norms." *Business Ethics Quarterly* 9:127–155.

Bikhchandani, Sushil, David Hirshleifer, and Ivo Welch. 1992. "A Theory of Fads, Fashion, Custom, and Cultural Change as Informational Cascades." *Journal of Political Economy* 100:992–1026.

Blume, Lawrence, and Steven N. Durlauf. 2003. "Equilibrium Concepts for Social Interaction Models." *International Game Theory Review* 5:193–209.

Blumer, Herbert. 1969. "Fashion: From Class Differentiation to Collective Selection." *Sociological Quarterly* 10:275–291.

———. 1971. "Social Problems as Collective Behavior." *Social Problems* 18:298–306.

Borghesi, Christian, and Jean-Philippe Bouchaud. 2006. "Of songs and men: A model for multiple choice with herding." http://xxx.lanl.gov/pdf/physics/0606224, June 26.

Boudon, Raymond. 1998. "Limitations of Rational Choice Theory." *American Journal of Sociology* 104:817–828.

Brock, William A., and Steven N. Durlauf. 2001. "Discrete Choice with Social Interactions." *Review of Economic Studies* 68:235–260.

Calhoun, Craig. 1998. "Explanation in Historical Sociology: Narrative, General Theory, and Historically Specific Theory." *American Journal of Sociology* 104: 846–871.

Cialdini, Robert B., and Noah Goldstein, J. 2004. "Social Influence: Compliance and Conformity." *Annual Review of Psychology* 55:591–621.

Clark, Kenneth. 1973. "Mona Lisa." *The Burlington Magazine* 115:144–151.

Coleman, James Samuel, Elihu Katz, and Herbert Menzel. 1957. "The Diffusion of an Innovation among Physicians." *Sociometry* 20:253–270.

Danto, Arthur C. 1965. *Analytical Philosophy of History.* Cambridge, UK: Cambridge University Press.

Davis, Gerald F. 1991. "Agents without Principles? The Spread of the Poison Pill through the Intercorporate Network." *Administrative Science Quarterly* 36:583–613.

De Vany, Arthur, and W. David Walls. 1996. "Bose-Einstein Dynamics and Adaptive Contracting in the Motion Picture Industry." *The Economic Journal* 106: 1493–1514.

DiMaggio, P., and W. Powell. 1983. "The Iron Cage Revisited: Institutional Isomorphism and Collective Rationality in Organizational Fields." *American Sociological Review* 48:147–160.

Dobbin, Frank. 1994. "Cultural Models of Organization: The Social Construction of Rational Organizing Principles." Pp. 117–141 in *The Sociology of Culture: Emerging Theoretical Perspectives,* edited by D. Crane. Oxford, UK: Basil Blackwell.

Dodds, P. S., and D. J. Watts. 2004. "Universal behavior in a generalized model of contagion." *Physical Review Letters* 92:218701.

———. 2005. "A generalized model of social and biological contagion." *Journal of Theoretical Biology* 232:587–604.

Durlauf, Steven N. 2001. "A Framework for the Study of Individual Behavior and Social Interactions." *Sociological Methodology* 31:47–87.

Economides, Nicholas. 1996. "The Economics of Networks." *International Journal of Industrial Organization* 14:673–699.

Festinger, Leon. 1957. *A Theory of Cognitive Dissonance.* Stanford, CA: Stanford University Press.

Frank, Robert H., and Philip J. Cook. 1995. *The Winner-Take-All Society: Why the Few at the Top Get So Much More Than the Rest of Us.* New York: Free Press.

Friedman, Milton. 1953. *Essays in Positive Economics.* Chicago: University of Chicago Press.

Glaeser, Edward L., Bruce Sacerdote, and Jose A. Scheinkman. 1996. "Crime and Social Interaction." *Quarterly Journal of Economics* 111:507–548.

Goldstone, Jack A. 1998. "Initial Conditions, General Laws, Path Dependence, and Explanation in Historical Sociology." *American Journal of Sociology* 104:829–845.

Goldthorpe, John H. 2000. *On Sociology: Numbers, Narratives, and the Integration of Research and Theory.* Oxford, UK: Oxford University Press.

Granovetter, M. S. 1978. "Threshold models of collective behavior." *American Journal of Sociology* 83:1420–1443.

Griffin, Larry J. 1992. "Temporality, Events, and Explanation in Historical Sociology: An Introduction." *Sociological Methods & Research* 20:403–427.

Hedstrom, Peter. 1998. "Rational Imitation." Pp. 306–327 in *Social Mechanisms: An Analytical Approach to Social Theory,* edited by P. Hedstrom and R. Swedberg. Cambridge, UK: Cambridge University Press.

Huckfeldt, Robert, Paul E. Johnson, and John Sprague. 2004. *Political Disagreement: The Survival of Disagreement with Communication Networks.* Cambridge, UK: Cambridge University Press.

Kahan, Dan M. 1997. "Social Influence, Social Meaning, and Deterrance." *Virginia Law Review* 83:349–395.

Katz, Elihu, and Paul Felix Lazarsfeld. 1955. *Personal influence; the part played by people in the flow of mass communications.* Glencoe, IL: Free Press.

Katz, Michael L., and Carl Shapiro. 1985. "Network Externalities, Competition, and Compatibility." *American Economic Review* 75:424–440.

Keynes, John Maynard. 1936. *The General Theory of Employment, Interest, and Money.* New York: Harcourt Brace and Co.

Kirman, Alan D. 1992. "Whom or What Does the Representative Individual Represent?" *Journal of Economic Perspectives* 6:117–136.

Kiser, Edgar, and Michael Hechter. 1998. "The Debate on Historical Sociology: Rational Choice Theory and Its Critics." *American Journal of Sociology* 104:785–816.

Kuran, Timur. 1991. "Now Out of Never: The Element of Surprise in the East European Revolution of 1989." *World Politics* 44:7–48.

Lane, David. 1997. "Is what is good for each best for all? Learning from others in the information contagion model." Pp. 105–127 in *The Economy as an Evolving Complex System II,* vol. XXVII, *SFI Studies in the Sciences of Complexity,* edited by W. B. Arthur, S. N. Durlauf, and D. Lane. Cambridge, MA: Addison-Wesley.

Leibenstein, H. 1950. "Bandwagon, Snob, and Veblen Effects in the Theory of Consumers' Demand." *Quarterly Journal of Economics* 64:183–207.

Lieberson, Stanley. 1991. "Small N's and Big Conclusions: An Examination of the Reasoning in Comparative Studies Based on a Small Number of Cases." *Social Forces* 70:307–320.

——. 1994. "More on the Uneasy Case for Using Mill-Type Methods in Small-N Comparative Studies." *Social Forces* 72:1225–1237.

——. 1997a. "The big broad issues in society and social history: application of probabilistic perspective." Pp. 359–386 in *Causality in Crisis? Statistical Methods and the Search for Causal Knowledge in the Social Sciences,* vol. 4, *Studies in Science and the Humanities from the Reilly Center for Science, Technology, and Values,* edited by V. R. McKim and S. P. Turner. Notre Dame, IN: University of Notre Dame Press.

——. 1997b. "Modeling Social Processes: Some Lessons from Sports." *Sociological Forum* 12:11–35.

Liebowitz, Stanley J., and Stephen E. Margolis. 1998. "Network Effects and Externalities." Pp. 671–675 in *The New Palgrave's Dictionary of Economics and the Law*, vol. 2. New York: MacMillan.

Lohmann, Susanne. 1994. "The Dynamics of Informational Cascades: The Monday Demonstrations in Leipzig, East Germany, 1989–91." *World Politics* 47:42–101.

Lopez-Pintado, Dunia, and Duncan J. Watts. 2007. "Social Influence, binary decisions, and collective dynamics." Under Review.

Mackay, Charles. 1932. *Extraordinary popular delusions and the madness of crowds*. Boston: L. C. Page & Company.

McDonald, Terrence J. 1996. "The Historic Turn in the Human Sciences." Ann Arbor: University of Michigan Press.

Meyer, John W., and Brian Rowan. 1977. "Institutionalized organizations: Formal structure as myth and ceremony." *American Journal of Sociology* 83:340–363.

Meyersohn, Rolf, and Elihu Katz. 1957. "Notes on a Natural History of Fads." *American Journal of Sociology* 62:594–601.

Morris, S. 2000. "Contagion." *Review of Economic Studies* 67:57–78.

Noelle-Neumann, Elisabeth. 1993. *The Spiral of Silence: Public Opinion, Our Social Skin*. Chicago: University of Chicago Press.

Norris, Floyd. 2003. "When Palm Does a Deal, Prices Get Crazy." Pp. C1 in *New York Times*. New York, June 6.

Olick, Jeffery K. 1999. "Collective Memory: The Two Cultures." *Sociological Theory* 17:333–348.

Quadagno, Jill, and Stan J. Knapp. 1992. "Have Historical Sociologists Forsaken Theory? Thoughts on the History/Theory Relationship." *Sociological Methods & Research* 20:481–507.

Rosen, Sherwin. 1981. "The economics of superstars." *American Economic Review* 71:845–858.

Ryan, B., and N. C. Gross. 1943. "The Diffusion of Hybrid Seed Corn in Two Iowa Communities." *Rural Sociology* 8:15–23.

Salganik, Matthew J., Peter Sheridan Dodds, and Duncan J. Watts. 2006. "Experimental Study of Inequality and Unpredictability in an Artificial Cultural Market." *Science* 311:854–856.

Sassoon, Donald. 2001. *Becoming Mona Lisa: The Making of a Global Icon*. New York: Harcourt, Inc.

Schelling, Thomas C. 1969. *Neighborhood tipping*. Cambridge, MA: Harvard Institute of Economic Research, Harvard University.

———. 1973. "Hockey Helmets, Concealed Weapons, and Daylight Saving: A Study of Binary Choices with Externalities." *Journal of Conflict Resolution* 17:381–428.

———. 1978. *Micromotives and macrobehavior*. New York: Norton.

Sewell, William H. 1996a. "Historical Events as Transformations of Structures: Inventing Revolution at the Bastille." *Theory and Society* 25:841–881.

———. 1996b. "Three Temporalities: Toward an Eventful Sociology." Pp. 245–280 in *The Historic Turn in the Human Sciences*, edited by T. J. McDonald. Ann Arbor: University of Michigan Press.

Sherif, Muzafer. 1937. "An experimental approach to the study of attitudes." *Sociometry* 1:90–98.

Simmel, Georg. 1957. "Fashion." *American Journal of Sociology* 62:541–558.

Skocpol, Theda. 1979. *States and Revolutions: A Comparative Analysis of France, Russia, and China.* Cambridge, UK: Cambridge University Press.

Somers, Margaret R. 1998. "'We're No Angels': Realism, Rational Choice, and Relationality in Social Science." *American Journal of Sociology* 104:722–784.

Sperber, Irwin. 1990. *Fashions in Science: Opinion Leaders and Collective Behavior in the Social Sciences.* Minneapolis: University of Minnesota Press.

Steinmetz, George. 2004. "Odious Comparisons: Incommensurability, the Case Study, and 'Small N's' in Sociology." *Sociological Theory* 22:371–400.

Swedberg, Richard. 1998. *Max Weber and the Idea of Economic Sociology.* Princeton, NJ: Princeton University Press.

Tilly, Charles. 1984. *Big Structures, Large Processes, Huge Comparisons.* New York: Russell Sage Foundation.

Tucker, Nicholas. 1999. "The rise and rise of Harry Potter." *Children's Literature in Education* 30:221–234.

Warner, Melanie. 2004. "Is the Low-Carb Boom Over?" in *New York Times.* New York, Dec 5.

Watts, Duncan J. 2002. "A simple model of information cascades on random networks." *Proceedings of the National Academy of Science, U.S.A.* 99:5766–5771.

———. 2003. *Six Degrees: The Science of a Connected Age.* New York: W. W. Norton.

Watts, Duncan J., and Peter Sheridan Dodds. 2007. "Influentials., networks, and public opinion formation." *Journal of Consumer Research* (in press)

Weber, Max. 1958. *The Protestant Ethic and the Spirit of Capitalism.* New York: Charles Scribner's Sons.

Young, H. Peyton. 1993. "The Evolution of Conventions." *Econometrica: Journal of the Econometric Society* 61:57–84.

———. 1996. "The Economics of Convention." *The Journal of Economic Perspectives* 10:105–122.

Young, H. Peyton, and Mary A Burke. 2001. "Competition and Custom in Economic Contracts: A Case Study of Illinois Agriculture." *American Economic Review* 91:559–573.

Notes to Chapter Ten

1. I am grateful to Peter Bearman, Victoria Johnson, and Richard Swedberg for their comments on earlier drafts. I am also grateful to the members of the Collective Dynamics Group—especially Peter Dodds, Dunia-Lopez Pintado, and Matthew Salganik—for many stimulating discussions. Finally, I would like to thank R. S., Victor Nee, and the Templeton Foundation for inviting me to contribute this paper, and the National Science Foundation (SES-0094162 and SES-0339023) and the McDonnell Foundation for financial support.

2. It is worth noting that Weber's full argument is considerably more complex, and his aims more encompassing, than my simplistic sketch of it might imply. Very briefly, Weber's larger project (of which the *Protestant Ethic* is only one part) was to understand the rationalization of culture in modern Western societies—a phenomenon he saw as unique in history. His explanation was that all cultures can be characterized in terms of the relationship between three social "spheres"—religion, the polity, and the economy—each of which may or may not exhibit, in any given society, the hallmarks of rationalization, by which he meant the codification of social conduct, and its associated ends, in terms of an impersonal system of rules, roles, and relationships. In non-Western societies, Weber argued, one or two of these spheres may have experienced rationalization; but only in Western societies did the particular process of rationalization taking place in each sphere turn out to reinforce, rather than to undermine, the rationalization of the other two. In Indian culture, for example, Hinduism is highly rationalized, but the particular nature of the resulting belief system causes its adherents to withdraw from worldly economic activity, rather than actively pursuing it. Calvinism, by contrast, had precisely the opposite effect. It is thus the peculiar historical process by which rationalization appeared in all spheres of Western culture that Weber was seeking to understand in the Protestant Ethic—a process that, on account of the mutually reinforcing nature of its constituent parts (the so-called iron cage), continues to exert its influence even today. A full account of Weber's real project is well outside the scope of this essay, which aims to explore a problem that Weber's analysis exhibits but doesn't identify: the conflation of individual and collective logic. For the purpose of this essay, therefore, the simplistic version of the Protestant Ethic sketched out in the text will suffice. I am grateful, however, to Peter Bearman for clarifying the scope and subtlety of Weber's intellectual framework.

3. Ironically, Weber's argument also laid the foundations for rational choice theory: Because, at least in Western societies, individual action could be understood in terms of rational principles, it followed that theories of individual action could proceed on the basis of universal rational principles, unencumbered by the details of the particular social-cultural context. Thus Weber occupies the unusual position of intellectual progenitor of two opposing philosophies of human behavior.

4. See the special issues of *Sociological Methodology and Research,* 20(4) (1992) and *American Journal of Sociology,* 104(3) (1998), along with Tilly (1984), McDonald (1996), Abbott (2001), and Adams et al. (2005) for a range of viewpoints.

5. Much earlier, Danto (1965) made a similar but more general argument regarding the recording of all of history—that, in effect, history cannot be recorded at the time it is happening, because the meaning of what is happening now is only ever apparent later, and it is the meaning that is attributed to events, not the events themselves, that determines their historical significance.

6. Milton Friedman (1953), in fact, made more or less this same argument in defending the efficiency of free markets: Even if real people are cognitively incapable of computing rationally optimal strategies, over time nonrational behavior will be weeded out of the population via a process akin to natural selection, but operating on

strategies in place of genes; thus people will behave "as if" they are rational whether or not they satisfy the underlying assumptions of rational choice theory.

7. That is, "A causes B" now implies that A's presence merely increases the probability that B will occur, but does not imply that A is either necessary or sufficient.

8. For example, in discussing Crane Brinton's metaphor of revolution as a "fever," Tilly (1984, p. 102) notes "Despite all the qualifications he attached to it, the idea of fever suggests that revolution happens to something like a single person—to a society personified."

9. Skocpol (1979), for example, invokes a set of structural variables, which appear to correlate with shifts in political power in different countries. However, implicit in her argument is the assumption that some "actor"—a country, or population—is responding to its structural environment.

10. Technically speaking, this simplification applies only to situations in which each individual i responds directly only to some "aggregate" externality ϕ_i; that is, where $\phi_i(\vec{s})$ is a linear function of the set of actions $\vec{s}$ of all other individuals. The importance and validity of this relatively benign restriction are discussed in some detail in Lopez-Pintado and Watts (2007).

11. Kuran (1991) considers a similar example, and reaches essentially the same conclusion, in the context of discussing the East European revolution of 1989.

12. Blumer (1971) has made a similar argument, albeit in slightly different language, with respect to the identification of social problems.

13. The first Harry Potter book was rejected by several children's book publishers before being picked up finally by Bloomsbury, a small, independent press.

11 Analytical Individualism and the Explanation of Macrosocial Change

Ronald Jepperson, University of Tulsa, and John W. Meyer, Stanford University[1]

T HE ROLE OF CULTURAL AND INSTITUTIONAL FACTORS IN ECO-nomic development has attracted renewed attention. Reference to such factors is routine in the literature on Western modernization; explanatory ideas have expanded to consider long periods and broad institutional frameworks (Baechler et al. 1988, Engerman 2000). Running against these tendencies, however, one finds a prominent individualist theoretical discourse, with a strongly ideological character. Various magic bullets related to individuals are presented as keys to development: "trust," "achievement motives," "risk taking," or "entrepreneurship." These ideas seem to have a normative role in a modern society that celebrates the "cult of the individual" (Durkheim [1898] 1969).

This paper highlights the disjunction between substantive explanatory efforts—ideas that have become more macrosociological in character—and more formal theoretical efforts, which strongly feature doctrinal (or in some usages, methodological) individualism. Interestingly enough, both discussions refer back to Max Weber's various efforts to explain European development.

Accordingly, in the first section of the paper ("Background"), we discuss how a reified "Protestant Ethic thesis"—a meta-theoretical and deeply ideological version—has prospered throughout the last century as the canonical example of a macrosociological proposition. It has been used to celebrate the centrality of the individual actor in human history and the import of theoretical explanations reduced to the individual level. Weber's specialized essay has become an exemplar and proof text for analytical individualism.

We then step back to isolate the core intellectual issue involved: levels of analysis. In privileging one level of analysis, doctrinal individualism directs attention away from consideration of multiple possible causal processes—structural and institutional ones as well as individual-level ones. We illustrate how a doctrinal individualism, given standing as the sole grounding for proper social scientific explanation, distorted the substantive discussion of Protestantism and capitalism. It has also limited the explanation of a wide range of macrosocial outcomes: analyses of European economic history, European modernity in general, later modern and postmodern development, world economic development, and globalization generally. Throughout we emphasize how individualist imagery has led to a disconnection between imagined theory and actual explanation for many topics.

In our conclusion we contextualize the argument historically. The broad cultural movements surrounding the Reformation played a central role in the legitimation of all sorts of social action—not only economic action—seen as rooted in the individual person and in the resultant rationalization of society in terms of individual and collective "actors." Modern analytical individualism is embedded in this cultural matrix, and in the later and related liberalism, the rise of American power (which institutionalized Protestant and liberal cultural models), and the expansion of American social science (which conventionalized analytical individualism). We consider how contemporary shifts to more globalized cultural understandings of society reinforce both the emphasis on the human individual and the (now supranational) rationalization of society, and thus keep alive the emphases on the qualities and causal primacy of individuals.

Background

As is well known, Weber's general idea was that religious change—emphasizing the virtues of purposive rational action in the real world—supported similar changes in economic values and orientations. The specific idea that Protestantism was involved in the sweeping changes in Western economic life called "capitalism" was not especially remarkable. Even at the time of the Reformation, the idea (often an accusation) that the new doctrines supported economic rationalization was fairly routine (Viner 1978, Wuthnow 1989).

Weber published his essays on the parallels between the cultural logic of the Protestant Reformation and the economic logic of capitalism in 1904/5. By the time he gave his lectures on "General Economic History"—1919/20—the Protestant Ethic thesis as we now know it played a relatively minor role (Collins 1980). The legal and institutional changes aided by the Reformation were given great importance. The social psychological impact of Calvinism, however, was given a much more circumscribed place (see Weber [1923] 1950: 365ff).

The subsequent literature on Europe absorbed the narrow Protestant Ethic theme in much more general analyses of institutional conditions for development. There is the long-term bent of Christendom toward the demystification of nature (Eisenstadt 1999), carried along by a surprisingly rationalized monasticism (Collins 1986, 1999). There is the heritage of Roman law transmitted through the Church and sustaining political and organizational rationalization (Anderson 1974). There are the religious supports for the states system and the effects of that competitive system on economic rationalization (Strayer 1973; Wallerstein 1974; Tilly 1990). There is the extraordinary technological dynamism of a Western feudalism once conceived as dark and static (Mokyr 1992; Landes 1998). There is the organizational pluralism of Europe—including the development of relatively autonomous cities—fostering both "private" property and the rise of interstitial economic networks (McNeill 1963; Mann 1986). There is the role of representative traditions, together with the failure of imperial efforts, in creating more secure property rights in some zones (North 1981). Then there are all sorts of ecological factors (the physical layout of Europe, the Baltic and Atlantic economies) that weakened the controls of traditions (allowing the success of both Protestant heresy and protocapitalist trading systems) and provided incentives for improvement (Jones 1981; Landes 1998).

Given this intellectual history, it is striking that Weber's narrow essay remained alive through the entire twentieth century as the great and canonical example of an important macrosociological thesis. It survived, not as a substantive theory of European and world development, but as a meta-theoretical and ideological model. A reified "Protestant Ethic thesis" celebrated (a) conceptions of society as rooted in individual actors and (b) social scientific accounts representing social life as the purposive action of individual human actors.

Doctrinal Individualism

The conception of the individual as the central actor in society has strong intellectual and moral standing in a modern and liberal context. The liberal market economy, democratic polity, and open religious system are justified by the ideas of individual choice based upon prior goals and by the idea that individual choices in fact direct society. Modern society and much modern social science make cognitive and normative precommitments to a view of society as produced by purposive individual action.

In the first half of the twentieth century, the most prominent use of Weber's discussion of Protestantism was as an exemplification of the great truth that human society is driven by human choice—by purposes and ideas, beyond raw material forces. The theme was put forward against a nineteenth-century materialist determinism, emphasized in a variety of evolutionary and economistic theories. Mechanistic visions allowed no place for the emergent role of the individual in a modernity reorganizing around a "cult of the individual" (Durkheim [1898] 1969). In this context, the Protestant Ethic thesis held great attractions. Values and institutions and meanings mattered in human action, and should matter in the analysis of this action. Both this position and this reading of Weber were central to the position of Talcott Parsons, for instance (1937, 1951).

In the second half of the twentieth century, individualist uses of Weber's thesis shifted. Less emphasis was placed upon the idea that humans have real choices and purposes; now it was claimed that it was almost definitionally true that these choices, seen as properties of individual persons, drive society and social change. Further, it was emphasized that social scientific explanation was only properly scientific when it reached down to the level of the individual human.

Thus, Weber's narrow thesis has been employed many times as an exemplar of the scientific value of reductionist explanation—explanation reaching to the presumed individual bottom line. David McClelland (1967: esp. 47–57) built a major substantive thesis about personality and social change around a Protestant Ethic idea. Hans Zetterberg used it as an example of proper social scientific explanatory theory (1993, see also 1977: 67–69), as did Gudmund Hernes (1989, see also 1976). James Coleman (1986, 1990), drawing on earlier work, made it a major illustrative theme about how sociology should be done.

In their treatments, Zetterberg, Hernes, and Coleman were not substantively interested in explanations of the rise of the modern economy (though McClelland certainly was). They were advocating a certain style of explanation and trying to give it something close to monopoly status in social science. It is interesting to note that each of these analysts found some aspects of Weber's own formulations to be problematic, incomplete, and unclear. In each case, the alleged defects lay precisely in the fact that Weber's explanations were not exclusively individualist in character, but included more institutional conceptions and explanations.

The important point is less the emphasis on individual explanation than the discomfort with (even denial of) any other form of explanation. It is entirely reasonable, as we discuss in the next section, to imagine that a good many social processes work through individual-level independent and intervening variables. It is deeply problematic to imagine that all social processes, properly analyzed, must work this way. And it is a major error to imagine that scientific explanations of social life must be formulated in terms of individual-level processes.

Multiple Levels of Analysis

In Figure 11-1 we show the way in which the Protestant Ethic thesis is put forward by Coleman, following directly from his predecessors. The figure shows a very simple explanatory structure. Causal relations between historical and institutional structure occur through—and only through—individual persons in society. The matter is made practically axiomatic and is almost equated with scientific explanation itself.[2]

What is problematic about the figure is not what is there but what is not there. Notably, there is no direct casual connection between (macro-level) Protestantism and capitalism. But that is the point of analytical individualism— to picture society and social change in terms of, and only in terms of, individuals. Here, we highlight the distortions by filling in some sociological

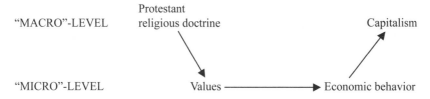

FIGURE 11-1 Typical Reconstruction of Weber's Protestant Ethic thesis (after Coleman 1986)

processes. Beyond individual-level linkages, we consider causal processes working through social-organizational arrangements and then processes occurring at very macrosociological, or institutional, levels.

Explanation at the Individual Level

It is certainly plausible to argue, as part of some broader account, that the rise of capitalism was facilitated by the increased "production of capitalistic individuals" (Weber [1923] 1950: 368-9). David Landes, in his recent overview of economic history, offers the reasonable argument that Protestantism "encouraged the appearance in numbers of a personality type that had been exceptional and adventitious before," a "new kind of businessman" that was an important ingredient in the expansion of the new manufacturing enterprises of the time (1998: 178, 175).

Weber himself offered different variants of an individual-level argument linking Protestantism and economic culture. It is the "salvation anxiety" formulation—that Calvinist ideas about predestination produced uncertainty, compelling self-discipline and hard work—that has been especially attractive to meta-theoretical users of Weber. Yet this idea was rather contrived and unconvincing from the start, and it has not fared well (Poggi 1983: 47; Parkin 1982: chap. 2; Hamilton 2000). In his later work, Weber emphasized a more general, and plausible, individual-level dynamic. Protestant sects, especially Calvinism (he thought) extended a more "rational mode of life," an ascetic mode of life, outside of monastic circles—in effect, bringing religious discipline to the masses (Weber [1923] 1950: 365; Collins 1980 for commentary). This more general formulation ended up as an individual-level component in Weber's much broader explanatory framework (again, Collins 1980).

Contemporary empirical social science has moved even further in this direction. Examine the causal pathways emphasized in Figure 11-1, and notice the contextualizations that are necessary. In the absence of institutionalized supports for changed individual orientations and behavior:

(a) It is not clear that the socializing effects of Protestant religious participation on a variety of individual attitudes were or are likely to be strong or effective.

(b) It is unlikely that the changed attitudes will remain over long periods. The literature is pessimistic about the durability of personality characteristics over long periods absent continuing reinforcement.

(c) It is unlikely that the changed attitudes will be translated into altered behavior. Altered behavior, for example in the workplace, requires much structural support.

(d) Finally, it is not at all clear that some changed individual attitudes or behaviors are likely to build up, through aggregation, into dramatic changes in the institutional rules of society. As Weber repeatedly stressed, a society can have many very calculative merchants and artisans without generating either capitalism or development.

So, to make the specific arguments depicted in Figure 11-1 plausible, one has to imagine a surrounding social structure that legitimates Protestant lines of thought, supports their transmission and retention in individuals, aids in the translation of the ideas into capitalist action, and treats such action—stigmatized in most human societies, after all—as centrally valuable to the collective good. However, if all this supportive social structure exists, at a minimum it should be analyzed as having effects of its own.

Explanation at Structural (or Social-Organizational) Levels

Sociologists tend to distinguish two levels of analysis above the individual level. One is social organizational, the other more institutional. Social-organizational processes are built around images of society as (a) a set of interrelated groups or roles and (b) arrangements of prestige and value attached to roles and their transactions. The term *role* tends to be central: Roles have both an organizational and a cultural character.

Weber's main social-organizational idea about Protestantism, as reconstructed by Poggi, has to do with the formation of a new collective actor or role (Poggi 1983; see also Bendix 1960, chap. 3; Parkin 1982: 60–62; Mann 1986). Protestantism facilitated the transformation of a preexisting collective actor—the urban commercial estate—into the burgher class of entrepreneurs (Poggi 1983).

Whatever the Protestant Reformation did to the motives of people, it certainly modified the available and legitimate roles for them. In the religious system, the roles of priest, bishop, cardinal, pope, monk, and nun were weakened or destroyed: Cathedral and monastery lost centrality. In the political system, the authority of landowners and aristocrats was weakened. In the economy, the old feudal roles of the pariah bankers and merchants were undercut, along with the whole complex of landowner-serf relations. On the other hand, whole classes of roles were created or strengthened. Politically, the rationalized state grew. In religion, the centrality both of the individual and of the church as an association of individuals was dramatically emphasized. In the economy, of course, the new roles included formally free individuals producing and exchanging in markets.

Structural explanations, in other words, give accounts of how changed distributions of social values and opportunities occur—in this case, supported by fairly dramatic religious changes. Much less causation is located in individual personality—people can be assumed simply to adapt to (and incorporate) changed values and opportunities in their environments.

Institutional Explanations

Explanations of the structural sort—in Weber's work and in the later history of explanation of early modern (or present-day) economic growth—tend to levels of generality considerably beyond the narrow structural argument of the *Protestant Ethic*. Essentially, this is because we, like Weber, have an expanded notion of the structures involved, seeing them as institutions. For instance, the destruction of the "priest," and the magical values attached to formerly stigmatized notions of the entrepreneur or the usurer, would be very imperfectly captured by dry network imagery. These roles have enormous cultural meaning, and they carry dramatic and substantial social authority. Such role packages involve big pictures—social programs, ideologies, and cosmologies given widespread meaning across time and space. Historically, sociology has pulled together conceptions of phenomena at this level under the heading "institutions": The state, its ideologies, and the law provide examples (Jepperson 1991).

It is clearly apparent that causal processes operate at the institutional level, beyond the levels discussed previously. Thus, the Reformation, working through the ideologies and organizational authority of elites (e.g., the state) had dramatic effects. It invested economizing with public moral significance and standing, turning private gain into a public good. It legitimized the national state and its development efforts (Mann 1986: 467ff.; Wuthnow 1989). It legitimized rational action toward progress (Poggi 1983: 70; Muench 1994: 183), supporting a whole array of public policies and their intellectual and social movement bases (e.g., the English, French, and American revolutionaries, and Adam Smith, Locke, and Rousseau). It weakened liturgical conceptions of society, and strengthened notions of a "social system" made up of empowered and responsible individual persons. In addition, it promoted the gradual rise of science as a central modern institution relevant for every collective purpose (Landes 1998: 178–179; also Weber [1923] 1950: 368; Mann 1986: 471; Foucault 1970; Drori et al. 2003).

The Reformation clearly involved institutional changes: changes in authoritative models of society, not necessarily the dispositions of individuals. As institutional changes they had long histories in Western development. These processes, absolutely central in substantive discussions, are not accommodated in the schemas of analytical individualism.

The Limiting Effects of Analytical Individualism

Real explanatory discussion, in historical and comparative research, has moved in broad and contextualizing directions, far removed from the formalisms of a doctrinal individualism. It necessarily relies upon social-organizational and institutional argumentation, as well as on individual-level ideas. Hence real theory, operative in actual intended explanations, tends to be sharply decoupled from theory in the more normative and scientistic sense.

In this section, we illustrate the limitations imposed by doctrinal individualism. As a transition, we begin with conceptualizations of European religious culture. We then give examples from discussions of European economic development, European modernity in general, postindustrial development, and world development and globalization. The intellectual limitations we are concerned with are notably: (a) an exaggerated emphasis upon individual-level causal formulations (often implausible ones); (b) failure to consider processes operating at other levels, including especially the most institutional and cultural levels; and (c) failure to consider interactions between more institutional and more individual-level processes.

Conceptualizing European Religious Culture In General

We note is passing, first, that the prominent but artificial Protestant Ethic thesis directed attention away from the substantive literature on Protestantism and its historical context. This literature, beginning with Weber himself, considered more institutional-level roles of Protestantism (e.g., Butterfield 1950, 1979; McNeill 1963; Walzer 1965; Merton 1973; more recently Fulbrook

1983; Zaret 1985; Wuthnow 1987; Gorski 2003). In this literature, Protestant-ism is represented (if in various ways) as a phase in a long-term process of European rationalization of social structures in terms of models of nature as lawful, and of society as a modifiable system, with a strong individual as its bottom-line element. Thus, far beyond the narrow economistic individual de-picted in the Protestant Ethic thesis, the ideological movements surrounding the Reformation built expanded models of nature (thus science) and of the human collective society (thus the national state) and set individuals in legiti-mated relation to both.

Second, the Protestant Ethic thesis has also deflected theoretical attention from the broader effects, including collective ideological effects, of Christi-anity itself. For instance, there are the ways that Christian models of society promoted (in comparative perspective) "the destruction of the extended fam-ily"—the "religious institutionalization of equality was the foundation upon which an autonomous bourgeoisie developed in the cities of western Europe" (Bendix 1960: 417; cf. Collins 1980, Goody 1983). There are the ways that Christianity constantly "promoted moral and social improvement" (Mann 1986: 398), one of the sources of the oft-noted "rational restlessness" (Weber) or "activism" (Eisenstadt 1987: 11–13) of European civilization. There are the ways that Christian religious orders developed ideologies of economic ra-tionalization (Collins 1986, 1999; Werner 1988). Points such as these have been well established in scholarly literatures, as the citations to central fig-ures suggest. However, such points, despite their substantive centrality, have not much entered into the dominant meta-theoretical discourses about Eu-ropean development.

The reason is that the narrow Protestant Ethic thesis conceptualized re-ligion, anachronistically, as a set of beliefs held by individual persons, not as a fundamental culture and organizational system of a European polity. This approach, by no means incidentally, treats religion in the preferred format of modern individualistic ideology. Looking through the wrong end of a his-torical telescope, it tends almost entirely to miss the institutional centrality of historical Christendom.

In this connection, and as background for the sections that follow, we wish to delineate three very basic changes in Western cultural models within Christendom. These changes help to capture long-term patterns in institu-tional development—patterns that have been sustained, as we will indicate, in the contemporary period. We refer to the evolution and institutionalization of a cultural model that envisions a *rationalized and progressive society,* made up of *empowered individuals,* and functioning in a *lawful nature* (cf. Eisenstadt 1999: 51–67).

Thus, one development involves the cultural-institutional shift toward what we now call individualism. In the cultural models of Christendom, intensified with Protestantism but antedating it, individual persons acting in a real world are placed at the center of things and are to be valued and empowered by themselves, others, and authorities. This feature is deeply institutionalized. For instance, it is located in principles of individual citizenship, which have an early origin, as Weber stressed (Bendix 1960; Bendix 1964; Collins 1980). In the contemporary period, these cultural principles are reformulated in broadened ideas of human rights (Ramirez and Meyer 2002). The underlying principles have been carried in sweeping social, cultural, and religious movements and lodged in legal and doctrinal systems (Meyer and Jepperson 2000; Frank and Meyer 2002). These movements have been relatively independent from economic developments, and the logic of capitalism has not been an especially important causal factor.

A second long-term cultural-institutional dynamic is the shift in models of collective society from liturgical to systemic (Duby 1980). Like the individual, society is envisioned as capable of improvement—it can and should progress, via rational strategies of action in a world that can be analyzed as lawful. This picture of society has a transcendent character, revealed for instance in the modern universalist assumption that development can occur anywhere. Through many transformations in Western history, from the Renaissance, Reformation, and Enlightenment down to contemporary development theories, an increasingly detailed analysis of society itself has been produced. In this analysis, society's components are desacralized (individuals aside) and seen as properly under systemic control.

A third change is indeed the long-term shift in conceptions of nature from fallen and disorderly and arbitrary to analyzable and lawful. The modern authority of science reflects a long-term outcome of this set of assumptions (Butterfield 1950; Huff 1995; Drori et al. 2003).

Integrating these components is the underlying principle of rationalization, taking three forms.[3] First, one can discern tightening organization of the Western European cultural ontology around its three primary elements: individual, society, and nature. Second, one can discern the ongoing elaboration of each element: expanded ideas (and constructions of) the individual;

expanded ideas (and "structuration" of) society; expanded ideas of (and technological interaction with) nature. Third, one can discern the ongoing systematization of the relations among the main elements—what is ordinarily meant by the term rationalization. So, in the evolving cultural model, the hard-wired individual and the systemic society can be linked together (and linked with nature) in elaborately rationalized structures. Society and individual are not fundamentally at odds. The proper individual can be integrated into the good society under the laws of nature, in ways that violate the integrity of none of these elements. This project naturally requires and justifies enormously expanded and differentiated organizational structures, to pursue technical relations with nature, and social ones between individual and society (cf. Giddens 1986 on "structuration"). In this project, a great many social structures of the premodern world are weakened and delegitimated (most prominently those linked to the old Church), and a great many new rationalized and differentiated ones are created (such as rationalized corporate organizations). We wish to invoke this evolving cultural-institutional framework in the sections that follow.

Accounting for European Economic History

For a long time, accounts of European economic development have been constrained by doctrinal individualism, taking the specific form of economism. Various analysts have detected an (Adam) "Smithian" imagery in the literature, a representation of European economic development as if it were the story of the liberation of a natural exchange system. (Marx famously complained about this tendency, of course.) Remarkable as it may seem, it is still probably accurate to say that the European economic system (and hence "capitalism" itself) has been taken for granted to some degree—and hence undertheorized. For instance, when the economic historian E. L. Jones reviewed the literature in 1980, he "found little directly on the rise of the market except in the oldest literature" (Jones 1981: 243). When Robert Brenner reviewed neo-Marxian work on capitalism, including the first volume of Wallerstein's *The Modern World System,* he found "neo-Smithians" who implicitly assumed that "capitalism was there before it emerged" (Macfarlane 1988: 191 epitomizing Brenner 1977). When Michael Mann completed his more recent synthesis of the historical literature, he observed that prominent neoclassical accounts (by North and Thomas, for instance) seemed to "assume the existence of a market in the first place" (Mann 1986: 411).

Jones pointed out that the explanandum for European economic development was obviously "much more than the usual conception of an economic process (Jones 1981: 238), involving structural changes normally held constant by economists (see North 1981: 57). Struggling with this issue earlier, Weber complained numerous times about what we would now call the naturalizing of capitalism. For instance, he criticized the tendency to see the "impulse to acquisition, pursuit of gain, of money, of the greatest possible amount of money" as the key to the European economic story: These have in themselves "nothing to do with capitalism. . . . It should be taught in the kindergarten of cultural history that this naïve idea of capitalism must be given up once and for all" (Weber [1920] 1996: 17).

For Weber, the essence of modern "rationalized" capitalism as an economic system was the expansion of production by the method of market-oriented "enterprise." When he tried to delineate this rationalized capitalism specifically, however, Weber found he had to describe an elaborate institutional complex of production arrangements, legal arrangements, markets, and financial structures (see Bendix 1960: esp. 53–54). Moreover, he had a hard time distinguishing these defining characteristics from their preconditions—that is, it was hard to isolate an economy, in any narrowly defined sense (Stinchcombe 2004: 429–431; also Bendix 1960). So, although Weber talked about "capitalism," following Marxian precedent, in practice his actual explanandum was a broad institutional system, including a normative order.[4] For instance, Weber reminded that capitalism may "even be identical with the restraint, or at least a rational tempering" of "unlimited greed for gain" (Weber [1920] 1996: 17). As a broadly defined institutional (and normative) system, this capitalism embodied an ideology of collective progress, one that entailed far more than mere support for individual accumulation. The legitimation of enterprise authority, and of freedom of contracting, was central to the expansion and stabilization of capitalism. This legitimation was provided by an ideology of economic and social progress that, as we have discussed, was bound up with the system (Stinchcombe 2004; Hirschman 1977).[5]

As later scholars problematized the European economic system, they have also followed Weber (consciously or not) in reconceptualizing the issue of explaining it. This move has occurred along two axes. First, causal reasoning has become broader and more systemic: More and more dimensions of institutional structure have been seen as centrally involved in the historical development. Second, causal forces have been conceived to operate over longer periods. We consider these points in turn.

First, in reasoning at the institutional level, one focuses upon broad organizational and cultural systems rather than more narrowly defined causal structures, such as shifts in the motives of some businessmen or the development of a few new technologies.[6] Because the explanandum, European development, is itself an institutional (and normative) system, broad political, religious, and cultural forces are likely to be intertwined with it. The evolution of Douglass North's work is illustrative. As North came to stress, "[t]he simple fact is that a dynamic theory of institutional change limited to the strictly neoclassical constraint of individualistic, rational purposive activity would never allow us to explain most secular [economic] change" (North 1981: 58). A proper account of the economic "rise of the West" seemed to require, he argued, a whole set of interrelated arguments: in his language, a theory of demographic change, a theory of the growth in the stock of knowledge, and a theory of institutions (including property rights, the state, and ideology) [1981: 7]. The details are not what is relevant here; the point is that the historical record motivated a move far beyond any standard economism. It is interesting to note that this move in a way recapitulates Weber's earlier investigations. For Weber, broad processes of political and cultural rationalization—as reflected in the development of the bureaucratic and representative state and of a more universalist economic ethic—became main causes of European economic development (see Collins's reconstruction [1980]). Both North and Weber were drawn from the details of production and exchange into delineations of broad sociocultural systems that give value and meaning to some activities and withdraw them from others. Their efforts are representative of current substantive discussion.

Second, the time frame for causal analysis has lengthened greatly. Ideas about a dramatic "industrial revolution" are no longer dominant in the substantive literature. For instance, in Mann's explicit discussion of possible formulations, the European economic explanandum becomes "an extraordinarily long and almost continuous process [of economic development] lasting from before AD 1000 to 1800" and beyond (Mann 1988: 9; cf. Jones 1987: xx–xxi, Cameron 1989, Maddison 2001).

These two shifts in the substantive discussion—both causal broadening and lengthening—have redirected attention to Christendom as a cultural and institutional complex. For some time one would not have heard about Christendom in theoretical talk about European "modernization." From the point of view of intendedly hardboiled European history, the history of the Church and of religion in general was properly located in a separate academic field. A modern scholar could be quite conversant with European history and know almost nothing about the religious component. From the point of view of analytical individualism, Christendom is too broad a construct, operating over too long a time frame. Broad institutional frameworks were to be bracketed (as too macrosociological) or were somehow seen as ineffable (as too cultural or "ideal").

However, in Mann's reconstruction—to stay with what must be the high point of recent substantive work—Christendom as a cultural-institutional framework operates as a cause in a number of fundamental institutional-level ways. For example, in Mann's account, Christendom created a "minimal society," with some "normative order" and (relative) "pacification." Early on, it institutionalized and legitimated effective local possession of autonomous economic resources and allowed goods to be commodities of exchange (Mann 1986: 406-407). Christian doctrine was a source of constant social (including economic) rationalization efforts. Complementary work by Collins stresses that Christendom's monastic orders (as in Asia) served as an initial "leading edge" of economic "breakout" from the existing coercive-agrarian economies; they were the initial commercial nodes and development engines (Collins 1986, 1999).

It is striking to note that current economic historians have featured long-term institutional-level processes too, in ways that have been missed. Economic theory tells economic historians that the engine of growth is economically useful knowledge (DeLong, forthcoming). This premise has directed their attention to knowledge systems, and then recently to science as a set of socially enabling institutions (Mokyr 2002). For example, Joel Mokyr says that economic historians, despite their differences, have one central agreement about European economic development: "Europeans knew more"—they "learned rather greedily" and wanted to apply what they learned (Mokyr 1999). Jones, in a related conclusion, noted that Europe always seemed to have "a number of individuals whose creative talents were directed to improving the means of production" (Jones 1981: 228).

This application of economic theory leads in directions that move far away from analytically individualist economism. The processes, involving knowledge systems, are institutional-level. Invocation of knowledge systems goes beyond the institutional effects called attention to by North to include the broader rationalization projects of European culture: monastic orders, scientific societies, universities, educational systems. As we discuss in detail in the following, the consequences of such rationalization projects and knowledge systems also extend far beyond the economic, creating all sorts of feedback effects (e.g., through institutions like democracy).

Talk about knowledge systems produces "analytic narratives" in economic theory that are not primarily individual-level ones, despite ideological attempts to argue that they must be (e.g., by Bates et al. 1998). And the "mechanisms," in the substantive literature, are not limited to individual-level ones. Knowledge systems include great institutions like science, the university, a whole educational apparatus, and a host of highly organized professions. These structures have roles and legitimating principles extending far beyond the motives of individual persons (Drori et al. 2003).

These intellectual developments are insufficiently recognized in self-consciously theoretical domains, given the discursive dominance of analytical individualism. Analysts fail to follow the theoretical implications of their own work. For instance, Mokyr often defaults to locating innovation in individuals, not in systems that select innovations, a far more plausible starting place for explanation (1992, 2002).[7] Landes has been criticized for invoking "culture" (in Landes 1998) as a master explanation in rather undisciplined ways, often involving vague "attitudes." We argue that analytical individualism hinders more substantial theoretical syntheses. For instance, (economic historian) Landes does not draw upon (macrosociologist) Mann's work, or upon (macrosociologist) Collins's directly relevant discussions comparing Chinese, Japanese, and European "religious capitalisms" (Collins 1986, 1999)—let alone upon sociological theory more broadly considered.

One simple way to review the preceding discussion is to note that the theory associated with analytic individualism has become more narrowly economistic (and individualistic) over time, to an impressively formalized degree. However, the substantive discussion of Western economic expansion has become less and less economistic (cf. Cameron 1989: 9–16, Engerman 2000). It has seen the Western economy as itself a broadly institutional and cultural construction, full of meanings and legitimations as much as instrumental motivations, and as intertwined with and embedded in long-lived institutional frameworks.

European Modernity in General

A core theme of analytical individualism—with its picture of history as produced by hard-wired, autonomous, and purposive individual actors—is that private instrumental goals represent the central mechanism driving historical change. For the most part, this theme gives pride of place to material economic forces in interpreting history. As modern society and its individualistic culture have developed over recent periods, this line of thought has become more extreme and intensified as formalized economistic theory. However, in striking opposition, substantive historical analyses focusing on the rise of Europe have gone in the opposite direction, seeing European rationalization and development as taking place in many different institutional sectors.

Economism, of course, is embedded in the broader narrative of modernity: Much intellectual and popular discourse has treated the core of that history as fundamentally economic. Modernity is "capitalism." The societies are "capitalist societies" or "industrial societies"—identifying societies with economic characteristics is common practice. The familiar materialist narratives rendered economic rationalization as the primary driving force, with other forms of rationalization as defensive consequences. Powerful economic forces of rationalization destroy an older society, the story went. Ultimately, in defensive balancing through multitudes of protests, political and cultural and educational rationalization arises from attempts to control the economic forces (a central version is Polanyi [1944] 1957). Mechanisms like anomie, or relative deprivation, or other defensive processes, were advanced (as in mass society theories, which despite empirical failure retain their many lives in the current period). The narrative was often given an individualist flavor, as if heroic (or demonic) capitalists and authentic (or explosively irrational) laborers, as individuals, were at the center of historical causation.

Mann finds that dominant neoclassical economic theories still "[see] history as capitalism writ large" (Mann 1986: 534). When Braudel reflected upon his own corpus of work, and upon European history writ large, he criticized Weber and the entire ensuing literature for its "exaggeration of capitalism's role as promoter of the modern world" (Braudel 1977: 67). Debates about the "transition from feudalism to capitalism," or about "the industrial revolution," located very sharply in space and time, became distillations of European modernity itself. Even the path-breaking works by Wallerstein (1974) and Perry Anderson (1974) largely identify the modern world system with the economy (in Anderson's case, by stretching the concept of "mode of production" to the breaking point). Some exceedingly narrow accounts of modernity offer economic magic bullets of one sort or another: new ploughs or ships or property rights.

The economistic imagery has not held up well under examination. Contemporary substantive work no longer treats as obvious that industrial capitalism in material production was the special breakthrough to modernity in history. The originating history has been pushed back, repeatedly: from nineteenth-century industrialization back through capitalism, Protestantism, science, urbanization, commercialization, medieval Christendom, agricultural revolution, into an institutional-ecological matrix preceding 1000 (see Mann's characterization of the literature [Mann 1988: 11–12], which is broadly concurrent with that of Landes [1998], Cameron [1989], and Maddison [2001]).

In following the record back, it has become clear that dominant theoretical narratives, in so focusing upon economic rationalization, elided Weber's other main dimension of European development: the long-term reconstruction of institutional life around rationalized bureaucracy, law, science, and individualism. In fact, the historical literature discusses social rationalization across a very broad front, one by no means especially concentrated upon economic matters. In the political system, there is the rise and legitimation of the national state in Europe's earliest periods (Strayer 1973), in its later development (Wuthnow 1989; Toulmin 1992), and in our own time (Meyer et al. 1997). There is rationalized education, which expanded dramatically after the Reformation and continues to expand at even greater rates in recent decades (Boli 1989; Schofer and Meyer 2005). There is rationalization in the religious system itself, with the rise of modern organizational forms in both denominations and congregations (e.g., Chaves and Sutton 2004). There is science, a core institution of the modern system, sometimes linked to economic activity, but typically not. Despite fashionable contemporary theoretical attempts to see close links, the capitalists are not really behind Galileo's search for moons around Jupiter and in our own time are not particularly behind the search for life on these moons. Expanding dramatically after the Reformation, science only acquired strong economic linkages in the late nineteenth and twentieth centuries (Merton 1973; Mann 1986: 471; Wuthnow 1987; Huff 1995). Even for our own time, theoretical and ideological literatures have greatly overstated the closeness of the linkages (Drori et al. 2003).

This situation is typical and reflects the defects of economistic analytical individualism. In analyzing science, education, or the rise of the (bureaucratic and democratic) state, theorists place heavy emphasis on the causal force of economic (or capitalist) development, just as they stress the putative services such institutions provide for the economy (or capitalist economy). The researchers who actually study the rise of these modern institutions do not generally find the theoretically assumed close linkages.[8] Researchers on educational expansion historically and in our own period, for example, were surprised to discover how weak the effects of economic development were (see Chabbott and Ramirez 2000 for a general review). In America and elsewhere, educational expansion preceded capitalist expansion. In the period since World War II, education expansion has been endemic, yet almost unrelated to economic conditions (Meyer et al. 1977; Meyer, Ramirez, and Soysal, 1992). The same conclusions are reached by those who actually study scientific (or political) development. The rationalized institutions of modernity, in short, arise out of long-term institutional developments in European history.

Classical economisms rested on the assumption, best articulated by Marx and Engels, that only material production revealed a true developmental history (Marx and Engels [1845-46] 1978: e.g., 154–155). This assumption, brought to light and measured against the full historical record, has not remained plausible. European political, cultural, and economic development has seemed too much of a piece, one not expressible in terms of any magic independent variable. The most intensive recent examination of the causal issues involved in explaining European modernity has undoubtedly been Mann's (1979, 1986, 1988, 1993). In grappling with historical materials, Mann found that he was compelled to distinguish four independent engines driving historical development: economic, political, military, and ideological (an imagery partly captured in the title of Ernest Gellner's complementary effort, *Plough, Sword, and Book* [Gellner 1990].) Further, Mann was unable to assign any general primacy among them: In one historical period, one driver seems the dominant "reorganizing, tracklaying force," at other times another one. Recall too that North, addressing economic outcomes only, was driven to invoke political and ideological histories, exogenous to his economic account.

Here we do not mean to endorse any particular formulation. We simply note that such substantive developments are not as theoretically prominent as they should be. When theory is so much at odds with substantive research, there are those who take the scientistic position that reality must quickly be modified (currently, in a variety of neoliberal projects). We take the scientific view that perhaps modern analytical individualist theory is imperfect and needs much repair.

Later Modernity and Postindustrial Development

Interpretations of our own societies and times show the same conspicuous disjunctions between doctrinal theory and more substantive analysis. There is a continuing overstatement of the centrality of economic rationalization and a great underemphasis on political, administrative, educational, scientific and medical rationalization. In analyzing rationalization, there is an overemphasis on the differentiation of structures and underattention to continuing social construction: the expansion of contemporary individuality, the ongoing elaboration of contemporary society. In analyzing the "economy" itself, there is too little attention to the institutional or cultural embeddedness of its activities and structure.

Empirical assessments of long institutional trends find several interrelated strands, not just one. There is indeed the ongoing expansion of the exchange system and rationalization of it. There is of course more and more elaborate monetarization and market coordination and financial structuration: Money has truly become a more generalized medium of exchange. With these changes is the associated expansion in *conceptions* of the economy—the imagined economy enlarges greatly—a cultural and institutional form now extending to a global level.

There is also the expansion of a host of noneconomic institutions, structures, and social strata, the extraordinary expansion of noneconomic criteria in assessments of social life and its goals, and the astonishing capacity of modern people (for better or worse) to act collectively in completely noneconomic ways. Theoretical discourse has concentrated upon the first strand: The common assumption has been that the dominant institutional trends in later modernity have been economic. Dominant narratives have missed (or downplayed unrealistically) the second strand: the expanded polity and the expanded society—that is, the continuation of institutional processes discussed in the previous section. Here we indicate main lacunae.

First, most basic, theoretical accounts still somehow leave out the expansion of sociopolitical controls over of the economy. All the contemporary "capitalisms" did truly become "political economies." With the rise of big government and the expansion of law, they are all more collectivist, in a sense more "communal," in Daniel Bell's formulation (Bell 1973). One forgets that Schumpeter and Polanyi were so struck by differences from the nineteenth century that they envisioned "the passing of the market economy," at least in the strict sense (Polanyi 1977). To them, the twentieth century primarily represented a massive growth in planning, what J. R. Hicks called the "administrative revolution" (Hicks 1969: chap. 10). In fact, in long-term perspective—and despite the current neoliberal period—"criteria of individual utility and profit maximization [have] become subordinated to broader conceptions of social welfare and community interest" (Bell 1973: 481). We would add that criteria of utility, both individual and collective, have been elaborated as well— there are many new forms of politically constructed value. Here, with Bell, we are referring to the expansion of explicitly conceived public goods and services: environmental protection, public health, individual health, education, and all sorts of media of self-expression.

Second, we engage in mental gymnastics to conceptualize our own society as if it were principally an economy in the old sense of commodity production (see Block 1990). This tendency involves an unfortunate equating of rationalization with monetarization, and monetarization with traditional meanings of the *economic*. However, most rationalization in the modern system, whether monetarized or not, is not traditionally economic in character (i.e., concerned with anything about commodity production or exchange). Most of it lies in rationalized educational arrangements (with their credentials and credits), medical arrangements (with their procedural definitions of care as a service, their elaborated professional and organizational forms), administrative structures in public and private life (with elaborate systems of authority and prestige), and so on. There is the rise of a whole set of institutions helping people manage a rationalized family life and, for that matter, a rationalized and elaborated life course (Meyer 1986; Meyer and Jepperson 2000). There is the now vast range of nonprofit organizations, principally engaged in the noneconomic rationalizations of the modern system, present in both national and world domains (Boli and Thomas 1999).

Within what is loosely called the economy itself the same processes of cultural elaboration and rationalization go on, little related to the logics of capitalism and the means of production. Modern firms have an astonishing array of management structures far removed from production and responding to political and cultural demands from the environment: safety people, environment people, legal officers, public relations people, accountants and economists, and so on and on. For none of these people can clear measures of economic productivity be established. All these managers, many trained in business schools with little hint of knowledge about or interest in productive forces, represent forms of rationalization very distant from what was once called, or thought of as, the economy.

Third, when rationalization involves monetarization—which it certainly often does—there is no reason to imagine that the money involved is a particularly economic commodity in the traditional sense of production and exchange. True, people are paid for something called *work* (a modern metaphor based in classic notions of labor), but think how far their activities depart from the archetypes of household or agricultural or industrial labor. People are paid, yes, but for activities that by only the greatest stretch can be called economic in any original sense—they are paid as schoolteachers, administrators, child care workers, medical personnel, counselors, and so on. Much of the money received in these activities is spent outside the commodity economy proper. A related observation can be made about profit. It is certainly a central mechanism (although with the expansion of government and nonprofits, obviously not an exclusive one), but firms accumulate it by producing not only commodities but the most broadly imaginable human services.

The point is that money, in the modern system, is far removed from any narrowly defined economy. Parsons argued that money is a generalized medium of exchange; it would be better to say, now, that it has become a generalized medium of value. Marx wrote about the power of money in bourgeois society, imagining that this power reflected economic causation in history, and modern people tend to think that way, too. (When we see the university, for instance, as too greatly influenced by considerations of money, we assume without reflection that this means by economic power.) It would be better to parallel Marx's insight with the idea that bourgeois society also developed enormous power over money: Money has, in a way, been socially appropriated, transforming it. Money, originally a narrowly economic commodity, is used to value pastors, teachers, professors, therapists, child care providers, "sex workers," students of the moons of Jupiter, and the widest variety of administrators. It is also used to support the widest array of identity activities and choices of modern persons, generated by the extraordinary legitimation of ideas of expansive personhood and its expression (Frank and Meyer 2002).

Is the monetarized economy dominating society? Or does society dominate the economy? *Both* economization and sociopolitical embeddedness have occurred and are consequences of long-run institutional developments. An analysis that focuses only on one question (like conventional economic thinking) is an interesting ideological outcome of the evolving system, but not one to be taken very seriously in substance.

Fourth, the expansion of money, as interpreted via analytically individualist ideology, has produced a vast imagined economy and an unclearly delineated one. At the extreme, the economy is thought to be present wherever exchange of any utilities is to be found. With such extraordinary concept stretching, arbitrary conflations are quick to follow. For instance, one looks for utilities—say, in family interaction—and then assumes that price-like dynamics are operative and predominant. Or, one defines the economic in terms of monetarization, and then assumes, say, that market dynamics are present—because the economic is also often associated with markets. Work is monetarized and incomes attached to jobs do have some market-like dynamics. So then one speaks freely of "labor markets" and treats pay patterns as straightforward market outcomes (as in sociology's "functional theory of stratification" and in conventional microeconomic characterizations). Yet we know from empirical research that pay is not principally established in markets (e.g., Granovetter and Tilly 1988). Educational status, for instance— a central definer of both individual and occupational positions in the modern order—has principally nonmarket bases. Somehow we imagine that the factors affecting pay— say, those producing the large cross-national differences in how much top executives make—are deflections from some sort of true underlying market value. The problematic reification of markets is readily apparent.

With such expansive conceptualization, the properties of money or markets or utilities—or any rationalization—are projected onto one another, in a way that forecloses serious analysis. Economism becomes child's play. For instance, note the current popularity of the concept *capital*: We now have human, cultural, social, and political capitals, routinely invoked in serious literatures. Although it is empirically the case that various factors affect whether (or where) a child goes to college, calling them capital, and then treating college attendance as an economic profit center, is a gross distortion. The economistic parlance of "capital" has great attraction, however, because economics is imagined as somehow most fundamental.

The vast imagined economy is an element, ultimately, of analytical individualism. Social structures that have been highly rationalized—like labor allocation and pay structures—are treated as merely economic and then built around individual choices (choice of a job, a career, a school). These choices can then be reified and focused upon, with institutional context and construction backgrounded, at best. We extend this point in our concluding section.

World Development and Globalization

Recent attention has shifted from national to regional and world levels of social organization and development. The term *globalization* has become intensely fashionable, along with a sense that forces operating at the world level have taken on lives of their own. Much of the discussion follows the familiar patterns of earlier discourse analyzing national-level developments.

Thus, globalization is commonly taken to mean economic globalization and the spread of a world capitalism. The discussion misses the rapid modern construction of a world society that transcends economic linkages (Meyer 2002). Much of modern world globalization builds its institutions not around economic controls, but around political and cultural ones (following the disaster of World War II and the crises of the Cold War). Thus we have an explosively expanding world organizational system (Boli and Thomas 1999), a network of standardizing controls over national states (Meyer et al. 1997), huge world human-rights and environmental mobilizations (Ramirez and Meyer 2003; Frank and Meyer 2002), and an exponentially growing world educational system built around common mass and elite institutions (Meyer and Ramirez 2000; Schofer and Meyer 2004). All of these institutional arrangements occur prior to, and relatively independently of, recent expansions in economic exchange. Many are actually sources of ongoing socioeconomic rationalization.

The world economy itself is a much more collectively oriented structure than we perceive: Its institutions are infused with ideas about world collective goods. Massive numbers of intergovernmental and nongovernmental associations pursue goals thought to benefit the world as a whole (Boli and Thomas 1999). Countries are routinely asked to change economic or environmental policies in the interests of the world rather than the country itself, and organizations like the World Bank proclaim and try to represent principles of ecology and of human rights.

We have, in short, a rapidly expanding global society, filled with all sorts of rationalized institutions. Nominally economic and noneconomic institutions clearly affect one another in all sorts of ways. For example, current world free-trade ideologies directly reflect ideas of the world as a single society. So do the forces that resist expanded world free trade—these groups too have a strikingly globalized character and act in terms of political and cultural norms that are now global in character. Oddly enough, both sides of the modern (and partly mock) globalization/antiglobalization battles pretend to agree with an entirely inadequate and traditional analysis. The globalization forces, in this primitive analysis, represent demonic (or virtuous) forces of world capitalism. The antiglobalization forces represent defensive or progressive (or irrational and reactionary) attempts by put-upon local communities beset by this capitalism—the old narrative, once again.

The whole analysis is distorted. It ignores the breadth of the global institutionalization process—the range of the institutional forces involved, and the extent to which they celebrate (in various and conflicting versions) models of a world society of free modern individuals. It also tends to ignore the extent to which these broader institutionalized cultural forces cause rather than simply reflect changed patterns of nominally economic relations. Faced with this expansive institutional system, producing rapid change everywhere in the world, theoretical analyses rooted in an economistic individualism have been bloodless. It is impossible to think seriously about all this change if it is seen merely in terms of economic globalization.

Conclusions and Reflections

In this paper, we presented the conventionalized Protestant Ethic thesis as an exemplar of a dominant intellectual culture of modern (especially American) social science—analytical individualism. Weber's narrow thesis, in the *Protestant Ethic,* has effectively been absorbed in a broad literature on Western rationalization. This rationalization covers many institutions, has long historical roots, and continues into our own time. It centrally involves the invention of stronger and stronger models of society as a social system. Even more centrally (at least in liberal forms), it involves the invention of stronger models of the individual as "actor" (Meyer and Jepperson 2000, Frank and Meyer 2002). In every institutional sector, processes of differentiation and rationalization have more and more tightly defined the goods of individual and society and created elaborate roles and organizational structures linking the two (and embedding both in a scientized Nature).

However, a prominent individualist theoretical discourse represents the social world as created and changed by something called "individuals," in quite a strong sense: This individual, in much Western theory, is the dramatic actor in history, and acquires this actorhood either through nature or through religious legitimation. This imagery is especially prominent in the liberal versions of Western ideology, which have been influential or dominant throughout the modern period. Corporatist or statist alternatives also focus on the individual (often more as imagined beneficiary than as creator of the social world), but to a lesser extent (see Jepperson 2002 for a typology and analysis).

In recent decades, during which the individualist and reductionist aspects of the Weber thesis have been given special attention, liberalism has turned quite triumphant.

The tendency to see the individual as a very real (i.e., natural and materially focused) center for the social universe goes far beyond a decorative metatheoretical individualism. It infuses (and, from an analytic point of view, distorts) the Western intellectual, social, and policy self-conceptions and analyses. We call anything rationalized "economic" and even more see anything monetarized as "economic." We root our explanations of these things in an individualist rhetoric, understating the extraordinary power of ideas (models, myths) of the collective good in modern social change. We become ideologues of the modern system's individualism, instead of analyzing this individualism and economism as something like a religious form.

The fact that contemporary social science operates within a vast and highly institutionalized system sustains individualist mythology. If they are so inclined, social scientists can simply take for granted the elaborate rationalization and institutionalization and then focus upon individual behaviors in investment, labor, innovation, management, and the like. One can rest content that such behaviors, construed as choices, somehow "ultimately" produce and reproduce the system. (One can likewise take for granted the role structure of organizations and institutions and treat people as merely typical individuals making decisions.) In fact, the more extensive and secure the institutionalization, the more that one can cultivate exclusively individualistic intellectual tastes. From a strictly scientific standpoint, the recurring causes of an institutionalized system are institutional reproduction routines, along with processes of institutional change (Jepperson 1991; Scott 2001). Yet this institutional reproduction (and change) may merely be set aside intellectually as somehow not truly fundamental. One can then imagine that all causation is merely individual action subject to constraints. Taking for granted an elaborate system, one can also imagine that no cultural dynamics are present: just raw individuals— more truly natural now, in emancipated modernity—making their choices.

Until very recently, this mythology has been constructed around ideas of national societies. In recent decades, these ideas have come undone and cultural models have begun to depict society as global in character. This evolution destabilizes some social scientific thinking and in a curious way repeats at a world level some of the intellectual and ideological trends of the earlier evolution of the liberal national state and society.

The rapidly integrating world we observe is a strikingly liberal system, because it has almost no capacity for a strong state (Meyer 2002). Its political forms are thus like those observed by Tocqueville in the stateless nineteenth-century America. One such form is extraordinarily intensified liberal individualism—notions of the strong, socialized, involved, participatory individual human actor. Thus we get, on both right and left, very strong emphases on the individual in the modern globalized world. On the right, one finds sweeping doctrines about property rights, individual values, individual educational achievement, due process, and so on. On the left, one finds equally sweeping doctrines about human rights in other (more welfare-related) senses. The ideological uses of individualism, in other words, remain very much alive, and we can predict that Protestant Ethic–like theses—in the most individualist and reductionist forms—will continue to be a kind of proof text, now of global individualism. We can also predict that the distortions in social scientific analysis produced by such emphases will continue to shadow our analyses of the globalized world.

References

Anderson, Perry. 1974. *Lineages of the Absolutist State.* London: New Left Books.

Baechler, Jean, et al. 1988. *Europe and the Rise of Capitalism,* edited by Jean Baechler, John A. Hall, and Michael Mann. Oxford: Basil Blackwell.

Bates, Robert, Avner Greif, Margaret Levi, Jean-Laurent Rosenthal, and Barry R. Weingast. 1998. *Analytic Narratives.* Princeton: Princeton University Press.

Bell, Daniel. 1973. *The Coming of Post-Industrial Society.* New York: Basic Books.

Bendix, Reinhard. 1960. *Max Weber: An Intellectual Portrait.* Garden City, NY: Anchor.

———. 1964. *Nation-Building and Citizenship.* New York: John Wiley & Sons.

Berman, Harold J. 1983. *Law and Revolution: The Formation of the Western Legal Tradition.* Cambridge, MA: Harvard University Press.

Block, Fred. 1990. *Postindustrial Possibilities: A Critique of Economic Discourse.* Berkeley: University of California Press.

Boli, John. 1989. *New Citizens for a New Society.* Elmsford, NY: Pergamon.

Boli, John, and George Thomas. 1999. *Constructing World Culture: International Nongovernmental Organizations since 1875,* edited by John Boli and George M. Thomas. Stanford: Stanford University Press.

Braudel, Fernand. 1977. *Afterthoughts on Material Civilization and Capitalism.* Baltimore: Johns Hopkins University Press.

Brenner, Robert. 1977. "The Origins of Capitalist Development: A Critique of Neo-Smithian Marxism." *New Left Review* 104: 25-92.

Butterfield, Herbert. 1950. *The Origins of Modern Science, 1300–1800*. London: G. Bell and Sons.

———. 1979. *Herbert Butterfield: Writings on Christianity and History,* edited by C. T. McIntire. New York: Oxford University Press.

Cameron, Rondo. 1989. *A Concise Economic History of the World*. Oxford: Oxford University Press.

Chabbott, Colette, and Francisco Ramirez. 2000. "Development and Education." Pp.163–187 in *Handbook of the Sociology of Education,* edited by Maureen Hallinan. New York: Plenum.

Chaves, Mark, and John Sutton. 2004. "Organizational Consolidation in American Protestant Denominations, 1870–1990." *Journal for the Scientific Study of Religion* 43: 41–66.

Coleman, James S. 1986. "Social Theory, Social Research, and a Theory of Action." *American Journal of Sociology* 91:1309–1335.

———. 1990. *Foundations of Social Theory*. Cambridge, MA: Harvard University Press.

Collins, Randall. 1980. "Weber's Last Theory of Capitalism: A Systematization." *American Sociological Review* 45:925–942.

———. 1986. *Weberian Sociological Theory*. Cambridge, UK: Cambridge University Press.

———. 1999. *Macrohistory*. Stanford: Stanford University Press.

DeLong, J. Bradford. Forthcoming. "What Do We Really Know about Economic Growth." In *Economic Growth,* edited by Michael Boskin. Stanford: Hoover Institution.

Drori, Gili, John W. Meyer, Francisco O. Ramirez, and Evan Schofer. 2003. *Science in the Modern World Polity: Institutionalization and Globalization*. Palo Alto, CA: Stanford University Press.

Duby, Georges. 1980. *The Three Orders: Feudal Society Imagined*. Chicago: University of Chicago Press.

Durkheim, Emile. [1898] 1969. "Individualism and the Intellectuals." *Political Studies* 17: 14–30.

Eisenstadt, S. N. 1987. "Centre Formation and Protest Movements." Pp. 7–23 in *Centre Formation, Protest Movements and Class Structure in Europe and the United States,* by S. N. Eisenstadt, L. Roniger, and A. Seligman. London: Frances Pinter.

———. 1999. *Fundamentalism, Sectarianism, and Revolution*. Cambridge, UK: Cambridge University Press.

Engerman, Stanley L. 2000. "Max Weber as Economist and Economic Historian." Pp. 256–271 in *The Cambridge Companion to Weber,* edited by Stephen Turner. Cambridge, UK: Cambridge University Press.

Foucault, Michel. 1970. *The Order of Things*. New York: Pantheon Books.

Frank, David, and John W. Meyer. 2002. "The Contemporary Identity Explosion: Individualizing Society in the Post-War Period." *Sociological Theory* 20: 86–105.

Fulbrook, Mary. 1983. *Piety and Politics*. Cambridge, UK: Cambridge University Press.

Gellner, Ernest. 1990. *Plough, Sword, and Book*. Chicago: University of Chicago Press.

Giddens, Anthony. 1986. *The Constitution of Society: Outline of a Theory of Structuration*. Berkeley: University of California Press.

Goody, Jack. 1983. *The Development of the Family and Marriage in Europe*. Cambridge, UK: Cambridge University Press.

Gorski, Philip S. 2003. *The Disciplinary Revolution*. Chicago: University of Chicago Press.

Granovetter, Mark, and Charles Tilly. 1988. "Inequality and Labor Processes." Pp. 175–221 in *Handbook of Sociology*, edited by Neil Smelser. Newbury Park, CA: Sage.

Hamilton, Alastair. 2000. "Max Weber's *Protestant Ethic and the Spirit of Capitalism*." Pp. 151–171 in *The Cambridge Companion to Weber*, edited by Stephen Turner. Cambridge, UK: Cambridge University Press.

Hernes, Gudmund. 1976. "Structural Change in Social Processes." *American Journal of Sociology*. 82: 513–54.

———. 1989. "The Logic of the Protestant Ethic." *Journal of Rationality and Society* 1: 122–161.

Hicks, John. 1969. *A Theory of Economic History*. Oxford, UK: Oxford University Press.

Hirschman, Albert. 1977. *The Passions and the Interests*. Princeton, NJ: Princeton University Press.

Hoff, Karla, and Joseph E. Stiglitz. 2000. "Modern Economic Theory and Development." Pp. 389–459 in *Frontiers of Development Economics*, edited by Gerald M. Meier and Joseph E. Stiglitz. New York: Oxford University Press.

Huff, Toby. 1995. *The Rise of Early Modern Science: Islam, China and the West*. Cambridge, UK: Cambridge University Press.

Jepperson, Ronald L. 1991. "Institutions, Institutional Effects, and Institutionalism." Pp. 143–63 in *The New Institutionalism in Organizational Analysis*, edited by Walter W. Powell and Paul J. DiMaggio. Chicago: University of Chicago Press.

———. 2002. "Political Modernities: Disentangling Two Underlying Dimensions of Institutional Differentiation." *Sociological Theory* 20: 61–85.

Jones, E. L. 1981. *The European Miracle*. New York: Cambridge University Press.

———. 1987. *The European Miracle*, 2nd edition. New York: Cambridge University Press.

Landes, David S. 1998. *The Wealth and Poverty of Nations*. New York: Norton.

Macfarlane, Alan.1988. "The Cradle of Capitalism: The Case of England." Pp. 185–203 in *Europe and the Rise of Capitalism*, edited by Jean Baechler, John A. Hall, and Michael Mann. Oxford, UK: Basil Blackwell.

Maddison, Angus. 2001. *The World Economy: A Millennial Perspective*. Paris: Organization for Economic Cooperation and Development.

Mann, Michael. 1979. "Idealism and Materialism in Sociological Theory." Pp. 97–120 in *Critical Sociology*, edited by J. W. Freiberg. New York: Irvington Publishers.

———. 1986. *The Sources of Social Power*, Volume 1. Cambridge, UK: Cambridge University Press.

———. 1988. "European Development: Approaching a Historical Explanation." Pp. 6–19 in *Europe and the Rise of Capitalism,* edited by Jean Baechler, John A. Hall, and Michael Mann. Oxford, UK: Basil Blackwell.

———. 1993. *The Sources of Social Power,* Volume 2. Cambridge, UK: Cambridge University Press.

Marx, Karl, and Friedrich Engels. [1845–46] 1978. "The German Ideology." Pp. 146–200 in *The Marx-Engels Reader,* 2nd edition, edited by Robert C. Tucker. New York: Norton.

McClelland, David. 1967. *The Achieving Society.* New York: Free Press.

McNeill, William. 1963. *The Rise of the West.* Chicago: University of Chicago Press.

Merton, Robert. 1973. *The Sociology of Science.* Chicago: University of Chicago Press.

Meyer, John W. 1986. "The Self and the Life Course: Institutionalization and Its Effects." Pp. 199–216 in *Human Development and the Life Course,* edited by A. Sorensen, F. Weinert, and L. Sherrod. Hillsdale, NJ: Erlbaum.

———. 2002. "Globalization, National Culture, and the Future of the World Polity." *Hong Kong Journal of Sociology* 3: 1–18.

Meyer, John W., John Boli, George Thomas, and Francisco Ramirez. 1997. "World Society and the Nation-State." *American Journal of Sociology* 103:144–81.

Meyer, John W., and Ronald L. Jepperson. 2000. "The 'Actors' of Modern Society: The Cultural Construction of Social Agency." *Sociological Theory* 18:100–120.

Meyer, John W., and Francisco Ramirez. 2000. "The World Institutionalization of Education." Pp. 111–32 in *Discourse Formation in Comparative Education,* edited by J. Schriewer. Frankfurt: Peter Lang.

Meyer, John W., Francisco Ramirez, Richard Rubinson, and John Boli-Bennett. 1977. "The World Educational Revolution, 1950–1970." *Sociology of Education* 50: 242–258.

Meyer, John W., Francisco Ramirez, and Yasemin Soysal. 1992. "World Expansion of Mass Education, 1870–1970." *Sociology of Education* 65: 128–149.

Mokyr, Joel. 1992. *The Lever of Riches.* Oxford, UK: Oxford University Press.

———. 1999. "Eurocentricity Triumphant." Published online in *The American Historical Review* 104 (4).

———. 2002. *The Gifts of Athena.* Princeton, NJ: Princeton University Press.

Muench, Richard. 1994. *Sociological Theory: From the 1850s to the 1920s.* Chicago: Nelson-Hall. New York: Plenum.

North, Douglass C. 1981. *Structure and Change in Economic History.* New York: Norton.

Parkin, Frank. 1982. *Max Weber.* London: Routledge.

Parsons, Talcott. 1937. *The Structure of Social Action.* New York: McGraw-Hill.

———. 1947. "Introduction." Pp. 3–86 in *Max Weber: The Theory of Social and Economic Organization,* translated by A. M. Henderson and Talcott Parsons, and edited with an introduction by Talcott Parsons. New York: Free Press.

———. 1951. *The Social System.* New York: Free Press.

Poggi, Gianfranco. 1983. *Calvinism and the Capitalist Spirit: Max's Weber's Protestant Ethic.* Amherst: The University of Massachusetts Press.

Polanyi, Karl. [1944] 1957. *The Great Transformation*. Boston: Beacon Press.

———. 1977. *The Livelihood of Man*. New York: Academic Press.

Ramirez, Francisco, and John W. Meyer. 2002. "Expansion and Impact of the World Human Rights Regime: Longitudinal and Cross-National Analyses over the Twentieth Century." National Science Foundation proposal (2002–2004).

Schofer, Evan, and John W. Meyer. 2005. "The World-Wide Expansion of Higher Education in the Twentieth Century." *American Sociological Review* 70: 898–920.

Scott, W. Richard. 2001. *Institutions and Organizations*, 2nd edition. Thousand Oaks, CA: Sage Publications.

Stinchcombe, Arthur. 2004. "The Preconditions of World Capitalism: Weber Updated." *The Journal of Political Philosophy* 11: 411–436.

Strayer, Joseph. 1973. *The Medieval Origins of the Modern State*. Princeton, NJ: Princeton University Press.

Tilly, Charles. 1990. *Coercion, Capital, and European States*. Cambridge, MA: Blackwell.

Toulmin, Stephen. 1992. *Cosmopolis : The Hidden Agenda of Modernity*. Chicago: The University of Chicago Press.

Viner, Jacob. 1978. *Religious Thought and Economic Society*, edited by J. Melitz and D. Winch. Durham, NC: Duke University Press.

Wallerstein, Immanuel. 1974. *The Modern World System*, Volume 1. New York: Academic Press.

Walzer, Michael. 1965. *The Revolution of the Saints*. Cambridge, MA: Harvard University Press.

Weber, Max. [1904/5] 1996. *The Protestant Ethic and the Spirit of Capitalism*. Los Angeles: Roxbury.

———. [1920] 1996. "Max Weber's Introduction to the Sociology of Religion (1920)." Pp. 13–31 in *The Protestant Ethic and the Spirit of Capitalism*, by Max Weber. Los Angeles: Roxbury.

———. [1923] 1950. *General Economic History*. Glencoe, IL: The Free Press.

———. [1925] 1954. *Max Weber on Law in Economy and Society*. Cambridge, MA: Harvard University Press.

Werner, Karl Ferdinand. 1988. "Political and Social Structures of the West." Pp. 169–184 in *Europe and the Rise of Capitalism*, edited by Jean Baechler, John A. Hall, and Michael Mann. Oxford, UK: Basil Blackwell.

Wuthnow, Robert. 1987. *Meaning and Moral Order*. Berkeley: University of California Press.

———. 1989. *Communities of Discourse: Ideology and Social Structure in the Reformation, the Enlightenment, and European Socialism*. Cambridge, MA: Harvard University Press.

Zaret, David. 1985. *The Heavenly Contract*. Chicago: University of Chicago Press.

Zetterberg, Hans L. 1977. *On Theory and Verification in Sociology*, 3rd edition. Totowa, NJ: Bedminster. 67–69.

———. 1993. "Rationalism and Capitalism: Max Weber." Chap. 2 of the Web publication *European Proponents of Sociology Prior To World War I*. Copyright 1993 Hans L. Zetterberg.

Notes to Chapter Eleven

1. We have benefited from comments from Al Bergesen, David Frank, Peter Meyer, Francisco Ramirez, Ann Swidler, and the participants at the 2004 conference upon which this book is based.

2. In an initial discussion of the Protestant Ethic, before his commitment to doctrinal individualism was intensified, Coleman indicated that causal effects can occur at multiple levels of analysis. He even gave an example of a collective effect (Coleman 1986: 198). The example disappeared in the subsequent development of his story (1990). In this later treatment, Coleman reifies the "macro to micro to macro" scheme and concentrates upon the issues associated with aggregation.

4. Weber used the term *rationalization* broadly to denote a wide range of projects of systematization and ordering: in his words, of "economic life, of technique, of scientific research, of military training, of law and administration," and even of "mystical contemplation" (Weber [1920] 1996: 26). He saw "Occidental rationalism" as itself a distinctive culture, propelled by various religious, political, and intellectual movements, and then institutionalized in various structures (like states, sciences, and professions—the great rationalizers of modern societies) [Muench 1994: chap. 9].

4. Parsons goes as far as to argue that "'Capitalism' in the sense in which Weber means it, must be regarded not as a form of economic organization alone, but as the distinctive pattern of a whole society. Terminologically this agreed with other schools of thought, notably the Marxian, of which Weber was acutely conscious." Parsons says that Weber often uses the term to refer to the "total institutional order" (Parsons 1947: 79).

5. Stinchcombe argues that the belief that capitalism brings progress was a "latent precondition" of capitalism in Weber's analysis. He gives reasons for concurring with Weber (Stinchcombe 2004: 429–431).

6. It is telling that a recent overview of "modern economic theory and development" opens by stating that "[d]evelopment is no longer seen primarily as a process of capital accumulation but rather as a process of organizational change" (Hoff and Stiglitz 2000: 389).

7. Our comments here parallel Braudel's criticism of Schumpeter for treating the entrepreneur as a "sort of *deus ex machina*" (1977: 63). However, we note that Mokyr in recent statements invokes explicitly macrocultural ideas, referring to the importance of an "epistemological" distinctiveness of Western culture and of an "industrial enlightenment" preceding nineteenth-century industrialization (Mokyr 2002).

8. For instance, Weber concluded that "capitalism has not been a decisive factor in the promotion of that form of 'rationalization' of the law which has been peculiar to the Continental West ever since the rise of Romanist studies in the medieval universities" (Weber [1925] 1954: 318). Contemporary studies have supported this judgment (e.g., Berman 1983: 538ff.).

12 Bootstrapping Development: Rethinking the Role of Public Intervention in Promoting Growth

Charles F. Sabel, Columbia University Law School

W EBER'S *THE PROTESTANT ETHIC AND THE SPIRIT OF CAPI-talism,* now a century old, is surely the most brilliant and influential statement of the dominant, endowment explanation of economic development. The disarmingly simple core of this view is that an economy grows if, and only if, it is endowed with those features that dispose economic actors to engage in market exchange, not least by protecting their interests when they do. In Weber's original formulation the emphasis is famously on motivational features, particularly the disposition to calculating entrepreneurial striving by which, he argued, members of certain Protestant sects tempered the tormenting theological uncertainty of their personal salvation. The currently dominant institutional variant of the endowment notion shifts the emphasis from (the preconditions to) individual motivation to the general conditions facilitating market exchange, especially the presence of legal rules that help induce investment by protecting property rights broadly understood, and the availability of courts and regulatory bodies capable of adjusting the rules to serve this end when circumstances demand. Such nuances aside, these views both assume that the features that favor or obstruct development are part of a society's fundamental constitution—its definitive endowments—and as such are all but inaccessible to deliberate revision. Thus, a society that has not spontaneously generated the growth-promoting endowments, or acquired them as a historical legacy (for instance, through colonization by a society that is so endowed) is likely to come into possession of them only when continuing stagnation renders it unable to resist the conforming pressure of more successful competitors.[1]

So tight has been the grip of this institutional endowment view on intellectual and policy circles in recent decades that, with few exceptions, debate has been limited to squabbles over how best to interpret it. The official interpretation—promulgated as the "Washington Consensus" by the International Monetary Fund and the World Bank—is that the only institutions favoring growth are those that directly prohibit market distortion or obstruct political manipulations with distortionary effects. Import duties and export subsidies are to be eliminated (liberalization); state-owned firms, managed for the benefit of electoral clienteles and their elite patrons, sold off (privatization); public spending, with its continuing temptation to populist excess, reduced and redirected to debt service (stabilization). Courts and other rule-interpreting and -enforcing entities—together, the rule of law—are added, in the current, "second-generation" version of the consensus, as indispensable market-making institutions, for without them, recent experience teaches, the prohibitions on and precautions against distortion have no effect.[2]

The heterodox interpretation of the institutional endowment view, associated with the early work of Rodrik and his collaborators,[3] also assumes that participation in the world economy—openness—is indispensable to growth. It finds, however, that the most effective means for a particular economy to enter world competition depend on idiosyncrasies of its context and may well involve (temporary) institutional innovations disallowed by the consensus. Thus, from the heterodox perspective, incentives to export (expeditious regulation for firms in export-processing exclaves, provision of sector-specific research and physical infrastructure) can be judiciously combined with protection of the nontraded sector (tariffs and minimum-wage laws) and with controls on capital flows to maximize the chances of effective opening while minimizing the chances of a sweeping domestic disruption through a flood of imports or an international financial shock.

In recent years failures of consensus-based reform programs in countries as different as Russia, Bolivia, and East Germany; successful heterodox openings in China, India, Mauritius, and Botswana (the last two being the post–World War II African success stories); and the detailed findings of empirical evaluations of the orthodox institutional view are moving proponents of the heterodox view to transform what began as an intramural challenge to the endowments school into (the beginnings of) an alternative to it. Where the consensus view sees market-favoring institutions as an all-or-nothing proposition, with still-to-develop economies typically endowed with nothing, the emergent process or bootstrapping view of growth sees developing economies as often, perhaps nearly always, disposing of many of the institutions and capacities needed for growth. At any moment what obstructs growth in a particular, currently stagnating economy, on this view, is some combination of two kinds of constraints. The first kind is the direct obstacles to market exchange (though these tend to be less frequent and daunting than the consensus holds). The second and often more important type of constraint is the absence of certain public goods: support institutions that help potential exporters determine where they should direct their efforts, and then provide the training, quality certification, physical infrastructure, and various stages of venture capital that new entrants to the export sector are unlikely to be able to provide themselves. Removal of the most pressing bundle of constraints, the argument continues, raises growth rates by several percentage points a year. Continued growth, and the gradual transformation of an economy into a reliably growing "tiger," depends on relaxing successive (and successively different) bundles.

The focus on relaxing successive constraints corresponds to a reinterpretation of the kinds of institutions that favor growth; this reinterpretation in turn undermines the claim that growth depends on institutional endowments in the familiar sense of a single, well-defined set of mutually supportive institutions. As a reform program, the goal of the consensus view is to create institutions that shape economic activity—directing it toward market transactions—yet are not shaped by it, except as may be required by (and limited through) the rule of law. Behind this idea of institutions as a kind of *deus absconditus* lies, as we shall see in more detail later, the economist's inveterate fear (periodically refueled by the failure of traditional government industrial policies for accelerating development) that the very possibility of changing the rules of the economic game provokes a power struggle among economic actors determined to advance their interests by political manipulation rather than competition in the market place.

The process or bootstrapping view, in contrast, assumes that even in the absence of market distortions, growth requires continuing social learning. The goal therefore is to create institutions that can learn to identify and mitigate different, successive constraints on growth, including of course such constraints as arise from defects in the current organization of the learning institutions themselves. Insofar as these institutional interventions go beyond rescission of the market-obstructing rules and aim to shape entrepreneurial behavior (if only by helping potential entrepreneurs clarify what their choices might be) they resemble the traditional industrial policies—the state-picking winners—that the consensus vehemently rejects. That is as far as the similarity between industrial policy in the traditional sense and the process view goes, however. Traditional industrial policy assumes that the state has a panoramic view of the economy, enabling it reliably to provide incentives, information, and services that less knowledgeable private actors cannot. There are no actors in the process or bootstrapping view with this kind of overarching vision. All vantage points are partial. So just as private actors typically need public help in overcoming information limits and coordination problems, the public actors who provide that help themselves routinely need assistance from other actors, private and public, in overcoming limitations of their own. Instead of trying to build inviolate public institutions whose perfection guarantees, once and for all, an equally inviolate, but wholly private, market order, the process view aims for corrigibility: institutions which, acknowledging the vanity of perfectibility from the beginning on can be rebuilt, again and again, by changing combinations of public and private actors, in light of the changing social constraints on market activity that their activity helps bring to notice.

If growth-favoring institutions are indeed built by a bootstrapping process where each move suggests the next, then such institutions are as much the outcome as the starting point of development. They cannot, in other words, be as the endowments view portrays them: a foundation upon which a market order must be built if it is to stand at all.

The only exception is when the rules, institutions, and distribution of political power in a particular economy all interlock in ways that make it impossible to identify and mitigate current constraints. When there are such infernal traps—market failures aggravating and aggravated by government failures aggravating and aggravated by political failures and failures of civil society—bootstrapping is stopped before it gets off to a (potentially) self-reinforcing start. This can be the case, for example, when political elites, seizing control of oil or other natural resources, prefer to live by predation and terror and actively block domestic development and the alternative centers of power it creates.[5] If such lock-ins are common, then the process view of the circumstances of economic development is just wrong, and the consensus emphasis on uprooting market-obstructing institutions and its disdain for heterodox solutions are easily understandable. However, as we will see, evidence is accumulating so rapidly against this possibility that the process view's program of institutional investigation and reform is arguably a better guide to reflection and action than that of the endowment school.

This essay aims to contribute to the emerging process agenda by detailing some of the key steps that lead to the new view and by specifying some organizational features of and open questions regarding the corrigible, learning institutions at its core. The following section traces the shift within the endowment school of development from the motivational perspective rooted in Weber's sociology to the institutional perspective currently associated with economics. The next section, "The New Stylized Facts of Economic Development," marshals the growing body of evidence weighing at once against the endowment view and for the bootstrapping alternative. "Developing Economies as Toyoda Production Systems" connects the discussion of learning institutions as it arises from evaluation of the evidence in developing economies to discussion of the rapid diffusion of like organizations in the private and public sectors of the advanced democracies, and shows how related ideas are coming to shape development policy.

From Motivation to Institutions: A Selective History of the Endowment View of Growth

Although the endowment school is presently focused on institutions as conceived by economists, the shift of attention from motivation to institutions in development was initiated by sociologists and historians, many of them reacting to Weber's *Protestant Ethic*. Reviewing the nub of their objections to Weber's thesis reminds us why the institutional perspective, whatever the difficulties that arise from its present association with endowments and foundations, is likely to remain central to our understanding of growth. Two episodes in an intricate, extended debate are especially illustrative.

The first concerns the relation between capitalism and Protestantism in Colonial New England.[5] As settlement of New England was led by Quakers and Puritans—two of the Reformed sects that embodied Weber's Protestant ethos—development there, if anywhere, should have demonstrated the economically transformative power of theologically induced worldly striving. The religious legacy of reform proved, on detailed investigation, more ambiguous than Weber claimed, however, and its effect on economic development correspondingly vexed.

There were, to be sure, prominent merchants for whom commerce was a calling, a this-worldly means of demonstrating in fact what sectarian doctrine denied in principle: the assurance of salvation. Set against this group of successful traders was a much larger body of artisans and farmers. Of much more modest means, they concluded from the same theological commitments that the striving for wealth, however motivated, must be subordinated to the preservation of an egalitarian spiritual commonwealth. Their spokesman was John Winthrop, governor, with brief interruptions, of the Massachusetts colony from its founding in 1630 to 1648, the year before he died. Winthrop's sermon on the "Model of Christian Charity" celebrated the virtues of traditional landed society, with its fixed social classes; condemned competitive, calculating self-seeking; and assigned the rich substantial responsibility for the well-being of the poor.[6] To meet their mutual ethical obligations, he concluded, the community of believers must "be knit together . . . as one man . . . in brotherly affection . . . willing to abridge ourselves of our superfluities, for the supply of other's necessities."[7] This communitarianism was given effect by the Massachusetts General Court in 1640 in laws favoring debtors over their merchant creditors.[8]

By the early eighteenth century the "merchant" interpretation of Puritanism, colored through intermarriage with Anglicans, was so influential among the Boston clergy that they remained neutral when conflict surged again between debtors and creditors. Not so in the countryside. There, despite harsh conditions, elaborate arranged marriages and careful inheritance strategies allowed a growing population to maintain the freehold tradition of the first settlers. But only just: By 1770 the average free, white person in New England had holdings valued at £33, whereas the corresponding figure was £51 in the wheat-exporting Middle Colonies of New York and Pennsylvania and £132 in the plantation economies further to the South. As Gary Nash puts it, "a peculiar Puritan blend of participatory involvement within a hierarchically structured society of lineal families on small community-oriented farms" produced "the least dynamic region of the British mainland colonies."[9]

The economically precarious New England countryside also proved especially susceptible to periodic calls to revive the ardor, rigor, and communitarian commitments of the founding religious sects. Of these revivals the Great Awakening of 1740 was the most extended and consequential. As the

American counterpart to English Methodism, the Great Awakening at first appealed to Protestants across class and doctrinal lines. The communitarian aspect soon came to dominate, however, as Evangelical preachers challenged the connection between divine grace and worldly activity more and more openly. Jonathan Edwards, one of the leading evangelical ministers, declared that "wicked debauched men" used commerce "to favor . . . covetousness and pride."[10] The outcome of the Great Awakening was to destroy even the tenuous link that had until that time existed between Calvinism and capitalism: Calvinism declined among the merchants in American seaports and European cities, while capitalism became even more suspect in congregations of rural New England and Virginia.

The triumph of the market order and the factory system that was its most visible manifestation came in the following century.[11] But this new order was much less the work of merchants (whether acting in pursuit of a calling or not) than of judges, who reshaped traditional common-law protection of property rights to favor economic development. Under common law, riparian owners, for instance, were entitled to the undiminished flow of water coursing by their property. Owners who dammed rivers to secure flows for water power were therefore traditionally required to compensate upstream neighbors for flooding caused by the dam. As the payment of damages reduced the return on the dam, the common law in this situation, and many others like it, slowed development in an early phase, when the uncertainty of a truly novel epoch— what would industrialization bring?—made investment especially risky in any case. During the first half of the nineteenth century, judges relaxed these constraints, allowing property owners who invested in efficiency-enhancing improvements to shift to others the costs of resultant harms (land submerged by reservoirs; fires ignited by sparks from passing locomotives).[12]

Thus, given the gap between individual or small-group behavior and the creation of institutional frameworks for social action, early American experience suggests that the Protestant ethos was not a sufficient condition for capitalist development. Indeed, given the complex and often contradictory implications of reform theology for ordering individual and social life, it is hard to see how, in any straightforward sense, it was a necessary condition either.

Investigation of economic development outside the Protestant ambit—first in Catholic countries, then Asia—led to convergent conclusions. If Weber was right to think that unlimited but calculating individual striving was the key to growth and religious questing key to this motivation, then there must be in all growing, non-Protestant economies some theological mechanism with motivational effects equivalent to those produced by Calvinist doubts about personal salvation. In Asia, to take the case that most directly influenced the debate under consideration here, such analogues abounded. Japan had Jodo and Zen Buddhists as well as the Hotoku and Shingaku movements; Java the Santri Muslims; India the Jains, Parsis, and various business or merchant castes. David C. McClelland grouped all those sects into a general category of "positive mysticisms," which included Weber's Protestant ethic.[13]

But as in the case of Puritanism in colonial America, the "positive mysticisms" or "achievement orientation" of Asian sects and social groups yielded capitalist economic development only in the context of supporting institutions that did not arise directly from their behavior, no matter how much religious conviction or social orientation might incline individual members of these groupings to enact capitalism in their own lives. Thus the Japanese samurai, prominent from the sixteenth century on, became paladins of capitalist enterprise only after the Meiji restoration freed them of their political obligations and removed legal barriers to their exercise of certain trades. Chinese merchants had limited success within the structure of Imperial China but became redoubtable capitalists in Southeast Asia. The Muslim Santri merchants of Java were becoming vigorous entrepreneurs in the early twentieth century, but relapsed into a more traditional trader role as institutional conditions became less favorable during the Great Depression. The implication for sociologists and anthropologists writing in the 1960s was clear enough. "Motivation," Bellah wrote, had to be considered "in close connection with institutional structure and its historical development." Geertz, with whom Bellah closely associated himself, concluded that economic development "demands a deep going transformation of the basic structure of society and, beyond that, perhaps even in the underlying value-system in terms of which that structure operates."[14] From this point of view Weber's *Protestant Ethic* was an elegant metonymy—an emblem of the encompassing Reformation of which it was only a part; and the challenge to the sociology of development or modernization was to produce an account of the conditions and consequences of the (evolutionary sequence of) such transformations.

Although this program had considerable resonance in social theory, for example in the work of Habermas,[15] in Anglo-American academic and policy debate it was, with the occasional brilliant, unrequited exception,[16] economists rather than sociologists who most assiduously investigated the institutional preconditions of capitalism. Responding to the stagnation of the social welfare states after the first oil crisis in 1973, the reverses suffered by developing economies in Latin American and elsewhere that had pursed interventionist industrial or import-substituting strategies, and the collapse of the plan economies, they articulated a view of market-making institutions that grew out of and gave theoretical legitimacy to the Washington Consensus.

The work of, Glaeser, La Porte, Schleifer, and their collaborators gives paradigmatic expression to this institutionalist view. The general and timeless assumption, as presented, for instance, in an influential essay on "Legal Origins," is that efficient rules of fair exchange arise naturally in communities of free and equal traders.[17] Efficient or market-favoring law is that which identifies and gives effect to these rules, thus protecting the traders who rely on them against coercion by politically powerful interests. Common law is the most efficient kind of law because its "independent" lay judges are both secure against meddling by political superiors and, given their reliance on oral argument and broad legal principles, especially receptive to the subtleties of emergent rules. Civil law, with its professional, "state-controlled" judges constrained by written codes, is both more susceptible to political influence and less open to spontaneous innovation. This is why "at the same level of development, French civil law countries exhibit heavier regulation, less secure property rights, more corrupt and less efficient governments, and even less political freedom than do the common-law countries."[18]

Because the persistence of civil law shows that power can trump efficiency for long periods, the argument continues, the emergence of common law in England can only be explained by a happy fortuity: In the tenth and eleventh centuries English magnates, fairly matched among themselves, feared their king more than they feared one another. So, in an exchange formalized in the Magna Charta, they pledged tax revenues to the King in return for the right to adjudicate their own disputes locally. In France, in contrast, the lesser magnates feared the greater ones more than the king so they preferred royal justice, even with the attendant risks of politicization, to local adjudication. Once reached, these settlements were hard to disentrench. In the very long term, however, pressure for increased institutional efficiency has led civil law jurisdictions to adopt rules that limit the discretion of judges (reducing the dangers of political meddling) while directing the codes to mimic the outcomes obtained by common-law winnowing of community norms. In this sense the cunning of reason, acting through the market, eventually mitigates the perversion of efficiency through politics. The lesson for contemporary policy is clear: The sooner a polity makes law a bulwark against, rather than an instrument of the powerful few, the sooner it will reap the bounty of the enterprising many.

Though plainly addressed to contemporary debate, this theory of the operation and origins of market-making institutions retells the most classic story in the economist's book: Adam Smith's account of the rise of market capitalism. Recall that in *The Wealth of Nations* Smith distinguished two paths to market society. The first was the "natural progress of opulence," where land was abundant and human institutions never thwarted "the natural inclinations of man" to truck and barter.[19] In this setting, best approximated for Smith by the American colonies, farmers improved their lands; their surplus became the subsistence of artisans in nearby towns. Improvements in the tools supplied by the artisans allowed the farmers to further increase their productivity, widening the market for the towns and so opening the way for further rounds of improvement, culminating in long-distance trade among centers of growing wealth. But in Continental Europe, where the powerful could perpetuate their extortionate grip on the land through their own law, this path was blocked. Their instruments were primogeniture, which prevented the subdivision of large estates through succession, and entails, which blocked division by sale. Thus secured the feudal lords could treat their estates as little principalities, taxing the peasants and conscripting them into military service. Lords aggrandized themselves not by improving their lands but by seizing others', thus enlarging their own military retinues and tax revenues and encouraging further predation. Only the nobles' boundless greed, and especially their childish desire to possess the luxurious baubles that long-distance trade dangled before them, eventually overcame aristocratic disdain for the economy. To afford their luxuries they began leasing lands to improving commoners, who soon enough bought out their betters and remade the law to protect their own interests as investors. Smith's "natural progress of opulence," where trade is not restrained by power cloaked in law, has become in the contemporary retelling the way of the common law and the Washington Consensus more generally. Smith's power-hungry lords, with their primogeniture and entails, have become rent-seeking officials and merchants, protecting themselves for too long, but not forever, with politicized justice, restrictive regulations, protective tariffs, and capital controls.

This strong family resemblance does not by itself discredit either account. We may indeed live in a Manichean world where power and efficiency, or the passions and the interests, struggle to determine our fate by controlling the law, with the cunning of selfish reason tipping the scales ever so slightly in favor of interest and efficiency. The preceding potted history of economic development in Colonial America, by calling attention to the shifting influences of communitarian legislatures and judges who promote growth despite the strictures of common law, suggests that even applied to the circumstances most favorable to the "natural" course of development, these accounts are parables: They express deep convictions about the proper subordination of power to prosperity, not empirically warranted laws of economic development.

Indeed, just as the discussion of Colonial development would lead us to expect, specialist opinion favors the view that the economic import of particular families of legal institutions that diffused at the time of the great waves of European colonization—common law or the civil code and its analogues—depends largely on the local context in which they operate. In the light of elegant recent studies by Acemoglu, Johnson, and Robinson, it seems that the hospitability of particular locations to European colonists shaped the colonists' economic strategies and choice of institutions. The institutional choices in turn influenced subsequent development. Where, for instance, high mortality rates from malaria or dense population by first peoples made a territory relatively inhospitable to colonists, the latter minimized settlement by pursuing extractive strategies based on plantations and mining, and selected institutions matched to the resulting concentration of property and power. Where conditions for settlement were more favorable, the Europeans colonized in larger numbers and replicated home-country institutions favoring dispersed property. The outcome as reflected in the long-term growth rate of the developing economy is thus not the result of an initial endowment with favorable or unfavorable, "natural" or "unnatural" institutions, but rather the interaction between the original setting, the strategic choice of development model, and the fixation of that choice in particular institutional arrangements.[20] Similarly Berglof and Bolton, in a recent review of economic outcomes in the transition economies, find that "the reason why some . . . were able to cross the Great Divide [separating self-reinforcing prosperity from poverty traps, cfs] while others did not must be sought to a large extent outside their financial and legal systems." Among the heterogeneous factors explaining success they list: prior relations with and proximity to Western markets, democratic traditions, candidacy for European Union membership, and low levels of integration into the Soviet plan economy with its huge factory towns and complex, fragile supply chains.[21] Again the common law does not by itself decide outcomes any more than the Protestant ethic does.

Even this contextualization of the endowments view does not go far
enough. For growth in different periods requires social mastery of new technologies and organizational forms, and the collective learning this supposes
is unlikely to be an automatic by-product of the institutions that facilitate
accumulation. In other words, whether market-making institutions actually produce growth in any particular epoch depends on the context of other
learning-related institutions in which they operate. In a recent survey of
growth theory that makes of institutions a key but ill-understood variable,
Helpman puts the point this way:

> Major changes in technology always induce major changes in economic organi-
> zations. The centralized factory in the late eighteenth century, the large business
> corporation in the late nineteenth century, the process of vertical integration
> at the beginning of the twentieth century, and the recent trend toward greater
> fragmentation of production exemplify organizational responses to technologi-
> cal change. As a result, the ability of a country to grow . . . depends on its ability
> to accommodate such changes, and the ability to accommodate change depends
> in turn on a country's economic and political institutions.[22]

And these latter institutions, Helpman concludes, are still so poorly understood as to count as the "mystery" of economic growth.

Even critical discussion of the inadequacy of this or that endowment view
assumes, with the arguments being criticized, that developing economies cluster into high-growth successes and low-growth failures, however, and that the
problem for growth theory and policy is to determine what sorts a particular
economy into one cluster rather than another. Stepping a bit away from these
debates, however, we find much contemporary evidence against the utility of
any sharp distinction of this kind at all, and hence *a fortiori* against the utility of explanations of success by reference to "common-law" institutions, in
all their extensions, or indeed any short list of endowments as determining
whether societies stagnate or prosper. This same evidence, to which we turn
next, supports the claim that growth requires social learning facilitated by
institutions that are built and rebuilt in the course of development itself.

The New Stylized Facts of Economic Development

The stylized facts of the consensus view are, we saw, that stagnating economies are enduringly and pervasively corrupted. That is why growth cannot

begin unless external intervention removes the institutional, cultural, or political sources of the corruption. However, there is compelling evidence that, with the exception of infernally trapped countries, less-developed economies are on many dimensions too internally heterogeneous and rapidly changing to have any essence at all, let alone to be essentially and enduringly corrupted. There is strong evidence, furthermore, that the institutions of developing economies are highly differentiated as well. Far from forming indissoluble wholes, they exist as connected but (often) detachable pieces, some performing well, or easily reformable, others badly broken and hard to repair. Because at least some parts of a developing economy are likely to be (on the verge of) doing well much of the time, and some of its surrounding institutions are likely to be serviceable, the problem of development is not starting growth, but using the functioning institutions to relax obstacles to the growth likely to be under way. In the most dramatic cases—of which China is the best current example—the outcome of this piecemeal reform is a thoroughgoing transformation of the economy and the institutions of development. Even when the outcome is far less transformative, however, the new facts of economic growth—heterogeneity of economic performance and institutions—suggest a new way of thinking of economic development, and corresponding strategies for encouraging it. This section looks at the new stylized facts, the next at ways of conceptualizing them with regard to new industrial policies.

To begin with, the growth rates of individual less-developed economies vary widely and abruptly, so that it is often misleading to classify such economies as either stagnant or growing. They are both in turn. More exactly, as Hausmann, Pritchett, and Rodrik have recently shown, spells of accelerated development often occur spontaneously, or with only marginal reforms. Counting conservatively,[23] they identified more than eighty episodes since 1950 in which a country's growth rate increased by at least 2 percentage points for at least seven years—the "vast majority" of these occurring in the absence of consensus-driven liberalization or opening. To the extent that acceleration *was* connected to reform, the latter was hesitant and often literally marginal: the introduction of market prices at the margins of Chinese agriculture in the late 1970s, an increase in interest rates and a currency devaluation that helped close the gap between the private and social returns on investment in South Korea in the early 1960s, and so on.[24] A first and fundamental new stylized fact of development, then, is that economic growth, although not ubiquitous and self-perpetuating, is not hard to start—certainly not as hard as the endowment view suggests it to be.

Just as the performance of less-developed economies is heterogeneous over time, so is it heterogeneous geographically, with some areas growing with occasional interruptions whereas others stagnate. It is a familiar fact that large developing countries such as Brazil, India, and China contain highly developed, "first-world" provinces (Saõ Paolo in Brazil, Bangalore in India) along with backward ones. Because development is uneven in space as well as time and occurs more frequently in general, and more nearly consistently in some places than normally supposed, there is a high likelihood that at least some parts of most developing societies will be growing, or on the verge of growth, much of the time. If national institutions, or endowments generally, had the preponderant effect attributed to them in the standard view, such stark regional disparities should be rare exceptions, not commonplace.

At higher degrees of resolution, moreover, the spatial differentiation of development becomes still more evident and some of its underpinnings at least partly intelligible. Growth in less-developed economies, as in advanced ones, often occurs in clusters: geographically compact agglomerations of firms, many small and medium sized, cooperating directly or otherwise drawing on common resources in one or several closely related areas of economic activity. By spontaneously recombining and augmenting fragmented specialized, and at least partly tacit, knowledge—know-how embedded in a way of life—a cooperative multiplicity of clustered firms adapts rapidly to changes in the economic environment. As the gains from these externalities are, within broad limits, self reinforcing—the more firms with complementary specializations, the greater the advantage to each from the presence of the others—spontaneous, accidental clustering will be self-perpetuating.[25] Insofar as it benefits from such network effects, economic activity will thus be by nature geographically lumpy. Since the turbulent, continuing transformation of products and markets now called globalization began to put a premium on such robustness in the mid 1980s, clusters have been widely regarded as a model, microcosm, or key component of the "new" economy, able to prosper in much more volatile conditions than the traditional, hierarchically organized large corporation. A good deal of the recent, detailed literature describing such growth as is actually occurring in developing economies (as opposed to accounts of aggregate performance and its supposed determinants) focuses on successes and difficulties of clusters of this kind—footwear in the Sinos

Valley of Rio Grande do Sul and aerospace in Saõ José dos Campos, in Brazil; wine growing in the province of Mendoza, in Argentina, or the Colchagu valley in Chile; computer components in Hinchu, Taiwan; garments in various locations in Vietnam; soccer balls in Sialkot, Pakistan—are prominent examples.[26] That such clusters can prosper at all in countries (once) thought to be obstructive, if not inimical, to development underscores that national institutions are less determinative than conventionally thought. Conversely, the frequently counterintuitive distribution of clusters within each country—the Mendoza wine industry has captured 2 percent of the $12 billion global market through continuing improvements in grape growing and wine making; the industry in the neighboring province of San Juan, with similar *terroire* and micro climates, has until recently stagnated—suggests that subtle variations in subnational institutions and arrangements count for more than the standard view allows.[27]

At still higher degrees of resolution it becomes clear that even *within* particular, geographically concentrated clusters there is great variability as well. For one thing, extremely careful studies of rates of return among "like" firms reveal great variability, not the convergence that conventional theory would predict.[28] Part of this dispersion is likely to be due to the differences in the firms' strategies and the capabilities that these suppose. Many of the cluster firms in less-developed economies are performing routine operations according to detailed instructions from, and under the close supervision of, multinational clients. Competition is on cost, and more exactly low costs of labor. Informal capacities for local adjustment are likely to be indispensable to survival, but occasions to develop the skills on which they rest are limited. It is also a common finding of current writing on these clusters, however, that alongside such firms there exist more capable ones. These more capable industrial firms, farms, fisheries, and forest producers have mastered various combinations of the just-in-time disciplines of quality control, continuous improvement, and co-design—about which more later. In so doing they learn to complement and transform their tacit skills and take on more and more demanding tasks within the global supply chains of multinational customers. Some gain access to final markets (first regional, then global) of their own.[29]

Pressure on developing economy suppliers to adapt the more advanced methods is by all accounts increasing. At the limit, mastery of these coproduction disciplines will be a precondition for any but the most subaltern participation in world markets. Just as plainly that ability varies from firm to firm, cluster to cluster and country to country in ways that have little direct connection to the general conditions thought to encourage international competitiveness on the standard view. For instance, El Salvador and Bangladesh rapidly expanded their garment industries to supply multinational customers with cheap, standard products such as t-shirts. They find, however, that this success does not automatically prepare small- and medium-sized firms to respond to customers' recent demands for specialization and rapid change-over from one fashion-sensitive product to another, including the ability to correct the customers' design errors and suggest improvements and source fabric and trim locally to avoid long production delays without paying high inventory costs.[30] Many electronics and metalworking clusters in Mexican *maquiladoras* or export zones are having trouble with an analogous transition, even though some of their constituent firms have been working with just-in-time methods for a decade or more.[31] On the other hand, some clusters (such as Mendoza) have successfully pursued "upgrading" strategies, involving hundreds of firms and novel associations among them and between them and state service providers, to meet the more stringent requirements.[32] Again the upshot is that developing economy institutions or endowments are more varied and, at least within some ranges of the variation, more permissive or less constraining than the standard view supposes.

We come, unsurprisingly, to a convergent conclusion if we shift the focus from the variation of the developing economy performance in time and space to general features of developing economy institutions themselves. On the standard view, we saw, these institutions are thought to have essences—being market sustaining or not—which, as it were, create their own context, determining, once and for all, the impact of any of their parts on the course of development. On closer inspection, these institutions prove to be heterogeneous assemblies: layered, composite, or otherwise decomposable into (recombinable) pieces, at least some of which function well, or at least well enough relative to others to serve as the starting points of reform. Comprehensive evidence of this heterogeneity is hard to come by. Responding to the evidentiary burdens assumed by the standard view, investigations of institutional performance typically take the form of league tables, ranking the aggregate ability of all government institutions in each country to deliver the rule of law (by, for example, eliminating corruption) and meet deregulatory goals.[33] Reports of state entities that perform well in particular functional domains or regions can be dismissed as anecdotal exceptions, if they are noted at all. Still, some of the cases of institutional variety and transformation are so substantial that they compel the kind of attention due when an exception may be swallowing a rule; other, more contained instances are linked to broader, underlying changes in ways that suggest that they, too, may have general significance.

The extraordinary, rule-defying case is, of course, China, which has manifestly created the institutions for growth through growing.[34] The cascade of institutional changes began in the 1970s with an agricultural reform recognizing the peasants' control over the plots they were currently working and permitting them to sell for their own account, at market prices, surplus above target levels. The result was a sustained increase in agricultural productivity and a rise in rural incomes. In the 1980s another wave of reform allowed investment of the proceeds of agricultural improvement in Town and Village Enterprises (TVEs): manufacturing firms, owned by municipalities or co-owned by them and private parties, and producing for both domestic and export markets. Again proceeds in excess of tax obligations to higher authorities were retained by the enterprise and available to its stakeholders. The TVEs continued to expand through the mid-1990s, competing with state-owned firms and adding to the modest pressure for their reform exerted by the central state. The changes were accompanied and accelerated by partial reforms of the financial system and the opening of export-processing enclaves to foreign firms and joint ventures. The upshot was a profusion of new institutions that created incentives for investment and efficiency-enhancing behavior in domain after domain without ever creating what, on the consensus view, seem to be the essentials of a capitalist economy: China is very haltingly privatizing state firms, only recently recognized private corporate property as a distinct legal category, and makes little pretense of an independent judiciary.

An incomparably smaller, but still arguably revealing, instance of this same type of change is the reform of the institutions responsible for assuring hygiene and food safety of the Nile perch fishery on Kenya's portion of Lake Victoria.[35] Exports of the fish, predominantly to the European Union (EU), increased from under barely $100,000 in 1985 to just under $44 million in 1996. Starting in that year, however, the EU and various member states began to restrict perch imports from Kenya because of concerns about pathogens and pesticide residues and, more generally, concerns that Kenyan producers could not assure food safety and hygiene by meeting EU regulations based on Hazard Analysis and Critical Control Points (HACCPs). Under this form of regulation producers identify the production steps where pathogens are most likely to be introduced; devise remedial measures; test to verify that these measures produce outcomes within parameters fixed by the regulator for the relevant class of product; correct remaining shortfalls; and regularly verify, by routine tests, the effectiveness of the eventual methods. A competent public authority in turn periodically verifies the reliability of this self-monitoring.

An EU technical assistance mission inspected the fishery with Kenyan counterparts and documented problems ranging from unhygienic storage of fish on the fishing vessels to spotty record keeping, especially of "own checks" and inadequate vermin control at processing facilities, to insufficient training of fisheries inspectors, to a wide variety of deficiencies in testing laboratory organization, maintenance, and equipment. In response, the Kenyan government concentrated oversight for the fisheries from three entities to one, and the fisheries producers formed a single association to treat with the government. The World Bank study on which this account draws noted substantial improvements not just in compliance with HACCP regulation, but also in the organization of many links in the supply chain and the public sector infrastructure. During the period of these reforms Kenya ranked around 80 of 117 counties on the World Economic Forum's competitiveness index: a poor enough showing in the league tables of institutional adequacy to cast doubt on its ability to accomplish any reform, let alone to effect, in a short period, a coordinated series of demanding changes within the public sector and between it and private firms. Again, aggregate assessments obscure the internal differentiation that both is a product of and creates the possibility for reform.

Despite its marginal economic significance—in good years Nile perch accounts for only 2.5 percent of Kenyan exports—the regulatory reform of the fishery reflects broad trends in development. The introduction of HACCPs is of piece with the shift to just-in-time production noted previously: The regulatory authorities in effect are requiring firms to demonstrate the same general capacities to detect and correct problems their customers require of them as well. Because they accord local actors great autonomy in determining how to meet general goals, rather than setting out universal and detailed rules for compliance, such regulatory systems are well-suited to ensure product safety when—as now—product life cycles are short, precise production arrangements vary greatly from place to place, and judgments regarding the acceptability of particular risks are frequently revised.

Partial reform, domain by domain, or, as in this case, one cluster at a time, also appears to be commonplace: the accounts of cluster development referred to previously almost invariably interweave discussion of restructuring of firms, and the relation among them, with reorganization in that particular cluster of the public infrastructure for verifying compliance with standards set both by public authorities and private buyers of the cluster's products. Likewise the EU's technical mission to Kenya to investigate problems and propose changes is part of broader pattern. Because developing country institutions are changed domain by domain and leading professionals in each domain are likely to participate from their student days on in international communities of interest, it is often opportune to create teams of local and foreign experts to address problems in context and propose correspondingly specific solutions. Thus, the EU routinely insists that candidate members create committees to review key governance domains with qualified EU counterpart teams of their own choosing. Close observers of such collaboration, among them the World Bank, judge this "twinning" to be one of the most reliably effective means of securing governance reform. From this vantage point the EU and Kenya were applying to the reorganization of the Nile perch fishery a tested method of piecemeal or place-by-place reform of the new, just-in-time type.[36]

A further and important tile in the mosaic of evidence suggesting the pervasiveness of step-by-step institutional reform (and the decomposability and adaptability of the ensemble of national institutions that it supposes) is the frequency of heterodox adjustment. As noted at the outset, Rodrik, Hausman, and others have shown that successful openings of developing economies to the discipline of world markets tend to violate consensus expectation. Three, closely related kinds of deviation are especially salient.

First, successful openings are generally partial in the dictionary sense that they are not comprehensive: in the successful cases, openings in some markets go hand in hand with continued closure of nonexporting sectors of the economy and of the financial system against external shocks. There is, conversely, little evidence that by itself reduction of tariffs, nontariff barriers, and capital controls—the deregulatory core of traditional free trade—raises growth rates.[37]

Second, successful openings are deviantly partial in that they include, from the consensus perspective, impermissibly selective, and therefore inherently biased, interventions in the economy. These interventions typically include public provision of infrastructure and other subsidies to exporters of just the kind the Kenyan government provided the Nile perch fishery or, on a grander scale, that Japan, South Korea, and Taiwan provided to sectors of their economies. Underscoring the pervasiveness of such selective interventions Rodrik finds in addition that, of the top five exports, excluding commodities, from Brazil, Chile, and Mexico to the United States, all benefited from such public support, as well as export subsidies, preferential tariffs, and the like.[38]

Third, successful openings tend to be deviant in pursuing indubitably important ends—assuring the security of investment—by what seem, from the consensus perspective, dubious or even impermissible institutional means. In China, we saw, some combination of bureaucratic tutelage or protection and a tiered system of tax targets with local retention of the surplus has substantially substituted for private property rights and courts as an instrument for encouraging investors. Taken together the tax and corporate law aligned the incentives of local and regional officials with those who invested in TVEs. Both prospered when the TVE did, and through the mid-1990s, the bulk of investment in China was made in this form. (Development in South Korea, Taiwan, and, more recently, Vietnam has arguably followed an analogous, if less conspicuously unconventional, course, though I will not make the case for this view here.)

However, this outcome is, at best, counterintuitive from the consensus or common-law view of institutions, according to which the key role of property law and courts is precisely to protect investors against bureaucrats. More vexing still to the consensus position, just as the classic measures of free trade do not, by themselves, increase growth, so mass privatizations and the introduction of sophisticated corporate law enforced by a nominally independent judiciary have produced mediocre results in Russia and many other transition economies that acted on the assumption of clear property rights as the foundation of growth.

Of course the partiality, selectivity, and institutional unconventionality of heterodox reforms are only deviant from the standpoint of the consensus assumption that the institutions of growth are by nature self-contained totalities with the special property of facilitating trade by restraining all interference with it, including interference resulting from the institutional restraints themselves. Indeed from this perspective, reform that leaves anything essential unchanged, or tries to vary interventions to take account of the particularities of the economic and institutional situation, raises the suspicion of being more of the usual self-interested meddling, or simply no reform at all. If heterodox reforms do from time to time succeed, it is only, on the standard view, by a lucky accident that mitigates the normally disastrous effects of their limits.

On the evidence just canvassed, however, this get things exactly backward. If developing economies and their institutions lack essences and are as internally differentiated and context-dependent in their effects as the new stylized facts show them to be, omnibus reforms that ignore this heterogeneity will likely fail by treating very different economic contexts as though they were all the same. In contrast, reforms that attend to constraints of local contexts by devising sequences of changes that extend patches of growth, without thereby opening the door to political predation, will be likely to succeed. Thus, in the really existing, new-stylized-facts world, successful reform is *normally* "heterodox," and heterodox adjustment succeeds *because* of, not despite, its partiality, selectivity, and contextuality. On this process view of development the fundamental conceptual problem is not specifying with more and more precision the foundations of growth, for the process creates its own "foundations," but rather clarifying in what sense and by what general means developing economies can influence this process to their advantage.

Developing Economies as Toyoda Production Systems

On the new stylized facts of development, growth is not hard to start, but neither is growth self perpetuating. In addition, institutions on the new facts are de- and recomposable, and their effects depend on their context, including the context of other institutions. The problem of development, given this much, is literally to institutionalize these results: to build institutions that can identify and relax the constraints on growth. What is needed, in still other words, are institutions that do not supplant their context, but rather use the growth-promoting strengths of the latter to overcome its growth-retarding weaknesses.

To get from a general understanding of the relevant institutional innovations to their application to the problem of development, we proceed in three steps. The first is to present the class of especially context-sensitive and context-modifying organizations that improve outcomes by routinely identifying and overcoming limits posed by current operating procedures or routines. If they exist at all, the growth-promoting institutions have to be a member of this class, and the distinguishing features of their operation are most conspicuous at this highest level of generality. The next step is to illustrate the operation of this class in the domain of new public services, whose novelty consists precisely in their ability to provide customized or contextualized bundles of educational and other services to heterogeneous groups—in other words, just the kind of contextual adjustment of means to complex and changing ends required for the new institutions of development. The last step is to suggest, by a Chilean illustration, how similar principles are indeed already informing economic policy making in developing economies.

As you will have surmised from innumerable hints along the way or a nodding acquaintance with the business pages of the newspaper, constraint-relaxing institutions have become broadly familiar under the name of the Toyoda production system. The specificity of the name notwithstanding, they have diffused vastly beyond the Japanese firms, the automobile industry, and the production-line settings in which they arose. Indeed it is almost impossible to survey recent writings about the new economy or reform of public administration—ranging from the reorganization public schooling to the provision of child protective services—without stumbling across extended reference to them. For present purposes three features of the Toyoda system are especially important. [39]

First, they identity constraints by stressing existing arrangements until (successive) weaknesses are revealed. A famous example is just-in-time production, in which all work-in-progress inventories are stripped away and parts are produced, at the limit, one at a time. Because defective work pieces cannot be replaced with good ones from inventory, a breakdown at any station disrupts all downstream production. The only way to resume production is to correct the problem causing the disruption. Continuous improvement in the sense of the elimination of successive sources of disruption becomes in this deliberately fragile or lean environment a by-product of producing any output at all.

In the design of new products, disruption of current expectations and routines is produced by benchmarking: an exacting comparison of current products and processes "like" the currently employed ones, but with some attractive features that current choices lack. The provisional design resulting from this first survey is refined by application of the same technique to its parts: The initial design is chunked into its major components—transmission, engine, and so on for automobiles. Each chunk is then benchmarked against alternatives by an appropriate specialist and adjusted to take account of changes produced by the benchmarking of the others—a process often called simultaneous engineering.

Once detected by this deliberate stressing, constraints in current arrangements are relaxed by problem-solving techniques that direct searches for solutions beyond the boundaries normally established by routine, yet limit them sufficiently to return useful results in the allowable time. In production such problem-solving disciplines often go by the general name of root-cause analysis, to underscore their common assumption that the source of a disruption may not be palpably linked to the breakdown it provokes. A familiar example of such root-cause analysis is found in the five why's:

Why is machine A broken?	No preventive maintenance was performed.
Why was the maintenance crew derelict?	It is always repairing machine B.
Why is machine B always broken?	The part it machines always jams.
Why does the jam recur?	The part warps from heat stress.
Why does the *part* overheat?	A design flaw.[40]

In design, an analogous routine-breaking but self-limiting search for solutions is entailed by benchmarking itself. The evaluation of which products are enough "like" the target design to count in comparison directs attention away from habitual preferences and toward a broad consideration of just what that target should be. The strengths and weakness of competing solutions are mutually illuminating, so that detailed consideration of the alternatives judged to be alike enough for comparison clarifies the currently feasible choices, producing a serviceable map of the available solution space.

Finally, the search for constraint-relaxing solutions beyond the confines of routine continuously reorganizes the institutions that undertake them. In traditional, hierarchical organizations, complex problems are solved by reducing them to simple tasks and then aggregating the results of the simplified operations. In the Toyoda production system, in contrast, the solution to a complex problem is in effect to find someone who is already solving (some part of) it. Benchmarking and simultaneous engineering do this explicitly by identifying pieces of the target design originally produced for other, perhaps distantly related purposes. Root-cause problem solving does this by effectively declaring each piece of the organization potentially relevant to the solution of the problems of the others. In this way the institution becomes an instrument for searching for solutions, changing its own organization and boundaries the better to do this. The hierarchy becomes a search network.

Although these features of the Toyoda production system bear on problem solving in general, their origin in the private sector may incorrectly suggest that they can only be applied there, and are thus irrelevant to public sector policies such as fostering growth. To better see the full generality of problem-solving by search, consider the application of this model to the organization of the new public services that provide customized (combinations) of services to help individuals and families mitigate life risks. What makes these services new in contrast to familiar public services is that defining and redefining what they should be is anything but straightforward. In economic theory, the purpose and value of a public service is self-evident enough to give rise to a characteristic free-rider problem: Each citizen assumes all the others want such public goods and that he or she can free ride on their willingness to pay for their provision. The result is that no one pays unless a joint decision obliges all to pay together. New public services, in contrast, are so idiosyncratic and mutable that they have to be codesigned by client users if they are to be useful at all. Financing for new public services is not, of course, automatic. The defining difference is simply that the free-rider problem in new public goods is no more important than the problem of specifying the service in the first place. The problem of effectively contextualizing general goals such as providing educational or health services is thus comparable—"like" in the benchmarking sense introduced above—the problem of identifying and relaxing constraints on growth.

School reform in the United States is a well-studied example of the routine invocation of the Toyoda production principles to address the new public service problem of determining what service to provide and how to provide it.[41] To respond to the needs of heterogeneous classes, with many students arriving without the whole panoply of middle-class family support, required a thorough reorganization of the school. This reorganization aimed at teaching pupils complex skills regardless of their starting point, rather than transmitting information to them on the assumption that they started with the knowledge to use the transmissions. After more than two decades of desperate experimentation, reformers settled in the mid-1990s on a variant of root-cause analysis that, fully in the spirit of the new stylized facts of development, allows effective reorganization to proceed by using partial solutions and without presupposing any definitive model of the ultimate goal: Use standard tests not only to reveal shortcomings in pupils' learning strategies and the staff's teaching strategies, but also the defects in the organization of schools and school districts that are the root cause of these shortcomings.

To see more concretely how this discipline operates in school reform, consider the teaching of literacy. Learning to read, like mastering any complex task, requires each learner to assemble her own idiosyncratic bundles of general skills. So in learning to read each kid must decode phoneme streams (phonics) while inferring the meaning of words in context (holistic semantics, or, if you read philosophy, semantic holism). Each combines these skills in her own way, reflecting her particular strengths and weaknesses in each. Thus some kids go from context to meaning and use the meaning to guess sounds. Others sound their way to the meaning. Many have trouble doing either, but could benefit greatly if strengths in one area could be used to bootstrap them past difficulties in the other (by, say, learning to decode a proper name that reveals a context, that then prompts more sounding out.) Standard tests can be used to diagnose individual learning problems as well as the systematic difficulties of some teachers, relative to others, in helping students overcome their particular blockages. The aim of the institutional reform is to rebuild classes, schools, and school systems so that these individual "defects" can be identified and remedied systematically.

Thus, the job of the teacher in this new public service is to organize the classroom to identify and remediate each pupil's difficulties. The job of the principal is to organize the school so that teams of teachers within and across grade levels help one another achieve this goal (new search networks). The job of the district or system head is to organize the system so that principals have the authority and autonomy to do this (more search networks).

Reform by these means gives rise almost naturally to new forms of school accountability. Teachers and school officials are accountable to one another through the performance measures that make diagnosis of problems possible in the first place. They are also accountable to the public. Thus, in many states in the United States, parents can compare the extent to which demographically comparable schools close the achievement gap between rich whites and other groups. This allows them to put pressure on school authorities, on politicians. It also allows them to take action as families: school rankings have demonstrable effects on real estate prices. To the extent that reduction of the achievement gap results from more and more effective responses to more and more precise self-diagnosis of problems under pressure of such accountability systems, reorganization of U.S. public schools is an instance of the HACCP family of reform.

There is, so far as I know, no strictly comparable institution routinely identifying and relaxing growth constraints in developing economies by such well-honed and formalized routines. To note only one conspicuously missing piece of such an institution: Data on economic performance in developing economies, as we saw, are still collected at such levels of aggregation, and in such form, as to make the data next to useless as a source of information for diagnosing the difficulties of—locating the constraints on—growth. Whereas the data on student performance on standard tests can be used to pick out districts, schools, classrooms, and student subgroups that are doing well or poorly, the league tables of competitiveness and other such rankings report national results and call for national action. This is not inadvertent. The league tables are conceived as an incentive system, with bad performers paying such a high price in forgone foreign investment and costly conditionality on borrowings that they are motivated to improve their showing by reform. (Standard tests of educational attainment were initially viewed the same way in the United States, and in some quarters they still are.) In the light of the new stylized facts of development, it is easy to see that such incentive devices are at best incomplete, at worst seriously misleading. They suppose, among other things, that the leaders of a low-ranking country verge on wanting to improve conditions (the incentives provide the last bit of necessary motivation) and know just how to get results once prompted to want them. The same stylized facts suggest the need for diagnostic indicators. Hausmann, Rodrik, and Velasco and others have begun to call for just such growth diagnostics, and given experience in many other domains, there is no reason in principle to think they will not be forthcoming.[42] Nonetheless, the call for these tools is as good an indication as any that the new institutions of development are still a long way from the routine context-changing operation documented in other, arguably related settings.

All this notwithstanding, there is good circumstantial evidence from, for instance, Chile, that in the current cohort of developing economies the ensemble of growth-promoting institutions works jointly as an economywide Toyoda production system—partially, selectively, and unconventionally locating and reducing one constraint after another on exports—and that at least some of these institutions more and more explicitly apply the principles of such organizations. Of the many Chilean development institutions that exemplify this tendency[43] it is the Foundation Chile whose evolution approximates it more and closely and explicitly to the Toyoda model.[44] The Foundation was created as a nonprofit corporation by the Chilean government in 1976 with a $50 million payment by ITT as part of an agreement indemnifying the conglomerate for expropriation of its national telephone subsidiary. Under the agreement, ITT was to manage the new facility for ten years. Its initial efforts were bumbling. The first director general wanted the new institution to provide social services such as school lunches and nutrition for infants, whereas his successor wanted to develop telecommunications equipment, for which there was no market, and foodstuffs, for which the markets were incipient. Criticism of his suggestions, however, drew attention to prospects in renewable resources—principally forestry, aquiculture, and horticulture—which became the foundation's enduring focus.

Only in the aftermath of the economic shock of 1982 did the foundation develop the activities that have defined its strategy. A combination of sharp devaluation, low domestic interest rates, and high uncertainty produced a situation favorable to domestic investment but too risky for domestic investors. Seeing an opportunity in salmon farming, the Foundation Chile launched firms itself, hoping that success would lead to imitation and complementary activities. It acquired the necessary technology, free, from specialist public agencies in the U.S. Pacific Northwest and founded one firm to produce smelts, another to develop hatching and ranching technology for Chilean waters, and a third for smoking fish. From these firms grew the Chilean salmon industry, which now produces $600 million in exports annually.

In the next two decades, the foundation's model of supporting development was refined in three crucial ways. First, the foundation shifted from creating start-ups itself to coventuring with outside partners. Between 1985 and 1993, 87 percent of the foundation's start-ups were wholly owned by the foundation itself (and only one of the joint ventures involved a foreign partner). Between 1994 to 2004, however, 75 percent of the start-ups were joint ventures, and six of these were with foreign firms. Thus, the foundation went from spinning out projects developed internally to networking with outsiders to create projects. Second, the technological complexity of projects increased, with biotechnology in particular becoming more and more important. Because projects in this area—new vaccines, development of pest-resistant fruit varieties—often required integration of scattered intellectual property and diverse technical tools for genetic manipulation, many of the external partners had to construct networks of their own to serve the specific needs of the emergent companies. Thus, the foundation went from building networks to building and rebuilding networks of networks: It became, that is, a search network.

Third, the foundation's own project-selection and review mechanism became more explicitly comparative or competitive: Staff members, hired on the basis of demonstrated technical knowledge and familiarity with the markets and business practices in a particular sector, apply for internal grants to develop a case for launching a new venture in some general area. The projects born of the winning proposals become the basis for applications for a second, longer-term grant to develop a business plan for a new venture, typically in partnership with outsiders. The contests continue until the protoventure becomes a candidate for seed capital and enters the familiar sequence of venture capital financing. Thus, as the Toyoda model would suggest, at every stage projects are benchmarked against internal and external alternatives, and the start-ups that result are the institutionalized expression of the searches provoked by that benchmarking. The start-ups fill in gaps and extend the reach of and otherwise relax constraints on the formation and growth of the clusters whose growth propels the Chilean economy. So far, at least, the transparency inherent in the broad and continual benchmarking of projects at every stage has also functioned as an effective governance mechanism, assuring that public funds are indeed directed toward public purposes, as best these can be defined at any moment. Here then is a concrete intimation of the possibility of institutionalizing the idea of a developing economy as a Toyoda production system.

Unbalanced Growth Then and Now

To conclude an essay that is by design and necessity inconclusive, it will be useful to look back briefly on the argument and underscore the novelty of Toyoda-inspired industrial policy by comparing it with a kindred, though in the end distinct, notion of encouraging development: Hirschman's view of unbalanced growth.

Hirschman's model addresses two closely related, perennial problems of market failure typical of developing economies and touched on repeatedly in the preceding sections.[45] The first is identification of potential markets, especially for exports, in the turbid and turbulent conditions of economic life distressingly close to subsistence levels. In a general equilibrium world, there would be markets for all possible products (sold at all possible dates). Investors in developing economies could thus easily determine the costs of producing and the revenues from selling potential products and choose the most profitable lines of business. In the real world, of course, it is very difficult for the first potential investor in some sector either to estimate the costs of adapting available technology to local conditions or to gauge the size of the market accessible to domestic producers, except by going some way toward actually realizing the project.[46] The second problem of market failure concerns the coordination of complementary investments. Potential producers of table grapes or stone fruits will hesitate to invest unless they can count on help with pest control, logistics, and compliance with photo-sanitary regulations that they cannot provide themselves. However, firms that could provide these services will not, unless there is some assurance of local demand.

In the 1950s, "big bang" theories of economic development argued that planned, simultaneous investment in all the key complements of a production process solved both problems. Massive joint investment—the big bang—created effective demand for all the goods to be supplied while simultaneously resolving all questions of complementarity.[47] The insurmountable problem, of course, was that this solution to the problem of development supposed that developing countries had precisely what they lacked: sufficiently abundant resources to plan and execute the massive intervention.

Hirschman's alterative was to address these problems by the mechanisms of *unbalanced* growth: If a large (say state) investor committed funds to a grand, indubitably useful project (say a steel mill), then the resulting backward and forward linkages (backward to the capital goods for making steel; forward to fabrication of steel girders or rails) would create easily identified local demand that could be met without undue risk by domestic entrepreneurs. A cascade of imbalances would thus create a sequence of opportunities motivating investors to fill in the missing pieces of the economic structure. This kind of solution lost its appeal as it became clear that public investors could all too easily be captured by selfish interests and that many projects that seemed indubitably good proved very dubious indeed. Our concern here, however, is not with these governance issues and the vicissitudes of industrial policy from the mid-1950s to now, but rather with the similarities and, above all, the differences between the unbalanced approach and the idea of developing economies as Toyoda production systems.

A key similarity, of course, is incrementalism. In both cases one of many possible initial disruptions of an equilibrium suggests another, and the cumulative effect of moving from disequilibrium to disequilibrium is a comprehensive transformation that could not have been achieved of a piece. A corollary is that there is, as Hirschman writes, no *"primum mobile,"* no "pre-requisite" to growth: no necessary and sufficient endowment, as has been argued here. All the familiar preconditions of development are endogenous to the process of development. Hirschman recites the list current in his day: Skills needed for new industries can be learned; savings for investment can result from growth itself; entrepreneurship can emerge when purposive behavior, ingredient in the most diverse value systems, is no longer diverted by short time horizons into trade and real-estate speculation.[48]

The key difference between the views has to do with their respective assumptions about the organization of firms and the relations among them. In unbalanced growth, both are taken to be fixed. For Hirschman, as for most of the leading development economists of his day, the core of these relations can be captured in input/output tables, which show how each stage of production of each good in the economy is linked to the others. What is not known is the efficient sequence for building, in any particular national setting, the structure captured in the input/output table. Having rejected the *primum mobile* or endowments view, Hirschman's insight is that the efficient sequence in any locale can be determined by accidental, or artfully induced, perturbations.

His example is fitting pieces to a jigsaw puzzle. Assuming that the time needed to fit each piece is inversely related to the number of adjacent pieces already placed, each fit of course attracts further, faster ones in the same neighborhood. Central neighborhoods can be identified by looking at the input/output table pictured, as it were, on the puzzle box. Taking advantage of knowledge of the overall picture and cues provided by local clustering of pieces, the player completes the puzzle as quickly as possible.

In the Toyoda production-system view, in contrast, both the internal organization of firms and the relations among them are continuously redefined by ongoing searches for (partial) solutions to emergent problems. Firms, singly and together, form search networks whose nodes are routinely reconnected by the searches they enable. The jigsaw analogy to the world of the Toyoda model would be a game in which players have to fit pieces together without having any clear, box-top image as an initial guide—indeed without knowing whether the heap of pieces before them is drawn from several different puzzles rather than from one. In this game the challenge is not getting to a known result in the shortest possible time, but determining what the outcome(s) will be. However, making sense of multiple, conflicting, but related outcomes, puzzling out what the puzzle is—benchmarking "likes"—is precisely what the Toyoda system is designed to do. If, as the new facts of economic development suggest, developing economies and their institutions are, in their internal heterogeneity, indeed jumbles of puzzle pieces from different puzzles—some fitting to prosperity, others to misery—then a Toyoda-model industrial policy may indeed prove a key to carefully and collaboratively sorting through these contrary possibilities, creating and re-creating the conditions for growth, in a way that makes progress possible regardless of initial endowments.

References

Acemoglu, Daron, Simon Johnson, and James A. Robinson (2001). "The Colonial Origins of Comparative Development: An Empirical Investigation." *American Economic Review* 91: 1369–1401.

Banerjee, Abhijit V. & Duflo, Esther (2005). "Growth Theory through the Lens of Development Economics," in *Handbook of Economic Growth*, Edition 1, Volume 1, Philippe Aghion and Steven Durlauf, eds., pp. 473–552. Amsterdam: Elsevier.

Bell, Emma, and Scott Taylor. (2003). "The Elevation of Work: Pastoral Power and the New Age Work Ethic." *Organization*. Vol. 10(2): 329–349.

Bellah, Robert N. (1963). "Reflections on the Protestant Ethic Analogy in Asia." *Journal of Social Issues*. Vol. 19: 52–60.

——— (1964). "Religious Evolution." *American Sociological Review*. Vol. 29: 358–374.

Benton, Lauren (2002). *Law and Colonial Cultures: Legal Regimes in World History, 1400–1900.* New York: Cambridge University Press.

Berger, Stephen D. (1971). "The Sects and the Breakthrough into the Modern World: On the Centrality of the Sects in Weber's Protestant Ethic Thesis." *The Sociological Quarterly*. Vol. 12: 486–499.

Berglof, Erik and Patrick Bolton. (Winter 2002) "The Great Divide and Beyond: Financial Architecture in Transition." *Journal of Economic Perspectives*. Vol. 16, no. 1: 77–100

Carr, Patricia. (2003). "Revisiting the Protestant Ethic and the Spirit of Capitalism: Understanding the Relationship between Ethics and Enterprise." *Journal of Business Ethics*. Vol. 47: 7–16.

Congdon Fors, Heather and Ola Olsson. (2005). "Property Rights Investment and Growth in Modern Africa." Working Paper, Department of Economics, Göteborg University.

Cull, Robert, Lixin Colin Xu, and Guanghua School of Management, Peking University. (2004). *Institutions, Ownership, and Finance: The Determinants of Profit*

Reinvestment among Chinese Firms. Washington, DC: Development Research Group, World Bank.

de Beule, Filip, Daniel van den Bulke, and Luodan Xu (2005). "Multinational Subsidiaries and Manufacturing Clusters in Guangdong, China," in *Clusters Facing Competition: The Importance of External Linkages,* Elisa Giuliani, Roberta Rabellotti, and Meine Pieter van Dijk, eds., pp. 107–133. Aldershot, UK: Ashgate Publishing.

Fundación Chile, "Una oportunidad para Promover la Creación de Negocios Innovadores en Clusters Claves," Unpublished Paper, Fundación Chile, Santiago, Chile n.d.

Fukuyama, Francis (2004). *State-Building: Governance and World Order in the 21st Century.* Ithaca, NY: Cornell University Press.

Giuliani, Elisa. (2003). *Knowledge in the Air and Its Uneven Distribution: A Story of a Chilean "Wine Cluster."* Paper presented at the DRUID Winter Conference 2003, Aalborg, Denmark, January 16–18, 2003.

——— (2005). "Technological Learning in a Chilean Wine Cluster and Its Linkages with the National System of Innovation," in *Clusters Facing Competition: The Importance of External Linkages,* Elisa Giuliani, Roberta Rabellotti, and Meine Pieter van Dijk, eds., pp. 155–176. Aldershot, UK: Ashgate Publishing.

Giuliani, Elisa, Roberta Rabellotti and Meine Pieter van Dijk, eds. (2005). *Clusters Facing Competition: The Importance of External Linkages.* Aldershot, England: Ashgate Publishing.

Glaeser, Edward L. and Andrei Shleifer. (November 2002). "Legal Origins." *Quarterly Journal of Economics.* President and Fellows of Harvard College and the Massachusetts Institute of Technology: 1193–1229.

Goldstein, Andrea (2005). "Lead Firms and Clusters in the North and in the South: A Comparison of the Aerospace Industry in Montreal and Sao Jose dos Campos," in *Clusters Facing Competition: The Importance of External Linkages,* Elisa Giuliani, Roberta Rabellotti, and Meine Pieter van Dijk, eds., pp. 135–153. Aldershot, UK: Ashgate Publishing.

Gore, Charles. (2000). "The Rise and Fall of the Washington Consensus as a Paradigm for Developing Countries." *World Development,* vol. 28, no. 5, 789–804.

Habermas, Jürgen. (1984). *The Theory of Communicative Action.* Thomas McCarthy, trans. Boston: Beacon Press.

Harrington, Christine B. and Sally Engle Merry. (1988). "Ideological Production: The Making of Community Mediation." *Law and Society Review* 22:709.

Hausmann, Ricardo and Dani Rodrik. (May 2002). "Economic Development as Self-Discovery," NBER Working Paper Series, Paper 8952.

Hausmann, Ricardo, Dani Rodrik, and Andres Velasco. (2004). *Growth Diagnostics.* Cambridge, MA: Harvard University Press.

Hausmann, Ricardo, Lant Pritchett and Dani Rodrik. (2004). *Growth Accelerations.* Cambridge, MA: Harvard University Press.

Helpman, Elhanan. (2004). *The Mystery of Economic Growth.* Cambridge, MA: The Belknap Press of Harvard University Press.

Henretta, James A. "The Protestant Ethic and the Reality of Capitalism in Colonial America," in *Weber's Protestant Ethic*, Hartmut Lehmann and Guenther Roth, eds., pp. 327–346. Cambridge, UK: Cambridge University Press, 1993.

Henson, Spencer, and Winnie Mitullah (2004). "Kenyan Exports of Nile Perch: The Impact of Food Safety Standards on an Export-Oriented Supply Chain." World Bank Policy Research Working Paper 3349, June 2004.

Hirschman, Albert O. (1958), *The Strategy of Economic Development*. New Haven, CT: Yale University Press.

Horwitz, Morton. (1977). *The Transformation of American Law, 1780–1860*. Cambridge, MA: Harvard University Press.

Inter-American Development Bank. (2005). "The Emergence of China: Opportunities and Challenges for Latin America and the Caribbean." Discussion draft, March 2005.

Lehmann, Hartmut, and Guenther Roth (eds). (1993). *Weber's Protestant Ethic: Origins, Evidence, Contexts*, pp. 332-346. Cambridge, UK: Cambridge University Press.

Liebman, James S., and Charles F. Sabel. (2003). "A Public Laboratory Dewey Barely Imagined: The Emerging Model of School Governance and Legal Reform." *NYU Review of Law and Social Change* 28, 2: 183–304

MacDuffie, John Paul. (1997). "The Road to 'Root Cause': Shop-Floor Problem-Solving at Three Auto Assembly Plants." *Management Science* 43 (1): 479–502.

McDermott, Gerald. (2005). "The Politics of Institutional Renovation and Competitive Upgrading: Lessons from the Transformation of the Argentine Wine Industry." Paper presented at the APSA Annual Meetings, Washington, DC, September 1–4, 2005.

Merry, Sally Engle. (2001). "Rights, Religion, and Community: Approaches to Violence against Women in the Context of Globalization." *Law and Society Review* 35 (1):39–88.

—— 1995). "Resistance and the Cultural Power of Law." 1994 Presidential Address. *Law and Society Review* 29 (1):11–26.

—— (1991). "Law and Colonialism." *Law and Society Review* 25:889–922.

—— (1990). Book Review: "The Culture of Judging." *Columbia Law Review* 90 (8):2311–2328.

—— (1988). "Legal Pluralism." *Law and Society Review* 22:869–896.

Meyer-Stamer, Jörg. (1999). "Regional and Local Locational Policy: What Can We Learn from the Ceramics and Textiles/Clothing Clusters of Santa Catarina, Brazil?" Paper prepared for Inter-American Development Bank Conference "Building a Modern and Effective Business Development Services Industry in Latin America and the Caribbean," Rio de Janeiro, Brazil.

Navas-Aleman, Lizbeth, and Luiza Bazan. (2005). "Making Value Chain Governance Work for the Implementation of Quality, Labor and Environmental Standards: Upgrading Challenges in the Footwear Industry," in *Clusters Facing Competition: The Importance of External Linkages*, Elisa Giuliani, Roberta Rabellotti, and Meine Pieter van Dijk, eds., pp. 39–60. Aldershot, UK: Ashgate Publishing.Nurkse,

Ragnar. (1953). *Problems of Capital Formation in Underdeveloped Countries*. Oxford, UK: Basil Blackwell.

Ohnesorge, John K. M. (2003). "China's Economic Transition and the New Legal Origins Literature." *China Economic Review*, vol. 14: 485–93.

Pietrobelli, Carlo, and Roberta Rabellotti. (2004). "Upgrading in Clusters and Value Chains in Latin America: The Role of Policies." Inter-American Development Bank, Sustainable Development Department Best Practices Series, Washington, DC.

Pistor, Katharina, Martin Raiser, and Stanislaw Gelfer. (2000). "Law and finance in transition economies," *Economics of Transition*, vol. 8 (2), 325–336.

—— "Upgrading in Global Value Chains: Lessons from Latin American Clusters," in *Clusters Facing Competition: The Importance of External Linkages*, pp. 13–37. Aldershot, UK: Ashgate Publishing.

Poggi, Gianfranco. (1983). *Calvinism and the Capitalist Spirit: Max Weber's Protestant Ethic*. Amherst: University of Massachusetts Press.

Reddy, Sanjay G., and Sabel, Charles Frederick, "Learning to Learn: Undoing the Gordian Knot of Development Today." Columbia Law and Economics Working Paper No. 308.

Rodriguez, Francisco, and Dani Rodrik. (1999). "Trade Policy and Economic Growth: A Skeptic's Guide to the Cross-National Evidence." Working Paper for the National Bureau of Economic Research.

Rodrik, Dani (ed.). (2003). *In Search of Prosperity*. Princeton, NJ: Princeton University Press.

—— (2004). Getting Institutions Right.

—— (2004). "Rethinking Growth Policies in the Developing World," draft of the Luca d'Agliano Lecture in Development Economics, delivered on October 8, 2004, in Torino, Italy.

—— (2004). "Growth Strategies." Paper for the *Handbook of Economic Growth*.

—— (2004). "Industrial Policy for the Twenty-First Century." Paper prepared for United Nations Industrial Development Organization (UNIDO).

—— (2001). "Development Strategies for the Next Century." World Bank, Annual World Bank Conference on Development Economics 2000.

—— (1999). *The New Global Economy and Developing Countries: Making Openness Work*. Baltimore, MD: Overseas Development Council, Johns Hopkins University Press.

Rodrik, Dani, and Ricardo Hausmann (2003). "Discovering El Salvador's Production Potential." Unpublished paper, September.

Sabel, Charles F. (2004). "The World in a Bottle, or, Window on the World? Open Questions about Industrial Districts in the Spirit of Sebastiano Brusco." Paper presented to the Conference on Clusters, Industrial Districts and Firms: The Challenge of Globalization, Modena, Italy, September 2003; in *Stato e Mercato* as *"Mondo in bottiglia o finestra sul mondo? Domande aperte sui distretti industriali nello spirito di Sebastiano Brusco,"* issue 70, 143–158.

——— (2006) "A Real Time Revolution in Routines," in *The Firm as a Collaborative Community*, Charles Heckscher and Paul Adler, eds., Oxford, UK: Oxford University Press.

Samstad, James G., and Seth Pipkin. (2005) "Bringing the Firm Back In: Local Decision Making and Human Capital Development in Mexico's Maquiladora Sector." *World Development*. Vol. 33, no. 5, 805–822.

Smith, Adam. (1976). *An Inquiry into the Nature and Causes of the Wealth of Nations*, edited by Edwin Cannan. Chicago: University of Chicago Press.

Srinivasan, T. N., and Jagdish Bhagwati. (1999). "Outward-Orientation and Development: Are Revisionists Right?" Center Discussion Paper No. 806 for Economic Growth Center: Yale University.

Thoburn, John, Khalid Nadvi, Chris Edwards, and Markus Eberhardt (2005). "Challenges to Vietnamese Firms in the Global Garment and Textile Value Chain," in *Clusters Facing Competition: The Importance of External Linkages*, Elisa Giuliani, Roberta Rabellotti, and Meine Pieter van Dijk, eds., pp. 85–105. Aldershot, UK: Ashgate Publishing.

Tulmets, Elsa. "The Introduction of the Open Method of Coordination in the European Enlargement Policy: Analysing the Impact of the New PHARE/Twinning Instrument." *European Political Economy Review*, vol. 3, no. 1 (Spring 2005), 54–90.

Notes to Chapter Twelve

1. This paper has benefited greatly from continuing discussion with Robert Unger. It has been scooped by Dani Rodrik, to whose work it is plainly and deeply indebted. He began to see the implications of his research for a new, processual type of industrial policy in just the months that I began to realize the possibility of interpreting his findings as an economywide variant of the Toyoda-inspired organizational changes I have been investigating in public and private institutions. His "Industrial Policy of the 21st Century" is a more compelling and authoritative statement of the emergent view than the first synthesis here.

2. For the Washington Consensus and its vicissitudes, see Gore, "The Rise and Fall of the Washington Consensus as a Paradigm for Developing Countries," 2000.

3. For an overview with case studies of development in key countries, including all those referred to immediately below except Russia and East Germany, see Dani Rodrik, ed., *In Search of Prosperity*, 2003.

4. On this "resource-curse" see Heather Congdon Fors and Ola Olsson, "Property Rights Investment and Growth in Modern Africa," 2005.

5. See generally Henretta, "The Protestant Ethic and the Reality of Capitalism in America," 1993.

6. Stephen Nissenbaum, "John Winthrop, 'A Model of Christian Charity,'" in David Nasaw, ed., *The Course of United States History* (Chicago, 1987), 35.

7. Ibid., 35–36, 50.

8. Larzer Ziff, *Puritanism in America: New Culture in a New World* (New York, 1973), 79–80; Bailyn, *New England Merchants,* 49–50.

9. Gary Nash, "Social Development," in Greene and Pole, *Colonial British America,* 237, 236

10. Cited in Henretta, 1993, p. 342.

11. "The triumph of capitalism in British America was a long, slow process. It took decades—indeed, more than a century—to translate the capitalist "spirit" of Puritan and Quaker merchants into concrete economic practices and legal institutions. Only in the early eighteenth century did a rational and routinized capitalist legal system extend its reach into the countryside; and only toward the end of the century had merchants amassed sufficient financial resources and organizational skills to initiate the American transition to a capitalist and industrializing society." Idem., pp. 343–344.

12. Horwitz, *The Transformation of American Law, 1780-1860,* 1977, especially, pp. 63–108.

13. This discussion follows Bellah, "Reflections on the Protestant Ethic Analogy in Asia," 1963, which contains extensive references to contemporaneous literature.

14. Idem, pp. 55–56, 1963.

15. Habermas, *The Theory of Communicative Action,* 1984.

16. Unger, *Politics.*

17. Glaeser and Shleifer, "Legal Origins," 2002.

18. Idem, p. 1194.

19. Smith, *Wealth of Nations,* Book III, "Of the Different Progress of Opulence in Different Nations," pp. 329–446, 1976.

20. Acemoglu, Daron, Simon Johnson, and James A. Robinson (2001). "The Colonial Origins of Comparative Development: An Empirical Investigation." *American Economic Review* 91: 1369-1401

21. Berglof and Bolton, 2002, p. 74–94, citation from p. 94.

22. Helpman, *The Mystery of Economic Growth,* p. 140.

23. Excluding, that is, very small countries, those with less than two decades of data, rebounds from crises, and accelerations that peaked at annual growth rates of less than 3.5 percent.

24. Hausmann et al., 2004; Rodrik and Subramanian 2004.

25. On clusters see Sabel, "The World in a Bottle, or, Window on the World? Open Questions about Industrial Districts in the Spirit of Sebastiano Brusco," 2003/ 2004.

26. For representative recent writing see Giuliani, Rabellotti, and van Dijk, eds., *Clusters Facing Competition,* 2005

27. McDermott, "The Politics of Institutional Renovation and Competitive Upgrading: Lessons from the Transformation of the Argentine Wine Industry," 2005

28. Banerjee and Duflo, "Growth Theory through the Lens of Development Economics," 2004.

29. For good case studies see Giuliani, Rabellotti, and van Dijk, eds., *Clusters Facing Competition,* 2005.

30. Author's interviews with garment producers in El Salvador. See also Rodrik and Hausmann (2003), "Discovering El Salvador's Production Potential," 2004.

31. Samstad, James G. and Seth Pipkin. "Bringing the Firm Back In: Local Decision Making and Human Capital Development in Mexico's Maquiladora Sector," (2005).

32. McDermott, 2005.

33. For the evidentiary problems associated with such league tables even in relatively limited domains such as shareholder and creditor rights see the analysis in Pistor, Raiser, and Gelfer, "Law and finance in transition economies," 2000.

34. The view of China presented here is widely accepted in policy circles close to the international financial institutions. See for instance the account in Inter-American Development Bank, "The Emergence of China: Opportunities and Challenges for Latin America and the Caribbean." Discussion draft, March 2005

35. The following is drawn from Henson and Mitullah, "Kenyan Exports of Nile Perch: The Impact of Food Safety Standards on an Export-Oriented Supply Chain," 2004.

36. On the institutional pairing that makes accession to the EU a mutually transformative process see Tulmets, "The Introduction of the Open Method of Coordination in the European Enlargement Policy: Analysing the Impact of the New PHARE/Twinning Instrument," 2005.

37. Rodrik, *The New Global Economy and Developing Countries: Making Openness Work,* 1999.

38. Rodrik, *Industrial Policy for the 21st Century* (2004), p. 15.

39. For elaboration of the following and detailed references, see Sabel, "A Real Time Revolution in Routines," 2006.

40. MacDuffie, "The Road to Root Cause: Shop-Floor Problem-Solving at Three Automotive Assembly Plants," 1997, p. 494.

41. These ideas are developed extensively, and fully referenced in, Liebman and Sabel, "A Public Laboratory Dewey Barely Imagined: The Emerging Model of School Governance and Legal Reform," 2003.

42. Hausmann, Rodrik and Velasco, *Growth Diagnostics,* 2004.

43. For development of, for instance, the fruit export sector, see Rodrik, *Industrial Policy for the 21st Century* (2004).

44. This account is taken from Fundación Chile, "Una oportunidad para Promover la Creación de Negocios Innovadores en Clusters Claves," Santiago, n.d., and supplemented by the authors' interviews with Fundación officials in November 2005.

45. The problems of market identification and assurance of complementarities to be discussed next are of course in a different form familiar to high-tech venture capitalists in the advanced economies.

46. Hausmann and Rodrik call this the problem of self identification—potential investors have to discover, by reference to their particular circumstances, that they are indeed entrepreneurs. See Hausmann and Rodrik, "Economic Development as Self-Discovery" (May 2002).

47. See Nurkse, *Problems of Capital Formation in Underdeveloped Countries,* 1953.

48. Hirschman, *The Strategy of Economic Development,* pp. 1–7.

Index